MARKETISATION AND PRIVATISATION IN CRIMINAL JUSTICE

Edited by
Kevin Albertson, Mary Corcoran
and Jake Phillips

P

First published in Great Britain in 2020 by

Policy Press
University of Bristol
1-9 Old Park Hill
Bristol
BS2 8BB
UK
t: +44 (0)117 954 5940
pp-info@bristol.ac.uk
www.policypress.co.uk

British Library Cataloguing in Publication Data
A catalogue record for this book is available from the British Library

ISBN 978-1-4473-4570-1 hardback
ISBN 978-1-4473-4581-7 paperback
ISBN 978-1-4473-4618-0 ePub
ISBN 978-1-4473-4617-3 ePDF

Cover design by Andrew Corbett
Front cover image: istockphoto-135360831-1024x1024

Contents

Contents

List of figures and tables

List of acronyms

AAMR	Alcohol Abstinence Monitoring Requirement
AMS	Alcohol Monitoring Services
AR	Accredited Representative
BCT	Barrow Cadbury Trust
BRDO	Better Regulation Delivery Office
CIEH	Chartered Institute of Environmental Health
CIFC	Corston Independent Funders' Coalition
CJC	Community Justice Court
CJS	Criminal Justice System
CPS	Crown Prosecution Service
CRC	Community Rehabilitation Company
CRESR	Centre for Regional Economic and Social Research
CrimPR	Criminal Procedure Rules
CVSL	Centre for Voluntary Sector Leadership
DCLG	Department for Communities and Local Government
DCO	Detention Custody Officers
DWP	Department of Work and Pensions
E&W	England and Wales
EHO	Environmental Health Officers
EM	Electronic Monitoring
EMAG	Electronic Monitoring Advisory Group
ESRC	Economic and Social Research Council
FE	Further Education
FIM	Financial Incentive Model
GAG	Grenfell Action Group
GM	Greater Manchester
GPS	Global Positioning System
GYDP	Garda Youth Diversion Project
HC/HoC	House of Commons
HDC	Home Detention Curfew
HMIC	Her Majesty's Inspectorate of Constabulary
HMIP	Her Majesty's Inspectorate Probation
HMP	Her Majesty's Prison
HMPPS	Her Majesty's Prison and Probation Service
HMSO	Her Majesty's Stationery Office
HSE	Health and Safety Executive
IOM	Integrated Offender Management
IRC	Immigration Removal Centre

IT	Information Technology
IYJS	Irish Youth Justice Service
KCTMO	Kensington and Chelsea Tenants' Management Organisation
LA	Local Authority
LAA	Legal Aid Agency
LiPs	Litigants-in-Person
MAPPA	Multi-Agency Public Protection Arrangements
MoJ	Ministry of Justice
MOPAC	[London] – Mayor's Office for Policing and Crime
NAO	National Audit Office
NCS	Norwegian Correctional Service
NCVO	National Council for Voluntary Organisations
NHS	National Health Service
NOMS	National Offender Management Service
NPM	New Public Management
NPS	National Probation Service
NYCP	New York City Police
OASys	Offender Assessment System
ORA	Offender Rehabilitation Act
PA	Primary Authority (scheme)
PAC	Parliamentary Accounts Committee
PACE	Police and Criminal Evidence Act
PbR	Payment by Results
PCT	Price Competitive Tendering
PDS	Public Defender Service
PFS	Pay for Success
PSM	Propensity Score Matching
RBKC	Royal Borough of Kensington and Chelsea
RCMP	Royal Canadian Mounted Police
RF	Radio Frequency
ROTL	Release on Temporary Licence
SIB	Social Impact Bond
SMART	Specific, Measurable, Achievable, Realistic and Time bound (goals)
SoS	Secretary of State
SPVM	Fondation du service de la ville de Montreal
SRB	Single Regeneration Budget
T2A	Transition to Adulthood
TMO	Tenants' Management Organisations
TNC	Transnational Company
TPIM	Terrorist Prevention and Investigation Measure

TSRC	Third Sector Research Centre
TR	Transforming Rehabilitation
TUC	Trades Union Congress
TUPE	Transfer of Undertakings (Protection of Employment) Regulations 2006
TWP	Together Women Programme
VPD	Vancouver Police Department
VS	Voluntary Sector
VSO	Voluntary Sector Organisation
WPR	What's the Problem Represented to be (approach)
WSA	Whole System Approach

Notes on contributors

Kevin Albertson is Professor of Economics at Manchester Metropolitan University. His background is in statistics, forecasting and evaluation. Kevin's recent academic work considers the political economy of social innovation and public policy, in particular the ways, means and implications of public sector commissioning in the areas of social policy and criminal justice.

Jill Annison is Honorary Fellow in Criminal Justice Studies at the University of Plymouth. She worked as a probation officer in her early career and then as an academic, teaching and researching in the field of interventions with adult offenders, with a particular focus on women in the criminal justice system.

Tim Auburn is Honorary Research Fellow in Psychology at the University of Plymouth. His research centres on discursive psychology and social institutions, in particular aspects of the criminal justice system that are socially constructed through talk-in-interaction. By using an approach based on conversation analysis and discursive psychology, he examines the everyday practices and routines through which criminal justice institutions are constituted by those involved in them.

Monish Bhatia is Lecturer in Criminology at Birkbeck, University of London. He has worked for over a decade on the rights of people seeking asylum and is a member of the Scottish Refugee Council and Right to Remain boards. In 2015, he won a Carnegie Trust grant to study destitution, drug use and 'crimes' among asylum seekers. In 2012–15, Monish was a co-coordinator of the European Group for the Study of Deviance and Social Control, and is currently an acting editor of its journal *Justice, Power and Resistance*. He co-edited *Media, Crime and Racism* (Palgrave, 2018) and *Minorities, Crime and (In) justice* (*Justice, Power and Resistance* journal, 2018).

Victoria Canning is Senior Lecturer in Criminology at the University of Bristol. She researches and campaigns against the impacts of borders on survivors of violence and torture, specifically in the lives of women seeking asylum in the UK, Denmark and Sweden. She is co-coordinator of the European Group for the Study of Deviance and Social Control, Trustee at Statewatch and Associate Director at Oxford University's Border Criminologies. Her book *Gendered Harm* *and Structural Violence in the British Asylum System* (Routledge) won the 2018 British Society of Criminology book prize.

Vickie Cooper is Lecturer in Social Policy and Criminology at the Open University. Vickie's research currently focuses on the harmful impacts of austerity, housing and evictions. Her previous research includes the geographical dispersal of homeless women in the criminal justice system, hostels and housing policy for people leaving prison and serving a supervision order in the community.

Mary Corcoran is Reader in Criminology at Keele University. Her research and publications cover prisons and community-based sanctions, with a particular focus on women's experience of justice. A second theme focuses on the changing relationships among markets, states and civil society and the consequences for criminal justice. Mary also researches on bereavement and loss, as well as well-being and life course in custody. She has been advisor to several voluntary sector and government agencies.

Gerry Czerniawski taught in secondary schools and colleges in London before teaching in higher education (Open University, University of Northampton, London Metropolitan University and London University's Institute of Education). In 2006 he joined the University of East London where he is currently Professor of Education. He has been humanities programme leader for secondary initial teacher education and currently runs the doctoral programmes in education. Gerry holds a National Teaching Fellowship and Principal Fellowship from the Higher Education Academy and is a trustee and council member of the British Educational Research Association (BERA). He is Lead Editor of the BERA Blog and Chair of the British Curriculum Forum.

Roxanna Dehaghani is Lecturer in Law at Cardiff School of Law and Politics. Her primary interests are in treatment of 'vulnerable' people in the criminal justice process, the police custody process and environment, police decision making and discretion and vulnerability theory/ies. She has published on various aspects of vulnerability in the *Howard Journal of Crime and Justice*, *Policing: A Journal of Policy and Practice*, *Journal of Social Welfare and Family Law*, *Oñati Socio-Legal Series* and *Criminal Law Review*. Her first monograph, *Vulnerability in Police Custody: Police Decision-Making and the Appropriate Adult Safeguard*, was published with Routledge in 2019.

Del Roy Fletcher is Professor of Labour Market Studies at the Centre for Regional Economic and Social Research at Sheffield Hallam University. Del specialises in research on welfare reform and labour market disadvantage. He is an expert on the problems faced by offenders in the labour market and was the Offender lead on a major Economic and Social Research Council study of the ethicality and efficacy of welfare conditionality. He has authored 27 academic articles including, with S. Wright (2018), 'A hand up or a slap down? Criminalising benefit claimants in Britain via strategies of surveillance, sanctions and deterrence', *Critical Social Policy* 38(2).

Chris Fox is Professor of Evaluation and Policy Analysis at Manchester Metropolitan University. He leads the Policy Evaluation and Research Unit and is co-lead of the think tank Metropolis. Chris is involved in a wide range of evaluation and research projects and is particularly interested in programme and policy evaluation, evidence-based policy and practice, and innovation in social policy, particularly the 'personalisation' of public services. His work cuts across a number of policy areas including criminal justice, social innovation, welfare reform and education. He has led approximately £5 million of evaluation and applied research projects in these areas.

James Gacek is Assistant Professor at the Department of Justice Studies at the University of Regina, Canada. He continues to publish in the areas of incarceration, genocidal carcerality, visual and media studies, the exploitation of human–animal relations, the regulation of obscenity and indecency and the broader politics of judicial reasoning. With Richard Jochelson, he has co-authored *Criminal Law and Precrime: Legal Studies in Canadian Punishment and Surveillance in Anticipation of Criminal Guilt* (Routledge, 2018).

Daniel Gilling is the current Head of School of Law, Criminology and Government at the University of Plymouth. He is a Reader in Criminology, and his area of expertise lies primarily in a critical analysis of late-modern approaches to governing crime, with a particular focus on the domains of community safety, policing and community justice more generally.

Gisella Hanley Santos has worked as a Lecturer in Criminology at the University of Plymouth since 2014. She has a long-standing interest in issues to do with drug use, rehabilitation and desistance, having carried out research with young offenders in their transition to adulthood, drug and alcohol users in a Community Justice Court, steroid users, and street children and young offenders in a Therapeutic Community in Brazil.

Joanna Hargreaves is a graduate of the Masters programme in Applied Criminology, Penology and Management, University of Cambridge, where she developed a particular interest in the interaction between public and private services. She previously worked at Her Majesty's Prison and Probation Service. Most recently, Joanna was a Strategy Development Manager working to establish a future vision and strategy for HMPPS. Joanna started a new role with the Ministry of Defence in Autumn 2019.

Ed Johnston is Senior Lecturer in Law and the Programme Lead for Criminology and Law at the University of the West of England, Bristol. His areas of interest include adversarialism, the role of the defence lawyer and the rise of managerialism. He recently submitted his PhD, entitled *The Role of the Defence Lawyer in the Modern Era*, which examines how defence lawyers view their role in the post-charge stages of the criminal justice system. The thesis charts the dilution of traditional adversarial values and examines the implications for the criminal justice process in light of the rise of managerial goals.

Randy K. Lippert is Professor in Criminology at the University of Windsor. His research is in the areas of law and society, policing/security, surveillance/privacy, governance and urban studies. Recent major research projects funded by the Social Sciences and Humanities Research Council of Canada focus on public policing in Canada and the US, condo governance in Toronto and New York City, and municipal corporate security in Canada. He was Thinker-in-Residence at Deakin University in Australia in 2015.

Amy Ludlow is Director of the MSt Programme in Criminology, Penology and Management and Senior Lecturer and Research Associate at the Institute of Criminology, University of Cambridge. She is concurrently Director of Studies in Law at Fitzwilliam College. Amy has conducted wide-ranging research in prisons, focusing especially on how organisational reforms in the sector, particularly marketisation and privatisation, affect prison staff culture and quality of life for staff and prisoners. Amy also co-founded and directs Learning Together, an action research initiative that is yielding new insights about the role of educational communities in supporting movements away from crime.

Rob Macmillan is a Principal Research Fellow at the Centre for Regional Economic and Social Research at Sheffield Hallam University. His main research interests are around the long-term qualitative dynamics of voluntary action, the application of field theory in the third sector, the relationships between markets and the third sector, and capacity building and third sector infrastructure. He was part of the 'TrackTR' partnership led by Clinks (2015–18) to chart the experiences of the voluntary sector in the Transforming Rehabilitation programme.

Mike Maguire is a part-time Professor of Criminology, University of South Wales, and Professor Emeritus, Cardiff University. His research and writing have covered many aspects of the criminal justice and penal systems, including policing, prisons and probation. He is a member of the Correctional Services Accreditation and Advice Panel and a former member of the Parole Board of England and Wales.

Maureen Mansfield is principally experienced in working within voluntary organisations for women. Maureen currently works with INQUEST as a Family Participation Officer. Prior to this she worked with Women's Resource Centre, at Women in Prison and Women at WISH, a counselling service for women. Maureen is one of the founding members of Reclaim Holloway campaign, and organises with Reclaim Justice Network. She also started the story collecting website Holloway Prison Stories, following the closure of the prison.

Mike Nellis is Emeritus Professor of Criminal and Community Justice in the Law School, University of Strathclyde. After completing a PhD at the Institute of Criminology in Cambridge, he became involved in the training of probation officers at the University of Birmingham, writing extensively on alternatives to imprisonment, and especially electronic monitoring (EM). Between 2005 and 2014 he co-organised the Confederation of European Probation EM conferences, and between 2011 and 2013 he was an expert adviser to a Council of Europe committee producing an ethical recommendation on EM. He is currently the international editor of the *Journal of Offender Monitoring*.

Jake Phillips is Reader in Criminology at Sheffield Hallam University. His research interests lie at the intersection of policy and practice with a particular focus on probation. He is currently undertaking research on the impact of inspection on probation policy and practice, people who die while under criminal justice supervision and the use of community hubs to deliver probation.

Tom Smith is Lecturer in Law at the University of the West of England, Bristol. His areas of interest include criminal legal aid and pretrial detention. Most recently, he contributed a chapter on the rise and fall of criminal legal aid in England and Wales (with Professor Ed Cape) to a cross-jurisdictional book on access to justice. He was also co-investigator on an EU-funded study examining pretrial detention practice in England and Wales – the first of its kind in over a decade – and an expert consultant for an overseas jurisdiction regarding pretrial detention reform.

Richard Sparks is Professor of Criminology at Edinburgh Law School, University of Edinburgh. He is author or editor of a number of books, latterly including (with Albert Dzur and Ian Loader, eds) *Mass Incarceration and Democratic Theory* (Oxford, 2016) and (with Jonathan Simon, eds) *The SAGE Handbook of Punishment and Society* (SAGE, 2012).

Katharina Swirak is Lecturer in Criminology in the Department of Sociology and Criminology at University College Cork. Underpinned by her theoretical interests in critical criminology and critiques of neo-liberal governing, she researches, teaches and publishes in the areas of criminalisation of social policy, the criminal justice voluntary sector and youth justice policy.

Steve Tombs is Professor of Criminology at The Open University. He has a long-standing interest in the incidence, nature and regulation of corporate and state crime and harm and has published widely in these areas. He has long worked with the Hazards movement in the UK, and is a Trustee and Board member of INQUEST.

Kevin Walby is Associate Professor and Chancellor's Research Chair (2015–18) in the Department of Criminal Justice at University of Winnipeg. His research is in the areas of freedom of information, policing/security, surveillance and urban studies. Recent major research projects funded by the Social Sciences and Humanities Research Council of Canada focus on public policing in Canada and the US, prison and police museums in Canada, police communications and municipal corporate security in Canada.

Adam White is Senior Lecturer in Criminology at the University of Sheffield. His research focuses on three interconnected themes: the rise of the private security and private military industries in the post-war era; corresponding issues of governance, regulation and legitimacy in the contemporary security sector; and the changing nature of state–market relations. He has published articles on police outsourcing in the *British Journal of Criminology*, *Criminology and Criminal Justice* and *Policing: A Journal of Policy and Practice*.

Kate Williams is Professor of Criminology at the University of South Wales and Director of the Welsh Centre for Crime and Social Justice. Her research and publishing activities have been varied but include youth justice and women in the system, policing, the criminal justice system and probation. Some of her work has focused on justice in rural areas. Kate also acts as an advisor to the Youth Justice Board Cymru's Practice Development Panel. She co-chairs Domestic Homicide Reviews in two local authority areas in Wales and has provided advice to the both the Westminster and Welsh governments.

Kevin Wong is Reader in Community Justice and Associate Director (Criminal Justice) at the Policy Evaluation and Research Unit at Manchester Metropolitan University. He has over 20 years' experience of voluntary sector involvement in the criminal justice system as a practitioner, commissioner, policy advisor and researcher. He was previously an Assistant Director at Nacro, the crime reduction charity. He has undertaken a wide range of evaluations of voluntary sector criminal justice services for government departments, charitable trusts and charities. His research interests include voluntary sector delivery of justice services, justice reinvestment and impact measurement and voluntary organisations.

Acknowledgements

As with all book projects, this one was influenced by the individuals and groups, too many to name, who are shaping the broader intellectual project by writing about, experiencing and working in the criminal justice sector. Particular thanks go to our contributors who have produced innovative chapters despite the constant pressure of their 'day jobs'. We are grateful to colleagues past and present who have supported our work in these fields.

We would also like to thank Professor John Lea and Dr Sam King for their foundation of the project, to compile an edited collection relating to Privatisation and Criminal Justice.

Ultimately we are grateful to the staff at Policy Press who have supported us throughout.

Introduction
Marketisation and privatisation in criminal justice: an overview

Kevin Albertson, Mary Corcoran and Jake Phillips

Introduction

Criminal justice used to be thought of as a field that ought to be autonomous from politics and the economy, with the management of crime and punishment being seen as essentially the responsibility of the state. Now, however, it is widely agreed that decades of marketisation and privatisation have blurred the institutional boundaries and functions of the public sector with those of for-profit and civil society interests in many parts of the penal/welfare complex. The 'mixed market' in criminal justice services, pursued by successive governments since the 1980s, accelerated sharply in the wake of the Austerity Agenda and the reconstruction of the social economy post the banking crisis of 2007 (Corcoran, 2014). The ascendancy of market imaginaries is such that their influence on policing, prisons, probation, legal services and the courts, let alone numerous ancillary services from prisoner transport to interpretation services, is seemingly irreversible.

The dominance of the market in the public sphere was by no means assured nor consensual. In her classic study of the rise of the life insurance business, *Morals and Markets* (1979/2017), the economic sociologist Viviana Zelizer observed that 'the introduction of calculative market principles into a sacred sphere provoked a surprisingly strong resistance that took time and effort to overcome' (Healy, 2017: xi–xii). The essence of Zelizer's thesis was that the great accomplishment of the life insurance industry entailed the structural and cultural transformations which it achieved in establishing 'monetary equivalents for those aspects of the social order, such as death, life, human organs and other generally ritualised items or behaviour considered sacred, [that had hitherto been considered] beyond the pale of monetary definition' (Zelizer, 1979/2017: xxii).

Zelizer's finding that there is no 'sacred sphere' which cannot eventually be penetrated by commercialism coincided with the 'experimental phase of neoliberalism' when governments in Western capitalist countries were – somewhat tentatively – working to 'roll back the state in various ways' (Prasad, 2006: 5). More recently, Sandel's (2000) exposition of the 'moral limits of the markets' illustrates the ways in which a market economy can distort human behaviour in such a way as to undermine the very aims of the organisation or context which the market was intended to 'fix'. This book explores the impact of both marketisation and privatisation whilst recognising that there is no global coherence or universal consistency that maps neatly onto services, sectors or national jurisdictions. In the chapters contained in this volume, a market economy logic is evident in a myriad of different case studies having initially been introduced in order to fix a perceived problem such as a perception that the service was too expensive or inefficient, ineffective or lacking in accountability. However, with that came unintended consequences impacting on the delivery of justice and the effectiveness of the system, as well as the legitimacy of the institutions concerned. In this introductory chapter we provide a brief history of marketisation and privatisation in criminal justice and offer some workable definitions of the two concepts which we see as different, but interlinked.

Although our history begins with that of prison and probation, we argue that our object of analysis should be wider than these two key penal institutions. Indeed, as the range of chapters in this volume shows, privatisation and marketisation have found their way into a much wider set of institutions than these two. What is more, these forces have taken on different iterations and have been introduced for different reasons. Therefore, this is not a book about how or why governments have systematically handed over formerly state assets to private companies. Rather, it is about the process of political innovation in which governments and other agencies and sectors have sought to achieve often complex goals, for example, through the transfer of political and/or financial risk, and through attempts to include and motivate non-state organisations in a range of ways. For it is this pursuit of *innovation* which underpins both the reasoning behind privatisation and marketisation, and the continued efforts to manage its unforeseen (and predicted) consequences.

Where did it begin, and where are we now?

Why do we need a book on privatisation *and* marketisation in criminal justice? As has been documented elsewhere (Whitehead and Crawshaw, 2012), privatisation has been an ongoing process in criminal justice since the early 1980s. By 1987, faced with a prison system in crisis, and vested in the pessimistic belief that 'nothing works', Margaret Thatcher's second government was more amenable to the case – led by the influential right-wing members of the 'Conservative Study Group on Crime' – to introduce a US-style 'privately run prison' as a forerunner to privatising 'as many prison services as possible' in the long run (Le Vay, 2016: 7).

In 1991, the first outsourced prison in England and Wales, HMP The Wolds, was in operation, and the programme of compulsory contracting out in other areas of criminal justice, notably probation, was in train. Thereafter, 'money was on the march' in the penal sphere (Le Vay, 2016: 7) and we have since seen, in England and Wales, the attempted marketisation of the community sanctions sector in England and Wales (see Chapters 4 and 5 of this volume) and the introduction of market forces into the welfare system which, as Wacquant (2009, 2010) argues, is as much a part of a system of penality as it is a safety net for the poor.

Some elements of the services provided by the police have been outsourced, and the opportunity to purchase police services has existed for many years to organisations (such as football clubs) who are willing to pay. The largest private prison corporations – Core Civic and GEO Group – manage over half of private prison contracts in the United States and in 2015 had combined revenues of $3.5 billion. It is necessary to appreciate that the characteristics of marketisation and privatisation may differ depending on jurisdiction, service and sector. Therefore, the chapters here explore relationships across (and distinctions between) a wide range of institutions in different countries in order to shed light on the myriad processes and structures which account for greater involvement by the non-state sector in the delivery of criminal justice.

To return to the causes and consequences of the pursuit of innovation as explored by Zelizer, there are, of course, obvious differences between life insurance and the evolution of criminal sanctions; the former was a novel scheme for protecting families and businesses from financial disaster in the event of a death. The profitable transaction in punishment, on the other hand, can be understood recursively, that is, as recourse to practices that had existed for millennia, prior to the nationalisation of many criminal justice functions from the mid-19th century, and which persisted in one form or another in many parts of the world. Thus, latter-day privatisation encompasses both primordial and (post-)modern characteristics.

As with Zelizer's study, the ethical and moral quandaries created by putting punishment on the market also elicited similar expressions of outrage and reservation, even among Conservatives. Indeed, initial reactions to privatisation in prison and probation services in the UK were borne out by a tide of objections to the encroachment into the sphere of civil and political independence, as well as the distortion of ethics and sensibility, which would follow.

This first phase in the debate about the place of for-profit interests in public justice may be framed in terms of a discursive mismatch, with objectors pointing to the potential erosion of democratic accountability, public answerability and the framework underlying the importance of a state-led justice system, subject to checks and balances, and disinterestedly administered by public servants (Ryan and Ward, 1989; Sparks, 1994).

Against this, defenders of privatisation adhered to the script of superior efficiency, technical superiority, the transparency of market efficiency and flexibility of performance in other public services that had been rendered 'quasi-markets' (Harding, 1997). Thus, the debate played out in parallel and rarely intersecting terms of engagement between the economic efficiency rationale and the 'social' ramifications, which continues to the present. This book is intended to address these tacit lacunae by foregrounding a few elementary perspectives.

Firstly, marketisation and privatisation, and other forms of commercialisation, did not arrive fully formed, were not inevitable and involved numerous struggles and strategies (including the opportunism of political and corporate actors) to be put in place. Secondly, the full picture of these struggles will be incomplete if one only looks to structural and economic conditions for explanation and overlooks the importance of 'moral persuasion'. After all, the capacity for market making in Britain was already in place: the political appetite existed under Thatcher's and successor governments; the necessary laws and administrative apparatus could be put in place; the technical means and expertise to monetise penal 'interventions' existed; other human services (education, care and health, for example) were already sold on the marketplace; the state had the means to pay; and the right sort of knowledge and data existed to support market planning. The key struggle arose where the punishment business had to establish legitimacy by convincing public servants, civil society actors and the public that marketisation 'was not merely technically efficient, but a morally superior system' (Zelizer, 1979/2017: 107). In sum, the missing links which converted service providers from being agents of rehabilitation to socially useful technocrats and partners in crime control were the tools of moral and cultural persuasion that came into play.

Explaining marketisation and privatisation

Of course, sociologists of crime and punishment have long recognised the indispensable considerations of theory (Canton, 2017), political economy (Rusche and Kirchheimer, 2003), ideology (Gramsci in Bates, 1975) and culture to economic life and to social change more widely.

The penal market nexus materialises both as quantifiable and qualifiable phenomena. It manifests where the expansion in the use of custody and the innovation of new services as 'products' can be empirically captured in ways that show the transformation of companies, state agencies and some charities into powerful corporate institutions. Additionally, the penal market nexus is subject to qualitative analysis in the way that marketisation acquires an operational apparatus and ethos which is consistent with the goals of generating surpluses. It is thus possible to examine marketisation and privatisation from a range of perspectives. This volume examines and critiques these perspectives to develop our knowledge and understanding of the process of privatisation and marketisation, the impact of it and the extent to which newly marketised and privatised services result in 'justice'.

Certainly, justice is a slippery concept, and again we explore this from various angles, ranging from the delivery of a punishment, to someone who has caused harm with little concern about the impact, to the potential for punishment to reduce the risk of someone causing further harm – through rehabilitation or therapeutic jurisprudence – to the potential for punishment to reduce the inequalities which caused the harm in the first place, via the concept of social justice. What is clear from the chapters in this volume is that a marketised and privatised criminal justice sector has implications for all of these types of justice.

We have deliberately cast our net widely in our definition of criminal justice agencies so that we do not solely focus on the obvious institutions and actors such as the prison, police and probation (although these institutions are still covered). The reason for this is, quite simply, that privatisation and marketisation have exerted (and reproduced) effects beyond the main penal institutions. Consequently, we include chapters which explore immigration detention, the role of detention officers in police stations and women's centres, for example. Not only does this add depth to our knowledge, it also serves to illustrate the way in which privatisation and marketisation is not simply about handing over state assets but is about *cultural change*. That is to say, marketisation entails significant cultural effort not just for eliciting 'entrepreneurial' responses from agencies, but for ensuring the social reproduction of market consciousness and behaviour among workforces, service users and regulators.

How do marketisation and privatisation differ?

The chapters in this volume consider the scale and impact of marketisation and privatisation in the area of criminal justice. These are understood as interconnected phenomena, but too often they are used interchangeably and reductively. For clarity, we define them accordingly: privatisation encapsulates the transfer of public resources and employment to (usually) for-profit enterprises by means of outsourcing public services on 'open' contract markets or selling or leasing public assets. Marketisation, or the conversion of public services into marketable commodities, entails a paradigmatic shift in all areas of criminal justice organisation at macro-, meso- and micro-levels, whether or not they have been formally privatised or remain (at least for now) under public ownership and management.

The shift towards market-centric goals involves the transformation of public goods, from education or health to welfare and justice, towards improved performance in mobile spheres of competition that are supposedly attuned to the laws of supply and demand. However, the question of whose demand it is that is being matched remains open.

Marketisation facilitates, in a Bourdieusian sense, deep socio-cultural alignments towards business models which require that organisations and individuals who work in or use public services adapt to entrepreneurial dispositions as 'providers', 'deliverers' and 'consumers'. Marketisation is also a technocratic enterprise which harnesses a plethora of toolkits and techniques for measuring efficient delivery, converting data into monetisable outputs, establishing league tables and performance mechanisms, as well as generating rituals for disciplining participants into becoming effective 'market players'.

Both concepts of marketisation are reflections of an increasingly monopolistic, neo-liberal hegemony which promises citizens a utopian political project for ensuring individual freedom (subject only to market forces), and private and social enterprise opportunities to bid as the state transforms from provider to auctioneer of public goods and services.

The structure of the volume

The chapters in this book analyse multiple layers of privatisation and marketisation and, together, account for the relationship between the two. Thus, the volume considers 'why' and 'how' these processes occur in different fields of practice. A wide net in terms of what counts as criminal justice, as well as a recognition that marketisation and privatisation are two distinct but related developments and processes, means we can look at the issues holistically. For example, it means we examine the 'cultural' side of marketisation through the role of the state in 'stepping in' to reframe policy and introduce mechanisms which allow for market forces and their attendant technologies (contestability, audit; performance mechanisms; managerialism; funding by private concerns). It also means we can examine the way in which the state seeks to legitimise the new structures of services, and we can analyse their effect on staff and 'service users'.

The volume is split into four parts. Part I comprises chapters which primarily take a theoretical view of marketisation and privatisation. Neo-liberalism is a key concept in understanding both privatisation and marketisation as it is seen to underpin the political ideology associated with many such reforms. Thus, in Chapter 1, Corcoran explores the roots of neo-liberal ideology through a re-reading of Polanyi's *Origins of Our Time*. By linking political ideology to broader cultural ideas and attitudes, Corcoran explores the processes by which neo-liberalism created a context in which marketised and privatised criminal justice came to be seen not just as acceptable but necessary and inevitable. In Chapter 2, Fox and Albertson consider a major aspect of marketisation 'outcomes-based contracts', particularly the related concepts of payment by results (PbR) Social Impact Bonds (SIBs). Such contracts link a public commissioner, financiers and service providers via outcomes metrics designed to align the incentive structures of the parties involved so as to achieve efficient results. PbR and SIBs are key instruments in the commodification of public sector social goals, and PbR in particular has formed an element of much public commissioning in the criminal justice sector under Transforming Rehabilitation (TR). In Chapter 3, Gacek and Sparks consider the range of competing interests – commercial, governmental and civic – that are at play in the criminal justice system. Ultimately, they argue that unless these interests are reconciled – a task that is easier said than done – the marketised penal system will simply continue to exist in its currently exclusionary form. Phillips's Chapter 4 shifts our attention back to the field of probation in England and Wales and uses the process of marketisation which occurred as part of the Coalition Government's Transforming Rehabilitation agenda as a case study to understand that process. Analysing the field through the lens of Bourdieu's field theory, Phillips argues that the government was able to push through its reforms with very little opposition because the preceding years had led to the depreciation of the forms of capital upon which probation practitioners could draw to oppose the reforms. In Chapter 5, Albertson and Fox explore what has been happening in England and Wales with a focus on processes of marketisation in prison and probation policy. It is here that we see the difference between marketisation and privatisation. For example, probation in England and Wales was not wholly privatised in TR. Rather, a sub-section of it was outsourced and turned into a for-profit exercise, with probation being partitioned along the distinctly neo-liberal lines of risk – a topic that is returned to later in the book. As well as exploring the drivers for marketisation in probation and prison policy, Albertson and Fox consider the success of such reforms, concluding that the government should abandon plans for continued involvement in the field of probation and instead focus on localised services which have local accountability at their heart.

In Part II our attention shifts to the specifics of how privatisation and marketisation have manifested and impacted on criminal justice in a range of institutional and jurisdictional contexts. Thus, in Chapter 6, Swirak explores the process of marketisation in the field of Irish youth justice. Her chapter provides an excellent example of marketisation which is not simply about transferring state assets to the private sector. Rather, she argues that it has a much subtler effect on the way in which 'problems' are understood and solutions are devised. Through analysis of youth justice practitioners' discussions about their work with young people, we see that the emphasis placed on outputs and productivity in the market society imbues youth justice workers with the idea that the same is needed for young people engaged with the criminal justice system. Next, in Chapter 7, Dehaghani and White illustrate the impact of privatisation on the identities of front-line workers working in outsourced and non-outsourced police stations. Here we see that the effect of outsourcing is not just about saving money for the state and making profit for the private sector. Rather, it results in a greater sense of labour force vulnerability among those working in outsourced environments. There are, thus, implications for staff as well as service users. Walby and Lippert, in Chapter 8, take us across the Atlantic to Canada and the US where they provide a discussion of corporatisation – as distinct from marketisation. While outright outsourcing in Canada is considered beyond the pale, a different process has been in train in recent years with potentially similar adverse effects. Their example of police foundations and user-pay policing illustrate the myriad ways that the private sector has become intertwined with the field of criminal justice. What is key, for us, to these developments is the way they enable the channelling of private funds into police operations which, ultimately, means that people with money have the opportunity to dictate what the police do, and how, when compared with those without such capital.

In England and Wales, the right to legal aid has been severely curtailed and, in Chapter 9, Smith and Johnston examine these developments in the context of marketisation. Their argument, that attempts to rationalise legal aid and make it more efficient are leading to injustice – through an increasing number of 'litigants in person' and outsourcing to agents – sheds even more light on the damage being done to the delivery of justice as a result of marketisation. Ludlow and Hargreaves, in Chapter 10, explore the ways in which private prisons are held to account through an analysis of the role of the prison 'Controller' in England and Wales. They argue that while this system of accountability is supposed to ensure consistency and fairness across the private prison estate, it is the relational element of the Controller's role in the prison which has the most impact on what happens in a prison. Thus, while private prisons have contractual arrangements to comply, quality assurance procedures to meet and profits to deliver to shareholders, it would seem that marketisation cannot overcome the importance of human interaction in ensuring that good-quality accountability is achieved. Chapter 11 explores the effect of Transforming Rehabilitation in probation in England and Wales. The argument that the decision to split the service along the lines of risk is closely aligned to the ideology of neo–liberalism through analysis of its proximity to Feeley and Simon's New Penology leads the authors to conclude that the reforms were destined to fail, something which has been borne out in recent announcements that some aspects of probation will now be reunified and renationalised.

Part III has the voluntary sector as its object of analysis. In Chapter 12, Corcoran, Maguire and Williams explore the impact of, and reactions to, the process of marketisation among those working in the penal voluntary sector. Chapter 13 takes a similar approach but this time looks at the impact of marketisation on the delivery of services for women engaged in the criminal justice system. Cooper and Mansfield's argument, that marketisation has had a significant and deleterious impact on these services, is something which should concern all of us who see gender-specific services as critical in overcoming the personal and institutional violence to which many women in the criminal justice system have been subjected. In Chapter 14, the final chapter in Part III, Wong and Macmillan also paint a mixed picture of the impact of marketisation on the voluntary sector. On the one hand, the voluntary sector did not do well out of the government's top-down approach to commissioning probation services. On the other hand, their case studies of two local voluntary sector organisations point to the potential for ways of commissioning more effectively. This chapter serves nicely to illustrate the complexities of marketisation, demonstrating that it is not only about introducing market forces but that the way this is done has a significant impact on the outcomes achieved.

Part IV turns our attention to institutions which are seen as peripheral to criminal justice but are still nonetheless part of the systems of power and punishment that people engaged with the criminal justice system experience as punitive. Thus, in Chapter 15, Nellis explores the history of GPS tracking in England and Wales with a focus on how a reliance on the market led to poor service commissioning and numerous delays in the implementation of this new form of electronic monitoring. In Chapter 16, Bhatia and Canning explore the role of privatisation in the field of immigration detention. Their analysis points to the worrying move towards making 'migrant misery' the foundation of a profit-making business model. By exploring the impact of this on individuals and the society which these centres serve, they argue that the only solution is abolition of immigration removal centres. Chapter 17 explores the delivery of education in the prison context. Through the use of comparative case studies, Czerniawski shows that the choice to deliver education or training is linked to the dominant political economy in a particular country. His argument that such a focus on training/education reflects broader penal sensibilities about the purpose of such provision: to offer training to increase people's chances of finding employment and becoming productive members of society; or delivering, through education, a humane and transformative endeavour which enables people to be citizens rather than 'just' workers. Chapter 18 moves us away from the delivery of punishment by the state to the way the state causes harm with impunity through a degradation of systems of regulation which are closely related to the influence of the market. Here, Tombs explores changes in the systems of regulation in local authorities and argues that austerity has led to the increased involvement of private sector forces. He then asks us to think about consequences of deregulation in terms of state harm and low levels of accountability. This becomes particularly stark when considered in relation to the fire at Grenfell Tower which killed 72 people as a result of reduced-cost, low-quality cladding that had been fitted to improve the 'look' of the tower. Thus, Tombs's chapter becomes about how marketisation impacts upon our ability to hold power-holders to account in cases where the state is complicit in the imposition of harm. Ultimately, in Chapter 19, the intersection between the penal and the welfare states comes under scrutiny. Fletcher articulates the ways in which the harm caused by prison is exacerbated by the welfare state's tendency to make it more difficult for people leaving prison to claim out-of-work benefits due to the increasing involvement of the private sector in both the field of prison and welfare. In closing this volume, we draw out themes and conclusions.

References

Bates, T.R. (1975) 'Gramsci and the Theory of Hegemony', *Journal of the History of Ideas*, 36(2): 351–66.

Canton, R. (2017) *Why Punish? An Introduction to the Philosophy of Punishment?*, Basingstoke: Palgrave Macmillan.

Corcoran, M.S. (2014) 'The trajectory of penal markets in an age of austerity: The case of England and Wales', *Sociology of Crime, Law and Deviance*, 19: 53–74.

Harding, R. (1997) *Private Prisons and Public Accountability*, Milton Keynes: Open University Press.

Healy, K. (2017) 'Foreword', in to V.A.R. Zelizer, *Morals and Markets: The Development of Life Insurance in the United States*, New York: Columbia University Press, pp ix–xviii.

Le Vay, J. (2016) *Competition for Prisons: Public or Private*, Bristol: Policy Press.

Prasad, M. (2006) *The Politics of Free Markets: The Rise of Neoliberal Economic Policies in Britain, France, Germany and the United States*, London: University of Chicago Press.

Ryan, M. and Ward, T. (1989) 'Privatization and the penal system: Britain misinterprets the American experience', *Criminal Justice Review*, 14(1): 1–12.

Rusche, G. and Kirchheimer, O. (2003) *Punishment and Social Structure*, Abingdon: Transaction Publishers.

Sandel, M.J. (2000) *What Money Can't Buy: The Moral Limits of Markets*, London: Allen Lane.

Sparks, R. (1994) 'Can prisons be legitimate? Penal politics, privatisation and the timeliness of an old idea', *British Journal of Criminology*, 34(S1): 14–28, available from: https://doi.org/10.1093/oxfordjournals.bjc.34.S1.14 [accessed 30 March 2020].

Wacquant, L. (2009). *Punishing the Poor: The Neoliberal Government of Social Insecurity*, Durham, NC: Duke University Press.

Wacquant, L. (2010). 'Crafting the neoliberal state: Workfare, prisonfare, and social insecurity', *Sociological Forum*, 25(2): 197–220. doi: 10.1111/j.1573-7861.2010.01173.x

Whitehead, P. and Crawshaw, P. (eds) (2012) *Organising Neoliberalism: Markets, Privatisation and Justice*, London: Anthem Press.

Zelizer, V.A.R. (1979/2017) *Morals and Markets: The Development of Life Insurance in the United States*, New York: Columbia University Press.

PART I

Introduction and theoretical frameworks

1

Market society utopianism in penal politics

Mary Corcoran

Introduction

All along the line, human society had become an accessory of the economic system.

(Polanyi, 1945: 75)

This chapter outlines the utopian intellectual project of contemporary free market thought and politics (what is generally referred to as 'new liberalism' or 'neo-liberalism') from its origins as an outsider critique of the post-war social democratic settlement to its triumph in the wake of economic and political crisis from the 1970s onwards. The discussion initially draws on some core ideas from Friedrich Hayek (1944, 1960) and associates, who provided the intellectual legitimacy for the political choices and ideas that predominated in recent decades. It then turns to Karl Polanyi's (1945) *Origins of Our Time: The Great Transformation*, where he first gave theoretical expression to the concept of a 'market society'. Published just after the Second World War and in the context of emerging social democratic welfare states, these thinkers marked out the ideological divisions that have dominated politics since. The chapter considers the relationships between neo-liberal epistemology and penal politics and thinking during and after the 1980s. It concludes by noting that the aftermath of the financial crisis of 2007–08 heralded a false dawn for those who predicted that such policies would wither away. However, recent political disruptions and scandals arising from public contract failures or the removal of private, for-profit companies providing prison and resettlement services may be contributing to a tipping point in the demise of faith in the putative ruling idea of our time, the efficiency of supposedly free markets.

The 'culture' of marketisation

At its essence, marketisation reflects a model of society that is rooted in restructuring the public sphere in accordance with radical utilitarian, individualistic and economistic values. Marketisation describes a manifestation of '"free market" or "neoliberal" policies, ... [comprising] taxation structures that favor capital accumulation over income redistribution, industrial policies that minimize the presence of the state in private industry, and retrenchment in welfare spending' (Prasad, 2006: 4). The ensuing cultural revolution was not historically predestined, however, and it is an open question whether free market ideas ever secured the degrees of popular consensus claimed for them by governments and policy makers. Prasad (2006: 21) notes, for example, that free market ideas were resoundingly unpopular in the 1970s and 1980s yet came to resonate in ideational, popular cultural, symbolic and psychological spheres partly because 'even quite narrowly defined economic ideas are polyvalent and ... self-contradictory, so that the same idea may come to mean quite different things at different times or to different audiences'. What appeared to be an all-conquering paradigm was, she continues, the result of right-wing political opportunism which promoted certain 'material and institutional incentives [in order to] determine which version of an idea prevails and is implemented' (Prasad, 2006: 21).[1] Colin Leys (2001: 17) adds that while this cultural turn was essentially a 'political project', it required a profound ideological momentum to win four critical arguments. These were: (i) the conversion of erstwhile 'uncommodifiable' public goods (education, social care, probation, court sanctions, custody) into commodities which could be valued and transacted along commercial lines; (ii) the public had to be persuaded there was no realistic alternative to securing these resources competitively and often through some form of eligibility test; (iii) the existing workforce or producers had to be redefined and motivated to become 'wage workers' producing commodities and to generate a surplus for profits (or reinvestment); (iv) the change to for-profit provision involved substantial investment and risk, which private capital tries to get the state to absorb.

---

[1] It has been objected that there is a distinction between neo-liberalism as an intellectual project and the manner in which certain aspects were cherry-picked to suit certain political agendas. However, the fact that many intellectuals and academic economists consciously positioned themselves as part of the movement for actively influencing politics renders this point somewhat moot (Williamson, 2004; Prasad, 2006: 21–2).

The central ontological justification underlying this cultural transformation is that personal and group behaviours are governed by rational self-interest, financial incentives and utility. Here, competition is endorsed as a neutral instrument of selection and reliable standard of promoting competence among alternative providers. The public, the proposition goes, gets the best deal because the market is not swayed by political or sentimental biases but by the criteria of price and efficiency. Such claims elide a mode of ideological masking whereby vested interests are supposedly curtailed by the superior operation of impersonal, rational mechanisms. Yet the very process of market making derives from blurring elite economic and political interests – a process which precedes and frames the technocratic options that are subsequently employed.

Consider, for example, a speech given by Sir Ian Lambert, the Director of the Confederation of British Industry, in the aftermath of the special G20 Summit in London in 2009 to address how the major world economies should respond to the financial crisis. Sir Ian hypothesised that 30 of years of market liberalism were over and that a new order was coming, with the state taking 'greater *control* over domestic markets' (the use of language here indicating Sir Ian's critical view of that prospect). A more beneficial state of affairs, he continued, could arise if 'the state should become a commissioning agent [which is] *indifferent* to whether services were delivered by the private sector, the public sector or the third sector'[2] (Financial Times, 2009: emphasis added). It is worthwhile probing the epistemology of the adjective 'indifferent'. At face value, it references lofty neutrality, yet it was and remains frequently used to underline the argument that the public do not care who owns or operates public services as long as they get the service they want (Public Administration Select Committee, 2004). Additionally, market 'indifference' entered political discourse as reassurance to financial markets that government holds no favourable predisposition towards any particular provider or sector in procuring public services, and that the state or commissioners of public services will not stand in the market's way.

From the 1990s, the mantra of competitive tendering, sensitivity to supply and demand, productivity targets and payment by results regimes became central features of a succession of reports and policies for

---

[2] Lambert's argument that the state ought to shift from being a direct 'monopolistic' provider of services to an outsourcer of services on open competitive markets was also echoed by business, some third sector/philanthropic representatives and Third Way political commentary at the time.

reforming prisons, probation and offender management. Proponents of greater competitiveness posit that it is not simply about applying economic levers to stimulate economic efficiency, but a project for instituting deep changes in the organisational values and responsibilities of public service providers, regardless of sector (Le Grand, 2003).

Greater sensitivity to consumer demand supposedly democratises public services by transferring the power of choice to consumers of publicly contracted services. Mechanisms of choice and demand, the argument runs, have the virtue of providing impartial stimuli to generate more responsible organisational behaviour or they will go out of business. The marketised allocation of contracts is suggested to be inherently fair under the assumption that the best enterprises attract the highest demand. Yet the principle of consumer sovereignty is fallacious when 'service users' are convicted and sentenced persons, in which case they have no effective 'choice'. The question as to who is the 'customer' (the state, courts, the public, victims or clients) is not satisfactorily resoluble, perhaps because 'in practice it may simply be inappropriate to do so' (Public Administration Select Committee, 2004: 4). Further, where democracy is actioned through the market, it is those with the most market power who have a greater say.

The logic that market competitiveness sets the benchmark of fairness for all is also internally inconsistent: charities and most of the public sector do not fit neatly within a profit-making model and are thus deemed to have weak market orientations and to lack sufficient commercial discipline to perform well in free markets. As a consequence, commissioners and contractors seek to incentivise – even coerce – these sectors into becoming 'fit for purpose' in competitive public service markets.[3] What are deemed to be 'counter cultural' forces, such as charities and the public sector or non-governmental organisations (NGOs) associated with redistributive justice or public service ethics, inhibit progress in the 'operation of markets for public goods', and therefore must be realigned to embrace 'market discipline' (McKay et al, 2011: 3).

---

[3] The 'carrots and sticks' approach to public service contracting is by now very well embedded in several fields from social care to health and education, and latterly criminal justice. Inducements may include incentive mechanisms such as 'payment by results' regimes or bonus payments for volume processing of clients, as well as approved contract status (being listed by government ministries as a fit contractor). Sanctions include punitive audit monitoring, loss of status as an approved contractor, withdrawal of contracts and fines for failure to deliver, for example.

Undoubtedly, while the headline message is that this is all in pursuit of efficiency, in reality the precondition to achieving these goals is driving down workers' pay and conditions. Julian Le Grand (2003), the academic advisor to the New Labour government on public sector modernisation, proposed that consumer-led models of public services should supplant provider-led public service hierarchies. This reassuring talk about 'empowering' consumer-citizens and coalitions of interest among all 'stakeholders' – funders, providers and consumers – consciously underlined the strategic disciplining (disempowering) of public service workers. In the process, 'Knavish' (professionally privileged and profiteering) interests are held in check by a combination of 'pawns' (clients and service users) and 'Knightish' (public-spirited, altruistic) actors from other sectors. This would bring about

> two fundamental ... changes ... One was essentially empirical; a change in beliefs in the way the world worked, in particular about what motivated individuals, especially those who worked within the public sector. The other involved a shift in values: service users ought not to be treated as passive recipients of welfare largesse but should have the lead role in determining the quantity and quality of the services they received. (Le Grand, 2003: 9)

The counterargument warns that free market concepts and techniques do not cleanly transfer to the non-profit arena. Market systems have historically failed to meet significant areas of human need where there is no obvious opportunity to accumulate profits, which is why public services historically evolved. Furthermore, there is no evidence generally that either the private sector or charities are inherently more virtuous than public sector agencies. They are at least as much disposed to 'implementation gaming' and 'cream skimming' (selecting the most profitable areas of work) while avoiding scrutiny in deregulated service markets. The largest providers of criminal justice services after the state are transnational companies (TNCs) with access to significant resources, which allows them to invest heavily in lobbying and contract chasing to increase their market share (Corcoran, 2014). The concentration of contracts in the hands of large providers exposes government contractors to business or delivery failures, which in turn has required remedial public refinancing if vital public services are not to collapse. Indeed, the inherent tendency of unregulated markets towards monopoly not only contradicts the rhetoric of merit and innovation, but 'the uncertainties of unrelenting change' tilts competitors towards risk aversion and uniformity. As a consequence. 'all organisations … develop similar norms and techniques of conduct, for without so doing, they will not survive' (du Gay, 2000: 80).

If marketisation is the practice, neo-liberalism is the theory

The revival of current criminological interest in the political economy beckons back to the origins of neo-liberalism as an intellectual movement in the interwar period of the 20th century (Bonefeld, 2012), but which gained ground as a political programme in response to global economic crises in the 1970s. Neo-liberalism is as much a philosophical doctrine as an economic theory, in that its central tenet is that economic freedom is an essential precondition for political and social liberty. In this context, it was posited that free markets were necessary both for guaranteeing capitalist democracy and as the most effective defence against fascist or communist totalitarianism (spectres which neo-liberals argue are the end to which welfare states tend). This is because, according to this perspective, a freely operating economy is the foundation of political liberty, wherein citizens find freedom through exercising choices and assuming responsibility through property ownership. (What is omitted in this proposition is that freedom to participate in the market depends on access to economic resources, which is denied to many.) Because markets are supposedly more virtuous than states in fostering social harmony, the primary role of government is to foster the conditions for markets to operate. This did not imply that the state should stand back from protecting the economy, as a 'strong state' is necessary to maintain the legal and institutional structures for optimising the space for markets to operate with minimal impediment.

Exemplified by Friedrich Hayek's *The Road to Serfdom* (1944/1999) and *The Constitution of Liberty* (1960/2006), neo-liberals associated with the Austrian School argued that market forces are ultimately the most efficient, democratic and free ways of organising societies.[4] Their economic writings influenced a generation of free market thinkers, such as Milton Friedman in the US and Keith Joseph in the UK,

---

[4] Founded by Ludwig von Mises in Vienna, this group of economists grappled with the causes of economic crisis in Europe in the interwar years, forming the most formidable intellectual opposition to Keynesian economic theory and welfare capitalism after the Second World War.

who helped to deliver a decisive blow to the post-war consensus.[5] From the 1980s, neo-liberal ideas gained significant political traction when they were adopted for the political projects of Thatcherism and Reaganism, whose political agendas were largely maintained by their successors in government, regardless of their professed political leanings (as Right, Left or Centrist) to the present (Leys, 2001; Harvey, 2007). This legacy was initially most prominent in countries where 'Anglo-Saxon' capitalist models predominate (US, England and Wales, Australia, New Zealand) (Albert, 1997), but has now assumed near-global hegemony.

In these jurisdictions, a particular strand of neo-liberal thinking, manifesting in the 'Washington Consensus' of 1989 (Williamson, 2004) for example, laid the basis for recasting the shortcomings of criminal justice agencies as the result of the flaws of social democracy. For neo-liberals, the expansion of welfare states and what was perceived to be counterproductive levels of regulation represented illegitimate encroachment on freedoms. In order to remedy this, the declared purposes of neo-liberal social policy became those of creating conditions that would restore libertarian freedoms by removing such distortions as 'big government', 'excessive' consumer protections, 'red tape' and organised labour, especially among public workers such as police, prison and probation workers, for example. Moreover, while it was conceded that free markets are prone to unstable economic cycles, these shocks were supposed eventually to correct themselves if governments resisted pressures to install welfare protections. Ultimately, it was argued, economic decline or crisis was caused by governments interfering in the markets, never by markets themselves.

The mythology of marketised criminal justice

As a successful ideology, neo-liberalism has sustained a credible mythology with regards to the economic basis of social order and the beliefs emanating from that tenet. From its origins in economic theory, the logic of the market is naturalised in the wider social imaginary which defines 'what constitutes our social existence [and provides] a basic infrastructure for meaning-making, reducing complexity, and ordering social reality' (Bartl, 2019: 4). In this context, the neo-liberal influence on crime and justice is interwoven with beliefs as to the

---

[5] The post-war consensus refers to the state welfarist social contract adopted in the major European industrial democracies as well as Australia and the US. This was often referred to as the 'cradle to grave' welfare state in the UK.

individualistic basis of morality, the emphasis on personal culpability for rule breaking, the uncoupling of criminality from social conditions, and strict limits as to social responses to crime and harm. A few examples (which are far from exhaustive) illustrate where aspects of criminological policy intersect with imaginaries of successful participation in market societies.

Law and order need a new 'social contract'

Neo-liberal economists were not directly concerned with questions about the state's penal function, although neo-liberal influence on the governance of crime has been extensive, if highly self-contradictory. However, critical criminologists have drawn attention to the materialisation of a 'new' moral order since the 1980s, which corresponds with a distinctively punitive approach towards socially and economically precarious groups (Hall, 2003; Simon, 2007; Standing, 2014). From this perspective, the 'material and symbolic construction of the penal state' is concerned with 're-establishing the state's grip over the populations pushed into the cracks and ditches' of late capitalism (Wacquant, 2009: 35). A neo-liberal social contract has been redrawn around societal norms which divide citizens into those who are integrated by virtue of their responsible life choices and independence from welfare, and those who allegedly exclude themselves from this bargain (Sim, 2009). Concurrently, and viewed via the lens of 'criminalisation of social policy' theories, the penal system remained, and expanded, as the dominant framework for responding to social crises. Put another way, tackling social exclusion, poverty or distress were reframed and subordinated to the higher goals of crime control, the sanctioning of lawbreakers and signalling public reassurances. The socially excluded, it is implied, deserve little if any support as they have effectively excluded themselves through their life choices. Rather, their plight ought not to be relieved, for the efficiency of the market relies on participants bearing the consequences of their choices.

There is such a thing as society – it is the market

Unlike critics who view neo-liberalism as antithetical to social cohesion, neo-liberals postulate that free market activities form the basis of many social interactions and therefore markets are innately social entities. Freedom is gained by the exercise of choice and through transactional, impersonal relations. In all other respects, the state inhibits freedoms by curtailing citizens' expression of preferences or access to social goods (by regulating how they are distributed). In famously pronouncing that there 'is no such thing as society', Margaret Thatcher was simply reiterating this belief about the nature of the neo-liberal social order – that people ought not to look to the state to support them. In sum, free markets are supposedly beneficial to all inasmuch as the theorised sustained economic growth which they are thought to facilitate improves the common wealth, and therefore happiness, of citizens. Thus, the interests of markets are held to be interchangeable with those of society as well as of the political and legal apparatus of the state. The expectation that radical individualism would somehow replace social solidarity reflects the sociological illiteracy, or more accurately, the political antipathy to socialised organisational forms, of Thatcherism.

Disorder can be countered by community 'resilience'

One of the tenets of neo-liberalism is that citizens must develop resilience to withstand the shocks of market cycles. It is acknowledged that exposure to unrelenting competitiveness unleashes alienation and social division. Traditional structures (family, community) and civil society are therefore all the more necessary to counteract the debilitating effects of unfettered markets. Continual exposure to unrelenting competitiveness has provoked states of insecurity among working people, who are exhorted to develop self-reliance and entrepreneurial mindsets, and by this means reduce the demand for social security. Criminal culpability is interwoven with narratives about deficient self-management and inadequate compliance with labour and wage discipline. Neo-liberals promulgate a political/financial morality which holds that the welfare state has trapped people in cycles of dependency, poverty and crime by divesting poor communities of the capacity to build self-help systems which would 'empower' them to take greater responsibility for tackling urban decline, crime, violence and anti-social behaviour in their neighbourhoods (Wilson and Kelling, 1982). The role of the state in supporting industry and employment, and therefore facilitating people's opportunities to make the 'right' choices, is neglected. The purpose of social reform (and by extension penal reform) is intrinsically connected with returning these excluded groups, if not to prosperity, then at least to functional resilience. This entails re-educating citizens to become self-reliant and enterprising through property ownership, minimising their demands on public welfare, adapting to more precarious labour markets and adhering to marketised norms and traditions. Such aspirations are also connected to the trend for 'returning' notional power to citizens via community crime control, all the while disempowering small stakeholders by withdrawing state funding from communities.

The 'small state' deceit

Neo-liberals have long taken aim at the failures and inefficiencies of the public sector, including criminal justice agencies, as deriving from the fact that they are state-owned, unaccountable 'monopolies' which are supposedly guilty of wastefulness and inefficiency. If necessary, it was argued, the imbalance between the economy and inefficient state sectors had to be corrected by turning over some public criminal justice functions to market competition. In this context, the private sector and (larger) charities should hypothetically be given optimal opportunity to work in the criminal justice 'space' as active competitors for public service contracts. In actuality, the objectionable part of *public* services related to the fact that they were *publicly* owned, managed and regulated. In their stead has emerged an oligopolistic grouping of commercial providers of many erstwhile public services which have proven to be no less immune to practising commercial self-preservation and inefficiency.

Markets <u>do</u> need state authorisation

Contrary to the claims of laissez-faire theorists, neo-liberal theory in its 'purest' (ordoliberal) form always favoured the idea of a strong state capable of implementing authoritarian measures to protect the economic status quo (Passavant, 2005; Bonefeld, 2012). The state preferentially concedes to the market in matters of material provision because the essential functions of the state lie with military security, preserving the rule of law and protecting the social order. A strong state, therefore, acts decisively to create conditions that are conducive to market freedom, and to protect them when threatened by social or political opposition. As Marquand (1997: 202) noted, every British government in the past 40 years used 'the formidable battery of powers of the central state to reconstruct civil society in the image of an enterprise culture'. The 'hand of the market' is far from invisible, and indeed requires the state to fit it in the glove of regulatory legitimacy.

The 'great transformation' in our time

Karl Polanyi's (1945) *Origins of Our Time: The Great Transformation* first gave theoretical shape to the concept of a 'market society' as an immanently anti-social and destructive influence. First published in 1945, it was then, and has been since, celebrated as a riposte to his neo-liberal contemporaries, particularly Hayek and the Austrian School and their ideological successors. It is not a conventional economic history but an exegesis and interpretation of what he called the 'great transformation' that was brought about by the rise of a market economy as the paradigm of the Western, and eventually global, evolution of society. Polanyi's central thesis is that the pre-eminence of market forces as the organising principle of societies is inherently destructive of the same societies. 'The idea of a self-adjusting market implies a stark utopia. Such an institution could not exist for any length of time without annihilating the human and natural substance of society' (Polanyi, 1945: 1).

Here, he posited that capitalism dynamically accumulated power by pushing for maximum penetration into the furthest reaches of social life. This occurred at the cost of competing communal relationships and institutions – kinship, community, class – to favour marketised free exchanges between citizens. Polanyi argued that the prevalence of an idea of society forged by the self-regulating market was ruinously disruptive of social systems where markets became predatory in the absence of checks and counterbalances. 'To allow market mechanisms to be sole director of the fate of human beings and their natural environment, indeed, even of the amount and use of purchasing power, would result in the demolition of society' (Polanyi in Harvey, 2007: 21)

Far from creating an innate state of freedom, Polanyi argued that the 'free market' was an ideological and historical construct which had emerged most disruptively during the era of industrial modernity for the purpose of concentrating economic and political power in the hands of elites. His was no Marxist theory of class dialectics, however.[6] Rather, Polanyi's object of analysis was focused on the historical uncoupling of economic thought and practice from their societal bonds which thrust 'the market' and 'society' into antagonistic, competitive relations. This resulted, he argued, in an epochal struggle between capitalist economic interests and the wider social good. Given

---

[6] There is not enough space to account for the singularity of Polanyi's thesis. He claimed that it was politically unaligned and he presented his book as an historical account of the relationships between 'society and markets'. That being said, he conceded that it was written as a utopian theory of society with elements of anarchism and socialism, although his conceptual separation of the social and political institutional forms from their basis in capitalism is a major departure from Marxist theories of historical materialism.

the capacity for runaway capital accumulation to wreak disruption, he argued, it was imperative that unregulated markets are restrained for the good of 'society'. In this context, however, governments were faced with a 'double-bind': historically, political authorities sought to stave off crises (such as unemployment, inflation or deflation, and so on), but their interventions in turn threw up unforeseen or unwanted outcomes. In short, attempts by either interventionist or laissez faire governments to rein in or liberate market forces have eventually come to some form of grief, 'thus reinforcing the alienation of society'. Accordingly, while 'society'

> inevitably ... took measures to protect itself ... whatever measures it took impaired the self-regulation of the market, disorganised industrial life, and thus endangered society in *yet another way*. It was this dilemma which forced the development of the market system into a definite groove and finally disrupted the social organisation based upon it. (Polanyi, 1945: 1, emphasis added)

The fate of capitalism is to be caught in a 'double movement' whereby hubristic, unregulated markets would destroy social institutions, paving the way for the further exploitation of natural resources and human activities. Inevitably, this would generate counter-tendencies aimed at defending society, values, community and security, which may themselves be fuelled by authoritarian and reactionary impulses. The history of modern political economy is thus motivated by a dialectic of forces and interests which lead to embedding market relations in one era followed by reactive uprooting in the next.

To conclude, Polanyi strongly contested the appropriation of freedom claims by economic liberals as mere advocacy of free enterprise, resulting in their failure to grasp social complexities. In answer, he found in favour of the 'supremacy of political institutions' (that is political, public and civil spheres) for subordinating economic to social interests. Market regulation was necessary to rescue markets from their hubris, or they were otherwise doomed to the appearance of populist or authoritarian counterforces, as had occurred in the 19th and 20th centuries. He concluded:

> On the balance of these freedoms, this necessitated regulation of the market, as the function of power is to ensure that measure of conformity which is needed for the survival of the group. Power and compulsion are a part of

that reality; an ideal [market utopianism] that would ban them from society must be invalid. (Polanyi, 1945: 248)

The 'great transformation' interrupted?

This summary does not do full justice to the richness and prescience of Polanyi's work (nor indeed that of Hayek's), especially as the revival of interest in these ideas has been sharpened by the aftershocks of the banking crisis (2007–08), followed by austerity, political instability and the rising appeal of authoritarian populism. Some contemporary lessons from Polanyi merit brief mention, as current events (not all progressive) resonate with his 'double movement' thesis. Firstly, we have not yet fully measured nor understood the impact of exposure to contemporary market fundamentalism in criminal justice fields. (The use of the term 'fundamentalism' here is not intentionally pejorative but reflects neo-liberal belief in the fundamental importance of 'free markets' to social, institutional and political formations). Whereas the impact of decades of marketisation has hitherto been a subfield of criminological inquiry, it is now clear that some form of public reclamation of criminal justice, penal and welfare fields is gathering pace. This renaissance is spurred on by the withdrawal of contracts to manage prisons from private sector providers (Guardian, 2016, 2018), the collapse of large companies such as Carillion at huge public expense and the early termination of outsourced contracts to run probation services from 2020. The financial difficulties of large charities such as Lifeline in 2017 (a nationwide drug services charity) and Working Links, which owned three probation services, likewise deprived parts of the country of services until new contractors could be found.

This countermovement is neither coherent nor guaranteed to be progressive, however. Immediately after the onset of the banking crisis in 2007, commentators began to talk about the resurgence of a post-neo-liberal narrative and momentum for asserting control over global markets. Britain, already one of the most radically marketised European countries, further accelerated in the direction of outsourcing and state-shrinking. While many remain persuaded by the zero-sum fallacy that markets succeed where the state gets out of the way, it is in periods of economic and social crises that the real nature of the relationships between corporations and states are revealed. As Monbiot (2016) remarked, the doctrine of the 'self-hating state' has denuded the capacity of political systems to counter contemporary 'zombie economics' (that is economic policies that are kept viable only through artificial means such as state support). The crux, as Polanyi indicated, hinges on whether the strong state that neo-liberals desire will prevail or what shape any alternative might take.

References

Albert, M. (1997) *Capitalism against Capitalism*, London: Whurr Publications.

Bartl, M. (2019) *Socioeconomic Imaginaries and European Private Law*, Centre for the Study of European Contract Law, Working Paper 2019–02, pp 1–24.

Bonefeld, W. (2012) 'Freedom and the strong state: on German ordoliberalism', *New Political Economy*, 17(5): 633–56.

Corcoran, M.S. (2014) 'The trajectory of penal markets in an age of austerity: the case of England and Wales', in M. Deflem (ed) *Sociology of Crime, Law and Deviance, special edition on 'Punishment and Incarceration: A Global Perspective'*, 19, pp 53–74.

du Gay, P. (2000) 'Entrepreneurial governance and public management: the anti-bureaucrats', in J. Clarke et al (eds) *New Managerialism, New Welfare?* London: Open University Press and Sage Publications, pp 62–80.

Financial Times (2009) 'CBI Chief sees new order in business', 3 April.

Guardian (2016) 'G4S should be a failed company by now: But the government won't allow it', 23 December, available from: https://www.theguardian.com/commentisfree/2016/dec/23/g4s-prisons-contracts-hmp-birmingham [accessed 13 December 2019].

Guardian (2018) 'Why HMP Birmingham has been brought back under state control', 20 August, available from: https://www.theguardian.com/society/2018/aug/20/why-hmp-birmingham-has-been-brought-back-under-state-control [accessed 13 December 2019].

Hall, S. (2003) 'New Labour's double-shuffle', *Soundings*, 24: 10–24.

Harvey, D. (2007) *A Brief History of Neoliberalism*, Oxford: Oxford University Press.

Hayek, F.A. (1944/1999) *The Road to Serfdom*, London: Routledge.

Hayek, F.A. (1960/2006) *The Constitution of Liberty*, London: Routledge.

Le Grand, J. (2003) *Motivation, Agency and Public Policy: Of Knights, Knaves, Pawns and Queens?* Oxford: Oxford University Press.

Leys, C. (2001) *Market-Driven Politics: Neoliberal Democracy and the Public Interest*, London: Verso.

McKay, S., Moro, D., Teasdale, S. and Clifford, D. (2011) *The Marketisation of Charities in England and Wales,* Third Sector Research Centre, Working paper 69. Birmingham University and Southampton University.

Marquand, D. (1997) *The New Reckoning: Capitalism, States and Citizens,* Cambridge: Polity Press.

Monbiot, G. (2016) *How Did We Get into This Mess?* London: Verso.

Passavant, P.A. (2005) 'The strong neoliberal state: crime, consumption, governance', *Theory & Event,* 8(3), *Project MUSE,* available from: http://muse.jhu.edu/article/187839

Polanyi, K. (1945) *Origins of Our Time: The Great Transformation,* London: Beacon Press.

Prasad, M. (2006) *The Politics of Free Markets: The Rise of Neoliberal Economic Policies in Britain, France, Germany and the United States,* London: University of Chicago Press.

Public Administration Select Committee (2004) *Choice, Voice and Public Services.* Written evidence to House of Commons Public Administration Select Cttee. HC 49-II, 21 December, London: The Stationery Office.

Sim, J. (2009) *Punishment and Prisons: Power and the Carceral State,* London: Sage.

Simon, J. (2007) *Governing through Crime,* Oxford: Oxford University Press.

Standing, G. (2014) *The Precariat: The New Precariat Class,* London: Bloomsbury.

Wacquant, L. (2009) *Punishing the Poor: The Neoliberal Government of Social Insecurity,* London: Duke University Press.

Williamson, J. (2004) 'A short history of the Washington Consensus', paper presented to the conference From the Washington Consensus towards a new Global Governance, Fundación CIDOB, Barcelona, 24–25 September, available from: https://www.piie.com/publications/papers/williamson0904-2.pdf [accessed 13 December 2019].

Wilson, J.Q. and Kelling, G.L. (1982) 'Broken windows: The police and neighborhood safety', *Atlantic Monthly,* March, pp 1–12, available from: https://urbanpolicy.net/wp-content/uploads/2012/11/Kelling+Wilson_1982_BrokenWindows_policing.pdf [accessed 31 October 2019].

2

Outcomes-based contracts in the UK public sector

Chris Fox and Kevin Albertson

Introduction

In the developed nations of the world, and in the UK in particular, the state increasingly has recourse to outcomes-based commissioning to address social needs (Albertson et al, 2018). The rationale of paying for specified outcomes is that it will supposedly reduce costs and increase the effectiveness of expenditure as it 'will link payment to the outcomes achieved, rather than the inputs, outputs or processes of a service' (Cabinet Office, 2011: 9).

The emphasis on outcomes arises, at least in part, from the consideration that the state faces the same social problems with which it has been wrestling for at least four decades: adults and families that experience multiple social, economic and health challenges, and further expected pressures of globalisation, ecological change, ageing populations, the digital revolution and the increasing precarity of employment.

A payment by results (PbR) contract contains three elements: a commissioner, a service provider and an outcomes metric designed, in theory, to align the incentive structures of the commissioner and the service delivery agency. However, for the PbR contractor, payment – at least in part – is made after outcomes are known; implicitly, after interventions are delivered. This delay is problematic for the service provider who needs working capital in order to fund the interventions in the first place.

A related policy innovation, Social Impact Bonds (SIBs), has been proposed to address this challenge (Mulgan et al, 2011) by facilitating access of PbR contractors to private finance. SIBs are not, strictly speaking, 'bonds' (that is, a debt security) in the financial sense of the term. An SIB does not represent public sector debt, it is rather a contract to pay financiers of social services dependent on the social value of such services.

Mulgan et al (2011) suggest SIBs will facilitate philanthropists or charitable trusts in raising funds from philanthropic sources. These will be invested in a special purpose 'vehicle' (organisation) which will sub-contract with non-governmental organisations to deliver services to achieve socially desired outcomes. Alternatively, they suggest an SIB may be initiated by a public sector organisation, for example, a local authority borrowing from existing commercial markets to deliver social innovation. The costs of delivery will be recouped from central government if the innovation achieves social savings.

In practice, however, the definition of an SIB has drifted somewhat since they were first proposed (Williams, 2019), with the state, financiers and service providers often holding differing concepts of the term. Nor has their use become as ubiquitous in public service provision as their proponents had hoped (Williams, 2019).

In this chapter we examine the theory, challenges and recent history arising in the implementation of PbR and SIB mechanisms. We start by providing a brief outline of the main attractions of PbR and SIBs. Next we provide an overview of some of the main challenges to outcomes-based contracts, identifying both conceptual difficulties and more practical challenges. Then we highlight previous and current examples of relevant initiatives in the UK public sector. Conclusions are drawn in the final section.

Advantages of outcomes-based commissioning

Outcomes-based commissioning, in theory, will allow public sector commissioners effectively to privatise the upfront costs of social services delivery, reduce taxpayer expenditure in the short term and supposedly reduce the risk of public money being spent on interventions which do not deliver desired outcomes. Through the focus on outcomes, proponents of PbR and SIBs argue these will drive greater efficiency, innovation and impact in tackling social problems while also reducing risk for government. We examine each of these suggested advantages in turn.

Efficiency

As with marketisation in general (see the Introduction to this volume) outcomes-based commissioning is thought to facilitate disaggregation and centralisation of decision making and service provision, competition between service providers, appropriate incentivisation, and the utilisation of digital and information technology. Further, outcomes-based commissioning may facilitate innovative service provision, as existing (public sector) modes of delivery are disrupted and new delivery modes are developed through the commissioning process.

In theory, therefore, outcomes-based commissioning may facilitate the allocation of resources to where they will achieve the most impact; however, this depends on whether, and the extent to which, social entrepreneurs prioritise the likely short-run return on SIBs, as distinct from longer-term social returns.

Transfer of risk and deferred payment

By making some or all of payment for the delivery of a service contingent on the delivery of agreed outcomes, the outcomes-based commissioning supposedly transfers both political and financial risk away from government and towards the service provider. The use of an SIB contract, where the private sector raises the upfront capital to fund innovation, will also reduce the headline debt liabilities of government compared with traditional state funding.

Encouraging new market entrants and innovation

Implicit in the concept of increasing innovation and the transfer of risk is the potential of outcomes-based commissioning models to encourage new market entrants, particularly from the private and voluntary sectors. This may result in cost reductions as private sector firms are more effective in general than government in putting pressure on workers' terms and conditions of employment; further, voluntary and third sector providers may utilise unpaid labour in providing public services (Albertson et al, 2018). On top of this, proponents of outcomes-based commissioning argue that this approach will allow providers to deliver services in different ways. The potential to adopt differing approaches will encourage greater innovation in service delivery. Those contractors which adopt effective innovations will prosper, while those which adopt ineffective delivery methods will not. Therefore it may be that greater efficiency will result from encouraging public, private and voluntary providers to compete.

Challenges of outcomes-based contracts

Analysis of the underlying concepts behind PbR suggests a number of challenges which must be faced if PbR mechanisms are to work effectively. Here, we outline three methodological challenges, before considering the practical challenges of implementing PbR projects.

Methodological challenges

Measuring outcomes

Key to PbR contracts is a clear definition of the outcome which is being purchased; this is not clear-cut. Consider, in the context of the criminal justice sector, the seemingly straightforward aim of reducing reoffending; this will generally be measured via the proxy of reconvictions (that is 'proven reoffending'). Thus, it would appear to matter little to the PbR model if offenders cease to offend, or merely become less easy to catch. Further, although it is recognised that desistance may be modelled as a process evolving over time, it may prove difficult to measure reductions in the frequency or severity of offending on the desistance journey.

The scale of improvement which defines a payable 'result' may also be difficult to achieve. In the first place, service providers will require a payment that reflects the level of risk assigned to them; likewise, an investor in an SIB will require additional compensation for their taking on the financial risks of failing to deliver 'results'. Thus, substantial improvements in social outcomes will be required to achieve sufficient savings from which to make these payments. Moreover, for such improvements to be statistically significant (that is, to be sure they do not merely result from chance), we require programmes not just to achieve their target, but to exceed it.

However, evidence from criminal justice evaluations indicates such improvements may be beyond the range of even well-executed projects and programmes (Mulgan et al, 2011). In this case, the ideal conditions for detecting marginal improvements in outcomes measures includes large intervention cohorts, which in turn demand an increase in upfront costs to operate programmes and devolving risks to prove success to service providers. Finally, all this must be achieved for less financial cost than simply maintaining public sector delivery of services.

Evaluating outcomes

The validity of outcomes-based contracts will depend in large part on the robustness of the measuring of outcomes. Thus, evaluation designs with high levels of internal validity (experiments and quasi-experiments) will be preferred to those with lower levels of internal validity. This will require evaluations which make use of appropriate comparator groups. Such evaluations are costly and require levels of comparison and scales of participation that are beyond the remit of most single contract providers. The degree of improvement in outcomes must therefore be such that its value covers not only the cost of service delivery, and the additional cost of private finance (in the case of an SIB), and not only an additional amount so we can be sure improvements do not result by chance, but also the cost of a robust evaluation.

One way to reduce evaluation costs would be for service providers to rely on delivering interventions where the efficacy has already been proven. However, this would undermine one of the goals of outcomes-based contracts, which is that it supposedly fosters innovation. In any event, it is unclear how long the evaluation of any given intervention remains valid given the continually changing nature of the economy.

Valuing outcomes

If PbR models are to become widespread, they will rely on the commissioner realising a monetisable saving from which to pay for the results. This implies taking a relatively narrow view of value, one that is limited to the fiscal benefits realised by the commissioning organisation and able to be accredited to the service contract. Consider, for example, the savings of reduced crime to the state: The savings to the criminal justice system, police, courts, prison, probation and so on may be estimated, but the state may not recover financially the reduction in costs to the private sector (for example, insurers) and the savings from reductions in victimisation. Given that the state will not recover all the social savings resulting from reduced crime, it is likely PbR contracts will either be underfunded or loss making.

It should further be borne in mind that, from the point of view of the state, not all potential savings can be practically converted into fiscal savings. The costs of crime, for example, will not decline proportionally as crime rates fall. The scale of impact which might allow savings to be realised from the closure of a whole wing of a prison, for example, might well be beyond the scope of a single PbR contract. In any event, we might consider that, in general, crime is currently lower in England and Wales than it was a decade ago, yet there seems to be no sign of the closure of large parts of the prisons estate. Thus, it is not clear that monetised savings will accrue in the criminal justice system even where there is a successful intervention.

Practical challenges

Those involved in setting up PbR schemes are also encountering a number of more practical challenges. Generally, these add to the complexity of establishing PbR and increase the risk of establishing perverse incentives which might encourage intervention providers away from achieving socially efficient outcomes.

Gaming

Incentive-based systems often suffer from corruption if the social outcome which is desired is more difficult to define than the specific indicator chosen. In this case, service providers do best if they concentrate on achieving those indicators specified in the output/outcome mechanism and neglect other measures, even those they know are also important. This is known in general parlance as 'hitting the target but missing the point', or 'gaming'.

Such gaming will be a particular problem where service deliverers' continued employment and profits depend on hitting a particular 'target'. Thus, the use of outcomes-based contracts carries with it the risk of corruption. Ultimately, any indicator which becomes a target can no longer then be used as an indicator (cf Albertson and Fox, 2019). In this regard PbR is no different from any other performance management system.

Individuals versus groups

A key choice for those setting up PbR contracts is whether to pay for the results achieved for individuals or the results for a group. When payments are based on the performance of individuals, one challenge will be to develop a monitoring and payment system which is not overly complex, bureaucratic and costly. However, when the 'result' involves the improvement of the prospects of a cohort, the heterogeneity of the group may cause problems.

In general we want the intervention group to be as homogeneous as possible, both to make the intervention itself easier to deliver and to improve the quality of the evaluation. A comparison group will be easier to find for a homogeneous intervention group, making evaluation more robust. In practice, however, where groups are homogeneous, they will also be smaller – making it more difficult to attribute any improvements in the 'results' to the intervention.

In practice those requiring public support are unlikely to all have the same set of issues. Where groups are not homogeneous, and the desired result is the improvement in the 'result' for the cohort as a whole, there is a potential that service providers will focus on those individuals who need the least help. This is known in PbR circles as 'parking' those with the greatest (and therefore most costly to address) needs and addressing the relatively fewer challenges faced by the least disadvantaged.

In theory, the incentive to 'park' some service users can be offset to some extent by the use of tariffs which specify set outcomes and tariffs for particularly disadvantaged groups. However, such a fine level of detail in contracts may actually increase the potential for gaming the system.

Allocating payments between organisations

Those citizens requiring social support are often a client group with complex needs requiring more than one intervention. The challenge this raises is how payments for results will be apportioned between providers given that the outcomes achieved by their respective services might be contingent on the performance of other service providers.

Commissioners might address this issue in one of two ways: One option is for commissioners to contract with a prime contractor and expect them to negotiate sub-contracts with smaller, more specialist service providers able to address particular needs or engage effectively with particular segments of the client group. From the point of view of the public sector commissioner, this has the attraction of negotiating fewer contracts directly. A second option is for commissioners to enter into separate contracts with a range of providers. This latter approach will also have a potential for delivering a rather more localised service; however, it adds another layer of costly complexity and negotiation.

The transfer of risk

Part of the aim of a PbR model is to transfer risk from the public commissioner of a service to the private sector provider. However, under the prime contractor model, a large prime contractor might be deemed 'too big to fail'. In this case the commissioner may still implicitly be underwriting the financial risk of the project, for the larger contractors at any rate.

In general, it is worth noting that the smaller the risk-bearing organisation, the greater the practical risk to the service provider in the sense that one adverse result can have disproportionate effects – perhaps even putting the service provider out of business. Conversely, larger providers may spread risk across a portfolio of activities. Thus, outcomes-based commissioning may deter, and therefore effectively exclude, smaller organisations and voluntary and public sector organisations from becoming providers of services.

The SIB mechanism supposedly facilitates risk being transferred away from smaller providers and towards the financier of the project (Albertson et al, 2018); in practice it is not clear by what mechanism this would operate. Given that, in a large PbR/SIB contract, prime contractors are likely to be the larger organisations which face less competition, and third sector providers rather more 'junior partners', it is clear the balance of power in negotiating terms of risk (and payment) is likely to reside with the prime contractor.

Examples of outcomes-based commissioning in the UK

In this section, following Albertson et al (2018), we outline three examples of programmes which illustrate the range of different approaches taken to applying outcomes-based commissioning across different sectors: the Work Programme, the Troubled Families programme and the Peterborough SIB.

The Work Programme

The Department of Work and Pensions (DWP) made extensive use of a PbR mechanism as part of its Work Programme, which brought together into a single scheme various programmes designed to help people into work. The Work Programme was a welfare-to-work intervention for job seekers who had usually been unemployed for between nine months and one year. It was delivered by 17 prime contractors and about 850 sub-contractors drawn from the public, private and voluntary sectors (National Audit Office, 2015).

The overall budget for the Work Programme was £3.3 billion over nine years from June 2011 and the DWP expected 80 per cent of payments made under the programme to be outcome-based (National Audit Office, 2015). In particular, prime contractors were paid an attachment fee when a job seeker started on the programme, a job outcome fee paid if they subsequently found work and sustainment payments if they managed to continue in employment. There was a range of tariffs for different job seeker groups which supposedly made allowances for the relative difficulty members of some marginalised groups have in finding and keeping employment (Work and Pensions Committee, 2015).

However, despite the range of tariffs being designed to incentivise contractors to support marginalised job seekers, the PbR model adopted by the DWP did not work well for those who required more intensive or specialised help. It was rather 'work ready' participants who were offered more support (Work and Pensions Committee, 2015: 7). In addition to the apparent 'gaming' of the PbR system, the programme was criticised for the scale of financial risks and reputational risks which were passed on to contractors, particularly third sector organisations (Rees et al, 2013). Further, there was little evidence of innovation in the types of support offered (Work and Pensions Committee, 2015: 8).

Notwithstanding that the Work Programme cost less per participant to deliver than the services it replaced, and produced at least as good results (Work and Pensions Committee, 2015), referrals ended on 31 March 2017.

The Troubled Families programme

The Troubled Families programme was launched in 2012 and allocated £448 million in funding with the aim of supporting 120,000 families with multiple and complex needs in England to 'turn around' their lives by 2015. These families were estimated to cost £9 billion per year in support under existing schemes.

Outcomes-based commissioning was at the heart of the Troubled Families programme, with local authorities being allocated 40 per cent of the cost of supporting troubled families on a PbR basis (HM Government, 2011). The 'Results' in question were:

- getting children back into school;
- reducing criminal and anti-social behaviour;
- supporting parents into paid employment; and
- reducing the cost of supporting these families.

However, the 120,000 'Families with Multiple Problems' were classified as such because they faced at least five of the following challenges (Levitas, 2012):

- no parent in the family in work;
- living in poor-quality or overcrowded housing;
- no parent has any qualifications;
- mother has mental health problems;
- at least one parent has a longstanding limiting illness, disability or infirmity;
- family has low income (below 60 per cent of the median); and
- family cannot afford a number of food and clothing items.

Clearly the results which might trigger payment to service providers were not well aligned with the underlying social needs of the families on the programme. The government, however, had high hopes and in 2013, three years before the evaluation report, announced Phase 2: an expansion of the programme to an additional 400,000 families supported by £200 million in funding in 2015/16 (Day et al, 2016).

When Phase 1 of the programme was evaluated, it was found that the 'PbR financial framework and targets were contentious in many local areas and were thought to have resulted in certain perverse incentives' (Day et al, 2016: 69). Overall, no significant evidence was found that it had any systematic impact on the key objectives. Some participants saw improvements in their conditions, but 'similar changes were observed for comparable non-participants' (Day et al, 2016: 49). Day et al also point out that payments are triggered for 'results', whether or not the improvement in participants' circumstances are attributable to their involvement with the programme.

The Peterborough SIB

In general, prior to the Transforming Rehabilitation (TR) agenda, adult prisoners serving short-term sentences (12 months or less) received no probation support on release from custody. The Peterborough SIB offered one year's post-release support through an intervention called the One Service to adult male prisoners released from short-term sentences at HMP Peterborough between 2010 and 2015 (Disley et al, 2015). Prisoners' engagement with the One Service was not mandatory; they were not required to engage with the intervention.

The intervention was coordinated by Social Finance, which raised capital to fund the One Service from 13 charitable trusts. Payments were to be made in two ways: service providers were directly paid for their services, while investors were paid on the basis of 'results', specifically the change in reoffending as measured by reconviction rates (Disley et al, 2015: iv). If reconviction was reduced by 7.5 per cent across the course of the intervention – or 10 per cent in any one of three cohorts – results-based payments would be made. Depending on the scale of the reduction, investors might receive a return of up to 13 per cent over an eight-year period. However, there was a significant downside risk: Investors could lose all their capital if reconviction did not fall by a sufficient amount to trigger payments.

An impact evaluation of the first cohort of offenders compared their reconviction rates with a counterfactual cohort selected using a propensity score matching (PSM) approach. The analysis found an

8.39 per cent reduction in reoffending rates within the first cohort compared with outcomes of 9,360 similar offenders released from other prisons. A similar evaluation of the second cohort also utilised a PSM approach. In this case, it was found that engagement with the One Service reduced the number of reconvictions by 9.7 per cent compared with a matched cohort.

The pilot was expected to run until 2017, but it was curtailed early, after only two cohorts, because all adult prisoners released from short-term sentences in England and Wales received probation support under the TR agenda. The reduction across both cohorts was estimated to be 9.0 per cent, which exceeded the threshold level of a 7.5 per cent reduction in reconvictions required across the life of the programme for results-based payments to be made. Thus early indications from this one project indicated that SIBs was a potentially viable approach for funding additional criminal justice services.

Despite the early curtailment of the Peterborough SIB, it is considered to have been a successful experiment. Reconviction rates were reduced – though it is not clear whether evaluators allowed adequately for the impact of self-selection into the programme – and those who engaged with the One Service spoke highly of it (Disley et al, 2015). However, there is little indication from this example whether the SIB approach in and of itself fostered innovation (Disley et al, 2015). Such an improvement in reconviction as was observed might have been achieved through offering additional support financed directly by the state rather than through an SIB.

Recent development in the outcomes-based contracts market

It is clear from the previous discussion that the inconsistencies between the incentive structures faced by commissioners, service deliverers and financiers may lead to less than efficient outcomes in outcomes-based contracts. As a result, both PbR and SIB concepts continue to develop.

The evidence base for PbR is limited in the UK as the government maintains no inventory of PbR schemes across the public sector (National Audit Office, 2015). Of those schemes which might be classified as PbR, Albertson et al (2018) identify 16 PbR schemes which have been used as a means of delivering mainstream public services. The size and duration of these programmes varies considerably, from some programmes under £10 million to some worth several billion pounds. However, it may be that the government's enthusiasm for PbR contracting has decreased (Albertson et al, 2018). For example, the PbR elements of the contracts made with Community Rehabilitation

Companies (CRCs) to deliver probation services have been linked to the financial difficulties faced by some of the prime contractors, and this model is being adapted as the TR agenda develops (see Albertson and Fox, Chapter 5, this volume).

Similarly, the SIB approach has evolved in the decade since Peterborough and is reputedly less focused on attracting private capital into public provision and relatively more on encouraging an outcomes-focused mindset (Williams, 2019). Given the austerity agenda pursued by the UK government, SIBs have thus become identified more with the achieving of 'more for less' than with promoting social innovation. Ultimately, SIBs have not become so widely adopted as their proponents envisaged. Of the 32 SIBs identified in the UK by Albertson et al (2018), approximately two thirds had received investment of less than £1 million; the initial investment across all 32 SIBs averaged only £1.71 million. In the UK at least, the momentum for SIBs still comes largely from public sector bodies and they are utilised in only a few areas of public provision, particularly looked-after children, youth unemployment and homelessness (Albertson et al, 2018).

Discussion: the limits of outcomes-based contracts

Outcomes-based commissioning has a part to play in the provision of public services (Albertson et al, 2018). Where the potential client group is homogeneous and large, measurement of outcomes is straightforward and inexpensive, the fiscal return on achievement of outcomes is easy to establish and service provision is highly integrated, a PbR or SIB approach may be attractive to commissioners, service providers and financiers. Similarly, an SIB may be useful in funding an extension to – or innovation in – existing provision if more conventional public sector funding is not available.

However, as the complexity of commissioning and PbR contracts increases, so does the risk of the approach. Therefore, where client groups are heterogeneous and relatively small, if outcomes are relatively difficult to measure and expensive to evaluate, where service provision is complex with benefits and attributions shared across a number of different stakeholders and existing evidence on what works is sparse, outcomes-based commissioning is unlikely to be useful as a driver of service reform.

Nor is it straightforward to transfer financial risks from the state to the private sector. In general, the public sector is more able to bear risks, and can borrow more cheaply, than the private sector. Where financial risks are transferred to the private sector from the public sector, commissioners are likely to have to pay a premium or underwrite contracts to motivate the private sector to take on such risks.

As evaluation and appropriate evidence of impact is a key aspect of outcomes-based commissioning, as the approach is implemented we might expect an increase in the evidence base of 'what works' (and what does not). Such an evidence base will facilitate the growth of the outcomes-based commissioning market. However, there has been relatively little empirical support of these commissioning tools to date (National Audit Office, 2015) and little evidence in the UK of outcomes-based commissioning driving innovation. Thus,

> While supporters argue that by its nature PbR offers value for money, PbR contracts are hard to get right, which makes them risky and costly for commissioners. If PbR can deliver the benefits its supporters claim – such as innovative solutions to intractable problems – then the increased cost and risk may be justified, but this requires credible evidence. Without such evidence, commissioners may be using PbR in circumstances to which it is ill-suited, with a consequent negative impact on value for money. (National Audit Office, 2015: 8)

References

Albertson, K., Bailey, K., Fox, C., LaBarbera, J., O'Leary, C. and Painter, G. (2018) *Payment by Results and Social Impact Bonds: Outcome-Based Payment Systems in the UK and US*, Bristol: Policy Press.

Albertson, K. and Fox, C. (2019) 'The marketisation of rehabilitation: some economic considerations', *Probation Journal*, 66(1): 25–42.

Cabinet Office (2011) 'Modernising commissioning: Increasing the role of charities, social enterprises, mutuals and cooperatives in public service delivery', London: Cabinet Office, available from: https://assets.publishing.service.gov.uk/government/uploads/system/uploads/attachment_data/file/78924/commissioning-green-paper.pdf [accessed 16 July 2019].

Day, L., Bryson, C., White, C., Purdon, S., Bewley, H., Sala, L.K. and Portes, J. (2016) 'National evaluation of the Troubled Families programme: final synthesis report', London: Department for Communities and Local Government, available from: https://assets.publishing.service.gov.uk/government/uploads/system/uploads/attachment_data/file/786889/National_evaluation_of_the_Troubled_Families_Programme_2015_to_2020_evaluation_overview_policy_report.pdf [accessed 18 July 2019].

Disley, E., Giacomantonio, C., Kruithof, K. and Sim, M. (2015) 'The payment by results Social Impact Bond pilot at HMP Peterborough: final process evaluation report', London: RAND Europe for Ministry of Justice, available from: https://assets.publishing.service.gov.uk/government/uploads/system/uploads/attachment_data/file/486512/social-impact-bond-pilot-peterborough-report.pdf [accessed 22 July 2019].

HM Government (2011) 'Tackling troubled families', available from: https://www.gov.uk/government/news/tackling-troubled-families [accessed 18 July 2019].

Levitas, R. (2012) 'There may be "trouble" ahead: what we know about those 120,000 "troubled" families', Poverty and Social Exclusion in the UK, Policy Response Series No. 3, available from: http://www.poverty.ac.uk/sites/default/files/attachments/WP%20Policy%20Response%20No.3-%20%20%27Trouble%27%20ahead%20%28Levitas%20Final%2021April2012%29.pdf [accessed 18 July 2019].

Mulgan, G., Reeder, N., Aylott, M. and Bo'sher, L. (2011) *Social Impact Investment: The Challenge and Opportunity of Social Impact Bonds*, London: the Young Foundation, available from: https://youngfoundation.org/wp-content/uploads/2012/10/Social-Impact-Investment-The-opportunity-and-challenge-of-Social-Impact-Bonds-March-2011.pdf [accessed 16 July 2019].

National Audit Office (2015) *Outcome-Based Payment Schemes: Government's Use of Payment by Results*, London: National Audit Office, available from: https://www.nao.org.uk/wp-content/uploads/2015/06/Outcome-based-payment-schemes-governments-use-of-payment-by-results.pdf [accessed 16 July 2019].

Rees, J., Taylor, R. and Damm, C. (2013) 'Does sector matter? Understanding the experiences of providers in the Work Programme', The Third Sector Research Centre (TSRC) Briefing Paper 92, University of Birmingham, available from: https://www.birmingham.ac.uk/Documents/college-social-sciences/social-policy/tsrc/working-papers/briefing-paper-92.pdf [accessed 18 July 2019].

Williams, J.W. (2019) 'From visions of promise to signs of struggle: exploring social impact bonds and the funding of social services in Canada, the US, and the UK', available from: https://golab.bsg. ox.ac.uk/documents/234/Williams-2019-Final-Report.pdf [accessed 26 July 2019].

Work and Pensions Committee (2015) *Welfare-to-Work: Second Report of Session 2015–16*, London: The Stationary Office, available from: https://publications.parliament.uk/pa/cm201516/cmselect/ cmworpen/363/363.pdf [accessed 18 July 2019].

3

The carceral state and the interpenetration of interests: commercial, governmental and civil society interests in criminal justice

James Gacek and Richard Sparks

Introduction

There is something rotten in the state of criminal justice. Let us not mince words here: this smell is none other than the pungent aroma of the commercialisation of the penal realm, and it is through our current developments in penal politics (especially the expansion and intensity of mass incarceration, and its counterpart mass supervision) (McNeill, 2018) that this odour has exasperatingly wafted into governmental and civil society interests. Perhaps to us and our fellow criminologists (and certainly to most non-specialists), this miasma of commercialisation is no more than an irksome bother, an annoyance in our atmosphere. It does not impact us intensely, and we may even be persuaded to accept the claim that it is a necessary by-product of the smooth and efficient delivery of criminal justice services. There are doubtless many such odour-neutralising arguments to hand. However, in the lives of many already marginalised people in our society, it is sometimes the case that the interaction of state and commercial interests can produce hazardous, even noxious, effects. The question here is whether the permeation of the everyday lifeworld of very large populations of people through practices of supervision and surveillance is of this kind. Such effects may well be a debilitating smog; an overpowering feeling of exhaustion and strife these individuals endure, a darkened hazy fog which stops them in their tracks, making it difficult for them to breathe and flourish. This rot continues to pollute their lives and the lives of their loved ones, and as our chapter contends, now is the time seriously to reconsider the polluted path of commercial interests in criminal justice and query where it is taking us. We have resolved, in short, to get off the fence.

To be more precise, we need to think harder about whether the market provides – or does not provide – an adequate form of public accountability in this sphere, and about the ways the public are empowered or otherwise to engage in democratic decision making.

We think it is probable that confluent interests from the commercial, governmental and civil society sectors will, in the absence of robust interrogation, continue to extend the scope of penal supervision in the lives and communities of already marginalised people. If that is the case, failure to provide such interrogation becomes an evasion of the responsibilities of scholars of criminal justice to inform policy communities and the wider public of the foreseeable consequences of decisions taken at least nominally in our name. Not to do this is to allow the market – and those whom it empowers – to make relatively invisible and unaccountable decisions. As Stanley Cohen made eloquently clear in another context (Cohen, 2001), there are a variety of ways of not knowing, or avoiding knowledge, about the suffering of others. But the challenge of recognising such suffering is always exacerbated by opacity, just as the alibis of not knowing are rendered more difficult by visibility.

Democracy encompasses a wide and variable set of values and claims, and we recognise that particular models of democracy are appropriate for different political communities at different times. Such values and claims will depend not on abstract theorising (although it is clear that theoretical principles and formal arguments certainly will have their place), but on the structural, societal conditions faced by a particular polity at a particular moment in history. Perhaps it is time to listen to the electorate – or, more particularly, to communities directly affected by policy choices of various kinds – more intensely and the market experts less.

While we endeavour to examine the interpenetration of interests in the marketisation of criminal justice, our chapter also entails the classic social theoretical task of making the familiar strange. Generations of social inquiry acknowledge, in widely differing ways, both the centrality and the difficulty of resisting the weight of that to which we are habituated (for example Bourdieu, 1990; Harding, 1991). Harding (1991) influentially argues that cultivating the capacity to see familiar things as odd is the very beginning of scientific inquiry. After more than a generation of desensitisation to an expansive criminal justice state, and to rates of incarceration that are exceptional by historical standards, inhabitants of some

Western countries may stand in danger of losing the capacity to see these things, in the sense of bearing witness to their abnormality. It is for this reason that Dzur et al (2016) speak of contemporary criminological work taking place *in the shadow* of mass incarceration, critically querying how 'to fix what is broken about a dysfunctional system that implicates all of us who have grown accustomed to it and in whose name it was assembled' (Dzur et al, 2016: 2). As one of us has previously argued, 'the arguments over the justification of *any* practice of imprisonment (private or otherwise) need to be more strenuously pursued than contemporary rhetorics allow' (Sparks, 1994: 14; emphasis in original). If the argument is that the route towards a better penal politics involves investigating how the ideals and institutions of democracy can be given practical effects in reshaping criminal justice and penal arrangements, then one key dimension of that project concerns analysing the scope and limits of commercialisation in respect of public questions and public goods.

Yet a system which implicates all of us rests on the presumption that all of us form a 'public' in society. It is not entirely correct to presume that as the 'public', 'we' all have equal access to participating in political, civic life. While we the public, as an imagined collective, may frequently be invoked or enjoined, opportunities for informed participation and voice are relatively few, and by no means equally distributed. While some accredited (or wealthy) voices ring out, others are barely an audible whisper.

In terms of criminal justice, crime and punishment may saturate the public's news and entertainment media, but we have not been provided many or equal opportunities to think seriously about how our institutions deal with crime and punishment (Dzur et al, 2016: 6). Criminal justice work is often physically removed from the lay public. Some of it is literally sequestered behind walls. Other aspects are delegated to expert professionals in relatively low-visibility spaces. There may often be good reasons for this, but it nevertheless raises unresolved difficulties for cultivating public awareness of penal politics or offering opportunities for people to involve themselves in informed deliberation about it. If this favours the view that much work in the criminal justice arena consists of discrete, specialised tasks, often performed on people we view with distaste, then it becomes increasingly plausible to delegate such work to proficient providers of services (including those offering such services as private contractors) rather than viewing it as intrinsically public, visible and accountable.

Electronic monitoring (EM) of offenders in the community, for example, has become an increasingly complex entity within the expanding carceral state (a notion which we use here to refer to a series of institutional configurations and actors that prioritise punishment, containment, detention and/or incarceration for treating social inequality such as poverty and marginalisation) (see Sparks and Gacek, 2019). We should not underestimate the reach and embeddedness of the carceral state on either side of the Atlantic today. We now know a great deal about the structural causes of this phenomenon and about the political dynamics that have fuelled and shaped it. As Gottschalk (2015: 34) contends, the construction of the carceral state resulted from a complex set of developments: 'No single factor explains its rise, and no single factor will bring about its demise.'

To date, the greater part of criminological scholarship and counterpart forms of political engagement has been devoted to examining the effects of imprisonment, latterly most obviously the phenomenon of mass incarceration in the United States. This seems hardly surprising since the effects of that development have been so far-reaching, and have entailed consequences for other societal institutions including local economies, families, communities, political processes and democracy making. However, the scope and effects of the carceral state are by no means limited to the prison, and increasing proportions of its work are carried out by private actors. The resiliency of the carceral state owes much to the elasticity of its web, insofar as 'the various permutations of the carceral state suggests that it is informed by and contours itself around the ways in which the economic, political, and social structures interrelate to each other at different moments in time' (Kato, 2017: 217).

Such structures can connect to the everyday life of marginalised groups engaging with surveillant technologies. In effect, EM and other technology-driven surveillance and management innovations extend carceral space into everyday life, rendering carcerality and surveillance commonplace within the legal and regulatory operations of the contemporary state (Gacek, 2019a).

Recent scholarship also highlights multiple forms of confinement and mobility, examining how they coalesce in particular ways within the shadows of the carceral state (for select examples, see Gacek, 2019a; Sparks and Gacek, 2019). For instance, the use of the private security firm G4S Scotland by the Scottish government to monitor offenders in the community through EM could be rightly argued to be one governmental tool of the carceral state's arsenal. Put differently, the penal arm of the state is chronically overburdened, and apt to seek to generate additional capacity through innovative extensions, technologies and socio-technical assemblages.

Indeed, the multi-scalar effects of the carceral state call for greater attention towards the extension of carceral logics outside of prison walls and the larger, punitive governance of social marginality through carceral expansion (Gacek, 2019b). It now includes not only a country's 'vast archipelago of jails and prisons but also the far-reaching and growing range of penal punishments and controls that lie in the never-never land between the gate of the prison and full citizenship' for the excluded of society (Gottschalk, 2014: 289). Fletcher's (Chapter 19, this volume) research on the efficacy and ethicality of welfare conditionality in England and Scotland suggests that long-term imprisonment leaves a lasting legacy on benefits claimants, a kind of 'perpetual punishment' which risks pushing post-release individuals out of the welfare system and into criminal activity. Similarly, Thorpe (2016: 22) rightly contends that people who have served time in prison are less likely to be eligible to vote, find stable employment, receive public housing or educational benefits and maintain family ties. To make matters worse, predominantly poor, urban neighbourhoods where outsized numbers of young men have a prison record are subject to chronic instability, heightened social isolation and greater levels of civic distrust (Thorpe, 2016: 22).

The costs of carceral expansion now extend well beyond the length of a prison term. The price for the marketisation of criminal justice is levied in the lives of the vulnerable, marginalised communities which commercial interests require to make marketisation happen. Notable criminological scholars anticipated these developments; standing on this solid criminological bedrock, it is now our turn to take up the torch and proceed into the thick of the carceral state smog before us.

Reduce, reverse, or raze? Reconsidering the reign of the carceral state

One could argue that our current carceral 'fix' in some Western countries is an extreme one. Perhaps it is now so dire that we have no choice but to reconsider our predominant philosophical trajectory and the path of punishment down which it seems to be taking us. Do we allow the carceral state to continue its reign? Or can it be possible to rein it in and reduce the harms and failures it has produced thus far? Moreover, can we philosophically reverse the expansion of the carceral state, or raze it altogether, as Gottschalk (2015) contends?

From the outset it is no mystery that the situation of the carceral states in the US and the UK have become worrisome leviathans of confinement. According to the World Prison Brief, estimated numbers based on the end of April 2018 suggest that the current prison population rate for England and Wales is an estimated 139 people incarcerated in jails or prisons per 100,000 residents; the rate in Northern Ireland is 76 people per 100,000 residents; in Scotland the rate is 150 people per 100,000 residents; and in the US a staggering 655 people per 100,000 residents are presently imprisoned (World Prison Brief, 2018). Yet the carceral state is no longer just a problem largely confined to the prison cell and prison yard. For example, data as recent as late 2016 suggest that not only are roughly 2.2 million people incarcerated in jails and prisons throughout the US, but when one factors in the 4.5 million people supervised in the community by a parole or probation agency, it is estimated that one in 38 adults in the US are under some form of correctional supervision (Schiraldi, 2018). Similarly, recent statistics collated for the Council of Europe indicate that some jurisdictions that make extensive use of supervision in the community – such as Scotland – have among the highest aggregate correctional populations (well over 500 persons per 100,000 in the Scottish case).[1]

In effect, community corrections 'has turned into an add-on, rather than a relief valve, to the mass incarceration dilemma in the [US]' (Schiraldi, 2018: np) and in a number of other countries. Indeed, the situation has become so extensive that the carceral state 'has begun to metastasise' (Gottschalk, 2014: 289), leaching into the everyday spaces and places of life for impoverished, marginalised groups and communities alike. It has altered how essential governing and public institutions operate, as well as distorting key demographic, political and socio-economic databases, 'leading to misleading findings about trends in vital areas such as economic growth, political participation, unemployment, poverty, public health, and educational attainment', to name a few (Gottschalk, 2014: 290). Simultaneously, the carceral state is both bluntly and subtly 'remaking conceptions of citizenship' insofar as it creates an ever growing and permanent group of political, economic and social outcasts within our society, condemning hundreds of thousands (if not millions) of people to 'civil death' by way of denied core civil liberties and social benefits because of a criminal conviction, irrespective of the severity of the crime committed (Gottschalk, 2014: 290).

In our increasing eagerness to resolve this current carceral situation, EM offers itself as a handy technology and a viable alternative, able to

---

[1] See further the Council of Europe's (undated) Annual Penal Statistics: http://wp.unil.ch/space

increase diversion from prison and thus to decrease incarceration rates and costs. However, as Gottschalk (2014: 291) contends, 'the optimism that we are at the beginning of the end of the carceral state because the fiscal costs have become too high to sustain are unwarranted' and will not single-handedly uproot the carceral state from its place in our society. Many of the political, social and economic factors that conceived the carceral state remain fundamentally unchallenged and unchanged.

Kato (2017: 198) argues that even though demands in the West to dismantle mass incarceration 'are increasingly gaining traction, it will not necessarily lead to a reduction of the carceral state'. Emerging trends which centre on surveillance and security, coupled with how policy making is negotiated and social upheavals are managed, puts more of the onus upon the controlling aspects associated with the carceral state and less upon the enclosing characteristics of traditional incarceration. Therefore, decreased levels of incarceration and increases in EM 'should be seen as more of a realignment than an end to the carceral state' (Kato, 2017: 198), and while people may elude incarceration it is through EM that 'they are nevertheless *enmeshed within a carceral web that is more widening and diffuse*' (Kato, 2017: 217; emphasis added).

While we recognise arguments on behalf of EM as a fruitful endeavour to deal with mass incarceration in the West, we query whether a focus upon population rates and costs of prison on the one end and EM on the other gets to the heart of the matter, especially concerning the legitimacy of current penal developments in our society (Gacek, 2019b). Such a focus, we contend, merely obscures the underlying culture of control pervading our understandings of the scope of the penal realm (see also Gacek, 2019a; Sparks and Gacek, 2019), especially if it leads us away from interrogating the realities of mass supervision in everyday life (McNeill, 2018).

EM, and the marketisation of other technologically mediated penal sanctions, is not the silver bullet that will fix the problems of mass incarceration, nor will it ever be. Cognitive assumptions, normative commitments and emotional sensibilities continue to coordinate crime and social control in such a way as to reshape how we feel about marginalised groups and how they are made to feel punished, excluded, isolated or immobile within the carceral web in numerous ways (for examples, see Gacek, 2019a, 2019b).

Debating the use of prison *versus* the use of EM is of limited value if such penalties merely represent two sides of the same coin, that is, the legitimation of the carceral state's continued management of impoverished and marginalised groups with little to no consideration of ameliorating these social issues outright. While commercial interests may persuade governments and civil society that through their services punishment is served effectively and efficiently, the fact remains that EM does nothing to assist or support the excluded in a meaningful way that could lead to their fuller inclusion in society. Nor does it redress the collateral effects of imprisonment imposed upon the loved ones of the offender (Gacek, 2019a).

EM is not a meaningful alternative unless and until it is used as such. At present it represents a form of confinement similar to the prison while simultaneously widening the carceral web across a diverse range of socio-political and geographic scales (Gacek, 2019b). While we remain cognisant that such redress may be within neither the nature of the technology nor the parameters of its use (Gacek, 2019b), simply returning the offender to their community without adequate supports in place merely band-aids a wound that requires greater attention. Should we the public decide that EM is to be allowed to expand further (both in technological prowess and punitive means), it must be paired with appropriate social policies and programmes which directly redress the actual needs of the offender and assist them in ameliorating their particular social circumstances (Sparks and Gacek, 2019), a discussion to which we now turn.

Alternative paths and policy implications

The marketisation of criminal justice represents a kind of degradation of an important form of interaction that we, as scholars working in criminology and criminal justice, have a responsibility to defend alongside and for our fellow citizens. Yet this begs the question of how we are to further defend this interaction from future carceral campaigns: Is there a solution beyond the marketisation of criminal justice that will rescue us from the stretch of the carceral state?

Criminology urgently needs to overcome its discomfort in the face of democracy and its dubiety towards public participation. Citizens must no longer be treated as a befuddled herd of passive fools and hysterical hotheads; instead, they must be accorded a window of opportunity to struggle with the complex trade-offs that animate decisions about crime control and punishment. As scholars have pointed out (in a plethora of ways), the expansion of meaningful public involvement in governance has been shown to increase government legitimacy, social capital, civic participation and trust (for example, see Dzur et al, 2016). The toxic mix of market interests and criminal justice dehumanises (arguably, to an even greater extent) populations which are already doubly marginalised within the criminal justice domain.

There is a need to identify ways in which the philosophical rationales and justifications for particular crime control and penal policies can be drawn out into the open, public sphere, where citizens can be given the opportunity to consider the pros and cons of how their interests interpenetrate with government and commerce (Sparks and Gacek, 2019). Elected officials would then be able to grasp the wisdom and feasibility of sponsoring an alternative mode of politics that expands opportunities for greater democratic participation. Citizens, in turn, would then be able to contribute more meaningfully to government decision making, to the possible benefit of policy outcomes and social justice. Marketising criminal justice does not inherently provide citizens this ability, nor does it automatically render commercial interests in criminal justice transparent and open to public scrutiny. Those democratic gains only occur when conscious choices are made to ensure not just that accountability is formally stringent but also where both state and private actors are required to render accounts in public and to engage in deliberation with people affected by their decisions.

If criminology is to have an impact on public and criminal justice policy, then presumably it should take steps to encourage research that not only is relevant to policy discussions and debates but, following on from our previous discussion, makes the familiar strange. While such considerations may seem obvious and self-evident at first glance – that yes, attempts to robustly interrogate social phenomena are indeed part and parcel of questioning how our world works – we do not make this statement lightly. As Nellis (Chapter 15, this volume) contends, progressive penal reformers must continue to question 'all penal imaginaries', especially if such imaginaries prioritise tracking technology over properly resourced probation services and trained human supervisors. Indeed, we remain vigorously critical in our perspective that such endeavours to query the legitimacy of current penal developments remain paramount (Gacek, 2019a; Sparks and Gacek, 2019). Doing so has the potential fiercely and formidably to re-ignite public conversations concerning the implementation of penal supervision into the lives of already marginalised persons and groups in society.

Moreover, rhetoric matters in the process of educating democrats. It is necessary to reach beyond criminology's self-image as a 'dismal science', in order to see that in certain respects the strengths our discipline has in challenging and changing criminal justice can be profound. Our most powerful and compelling stories of penal change are narratives of decline and disaster, for it is within them that we document, warn, alert and critique the social world as it is and reimagine what it could be for all of its citizens with better penal reforms – where 'better' means 'something along the lines of more moderate, milder, rights-respecting, liberal, or principled' (Dzur et al, 2016: 4).

Rather than simply thinking in terms of crime control and punishment, we must think democratically about criminal justice, insofar as we 'seek to ask sharper questions about the collateral effects of the transformations of the carceral state upon political participation, the formulation of civic identities and the associational life of impacted communities' (Dzur et al, 2016: 8). In other words, direct human vulnerability maintained by the carceral state mandates more comprehensive forms of public participation to resist it.

Since the onset of the economic recession in 2008, the unsustainable fiscal costs of the carceral state have spurred greater demands for criminal justice reform from fiscal hawks and civil libertarians (Thorpe, 2016: 23). Yet fiscal pressures alone will not be enough to spur communities and governments to make significant shifts in how they perceive punishment in nature, form and function. As the carceral state has grown, 'so has the political clout and political acumen of groups, institutions, and organisations with vested economic interests in maintaining [it]' (Gottschalk, 2015: 35). Yet policy makers on both the political Left and Right continue to ignore the government's role in creating conditions in which social blight and degrading forms of punishment and crime control would metastasise. This makes it difficult to assist the impoverished, marginalised and/or incarcerated in society, and makes the carceral state particularly difficult to dismantle. The vastness of social control and punishment practices have brought the experiences of incarceration closer to the lives of the poor and communities of colour than ever before. Moreover, the expansion of surveillance and control through criminal justice systems, including probation and parole, mandated substance abuse treatment and practices of 'banishment', suggest creative and extensive reaches of the carceral state beyond the conventional threat of incarceration into these same lives (for example, see Sparks and Gacek, 2019). When commercial interests in the marketisation of criminal justice interpenetrate with government and civil society, the carceral state is then deployed to combat various (vividly depicted, yet often misleadingly simplified) social ills. We can no longer accept this. These communities remain key targets of the carceral state and therefore should be rightly heard within public policy debates and penal reforms.

Conclusion

The perfect is the enemy of the good, according to Voltaire. A perfect understanding of the pairing of punishment with the marketisation of criminal justice is a distant goal, as is a perfect comprehension of the legitimacy of current penal developments (Sparks and Gacek, 2019). Yet this is not a counsel of despair. To the contrary, it just might help clarify precisely what commercial, governmental and civil society interests in criminal justice are, and what outcomes are relevant to assessing the legitimacy of current penal developments and the predicaments facing the reduction, reversal or outright razing of the carceral state.

Our chapter has illustrated that the twists and turns of recent penal discourse are no less serpentine than ever. While political winds can shift quickly, the situation of the carceral state is more durable; the carceral state has expanded and diffused into various sectors of society, drawing upon the interpenetration of interests to maintain its permanency and legitimacy. Perhaps by making the familiar strange we can begin to query the carceral state's resiliency; perhaps with making the familiar strange, we can begin critically to open further discussion which redresses the creative carceral extensions of the state and its penal reach beyond the typical and conventional spaces of incarceration (Gacek, 2019a). The smog of the carceral state may be no less thick, but our attempts to clean and clear our air of this rotting stench are no less important.

We remain firm in the view that 'more socially conscious and morally charged perceptions of penal affairs' are as urgently required now as they have ever been (Garland, 1990: 161; Sparks and Gacek, 2019). Continued progress in public awareness and engagement opens the public (comprising *all* of its citizens, *and* wherever possible those non-citizens who are directly affected by its decisions and practices) to potentially fruitful outcomes in criminal justice reform and deliverables, and promotes a constructively welcoming civic participation and action within criminal justice issues. Criminal justice is inextricably entangled with concerns of how to bolster and maintain better democratic governance.

References

Bourdieu, P. (1990) *The Logic of Practice*, Stanford, CA: Stanford University Press.

Cohen, S. (2001) *States of Denial: Knowing about Atrocities and Suffering*, London: Polity Press.

Council of Europe (undated) *Council of Europe Annual Penal Statistics*, available from: http://wp.unil.ch/space [accessed 30 October 2019].

Dzur, A.W., Loader, I. and Sparks, R. (eds) (2016) *Democratic Theory and Mass Incarceration*, New York: Oxford University Press.

Gacek, J. (2019a) *Carceral Territory: Experiences of Electronic Monitoring Practices in Scotland*, Unpublished PhD Dissertation: University of Edinburgh.

Gacek, J. (2019b) 'Stuck in the carceral web: Inmates' experiences of electronic monitoring', *Criminological Encounters*, 2(1): 35–52.

Garland, D. (1990) *Punishment and Modern Society: A Study in Social Theory*, Oxford: Clarendon Press.

Gottschalk, M. (2014) 'Democracy and the carceral state in America', *The Annals of the American Academy of Political and Social Science*, 651: 288–95.

Gottschalk, M. (2015) 'Razing the carceral state'. *Social Justice*, 42(2): 31–51.

Harding, S. (1991) *Whose Science? Whose Knowledge? Thinking from Women's Lives*, Ithaca, NY: Cornell University Press.

Kato, D. (2017) 'Carceral state 2.0? From enclosure to control & punishment to surveillance', *New Political Science*, 39(2): 198–217.

McNeill, F. (2018) *Pervasive Punishment: Making Sense of Mass Supervision*, Bingley: Emerald Publishing.

Schiraldi, V. (2018) 'Parole and probation have grown far beyond the resources allocated to support them', *The Conversation*, 16 August, available from: http://theconversation.com/parole-and-probation-have-grown-far-beyond-resources-allocated-to-support-them-98372 [accessed 30 October 2019].

Sparks, R. (1994) 'Can prisons be legitimate? Penal politics, privatization, and the timeliness of an old idea', *British Journal of Criminology*, 34: 14–28.

Sparks, R. and Gacek, J. (2019) 'Persistent puzzles: the philosophy and ethics of private corrections in the context of contemporary penality', *Criminology & Public Policy*, 18(2): 379–99. DOI: 10.1111/1745-9133.12445

Thorpe, R.U. (2016) 'Democratic politics in an age of mass incarceration', in A.W. Dzur, I. Loader and R. Sparks (eds) *Democratic Theory and Mass Incarceration*, New York: Oxford University Press, pp 18–32.

World Prison Brief (2018) *World Prison Brief Data*, Institute for Criminal Policy Research, London: Birkbeck University of London, available from: http://www.prisonstudies.org/ [accessed 30 October 2019].

4

Understanding the privatisation of probation through the lens of Bourdieu's field theory

Jake Phillips

Transforming Rehabilitation: Grayling's brainchild or endpoint of a long process?

There is no need to go into great detail about Transforming Rehabilitation (TR) here, as it has been dealt with in several other places, including in this volume. Suffice it to say that in 2014 around 60–70 per cent of the work of the erstwhile Probation Trusts was outsourced to Community Rehabilitation Companies (CRCs), which became responsible for supervising 'low-' and 'medium-risk' offenders while the publicly run National Probation Service (NPS) took over supervision of high-risk offenders. CRCs were contracted partly on a payment by results (PbR) basis, firmly cementing the profit motive into the delivery of community sanctions (although one CRC, Durham and Tees Valley, is run on a not-for-profit basis). It is also unnecessary to go over the reasons for the reforms and how they were implemented, as this has been covered elsewhere.[1] There is now widespread acceptance that TR was unsuccessful in achieving either a reduction of reoffending or greater efficiencies in terms of delivering community sanctions. Indeed, a spate of government reports have highlighted serious concerns about the efficacy of the reforms and the government is in the process of redesigning the system.

One of the main criticisms of the reforms was that they were implemented with great speed, and with little by way of piloting or

---

[1] In 2013 a *British Journal of Community Justice* special issue focused on the arguments against TR and includes several pieces which raised concerns and made predictions about what might come to pass. The theme of a special issue of *Probation Journal* in 2016 was 'TR 2 Years On' (Burke, 2016) while a follow-up special issue in 2019 examined the TR five years after the reforms had been implemented (Corcoran and Carr, 2019).

testing. Indeed, after being appointed Secretary of State for Justice in October 2012 it took Chris Grayling just 20 months to privatise a substantial proportion of the probation service in England and Wales. Grayling was quick to publish a consultation, *Transforming Rehabilitation: A Revolution in the Way We Manage Offenders* (Ministry of Justice, 2013a), which talked of:

> The majority of rehabilitative and punitive services in the community [being] opened up to a diverse market of providers. We currently spend around £1 billion on delivering these services. Through competition and payment by results, we will introduce more efficient and effective services, specifically targeting a significant reduction in reoffending rates.

It was at this point in time that interested parties began to express a more serious concern regarding the government's plans and a visible opposition began to appear. The Prison Reform Trust (nd) argued that the 'speed of implementation could lead to some unintended consequences, which run counter to the objectives set out in the consultation' and Nacro (2013), while broadly supportive of the proposals because it would open up the potential for them (and other similar organisations) to expand their work with people on probation, warned that the government should 'not underestimate the challenge of getting offenders to stop especially when we are seeking to do this, on scale, with high volumes of offenders, over large geographical areas'. Napo, the probation officers' union and professional association, began to make headlines with warnings about the risk to public protection that the reforms posed. Practitioners on social media displayed high levels of antipathy towards what the government was proposing, and academics reinforced the argument that many of the reforms were not underpinned by evidence. The view among many was that these reforms signalled the potential 'death knell of a much cherished service' (Senior, 2016: 428).

The government published its response to the final consultation in May 2013 (Ministry of Justice, 2013b) and within less than a year, the necessary structural reform had been legislated for in the Offender Rehabilitation Act (2014). On 1 June 2014, Probation Trusts were disbanded and replaced with 21 CRCs and a National Probation Service. In spite of the failure of the new delivery model there can be no doubt that the government was highly effective in achieving its aims of marketising the field of community sanctions, and at great speed.

The defenders of a wholly public probation service could draw on over 100 years of evidence-based practice; a body of practitioners with graduate-level skills; a well-organised and respected professional organisation in the form of Napo; a small but committed group of academics; and a range of lobby groups and charities all of whom were vociferously opposed to the reforms. Nevertheless, the reforms proceeded as though there was very little opposition. How, then, did it come to be that on 30 May 2014, the eve of the dissolution of Probation Trusts, an anonymous probation officer published the following comment on the *Probation et al* blog:

> This [period of reform] has been a strain on every staff member and their families, and has tested our resilience … That being said we must move forwards. *I no longer have any faith in probation leaders who mostly failed to fight against these 'reforms' they knew would end the probation service as we know it, or in probation unions who have been consistently ineffective in the campaign to save probation.* (Anonymous, 2014; emphasis added)

This view has persisted, with the recent National Audit Office (2019) report being met with criticism from practitioners that senior leaders failed to defend a public probation service. But this explanation fails to acknowledge the context surrounding a profession which went from being in receipt of full cross-party parliamentary support during the 'rehabilitative ideal' to one which was sidelined and ignored in the face of reforms which would prove more disruptive than anything that had come before. Thus, this chapter seeks to answer the question: Why were opponents to the government's TR agenda unable to mount a successful opposition to the reforms in question? In answering the question it becomes clear that the issues are more complex than a simple failure to act. Rather, the people who were castigated by this anonymous practitioner had, in many ways, been silenced in myriad ways prior to the introduction of these reforms.

Bourdieu's field theory

In addressing this issue I draw on the work of Bourdieu's 'field theory' to argue that to understand the means with which policy reform is, or is not, implemented, resisted and opposed we need to understand and analyse the role of capital in the subfield of community sanctions. Field theory is a diverse analytical framework which attempts to explain how institutions, in the broadest sense of the word, are structured. Through this lens, Bourdieu draws attention to the unique 'logic' of each field; in essence it is the 'way it works'. In order to identify what the logic of a field is and how it functions, Bourdieu relies on three key concepts: field, capital and habitus.

The field is the broadest of Bourdieu's concepts and is used as a tool for visualising society as a 'series of relations' which exist in two forms:

> first, reified as sets of objective positions that persons occupy (institutions or 'fields') and which externally constrain perception and action; and, second, deposited inside individual bodies in the form of mental schemata of perception and appreciation (whose layered articulation compose the 'habitus') through which we internally experience and actively construct the lived world. (Wacquant, 2013: 275)

Bourdieu asks us to think about how these fields function and how they relate to one another. All fields are subordinate to the field of power, which is seen to transcend other fields and comprises a range of subfields.[2] This mode of analysis has been adopted by criminologists to examine, for example, the role of the prison officers' union in the US (Page, 2011), and the position of poor people in being punished (Wacquant, 2009). For the purposes of this chapter I focus on the penal field (Page, 2012), which is made up of a series of subfields such as the field of incarceration (that is prison) and the field of community sanctions (that is probation) (McNeill and Beyens, 2013).

In his work on the field of cultural production and the literary field, Bourdieu argues that there are different forms of art: aesthetic art and art produced for economic reasons. In discerning the way in which the field is structured (the logic of the field) he likewise identifies two poles – the heteronomous pole, and the autonomous pole:

> At the heteronomous pole artistic production is treated much like any other form of production: the work is made for a pre-established market, with the aim of achieving commercial success ... The principles of production at the autonomous pole include imagination, truth and freedom

---

[2] Bourdieu analysed an array of different subfields during his lifetime including, inter alia, higher education, cultural, literature and the juridical fields.

> from social or economic influence … the rewards in this part
> of the field are symbolic capital. (Webb et al, 2002: 159–61)

Thus an agent's position in the field imbues that agent with a specific form of capital. Similarly to the field of cultural production, the subfield of community sanctions has two poles. At the heteronomous pole, practitioners work to 'pre-established forms' that are defined by the structure of the field which derives from things such as politics or public opinion. This might be, for example, the drive to reduce reoffending, protect the public and work on behalf of the public rather than adopting the Kantian ethic of seeing offenders as people in their own right. The aim of practice at this pole is to garner legitimacy (or capital) from external stakeholders such as politicians and the general public (Robinson et al, 2017). Prior to TR probation workers accrued capital at this pole by demonstrating success through concrete measures of 'success' such as reductions in reoffending or meeting key performance indicators. At the autonomous pole, probation practice can be structured by its own internal logic which is underpinned by what we might call the 'values', or habitus, of probation. This might include: working on behalf of the offender, believing in an individual's capacity to change or measuring 'quality' in different ways to those defined by the field. Here, such work adds weight to the claim to protect the public; but this is not the be-all and end-all of such claims. Rather, the exercise of this form of practice results in capital, but not capital which is valued at the heteronomous pole – fellow colleagues might value this work, but those with the power to structure the field (that is politicians and policy makers) do not. This partly explains the privileged status which hitting targets obtains in policy thinking, as they seem to offer 'solid' evidence, such as delivering a piece of work on time, over the more ineffable notion of quality, for example.

Thus, the way in which the penal field is structured by, and structures, what happens within these subfields needs to be understood with reference to the concept of capital 'in all its forms and not solely in the one form recognized by economic theory' (Bourdieu, 2006: 105). Capital therefore incorporates financial means as well as other well-known forms of capital such as social, human and cultural. In the subfield of community sanctions this might be thought of as penal capital, defined by Page as 'the legitimate authority to determine penal policies and priorities' (Page, 2012: 159).

We can break penal capital down into three forms of capital in order to assess the extent to which actors have authority to determine policy change and priorities. Firstly, cultural capital denotes the cultural skills and competencies of actors – this would be signalled by titles, qualifications and the extent to which agents are seen as 'professionals'. Secondly, Bourdieu identifies social capital as the useful networks which agents can draw upon to further their own interests. And finally there is symbolic capital, which is the prestige which agents have in society. These three forms of capital, which make up penal capital, are critical to understanding the subsequent analysis of probation privatisation.

Habitus is 'at the basis of strategies of reproduction that tend to maintain separations, distances and relations of order(ing)' (Bourdieu, 1996: 3). In turn, capital is determined by those who have a 'well-formed' habitus which, in Bourdieu's terms, is one which is attuned to the logic of the field. Capitals are valued differently within different fields and across time, and so capital is entirely contingent upon the field in which it exists. There is constant contestation over capital, and those with the 'right' kind of capital have the power to transform, maintain or reproduce the structured relations in the field. Moreover, habitus is a product of relations: 'the value of each member depends on the contribution of all the others as well as on the possibility of actually mobilising the capital of the group' (Bourdieu, 1996: 286). Thus, the ability of, for example, senior managers and union representatives to oppose the reforms was always reliant, to some extent, upon the habitus of the practitioners they were representing. It is the contention in this chapter that the capital upon which opponents to TR could draw upon had become increasingly less 'well formed' and thus less 'valuable' in the years running up to TR.

The changing value of probation practitioners' capital

In this section I outline the changing value placed on the type of penal capital with which probation practitioners were imbued in the run-up to TR. Thus, this section is about how people define and implement the subfield of community sanctions' aims and priorities. In his seminal quartet of articles on the history of probation policy and practice, McWilliams argued that up until the early 1980s, probation officers and the service for which they worked were virtually synonymous: 'for most purposes the probation officer was the probation service'. There was, he argued, a 'large measure of consensus about the probation system, its purposes and its tasks [which] meant that the probation officer encapsulated the probation service in propria persona' (1987: 99). He went on to say that as the 1980s progressed, it became 'simply not possible to comprehend the modern service purely, or even mainly, by reference to its officers' because the organisation had changed in terms of its size, its composition and its aims, with the service taking on some additional responsibilities (in the form of post-custodial supervision) and losing others (such as working with fewer numbers of people on community service). This period in probation's history represented the beginning of a growing gap between what the organisation was intending to do, as defined by the broader penal field, and what the people who worked for the organisation wanted to do within that organisation. There began to appear a heterodox within the subfield of community sanctions, for it was at this point that probation officers started to move slowly towards the autonomous pole of the subfield of community sanctions, as the heteronomous pole began to be structured according to the ideals of, first, managerialism, then contestability and finally privatisation. In brief, the aims of probation practitioners remained relatively static while the logic of the field as defined by the heteronomous pole changed considerably.

The consensus in the penal field which existed prior to the 1970s and 1980s meant that the forms of capital, the habitus of practitioners and the field in which they practised were attuned to one another. Thus, practitioners' structured and structuring dispositions (that is habitus) were, broadly speaking, aligned with the organisation's aims, and so practitioners' habitus and the broader aims of the penal field were mutually supportive:

> when the 'rehabilitative ideal' was the dominant orientation ... in the years following World War II, it was 'thinkable' that prisoners should have access to higher education ... Today, however, when 'punitive segregation' ... is the dominant orientation in the penal field, college education for prisoners ... seems unthinkable if not 'taboo' or 'crazy'. (Page, 2011: 11)

However, we are now a long way from such consensus. The way in which policy defines and measures the aims of probation has changed significantly over the last 50 years, yet the way in which practitioners do so has not. Despite the claims of some that 'nothing works', rehabilitation survived as a purpose of probation when one looked to front-line practice and practitioners' beliefs (Raynor and Vanstone, 2007). Similarly, Humphrey and Pease (1992) found that probation practitioners justified their effectiveness in terms of being able to divert people away from custody, the ability to give clear recommendations to the court and the slowing of criminal careers, which contrasted with the attention paid to input and output targets by the Home Office. Robinson and McNeill (2004) found a similar inconsistency between practitioners' definitions of probation and the way in which probation's aims were measured by the 'system'. At both official and unofficial levels, public protection was seen to be a legitimate aim of probation, but it was the means with which public protection might be achieved where divergence was identified. Thus, 'interviewees tended to frame rehabilitative interventions and the reduction of reoffending in the context of the "more general" quest for public protection' while official documents adopted a more punitive rhetoric (Robinson and McNeill, 2004: 294). In the late 2000s, Annison et al (2008) found that probation trainees still put their offenders first, despite a distinct punitive shift in terms of probation policy, and Deering (2010) argued that a 'new breed' of probation trainees had, perhaps surprisingly, not emerged despite the extent to which probation could be understood as being underpinned by Feeley and Simon's (1992) actuarial new penology and the management of 'risk'. In more recent work, Robinson et al (2014) identify an inconsistency between the official and unofficial aims of probation, with practitioners being more concerned with flexibility, outcomes, individualisation and the working relationship. Since the 1960s there has been increasing divergence between official and unofficial accounts of probation so that by the time of Grayling's consultation in 2013, there was a distinct heterodox in the subfield of community sanctions. We can also see that probation practitioners have defined the aims of their work in relatively static terms over time:

> practitioner accounts of what matters most in the routine
> supervision of offenders can survive significant periods of
> social, political, cultural and even economic fluctuation
> – indicating that agency and discretion survive within
> contemporary practice. (Grant and McNeill, 2014: 1999)

It might be argued that practitioners have internalised managerialism to some degree (Phillips, 2011), and there have been adaptations in practice in response to changes in policy (Robinson et al, 2014). It is here that we can see the ways in which the field inculcates particular dispositions over and above the values that are absorbed through early childhood experiences (habitus) or occupational acculturation (secondary habitus). That said, despite myriad 'penal turns' practitioners seem to define success in similar ways to their predecessors, and work in similar ways (Grant, 2016). It is these 'welfarist' facets of probation practice which serve to constitute the probation habitus, and it is the case that practitioners have been resilient to changes in emphasis in the field in which they operate:

> The Scottish and English fields of criminal justice appear less successful in shaping more punitive dispositions amongst penal agents involved in the community side of punishment. (Grant, 2016: 763)

Such an argument, which sees probation workers as 'durable agents', is often presented in positive ways, as a 'curious ability ... to resist the influence of punitive discourse in their attitudes, actions and approaches to practice' (Grant, 2016: 764). While Grant's analysis may be accurate here, a Bourdieusian analysis draws our attention to the fact that practitioners were, in the run-up to TR, operating at a pole in the field which was not imbuing them with the capital needed to influence policy and priorities. Probation practitioners *did* acknowledge the importance of public protection and meeting targets, but this was not, for them, the main motivation for working in probation.

Alongside the durability of practitioners' habitus has come a considerable change in the logic of the field in which they are working. The subfield of community sanctions gains legitimacy from a range of stakeholders such as the public, offenders, victims, politicians and so on. Over the last 30 years, actors at the autonomous pole of the subfield of community sanctions have increasingly attempted to legitimate probation through tougher enforcement action, more punitive community sentences and a greater focus on binary measures of reoffending rates (Robinson and Ugwudike, 2012). Prior to TR, success was defined in terms of reduced reconviction rates, rates of enforcement, compliance rates and key performance indicators such as numbers of people put through a programme or timeliness targets. Meanwhile, practitioners remained focused on the ineffable nature of probation practice and its effects (Whitehead and Statham, 2006; Canton, 2013). Rather than focusing on, for example, 'the slowing of criminal careers' as a legitimate objective of probation practice (Robinson et al, 2014), the logic of the field was becoming structured in such a way that legitimacy was garnered through rewarding providers with reducing the reoffending rate, protecting the public from crime, working with victims or providing suitable sentences to the courts (Robinson et al, 2017). Thus, while Robinson et al (2017: 16) argue that 'the moral obligation to help improve offenders' lives which has animated probation work throughout its history is now sharpened by a new instrumental imperative to deliver profits for shareholders', one could also suggest that this moral obligation bears little relationship to the way in which the autonomous pole of the field is structured. In turn, this means that the habitus of probation, which is still very much predicated on this moral obligation, results in a form of capital which is undervalued by the logic of the field.

Alongside the effect of a durable habitus on the forms of capital with which agents are imbued, we can also take a closer look at specific forms of capital. During the 1990s and 2000s the legal, policy and training framework worked to turn probation officers into enforcement officers who did the bidding of the court rather than being an arm of the court and removed them from the social work profession. Being an 'arm of the court' meant probation staff could draw significant levels of capital from this group of important penal actors. Probation has slowly had its role in the court weakened through an increased emphasis on oral reports and what Robinson (2019) has characterised as the McDonaldisation of court work, whereby jobs are deskilled and transformed to achieve efficiency, calculability, predictability and control.

The requirement that they possess a university degree or equivalent qualification in social work linked probation officers with the social work profession until that requirement for probation officers was removed in the mid-1990s. This led to the depreciation of practitioners' symbolic capital because they no longer needed to be registered with a professional body. Moreover, the Criminal Justice Act 2003 worked to turn probation workers into brokers rather than providers of services, which further reduced their social capital because the links to professions such as psychology and social work became less important in the day-to-day delivery of the work. This further exacerbated the impact of the government's decision to remove the requirement to be social work qualified. One might also add that the emergence of initiatives such as What Works, the reliance on accredited programmes which are delivered according to a manual and the deprofessionalisation of probation practitioners is manifold. Other examples of how probation practitioners' various forms of capital depreciated over the years include, for example, the loss of a number of Chief Probation Officers in the run-up to the creation of the first National Probation Service in 2001 which left the service lacking in terms of valuable human and cultural capital. Other research has suggested that probation officers see themselves as doing the dirty work of society (Worrall and Mawby, 2013), which in turn results in less prestige and symbolic capital. This whole process could be summarised by Robinson's characterisation of probation as the 'Cinderella' of the criminal justice system (2016). Despite being focused on probation scholarship (rather than practice), Robinson highlights the invisibility of the field and questions over probation's role in the delivery of punishment as explanatory factors for a neglect of probation, and therefore also its practitioners. The central point, though, is that these changes in the field worked, in conjunction with a habitus which did not 'keep up' with changes in the field, to leave probation practitioners and their allies with a significant deficit in penal capital.

Capital can, in many respects, be likened to power, and all forms of capital can be exchanged for power if the conditions of the field allow. Thus it allows us to analyse not just what capital people in a field might have, but also how it is valued and what its exchange value might be. It is clear from the preceding discussion that probation practitioners lacked the 'right' forms of capital with which to influence penal policy and determine priorities in the run-up to TR. That said, probation practitioners had begun to 'catch up' with the changing field – as seen previously, practitioners had come round to accepting public protection as a key aim of probation and had, to some degree, internalised managerialism as a way of governing probation. In some respects, this reflects an acceptance of their diminished influence – acquiescing to managerialism meant they were less able to resist yet more managerialism in the form of marketisation.

However, as TR emerged as a piece of policy reform the field shifted again, and defenders of a public probation service were unable to keep up. TR was not 'sold' to the public by the government in terms of public protection and meeting key targets. Rather, the rationale, ostensibly at least, was saving money (in line with the Coalition government's austerity agenda) and reducing reoffending. Opponents of the reforms did not mount a defence on those terms. Rather, as discussed in Phillips (2014), they focused on the potential 'dangers' of TR (that is public protection) as well as the case that probation did not need reforming because Trusts were meeting key targets. The defence was laid down, but in the managerialist terms which had characterised probation in the first decade of the 21st century. Actors had 'caught up' with the heteronomous pole of the field as defined by the New Labour government but not with the way it was being structured by the Conservative–Liberal Democrat Coalition government. Thus, they were left stranded with the wrong form of capital to mobilise in their defence of a public probation service. The conditions for change were very much in the government's favour and so the reforms occurred not because of a failure to act but because the logic of the field was structured in a way which worked to silence opposition and bolster supporting voices.

Conclusion

This chapter has brought together the concepts of habitus and field in the field of community sanctions to highlight the ways in which agents' positions in the field shapes their actions and subsequent ability to shape the field. Such an analysis allows us to identify ways in which different actors, or groups of actors, in any subfield are positioned to influence, prevent or succumb to change that is being imposed by actors at the heteronomous pole. This chapter demonstrates that if we use Bourdieu's analytic framework to think about where agents are situated in any given field and the forms of capital which they possess and mobilise, we can better understand how policies and priorities might be influenced and resisted in future attempts to privatise sections of the criminal justice system (or any area of social policy, for that matter). This chapter needs to be understood as a case study of probation privatisation. This type of analysis can, and should, be conducted with other subfields to better understand how and why opposition to reforms will result in varying degrees of success.

Finally, and to put it bluntly, the failed reforms of the government were unable to be resisted at the time of their imposition, because the government had chosen and prepared the field of battle in advance. By limiting discussion to arguments relating to metrics and efficiency, probation practitioners were effectively outflanked by a government which made its stand in terms of reducing reoffending and protecting victims, albeit in a system which turned out to be fundamentally flawed.

References

Annison, J., Eadie, T. and Knight, C. (2008) 'People first: probation officer perspectives on probation work', *Probation Journal*, 55(3): 259–71.

Anonymous (2014) 'The probation service: final thoughts', *Probation et al.*, available from: http://offendersupervision.blogspot. co.uk/2014/05/the-probation-service-final-thoughts.html?m=1 [accessed 1 June 2014].

Bourdieu, P. (1996) *The State Nobility: Elite Schools in the Field of Power*, Cambridge: Polity Press.

Bourdieu, P. (2006) 'The forms of capital', in H. Lauder, P. Brown, J.A. Dillabough and A.H. Halsey (eds) *Education, Globalization, and Social Change*, Oxford: Oxford University Press, pp 105–18.

Burke, L. (2016) 'Transforming Rehabilitation: Reflections two years on' [Special issue], *Probation Journal,* 63(2).

Canton, R. (2013) 'The point of probation: On effectiveness, human rights and the virtues of obliquity', *Criminology and Criminal Justice,* 13(5): 577–93. DOI: 10.1177/1748895812462596

Corcoran, M. and Carr, N. (2019) 'Five years of transforming rehabilitation: markets, management and values' [Special issue], *Probation Journal,* 66(1).

Deering, J. (2010) 'Attitudes and beliefs of trainee probation officers: a "new breed"?' *Probation Journal,* 57(1): 9–26.

Feeley, M.M. and Simon, J. (1992) 'The new penology: notes on the emerging strategy of corrections and its implications', *Criminology,* 30(4): 449–74.

Grant, S. (2016) Constructing the durable penal agent: tracing the development of habitus within English probation officers and Scottish criminal justice social workers', *British Journal of Criminology,* 56(4): 750–68. DOI: 10.1093/bjc/azv075

Grant, S. and McNeill, F. (2014) 'What matters in practice? Understanding "quality" in the routine supervision of offenders in Scotland', *British Journal of Social Work,* 45(7): 1985–2002. DOI: 10.1093/bjsw/bcu056

Humphrey, C. and Pease, K. (1992) 'Effectiveness measurement in probation: A view from the troops', *Howard Journal of Criminal Justice,* 31(1): 31–52.

McNeill, F. and Beyens, K. (2013) *Offender Supervision in Europe,* Basingstoke: Palgrave Macmillan.

McWilliams, W. (1987) 'Probation, pragmatism and policy', *Howard Journal of Criminal Justice,* 26(2): 97–121.

Ministry of Justice (2013a) *Transforming Rehabilitation: A Revolution in the Way We Manage Offenders,* London: Ministry of Justice.

Ministry of Justice (2013b) *Transforming Rehabilitation: A Strategy for Reform,* London: Ministry of Justice, available from: https://consult.justice.gov.uk/digital-communications/transforming-rehabilitation/results/transforming-rehabilitation-response.pdf [accessed 31 October 2019].

Nacro (2013) 'Nacro's initial response to the "Transforming Rehabilitation" consultation', *Nacro News,* available from: https://www.nacro.org.uk/news/nacro-news/nacros-initial-response-to-the-transforming-rehabilitation-consultation/ [accessed 19 June 2019].

National Audit Office (2019) *Transforming Rehabilitation: Progress Review,* London: National Audit Office.

Page, J. (2011) *The Toughest Beat: Politics, Punishment, and the Prison Officers Union in California*, Oxford; New York: Oxford University Press.

Page, J. (2012) 'Punishment and the penal field', in J. Simon and R. Sparks (eds) *The Sage Handbook of Punishment and Society*, London: SAGE, pp 152–66.

Phillips, J. (2011) 'Target, audit and risk assessment cultures in the probation service', *European Journal of Probation*, 3(3): 108–22.

Phillips, J. (2014) 'Probation in the news: Transforming rehabilitation', *British Journal of Community Justice*, 12(1): 27–48.

Prison Reform Trust (nd) *Prison Reform Trust response to Transforming Rehabilitation*, London: Prison Reform Trust, available from: http:// www.prisonreformtrust.org.uk/Portals/0/Documents/Prison%20 Reform%20Trust%20response%20to%20Transforming%20 Rehabilitation.pdf [accessed 31 October 2019].

Raynor, P. and Vanstone, M. (2007) 'Towards a correctional service', in L. Gelsthorpe and R. Morgan (eds) *Handbook of Probation*, Cullompton: Willan, pp 59–89.

Robinson, G. (2016) 'The Cinderella complex: Punishment, society and community sanctions', *Punishment & Society*, 18(1): 95–112. DOI: 10.1177/1462474515623105

Robinson, G. (2019) 'Delivering McJustice? The probation factory at the Magistrates' court', *Criminology & Criminal Justice*, 19(5): 605–21. DOI: 10.1177/1748895818786997

Robinson, G. and McNeill, F. (2004) 'Purposes matter: Examining the "ends" of probation', in G. Mair (ed) *What Matters in Probation*, Cullompton: Willan Publishing, pp 277–304.

Robinson, G. and Ugwudike, P. (2012) Investing in "toughness": Probation, enforcement and legitimacy', *Howard Journal of Criminal Justice*, 51(3): 300–16. DOI: 10.1111/j.1468-2311.2012.00707.x

Robinson, G., Burke, L. and Millings, M. (2017) 'Probation, privatisation and legitimacy', *Howard Journal of Crime and Justice*, 56(2): 137–57. DOI: 10.1111/hojo.12198

Robinson, G., Priede, C., Farrall, S., Shapland, J. and McNeill, F. (2014) 'Understanding "quality" in probation practice: Frontline perspectives in England & Wales', *Criminology and Criminal Justice*, 14(2): 123–42. DOI: 10.1177/1748895813483763

Senior, P. (2016) 'Privatising probation: the death knell of a much-cherished public service?' *Howard Journal of Crime and Justice*, 55(4): 414–31. DOI: 10.1111/hojo.12179

Wacquant, L. (2009) *Punishing the Poor: The Neoliberal Government of Social Insecurity (Politics, History, and Culture)*. Durham, NC: Duke University Press.

Wacquant, L. (2013) 'Symbolic power and group-making: on Pierre Bourdieu's reframing of class', *Journal of Classical Sociology*, 13(2): 274–91. DOI: 10.1177/1468795X12468737

Webb, J., Schirato, T. and Danaher, G. (2002) *Understanding Bourdieu*, London: SAGE.

Whitehead, P. and Statham, R. (2006) *The History of Probation: Politics, Power and Cultural Change 1876–2005*, Crayford: Shaw & Sons.

Worrall, A. and Mawby, R.C. (2013) 'Probation worker responses to turbulent conditions: constructing identity in a tainted occupation', *Australian & New Zealand Journal of Criminology*, 46(1): 101–18.

5

The progress of marketisation: the prison and probation experience

Kevin Albertson and Chris Fox

Introduction

We have noted in the Introduction to this volume that there is a distinction between privatisation – the sale of public assets to the private sector or foreign governments – and marketisation – the purchase by the state of public services in markets or pseudo markets (that is, markets which are created and maintained by government regulation). In particular, marketisation often refers to the purchase of those services which the state formerly provided directly. In practice, this often amounts to a form of public outsourcing or sub-contracting by public sector commissioners.

It is often claimed that the process of marketisation in general, and in criminal justice specifically, results from politicians' adoption of a (so-called) 'neo-liberal' ideology. However, we should be wary in making such a claim; it is not even clear such an ideology exists. The term neo-liberalism itself is much contested; it is used widely in a pejorative sense – people seldom use it to describe their own outlook.[1] What is clear is that the remit of the state has changed in recent decades from direct ownership and operation of public assets to an increasing reliance on the utilisation of market mechanisms and market-based mechanisms to provide public goods and services. Such a move, we contend, may be theorised as reflecting policy makers' responses to prevailing incentive structures rather than the adoption of a coherent ideological stance. We examine such incentives in the next section. We then go on to outline the process of marketisation in the prisons and probation service. Next we consider whether the application of

---

[1] The Adam Smith Institute is a notable exception, although they distinguish neo-liberalism from the promotion of free markets – conversely, Mrs Thatcher, Prime Minister of the UK from 1979 to 1990, identified neo-liberalism with free markets.

marketisation has facilitated the realisation of stated and assumed policy goals. Discussions and conclusions follow.

Drivers of marketisation

In their recent summary of outcomes-based commissioning, Albertson et al (2018) identify five political drivers of marketisation in general, and in criminal justice commissioning in particular. To these we might add two drivers from the point of view of the private sector. It should be noted that these drivers operate on a sub-theoretical level; they are realised as individual political-economic actors maximise their returns through the prevailing incentive structure and current global liberal market economy.

Public sector drivers

The rate of real economic growth per capita in the global economy has been in decline for over four decades. While some nations are still benefiting from growth – for example, the Peoples' Republic of China – the developed world in general is not so fortunate. Further, globalisation has facilitated the avoidance (and in some cases evasion) of tax obligations by many large multinational corporations. As a result, democratic governments are faced with stagnant (at best) real per capita resources, even as populations age and public expectations of public services increase. The political response is to seek ways of delivering 'more for less'. That is to say, governments seek to drive down costs while modernising and improving outcomes through refining public service delivery.

In some cases, such innovations occur within the public sector, in which case they are generally known as New Public Management (NPM) (see Albertson et al, 2018 and references therein). Although it should be borne in mind that there is no one conception of NPM, most commentators summarise it as being about: markets; managers; and measurement.

It seems reasonable to suppose, therefore, that the theoretical motivation of NPM will also serve to motivate marketisation more generally. From the point of view of government, marketisation supposedly facilitates:

- Disaggregation: decentralisation and the devolution of decision making and service provision to lower levels of government. It is supposed that service provision will be more responsive to local needs if decisions are made locally by smaller, less hierarchical organisations than central government.

- Competition: the introduction of a purchaser–provider split and the enabling of different forms of provision is supposed to lead to new providers entering the market. In the case of TR, this included increasing involvement of the not-for-profit sector. Improvements follow, in theory, from the quasi-evolutionary process of market forces rewarding the most efficient provider (at least in the short term) and driving out of business the less efficient.
- Incentivisation: this occurs particularly through outcomes-based commissioning. Under outcomes-based commissioning, public sector procurement becomes based on the specification of desired outcomes. Payment for these is contingent (in theory) on evaluation, hence the term payment by results (PbR). Providers will therefore innovate and experiment to determine what services are most effective in terms of delivering the result which will trigger payment.
- Modernisation: which is to say, motivating the utilisation of digital and information technology. In theory, competitive pressures will motivate the innovation by service providers. Further, the private sector might be better placed to drive down the costs of labour – through, for example, the adoption of cutting-edge IT – than the public sector, which is more heavily unionised.

As well as these points, which relate to improving the efficiency of public services delivery, marketisation may also facilitate:

- The transfer of risk: both political and financial risk may, in theory, be transferred from government to the private sector in situations where private sector organisations are responsible for the delivery of public services. Many of the social problems to which governments respond are made more complex by the impact of rapid technological change and globalised markets on citizens and communities. Further, it may be that politicians are held more immediately to account through the rise of social media. This increased complexity may reduce the risk appetite of policy makers, motivating them to seek commissioning arrangements which transfer risk to third parties.

Private sector drivers

The providers of public goods and services have their own incentives. These are, however, less complex than those faced by government and public servants. The motivations, in general, of the private (both for-profit and not-for-profit) sector in engaging with marketisation, that is in bidding to provide marketised public services, is summed up in the phrase 'doing well by doing good'.

- Doing well: business, in general, seeks to increase its profits. As real per capita incomes in the developed world have stagnated over the last four decades, there is less profit to be made from providing goods and services directly to the public. New sources of revenue must therefore be sought; these will include the provision of goods and services indirectly to the public through the winning of government contracts.
- Doing good: business in general, and not-for-profit firms in particular, also have a motivation to contribute to social progress (or at least to appear to do so). As well as the satisfaction private sector providers and employees may realise from facilitating social progress – doing good is often the *raison d'être* of the not-for-profit sector – such progress provides favourable publicity for, and therefore lends legitimacy to, the profitability of the for-profit sector.

Misaligned incentives

It is clear there is a distinction between the motivations behind the public and private approaches to the marketisation of public services. This may well lead to incentive structures being misaligned. Osborne (2018) highlights several examples to make clear these differences.

In the first instance, private sector service firms desire repeat business and the retention of customers. By contrast, repeat business is likely to be a sign of service failure in public services, of which the rehabilitation of offenders is an example. Secondly, while private for-profit firms are generally more aligned to dealing with voluntary service users – that is to say, people who desire a particular service to be delivered – conversely users of public services are often 'coerced'. Again, this will be particularly pertinent in the area of the provision of criminal justice services. Thirdly, there is an added complication in that it is not clear who is the customer – for example, the public, the state, sub-contractors or the service user. The creation of value in response to payment received is thus complex and not easily dealt with in traditional markets. The definition of a 'successful' transaction may well also be contested. The 'success' or otherwise of the transaction may well depend on wider social factors beyond the control or remit of the private sector provider.

We may note that, further, the transfer of financial risk to the private sector is unlikely to be in the interests of private corporations, particularly if it is uncompensated financially, as seems likely if the government is consistent in pursuing an overarching policy goal of achieving 'more for less'. Such a goal will also restrict the private sector profits which may be made through public service provision. In any event, it is unclear how much risk may be transferred from the public to the private sector. In general, the public require essential services to be provided and will hold government to account for publicly funded services, irrespective of who is the ultimate supplier.

The prison experience

In the early 1990s, John Major's Conservative government began the process of marketising prisons by awarding short-term contracts to security companies. The first such was HMP Wolds in 1992. By the late 1990s the first fully privately designed, built and run prison, HMP Altcourse, was open to, if not the public, then selected members thereof. The marketisation process continued under Tony Blair's New Labour government, elected in 1997, despite their being opposed to marketisation while in opposition. In its first five years the New Labour government oversaw the opening of eight privately financed prisons (Panchamia, 2012). In 2003, the Carter Report argued for the creation of the National Offender Management Service (NOMS) with a mandate to increase contestability in prison and probation services. Contestability, in this sense, indicates the fostering of competition, supposedly between the public, for-profit and not-for-profit sectors, in delivering public services.

A competition was started in 2011 inviting bids for eight public sector prisons and one private sector prison that had come to the end of its contract period. At the same time a competition for 'innovation pilots' was launched: one 'lot' in the bidding round being designed to find innovative approaches to reducing reoffending of those who had served prison sentences of less than 12 months; and the other being more loosely specified. Both the prison bids and the innovation pilots included outcomes-based commissioning elements (Ministry of Justice, 2011). Part of the way through the process, both the prison and the innovation pilot competitions were aborted (Ministerial Statement, 2012). In November 2013, the privatisation of three further prisons in south Yorkshire was abandoned, as the leading bidder was under investigation for alleged fraud (House of Commons Library, 2014).

Alongside this, in 2016, prisons were given the opportunity to begin to operate as independent legal entities. The measures, announced in the Queen's Speech of 18 May 2016, saw the introduction of 'reform prisons' organised along the same lines as the UK's school system, with league tables for prisoners' reoffending, employment rates (after release), violence and self-harm. The first cohort of these reform prisons, six so-called Trailblazers, involved the granting of unprecedented freedoms to governors, including 'financial and legal freedoms, such as how the prison budget is spent and whether to opt-out of national contracts'.

Although initially it was intended that reform prisons would facilitate more localised and independent institutions, this vision did not long survive the departure (post-Brexit referendum) of the Secretary of State who had promoted it. Reform prisons ultimately did not become separate legal entities and their agency to act independently was curtailed (Bennett, 2019). Further, in 2017 it was announced that reform prisons would essentially be piloting arrangements for the reorganisation of the prison estate into clusters of four to six prisons, with prison governors managed by a group director. It appears likely, therefore, that the reform prison process will facilitate rather less independent policy (Bennett, 2019).

Currently, the UK maintains the most marketised prison system in Europe. On 26 October 2018 (before the contract for Birmingham prison was ended in April 2019), in England and Wales 15,813 prisoners (19 per cent of the prisoner population) were held in privately run prisons (Bromley Briefings, 2018). Ten of these are relatively new prisons, having been planned, financed, built and operated by private sector operators on contracts of 25 years or more. As noted, in April 2019 the contract to run Birmingham prison was terminated, with the agreement of the contractor. The public sector, so it has been argued, is better placed to provide the stability and continuity which is required to drive the long-term improvements the prison requires (Ministry of Justice, 2019a).

However, the government remains committed to a 'mixed economy of providers', which is to say, to the principles of marketisation (Ministry of Justice, 2019a). Two new prisons have recently been announced by the government, both of which will be built with public, not private, capital. The government expects private operators to run these facilities; HM Prisons and Probation Service will not take part in the competition to run the prisons. Notwithstanding, the public sector may take on the operation of the prisons if the private sector bids do not compare favourably with public sector benchmarks.

Ultimately, both in the reform prisons and across the prison estate in general, the emphasis on league tables, ratings and performance targets, including the national custodial performance tool, have an impact beyond the merely technical. Considered as a whole, it has been argued these have pushed prison managers and staff towards more managerial responses as they come under increasing surveillance through performance metrics (Bennett, 2019). The undoubted attractiveness of innovation in rehabilitation has thus been counterbalanced with the risk of failure to hit targets. This has led to more centralised control, monitoring and an emphasis on compliance (Bennett, 2019) rather than the promotion of desistence and agency.

Overall, it is not straightforward to assess the impact of marketisation on the prison estate as many of the innovations have coincided with the impact of austerity imposed by the government since 2010, in response to the global financial crisis. While the England and Wales prison system has become an increasingly crowded and dangerous place (Bromley Briefings, 2018), the extent to which this has arisen as a result of cost-saving measures, and the extent to which the impact of these has been exacerbated or mitigated by marketisation, is unclear.

The probation experience

Under the UK Coalition government (2010–15), early ideas on reform of the probation service envisaged probation innovation pilot projects subject to outcomes-based commissioning and devolution of the commissioning of community offender services to the existing 35 Probation Trusts.

However, after a change in Secretary of State, the government embarked on the more radical Transforming Rehabilitation (TR) agenda (Ministry of Justice, 2013). The Ministry's rationale for promoting transformational change was to reduce reoffending rates in the context of increasing efficiency (that is, reducing cost; p 9). These results were to arise from:

> greater flexibility in delivery, incentivised, at least in part by outcomes-based commissioning; extending post-release supervision to offenders released after serving short-sentences – this was to be resourced by the efficiency gains which were to result from marketisation; more efficient services resulting from increasing competition between service providers through the creation of a market for the provision of criminal justice services; increasing the number

of providers in the market, in particular to benefit from the supposed innovation of the private and voluntary sector; and enable co-commissioning to facilitate collaboration between providers to facilitate partnership working at a local level. (Ministry of Justice, 2013: 8–9)

Under TR, Probation Trusts were abolished and provision of the majority of community-based offender services, those to offenders who pose a low or medium risk of harm, were sub-contracted to geographically defined Community Rehabilitation Companies (CRCs). Work with high-risk offenders, assessments and court reports passed to a new (public sector) National Probation Service (NPS).

Although an emphasis was placed on the provision and support of local services in the TR agenda, in practice this was undermined by the way the contracts were awarded. In the first place, 21 CRCs and a single NPS were intended to replace the 35 Trusts which were abolished. Secondly, despite their sectoral experience, existing Probation Trusts were excluded from bidding in the national competition to commission probation services. In theory probation staff might bid through setting up new independent entities such as employee-led mutuals, but in practice, the formation of such mutuals was regulated and thus few were formed (Albertson and Fox, 2019). Ultimately all the main CRC contractors were from the private sector; only one CRC was to be led by a consortium in which the main or 'prime contractor' was a not-for-profit organisation, and employee-led mutuals or staff Community Interest Companies were involved in only seven out of the 21 winning bids (Albertson and Fox, 2019).

The new organisations, the CRCs and the NPS, were launched in June 2014, originally publicly run. In February 2015, the 21 CRCs were transferred to eight suppliers working under contracts which were intended to run to 2021–22. The Ministry considered that its reforms would deliver reductions in reoffending corresponding to £10.4 billion in net economic benefits to society over the seven-year period of the contracts (National Audit Office, 2019). However, the TR revolution failed to deliver on either public or private aspirations.

From the point of view of the private sector contractors' aspirations to doing well, the financial returns on probation provision have been disappointing, to say the least. In the first instance, there has been a decline in the number of community sentences since 2015 (HM Inspectorate of Probation, 2019), which is consistent with the supposition of a reduction in judicial confidence in such sentences. Notwithstanding, under TR there were more people on probation than would otherwise have been the case as a result of extending supervision to those released after short-term sentences. This extension in supervision was expected to have been paid for by the efficiency gains assumed to arise from marketisation. However, if fewer community sentences are handed down, there is a corresponding reduction in the opportunity to make such efficiency savings.

Further, the mix of offenders for whom the CRCs provided probation services had changed since the original benchmarking in 2011. There were fewer than expected low-risk and more than the expected number of high-risk offenders. Again, this has reduced the opportunities for achieving efficiency gains.

There were also problems with the payments which might have accrued through outcomes-based commissioning. In the first place, the degree to which CRCs' cost base could be considered 'fixed' had been incorrectly assessed (House of Commons Justice Committee 2018) in the winning contracts. This implies too much emphasis had been placed on payments which might have resulted from outcomes-based commissioning had targets been met. However, these targets were not consistently met. Although reoffending has reduced slightly, the number of offences committed by reoffenders has increased (HM Inspectorate of Probation, 2019). Ultimately, none of the CRCs managed to meet all their performance targets (HM Inspectorate of Probation 2019), with severe implications for income.

By 2017 it was clear contractors had underbid to run CRCs and were struggling financially. Although one of the motivators of the marketisation agenda is said to be the transfer of operational risk to providers (House of Commons Justice Committee 2018), in practice there are some services which are too important to fail – and probation is clearly one of these. The Ministry of Justice responded by cutting the length of the contracts by two years to 2020 and attempted to stabilise the CRCs financially with additional taxpayer funds to the tune of some £500 million (Albertson and Fox, 2019). This has proved an insufficient boost to at least one CRC contractor. In February 2019, one contractor, and the three CRCs for which it was responsible, went into administration; staff and services have since been transferred to another CRC. Another prime contractor entered a period of administration in March 2019 – though its financial problems were not primarily related to its criminal justice portfolio.

From the point of view of the Ministry, the TR experiment has proved disappointing. In general, the benefits of stability are seldom considered in the evaluation of innovation and, as the House of Commons Justice Committee (2018) notes, TR reforms were imposed without thorough piloting. The speed of introduction of the reform gave rise to risks to the system, to the public and to offenders that have been described (House of Commons Committee of Public Accounts, 2019: 5) as 'unacceptable'. According to the most recent data, the overall reoffending rate has risen slightly (Ministry of Justice, 2019b); in particular, the extension of supervision to offenders released after serving short sentences has not reduced reoffending, rather the opposite (Ministry of Justice, 2019b).

Far from incentivising a greater flexibility in delivery, the House of Commons Justice Committee (2018), HM Inspectorate of Probation (2019) and National Audit Office (2019) all note that outcomes-based commissioning may not be appropriate for delivering probation services as there is evidence it leads to outcomes other than those intended. The House of Commons Justice Committee (2018) has criticised the inflexibility of this approach and called on the government to consider getting rid of this requirement.

The TR agenda ultimately failed to create a growing and sustainable market in the provision of probation services. On the contrary, the voluntary sector is less involved in providing probation services than before TR (House of Commons Justice Committee, 2018; House of Commons Committee of Public Accounts, 2019), and the market TR created is 'underfunded and fragile' (House of Commons Committee of Public Accounts, 2019: 5). Ultimately, according to HM Inspectorate of Probation (2019), the 'probation model delivered by Transforming Rehabilitation is irredeemably flawed' and neither incentivises continuing improvement nor has proven cost effective.

Lessons learned

In their recent analysis of the process of marketisation in probation, Albertson and Fox (2019) point out that the utilisation of market forces in delivering public goods is by no means a benign technocratic decision. There are social consequences which echo beyond the simple provision of services. They argue the scale of marketisation matters, and that local contracting is more likely to create a sustainable mixed market that national contracting to a few prime contractors. They suggest, in the first place:

- Overall responsibility for probation ought to be retained by the public sector so as to provide stability at the core of the service. A mixed economy of private for-profit and not-for-profit contractors might be fostered to compete at a very local level.

This is indeed the import of the government's current approach, as the supervision of all offenders in England and Wales will be undertaken by the NPS, in partnership, it is hoped, with private sector organisations. However, there remains the issue of localism. Under the currently proposed arrangements 11 publicly run probation regions in England and Wales will replace the former NPS and 21 CRCs, reducing further the level of localism in the service. According to Albertson and Fox (2019), the ministry should:

- Create a system which fosters localism. While improving local accountability was supposedly one of the goals of TR, in practice current centralised subcontracting of probation services to a very few prime-contractors undermined this. An alternative to contracting to 'primes' at the national level would be to allow Police and Crime Commissioners, whose role has been minimal under TR, to contract at the local level.

Ultimately, with respect to marketisation in general, the government ought to:

- Establish a system which emphasises relational, rather than financial, transactions. Offenders ought to be the responsibility of a specified probation officer throughout supervision, for example.

Conclusions

The drive for marketisation is linked with the stated need across government generally to achieve 'more for less': more output for less resource. Thus marketisation, at least since 2010, is linked to the austerity agenda in the UK. To some extent this has been successful. The cost of a prison place has fallen (Bromley Briefings, 2018) and the cost of probation delivered by CRCs is less than was envisaged when the contracts were first signed (National Audit Office, 2019) – though, given the much reduced demand for CRC services, it is not clear whether cost savings have been achieved relative to what pre-existing provision would have cost.

Against these financial advantages we must consider, however, that the prison estate is becoming more dangerous, more crowded and faces a financial shortfall of *c.* £500 million over the next few years (Bromley Briefings, 2018). Similarly, probation services, as delivered by CRCs, failed to achieve either the aspirations of the public in reducing reoffending, or the aspirations of private providers in achieving financial surplus. The probation system is, however, too important to fail, and the effective bailout of the private providers cost the public purse *c.* £500 million. Following the failure of TR to deliver on its promise, the Ministry of Justice intends, at the time of writing, effectively to renationalise (but not relocalise) the delivery of probation.

It is, of course, possible to make any system of rehabilitation workable if sufficient additional public funds are made available to sustain it. However, in the current and ongoing financial climate, this is not an option; efficiency savings are required. Marketisation was postulated as a key part of achieving these savings. However, it is not at all clear it has delivered, or is capable of delivering, a service which improves protection of the public, delivers justice, reduces reoffending and increases efficiency.

References

Albertson, K. and Fox, C. (2019) 'The marketisation of rehabilitation: some economic considerations', *Probation Journal*, 66(1): 25–42.

Albertson, K., Bailey, K., Fox, C., LaBarbera, J., O'Leary, C. and Painter, G. (2018) *Payment by Results and Social Impact Bonds: Outcome-based payment systems in the UK and US*, Bristol: Policy Press.

Bennett, J. (2019) 'Reform, resistance and managerial clawback: the evolution of "reform prisons" in England', *Howard Journal of Crime and Justice*, 58(1): 45–64.

Bromley Briefings (2018) 'Bromley Briefings prison factfile Autumn 2018', available from: http://www.prisonreformtrust.org.uk/Portals/0/Documents/Bromley%20Briefings/Autumn%202018%20Factfile.pdf [accessed 8 April 2019].

HM Inspectorate of Probation (2019) 'Report of the Chief Inspector of Probation March 2019', available from: https://www.justiceinspectorates.gov.uk/hmiprobation/wp-content/uploads/sites/5/2019/03/HMI-Probation-Chief-Inspectors-Report.pdf [accessed 10 April 2019].

House of Commons Committee of Public Accounts (2019) 'Transforming Rehabilitation: Progress review, Ninety-Fourth Report of Session 2017–19', available from: https://publications.parliament.uk/pa/cm201719/cmselect/cmpubacc/1747/1747.pdf [accessed 12 July 2019].

House of Commons Justice Committee (2018) 'Transforming Rehabilitation', available from: https://publications.parliament.uk/pa/cm201719/cmselect/cmjust/482/48202.htm [accessed 10 April 2019].

House of Commons Library (2014) 'Prisons: The role of the private sector', House of Commons Library, Standard Note: SN/HA/6811, available from: https://researchbriefings.files.parliament.uk/documents/SN06811/SN06811.pdf [accessed 10 April 2019].

Ministerial Statement (2012) 'Written Ministerial Statement (8th Nov)', available from: http://www.publications.parliament.uk/pa/cm201213/cmhansrd/cm121108/wmstext/121108m0001.htm [accessed 10 April 2019].

Ministry of Justice (2011) 'Contract Notice 2011/S 206-336076 and 2011/S 235-381192', in *Supplement to the Official Journal of the European Union*, London: Ministry of Justice.

Ministry of Justice (2013) *Transforming Rehabilitation: A Revolution in the Way We Manage Offenders*, London: Ministry of Justice, available from: https://assets.publishing.service.gov.uk/government/uploads/system/uploads/attachment data/file/228580/8517.pdf [accessed 10 April 2019].

Ministry of Justice (2019a) 'Birmingham prison contract ended (1st April)', available from: https://www.gov.uk/government/news/birmingham-prison-contract-ended [accessed 11 April 2019].

Ministry of Justice (2019b) 'Proven Reoffending Statistics Quarterly Bulletin, April 2017 to June 2017', available from: https://assets.publishing.service.gov.uk/government/uploads/system/uploads/attachment data/file/797439/proven reoffending bulletin April to June 17.pdf [accessed 12 July 2019].

National Audit Office (2019) 'Transforming Rehabilitation: Progress review', available from: https://www.nao.org.uk/wp-content/uploads/2019/02/Transforming-Rehabilitation-Progress-review.pdf [accessed 10 April 2019].

Osborne, S.P. (2018) 'From public service-dominant logic to public service logic: are public service organizations capable of co-production and value co-creation?' *Public Management Review*, 20(2): 225–31. DOI: 210.1080/14719037.14712017.11350461

Panchamia, N. (2012) 'Competition in prisons', Institute for Government, available from: http://www.instituteforgovernment.org.uk/sites/default/files/publications/Prisons briefing final.pdf [accessed 10 April 2019].

PART II

Experiences of marketisation in the public sector

6

The 'soft power' of marketisation: the administrative assembling of Irish youth justice work

Katharina Swirak

Introduction

They can be anything they want to be ...

At the end of the day, their potential they reach that themselves, and they make the decisions to get there themselves ...

Okay, academically, they might not go to Trinity but that doesn't mean they can't be productive young people within the mainstream.[1]

These quotes from Irish youth justice workers about young people in trouble with the law and their possible futures are benign and well intentioned. At first sight, they could be interpreted as typical of meritocratic discourses that emphasise an equal-level playing field of life chances, when coupled with individual will and effort. Yet I will argue in this chapter that these quotes exemplify the diffusion of marketised governance from administrative policy discourse to professionals' constructions of young people and their offending behaviour. I will show how the prioritisation of marketising principles 'traverses' from policy to practice discourse, thus shaping contemporary realities of Irish youth justice work. More broadly, this chapter is based on the premise that marketisation understood as a governmental regime (Corcoran, 2014: 57) encompasses more insidious, subtle and softer aspects than 'hard' marketisation strategies such as 'privatisation' or 'monetisation'. Borrowing from Carol Bacchi's seminal 'What's the Problem Represented to Be' (WPR) approach (Bacchi, 2009), I also suggest that these softer aspects of marketisation become visible

---

[1] The University of Dublin is also known as Trinity College Dublin.

in the way that 'problems' and 'solutions to problems' are written or talked about. The importance of language and discourse as a vehicle through which marketisation operates also chimes with Wendy Brown's observations on the antipolitical language of governance. She argues that its presence is indicative of the fact that 'economics has become the science of government' (Brown, 2015: 77) as part of neo-liberalism's 'stealth revolution' (Brown, 2015). It is therefore important to problematise this antipolitical discourse of governance, as I attempt to do in this chapter in relation to contemporary Irish youth justice policy.

I will first outline how I use both Brown's and Bacchi's work as scaffolding to deconstruct governance reforms undertaken as part of the modernisation of the Irish youth justice system. The next section will then show how these reforms are exemplary of the soft power that marketisation entails and how administrative governance alters the relationship between the state, the voluntary sector and citizens. In particular, I will argue that administrative governance reinforces the subjectification of young people in conflict with the law primarily as flat stick figures, understood through reductive parameters that fit the marketised imaginary. This in turn renders the 'youth crime problem' and young people open to interventions that reinforce the marketisation paradigm and make alternatives seem more utopian. Importantly, administrative governance promotes a vision of social change that focuses on the creation of opportunities and individual empowerment, while effacing wider political struggles for equality and justice. Ultimately, the critical interrogation of administrative governance is important as it highlights the creeping normalisation of the economisation of 'other heretofore noneconomic spheres and activities' (Brown, 2015: 17), reaching from abstract forms of administration into the imaginations, narratives and souls of those working in and experiencing the youth justice system.

Administrative governance reform as the reshaping of democracy

Wendy Brown's key propositions on the impact of neo-liberalism on contemporary societies are highly relevant to thinking more deeply about marketisation of criminal justice generally and administrative governance in the Irish youth justice system more specifically. Mindful of the particularities of different national contexts, Brown maintains that neo-liberalism possesses 'ubiquitous' features: 'Neoliberalism takes diverse shapes and spawns diverse content and normative details, even different idioms. It is globally ubiquitous, yet disunified and nonidentical with itself in space and over time' (Brown, 2015: 21). In addition to describing a historically specific response to Keynesianism and democratic socialism, she suggests that neo-liberalism is best understood as a 'more generalized practice of "economizing" spheres and activities heretofore governed by other tables of value' (Brown, 2015: 21). As a consequence, we can refer to 'marketisation' or 'economisation' not only with reference to strategies such as 'privatisation' or 'monetisation', but more broadly to its encroachment of our lifeworlds. Marketisation unfolds itself unnoticed and becomes an unquestioned way of operating and being in our public and private life domains. Due to this 'termitelike' rather than 'lionlike' 'mode of reason, boring in capillary fashion in trunks and branches of workplaces, schools, public agencies, social and political discourse, and above all, the subject' (Brown, 2015: 35–6), these softer features and workings of marketisation often go unnoticed or unquestioned. Progressive 'governance reform' in the name of accountability and efficiency 'governs as sophisticated common sense' (Brown, 2015: 35) and is promoted by political and intellectual elites. However, exposing its workings and limitations goes against the grain of dominant ideological norms, which makes it all the more important as an exercise.

According to Brown, the very presence of the term 'governance' is indicative of the successful diffusion of neoliberalism in the field of public administration and the organisation of the welfare state: 'this interchangeability and promiscuity [of the lexical terms governance and management] suggest that governance comprises and indexes an important fusion of political and business practices, both at the level of administration and at the level of providing goods and services' (Brown, 2015: 123). Under marketised governance, the administration of the public good of justice becomes infused and infiltrated by working principles of the private sector so that 'the conduct of government and the conduct of firms are now fundamentally identical' (Brown, 2015: 27). Administrative governance 'replaces the opposition or tension between government and the private sector with collaboration and complementarity' (Brown, 2015: 126). The imposition of the ideals of administrative governance also significantly alters the relationship between various arms of the state, civil society and the private sector. If we consider the delivery of justice as a fundamental public good, its administration based on principles of 'governance' borrowed from the profit-oriented private sector is enormously problematic. It is possibly, through its invisibility and corresponding incontestability, even more problematic than the outright privatisation or outsourcing of public sector services.

Fundamentally, neo-liberalism, together with its constituent element of administrative governance, carries with it important ramifications for how democracies work. Brown reminds us of Salamon's (2000) widely applied theory of governance and public administration, which emphasises the replacement of 'hierarchical, top-down mandates and enforcement with horizontal networks of invested stakeholders pursuing a common end' (Brown, 2015: 126). Governance removes contestation and public debate from its normative framework. Rather, the emphasis is shifted towards the fine-tuning of 'tools or instruments for achieving ends' (Brown, 2015: 126). However, consensus-oriented collaboration is never an equal-level playing field, so dominant elites are able to maintain agenda setting power in public sector reform and the endless cycle of fine-tuning administrative governance. One of the results of this dynamic is that those causes of social problems – structural inequalities – that generally suit elites are sidelined in public discourse and public reform.

Administrative governance is also achieved by and impacts on one of the other key aspects of neo-liberalism's distinctive mode of reason, the production of subjects. As aptly described by Foucault (2004), the contemporary *homo œconomicus* is shaped by neo-liberalism's 'scheme of valuation' (Brown, 2015: 21). Individual responsibility is emphasised and activation of the 'entrepreneurial self' (Kelly, 2006) is demanded in all spheres of life, including in youth justice. The neo-liberal subject is continuously 'seeking to strengthen its competitive positioning and appreciate its value' and different life domains are 'more increasingly configured as strategic decisions and practices related to enhancing the self's future value' (Brown, 2015: 33–4). As public and political life are folded into the dominant logic of market principles, human subjects are constructed in all spheres of life as *homo œconomicus* (Brown, 2015: 33). And indeed, my research shows that despite the best intentions, young people are continuously evaluated by professionals against the ideals of neo-liberal *homo œconomicus*, who is able to judge wisely and self-improve continuously.

The importance of language and discourse

If we understand marketisation as a governmental regime, then paying close attention to language and discourse becomes a central task for making neo-liberal governmental practices visible and exposing its limitations. Neo-liberalism does not govern through hard, but soft power and takes 'deeper root in subjects and in language, in ordinary practices and in consciousness' (Brown, 2015: 47).

It is often overlooked that neo-liberal governance unfolds itself in 'dry' administrative texts and associated reporting, management and auditing tools. Their importance is easily dismissed as bureaucratic detail that can be ignored, subverted or reappropriated. Similarly, policy makers themselves like to point out the pressures, lack of resources and well-meant intentions when faced with a deconstructive reading of 'their' policy documents. However, in a policy landscape where negotiation, consensus and consultation are central, administrative governance expressed in policy discourse serves as the very vehicle of marketisation. Brown argues that the language of administrative governance is 'expressly and intentionally antipolitical' (Brown, 2015: 77). Once it 'becomes the lingua franca of the state, corporations, schools, non-profits, indeed, of all public and private enterprise, economics has become the science of government' (Brown, 2015: 77).

As such, discursive spaces where administrative governance happens should be interpreted as 'textual sites of power' (Moss and Petrie, 2002: 98) that ultimately have powerful consequences for those individuals targeted by them. Rather than interpreting these at face value and understanding how they offer solutions to 'problems', they should be assumed to hold formative power in defining problems and corresponding solutions. Bacchi's seminal WPR approach to discourse analysis (Bacchi, 2009) reminds us of the different symbolic and material 'effects' that policy documents and other textual materials have. These include, firstly, discursive effects that limit what is thinkable or sayable. Secondly, they contain subjectification effects that define how we feel about ourselves and others. And thirdly, they importantly also refer to lived effects, 'such as the material impact of problem representations which can, for example, limit or enable access to resources, or cause or relieve emotional or material distress' (Goodwin, 2012: 33).

If we pay attention to how young people in trouble with the law are subjectified in administrative governance, we can not only understand how they are 'imagined' by policy makers, but we can unravel the larger issue at stake here, the pervasive infiltration of neo-liberal governance. Importantly, dominant discourses 'travel' from sites of administrative governance into the imaginations of front-line workers directly engaging with young people. Professionals draw on available discourses and position young people accordingly, ultimately with real effects on how young people can 'be' and which types of 'self' are valued. It is important to be subtle here. We cannot claim that '"discourse" or "talk" on a given subject has a direct and immediate effect on that subject. Rather, it signals a kind of embeddedness: a radical connection between our ways of knowing the world and our ways of occupying it – of "being" in it' (Bletsas, 2012: 43). It is these intricacies that we have to make visible and analyse, if we want to dismantle the 'soft' mechanisms of marketisation.

Irish youth justice reform: Governance as neo-liberal marketisation

Modern Irish youth justice policy really commences with the Children Act 2001. Informed by the international regime of children's rights, this long overdue piece of legislation brought Ireland in line with other European jurisdictions. The Act raised the age of criminal responsibility from seven to 12 years, and institutionalised diversion and the principle of detention as a last resort. Additionally, it introduced a wide range of noncustodial sentencing alternatives and set up a dedicated Children's Court as well as a child-friendly detention facility.

Commentators usually describe this modernised Irish youth justice system as welfarist in nature, albeit with remnants of more punitive and paternalistic attitudes towards young people remaining intact. However, I propose that in tandem with the modernisation of the Irish youth justice system, neo-liberal marketisation has become a key feature of Irish youth justice policy. Due to its 'termitelike' rather than 'lionlike' 'mode of reason' (Brown, 2015: 35), these developments have gone largely unnoticed or unquestioned. Equally, Irish youth justice reform took place at a time when broader public sector reform in Ireland was strongly and unequivocally driven by principles and practices of marketisation in areas such as workfare and health. As 'neoliberalism governs as sophisticated common sense' (Brown, 2015: 35), it is intuitively uncomfortable in a small jurisdiction to deconstruct progressive youth justice reform.

At an institutional level, the setting up of the Irish Youth Justice Service (IYJS) in 2005, with its main mission to coordinate and oversee Irish youth justice policy, is itself a hallmark of the institutionalisation of governance in the Irish youth justice system. Governance 'replaces orders with, orchestration, enforcement with benchmarks and inspection, and mandates with mobilisation and activation' (Brown, 20015: 127). Tellingly, the first high-level goal of the National Youth Justice Strategy 2008–2010, the first strategy document to be published by the IYJS, was aimed at making 'the youth justice system more effective through providing clear, unified and strategic leadership' (IYJS, 2008: 22). The prioritisation of governance mechanisms over the reduction of youth offending indicates this important shift towards orchestration and coordination, typical of administrative governance.

As a consequence of this new governance architecture, the IYJS's core task in the past 13 years has been to devise and coordinate youth justice policy. However, I argue that the IYJS has also been instrumental in introducing a new governance system (through the so-called Agenda of Change) to the management of Garda Youth Diversion Projects (GYDPs), heavily informed by principles of marketisation. GYDPs are a significant site where young people encounter the Irish youth justice system. Around 5,000 young people across 115 locations (compared with detention and remand rates of around 60 young people at any given time) are involved annually in these multi-agency diversion and youth crime prevention initiatives. The origins of GYDPs lie in a collaboration between civil society (voluntary youth work organisations) and the Irish police (Gardai) and until today, youth work organisations manage the majority of these projects. The projects are co-financed by the Department of Justice and the European Social Fund, with an annual total budget of around 11 million euros.

The Agenda of Change included the introduction of new reporting and auditing requirements, uniform risk assessments for tracing young people's participation in projects and the retraining of project workers and Juvenile Liaison Officers (police officers) in structured interventions. While at the surface these changes may be interpreted as a long overdue introduction of administrative oversight and alignment of a wide variety of reporting and working practices, I have suggested elsewhere that they have effectively created a new professional field of 'youth justice work' in Ireland (Swirak, 2016). Youth justice work favours highly interventionist programmes with young people, while decentring those which are based on principles of organic relationship building, young people's participation and other priorities reflected in more traditional types of 'youth work'. Youth justice work also chimes more closely with the new demands of marketised governance and does not always sit comfortably with professionals, as expressed by this youth justice worker: 'When I first started in this line of work … nothing was recorded but a lot of work was being done. And now we have to justify what we're doing, but to do it all statistically, I think it's wrong … we have to code young people and tick all of the boxes … and it dehumanises the whole process and I find that really, really frustrating.'

However, at another level, the Agenda of Change has also contributed to the deeper entrenchment of marketisation in Irish youth justice policy and is emblematic of its wider infiltration into Irish public policy. Again, it is important to remember here that marketisation understood as a governmental regime signifies the encroachment of business practices into other fields. In Irish youth justice, this has become evident through the emphasis in policy discourse that borrows heavily from the business sector. The economisation of discourse was strongly present throughout the Agenda of Change and has since become acceptable terminology across contemporary youth justice policy. Discursive signifiers such as 'measurable logics', 'auditing', 'performance' and 'value for money' were normalised throughout the Agenda of Change, and youth justice policy documents ever since have drawn regularly on such terms.

The discursive use of such an 'economic style of reasoning' (Garland, 2001: 88) is itself a powerful indicator of the infiltration of neo-liberal ideology. Its 'travelling' to the imaginations of professionals who deal with young people on a daily basis was very visible in my research and shows how discursive agenda setting provides a frame of reference from which it is difficult to deviate. Nearly all youth justice workers I spoke to had bought into the economic rationality of youth justice policy, emphasising and at times even championing the importance of accountability and 'value for money' as an acceptable principle around which GYDP reform should be orbiting. Youth justice workers were concerned with justifying 'taxpayers' investment' and with their responsibility to not waste this 'investment', as for example expressed by this youth justice worker: 'And it's very understandable as well why they are doing that [tighter reporting and auditing] because, they need to justify why they're funding us ... it has to be the number crunching game to a certain extent because, that's what funders look for.'

Importantly, youth justice workers' 'economic style of reasoning' nearly always universally included references to 'evidence-based' and 'best-practice' discourses of working with young people, in themselves expressive of the spread of governance. Best practices 'entail a never-ending loop' between researchers and practitioners and between diverse endeavours and institutions – firms, families, factories, schools, government and non-governmental organisations (NGOs) (Brown, 2015: 47). Ironically, once 'best practices' are established, they can never be questioned in their very essence, only fine-tuned and improved: 'best practices can be effectively contested only by postulating better practices, not by objecting to what they promulgate' (Brown, 2015: 47). Typically, this results in the sidelining of in-depth, qualitative and 'slow' types of evidence that are considered 'unscientific'. Many youth justice workers indeed bought into the idea that punctuated interventions with young people could be tangibly 'measured': 'Project participants were assessed in March. We are going to assess them again in July and August to see if there is going to be a change after all the interventions have been put in ... that should actually make a difference.'

The wide use and the 'meshing of political and business lexicons' are carriers through which 'neoliberal reason is disseminated' (Brown, 2015: 71). If we apply Brown's further argumentation to Irish youth justice policy, we face some deeply troubling questions. Brown suggests that the rolling out of 'governance' involves an inbuilt 'antipathy to politics' (Brown, 2015: 71). She argues that its introduction results in a 'very specific model of public life and politics', where 'deliberation about justice and other common goods, contestation over values and purposes, struggles over power, pursuit of visions for the good for the whole' move to the background and 'public life is reduced to problem solving and program implementation, a casting that brackets or eliminates politics, conflict, and deliberation about common values or ends' (Brown, 2015: 127).

And indeed, with its overarching emphasis on consensus-oriented governance, Irish youth justice policy has successfully depoliticised the 'youth crime problem'. By focusing on managerial and governance changes without paying attention to the uncertain knowledge around young people's offending behaviour for more than a decade, Irish youth justice policy seeks to govern through consensus, thereby 'downplaying to the point of disavowing structural stratifications in economy and society that could produce different political stakes and positions' (Brown, 2015: 129). Rather this consensual modus operandi has resulted in a sidelining of contextual factors such as neighbourhood disadvantage, a classed school system and a marketised social support system. Within the rationale of marketised governance, solutions to young people's offending behaviour are mostly located in the psyche of the individual. As one youth worker commented, 'at the end of the day, their potential they reach that themselves, and they make the decisions to get them there themselves with our support and guidance. Some of them make the right decisions and unfortunately others don't, you know.'

Ironically, where social stratification is acknowledged, addressing systemic changes is placed beyond the reach of youth justice policy and practice and within the realm of responsibility of other 'services'. Normative discussions around the extreme difficulty for young people from deprived areas to access the same opportunities as their middle-class peers are either not brought up, or downplayed by showcasing 'successful' persons from similar backgrounds. As one of the youth justice workers herself said:

> 'And I live in x – so it wouldn't be a nice area. Now like that again, there's good and bad in everything but, I always use myself as an example. Like when the lads heard that I went to college they were like, wow, you were into college and you're from Y and we didn't think people from Y went to college like so, I am constantly using myself as an example; that even though I'm not from an upper class area, I'm from like a very working class area that people can change and do good for themselves.' (Youth Justice Worker 1)

The Agenda of Change has also repositioned the Irish youth work sector as a responsible partner for implementing this depoliticised version of youth justice. This has been achieved by mutual agreement to sideline the social justice orientation of many youth work organisations and co-opting them into favouring interventions which can be easily measured. In line with governance's modus operandi of ruling through agreement, youth work organisations have been 'membershipped' (O'Sullivan, 2005: 38) into youth justice work through a research, consultation and piloting process. Through the implementation of the Agenda of Change, these small units of governance, while 'responsible for themselves', have been bound 'to the powers and project of the whole' (Brown, 2015: 129), the larger project of marketised youth justice. The GYDP reform process is therefore a prime example of successfully implemented neo-liberal governance, which 'operates through isolating and entrepreneurialising responsible units [GYDPs] and individuals [youth justice workers], through devolving authority, decision making, and the implementation of policies and norms of conduct' (Brown, 2015: 129).

Similarly to other national contexts, where voluntary sector organisations enter into contractual relationships with different degrees of marketisation, this Irish version of marketised governance has provoked differentiated responses. Depending on the respective organisational ethos as well as the youth justice workers' own professional and training background, youth justice workers also challenged, subverted and resisted the new governance framework. Nevertheless, it is strongly noticeable how the principles and practices of marketised governance have become the new frame of reference for organisations and professionals. Many GYDPs and their parent youth work organisations have been unable to escape 'mission drift' by displacing the original goal of young people's welfare with the goal to prevent crime. As Cohen (1985: 258) already outlined in relation to expansionary social control, positive side effects are not impossible. Nevertheless, the expansion of marketised governance signifies a reconfiguration of the relationship between the state, the voluntary sector and, as I will now go on to show, ultimately the young person involved in GYDPs.

Assembling the 'marketised' young person in conflict with the law

Marketised governance has direct ramifications as to how young people are subjectified. Under neo-liberal rule, *homo œconomicus* is turned into a citizen consumer, configured so as to render herself/ himself amenable to self-improvement and 'ethical reconstruction' (Rose, 2000). Bacchi reminds us to look for absences in discourse, and it was notable how with the Agenda of Change's prioritisation of effectiveness, coordination and accountability, young people in trouble with the law disappeared in policy discourse. No space was provided to describe their full range of capabilities, potential, strengths and resilience in the face of different kinds of hardships. Rather, similar to other jurisdictions, where the 'new governance of youth crime' (Gray, 2009: 443) has prioritised the pseudo-scientific risk and needs approach, Irish youth justice policy relies on this reductionist framework of describing and managing young people's offending behaviour. Risk factors relating to young people's education, family background and neighbourhoods are combined to assemble a young person who has to be intervened upon in the most efficient way. The Agenda of Change described young people as passive service recipients, and actuarialist language throughout dehumanised the complex relationships of young people and their social networks. In this vein, the lack of 'input' by parents had to be compensated by more intensive 'input' from GYDPs. And similarly to effective employees, it was envisaged that young persons should be trained in 'problem solving' by setting SMART, that is 'specific, measurable, achievable, realistic and time bound' goals.

What is important to remember here is that a youth justice system that relies on the collation of comparable statistics to govern interventions that are geographically dispersed, such as the GYDPs, must inherently rely on these reductionist frameworks of categorising and describing young people. Biesta (2010: 497) aptly refers to this reliance on tools that are supposedly able to demystify intangible human interactions and relationships as attempts of 'complexity reduction'. Similarly to modernist attempts of graphically differentiating the 'normal' from the 'abnormal' child, risk factor assessments as well as other visual categorisations of young people's behaviours have to be understood as an attempt to make the young person 'real'. The young person becomes a manageable part of a youth justice system that has at its core come to accept the norms of measurement, best practice and accountability. The tables and graphs used to depict young people's problem behaviours make the young person 'stable by constructing a perceptual system, a way of rendering the mobile and confusing manifold of the sensible into a legible, visual field' (Rose, 1990: 147).

However, as the values of accountability, comparability and traceability of interventions gain discursive precedence over the unpredictability and fragility of human behaviour, so do subjectivities of young people undergo permutation. Marketisation as a governmental regime 'swallows humanity ... by its form of valuation' (Brown, 2015: 44). One cannot help but juxtapose the administrative language of marketised youth justice and its representation of young people with other visions of what it means to be human. Brown reminds us that in John Stuart Mill's liberalism, human beings are subjectified through hopeful description: 'what makes humanity "a noble and beautiful object of contemplation is individuality, originality, fullness of life," and above all, cultivation of our "higher nature"' (Brown, 2015: 43–4). Marketised youth justice, just like neo-liberalism, 'retracts this "beyond" and eschews this "higher nature"' (Brown, 2015: 44) – in the search for oversimplified explanations of complex social, psychological, cultural and spatial contingencies in which offending behaviour is couched. The reader of marketised youth justice policy cannot escape an aftertaste of Kafkaesque hopelessness.

Compared with official policy discourse, youth justice workers were more imaginative and positive when it came to describing the young people with whom they worked. They sought to explain young people's offending behaviour through a variety of typical 'origin stories' (Griffin, 1993) related to a variety of developmental and psycho-social discourses. Notably, 'origin stories' set out to 'search for the cause(s) of a socially constructed phenomenon which is situated within the "deviant" individual (who is usually working-class, Black and/or male), their "deficient" cultural practices and/or family forms ... Such origin stories seldom construct "delinquency" as a product of poverty, racism or other structural forces' (Griffin, 1993: 106). As such, 'origin stories' present a level of sufficient complexity that satisfies marketisation's 'sophisticated common sense' (Brown, 2015: 35), but equally chime with the individualising rationality of marketised youth justice.

However, despite these different layers of complexity introduced in professionals' narratives, it was striking how the emphasis in terms of hopes for young people was expressed in limited terms, mainly referring to achievements in education and employment. Notwithstanding the well-documented role of education and employment in 'desisting' from crime, the linking of young people's success to primarily educational and employment outcomes also signifies the subjectification of the young person as *homo œconomicus*. Entrepreneurial selfhood is imagined in very limited ways: '"initiative", "enterprise", "responsibility" and "activity" are narrowly imagined in relation to the performance of exchange relations in the extended order of capitalist markets – of all sorts' (Kelly, 2006: 28). The subjectification as neo-liberal *homo œconomicus* means that there is 'no longer … an open question of how to craft the self or what paths to travel in life' (Brown, 2015: 109).

This process became even more evident as the majority of youth justice workers placed the responsibility of young people's pathways out of offending behaviour on self-improvement: 'I don't think there's any limit on their potential … once they kind of reach their confidence level in themselves, you know.' GYDPs were positioned as the location where opportunities were created, young people empowered, but in line with the assumption of 'free will' of *homo œconomicus* – it was seen as 'up to each individual young person' what to make of these offerings. This individualising version of young people's life choices was often also extended to young people's families:

> 'And I suppose kind of again it goes back to kind of family values and attitudes … it's the same with stolen goods like, I mean, there's no problem in these families with actually buying stolen goods … I mean, if you're getting a bargain at your door, you're not going to ask where it came from and so it's that kind of thing you know … they [young people] don't really see a major problem with some of that petty crime you know, robbing an ice cream or a bag of crisps … they don't really see an issue with that and that's kind of a really engrained attitude, that comes from a very early age … from their families.' (Youth Justice Worker 2)

Ultimately, the larger socio-political, cultural and economic forces at play were not deemed to be acceptable explanations, nor were they seen as loci for changing offending behaviour. In line with neo-liberal meritocracy, a large focus was placed on convincing young people that their poor living conditions and life chances were not entirely deterministic and that they could better their lives if only they tried hard enough. These assemblages of young people's subjectivities are useful to and typical of marketised governance, as they render the 'youth crime problem' open to interventions that fit and reinforce its norms and values. Self-activation, individual responsibility and participation in evidence-based interventions that can be measured and documented become foremost principles in a marketised youth justice landscape. Administrative governance of youth justice favours a young *homo œconomicus* who is open to self-investment, to not only become law-abiding, but also to become a productive citizen in a marketised political economy.

Conclusion

Brown argues that in order 'to understand how neoliberalism becomes a governing political rationality, we need to examine a set of developments in formulations and practices of governance' (Brown, 2015: 122). Neo-liberalism and governance are 'intertwined and synergistic', as 'contemporary neoliberalism is unthinkable without governance' (Brown, 2015: 122). Ireland's mixed economy of welfare has become increasingly dominated by clearly visible trends of marketisation and privatisation in the delivery of services, particularly in the areas of employment and training, housing, water and health. The Irish justice sector generally and the youth justice sector more specifically have shied away from large-scale marketisation, although this happened more due to political and economic exigencies rather than an ideological stance against marketisation as such.

Marketised *governance*, however, is rife throughout the entire Irish public sector, and by looking at a snapshot of Irish youth justice policy reform, I have sought to highlight how soft marketisation is indicative of the dissipation of neo-liberal ideology. By drawing on Brown's work, I have argued that in the area of youth justice policy this has several important ramifications. These include the repositioning of the voluntary youth work sector, the prioritisation of systems management and economising variables, individualising simplifications of young people and their offending behaviour and a concurrent sidelining of wider socio-political questions crucial for addressing youth offending. At the time of writing, the IYJS has started to focus on introducing more inclusive and participatory tools for evaluating the impact of GYDPs, with a view to capturing nuanced, qualitative and relational outcomes for policy makers' perusal. Maybe this is indicative of a realisation that administrative governance has its limitations, and it offers a glimpse of hope for the future.

References

Bacchi, C.L. (2009) *Analysing Policy: What's the Problem Represented to Be?* Canberra: Pearson Education.

Biesta, G. (2010) 'Why "what works" still won't work: from evidence-based education to value based education', *Studies in Philosophy and Education*, 29(5): 491–503.

Bletsas, A. (2012) 'Spaces between: Elaborating the theoretical underpinnings of the 'WPR' approach and its significance for contemporary scholarship', in A. Bletsas and C. Beasley (eds) *Engaging with Carol Bacchi: Strategic Interventions*, Adelaide: University of Adelaide Press, pp 37–52.

Brown, W. (2015) *Undoing the Demos: Neoliberalism's Stealth Revolution*, New York: Zone Books.

Cohen, S. (1985) *Visions of Social Control: Crime, Punishment and Classification*, Oxford: Polity Press.

Corcoran, M.S. (2014) 'The trajectory of penal markets in a period of austerity: the case of England and Wales', *Sociology of Crime, Law and Deviance*, 19: 53–74.

Foucault, M. (2004) *The Birth of Biopolitics: Lectures at the Collège de France, 1978–79* (ed M. Senellart, trans G. Burchell), New York: Picador.

Garland, D. (2001) *The Culture of Control: Crime and Social Order in Contemporary Society*, Oxford: Oxford University Press.

Goodwin, S. (2012) 'Women, policy and politics: recasting policy studies', in A. Bletsas and C. Beasley (eds) *Engaging with Carol Bacchi: Strategic Interventions*, Adelaide: University of Adelaide Press, pp 25–36.

Gray, P. (2009) 'The political economy of risk and the new governance of youth crime'. *Punishment and Society: The International Journal of Penology*, 11(4): 443–58.

Griffin, C. (1993) *Representations of Youth: The Study of Youth and Adolescence in Britain and America*, Cambridge: Polity Press.

IYJS (Irish Youth Justice Service) (2008) *National Youth Justice Strategy 2008–2010*, Dublin: Stationery Office.

Kelly, P. (2006) 'The entrepreneurial self and youth at-risk: exploring the horizons of identity in the 21st century', *Journal of Youth Studies*, 9(1): 17–32.

Moss, P. and Petrie, P. (2002) *From Children's Services to Children's Spaces: Public Policy, Children and Childhood*, London: Routledge Falmer.

O'Sullivan, D. (2005) *Cultural Politics and Irish Education since the 1950s: Policy Paradigms and Power*, Dublin: Institute of Public Administration.

Rose, N. (1990) *Governing the Soul: The Shaping of the Private Self*, London: Routledge.

Rose, N. (2000) 'Government and control', *British Journal of Criminology*, 40: 321–39.

Salamon, L.M. (2000) 'The new governance and the tools of public action: an introduction', *Fordham Urban Law Journal*, 28(5): 1611–74.

Swirak, K. (2016) 'Problematising advanced liberal youth crime prevention: the impacts of management reforms on Irish Garda Youth Diversion Projects', *Youth Justice: An International Journal*, 16(2): 162–80.

7

Police outsourcing and labour force vulnerability

Roxanna Dehaghani and Adam White

Introduction

The post-financial crisis politics of austerity have required police forces in England and Wales to make unprecedented savings at a rapid pace. In response, some forces have turned to the market, outsourcing back office and front-line functions to commercial enterprises which promise to deliver the same service (or more) for less. This trend has unsurprisingly captured the attention of policing scholars who have started to explore attendant issues of policy (Crawford, 2013), politics (White, 2015), accountability (Rogers and Gravelle, 2012) and service delivery (White, 2014, 2018). This chapter adds another variable into the equation: vulnerability in the labour force. It does so by comparing the experiences of front-line workers in non-outsourced and outsourced police custody suites. It argues that in addition to the common vulnerabilities in evidence across the traditional non-outsourced police labour force, those in outsourced roles confront a further set of vulnerabilities specific to the market for policing. This finding deepens our understanding of the implications arising from austerity-era police outsourcing.

The chapter develops this line of argumentation over four sections. The next section traces the impact of the post-financial crisis politics of austerity upon the policing landscape, focusing on budget cuts and cost reduction strategies. It also reviews the extant scholarship on this trend, highlighting a gap when it comes to issues of labour force vulnerability. The following section examines the common vulnerabilities experienced by front-line workers in traditional non-outsourced custody suites, such as the complexity of police work, limited resources, lack of training and feeling over-scrutinised – many of which, incidentally, have been exacerbated under conditions of austerity. The subsequent section investigates the additional vulnerabilities faced by front-line workers in austerity-era outsourced custody suites, such as identity crises, unwanted media attention and a particular kind of prejudice from detainees. At the same time, however, this section emphasises how outsourcing can also enhance resilience against these vulnerabilities through improved training programmes and opportunities for career progression. The final section highlights the original contribution of the chapter by connecting issues of labour force vulnerability to extant scholarship on police outsourcing and the privatisation of criminal justice.

Context

As the global financial crisis spread across the UK banking sector during the course of 2007 and 2008, the New Labour government took the unprecedented steps of nationalising Northern Rock and Bradford & Bingley and publicly funding capital investments in Lloyds TSB and the Royal Bank of Scotland, amounting to 'the largest UK government intervention in financial markets since the outbreak of the First World War' (Bank of England, 2008). While successful in its objective of stabilising the banking sector, this bailout left an enormous hole in the exchequer which required immediate attention. As a consequence, the central debate of the 2010 general election was not whether or not public spending should be cut, but how far. Upon assuming office, the newly formed Conservative–Liberal Democrat Coalition government duly initiated a Comprehensive Spending Review which, among a swath of other cuts, stipulated a 20 per cent reduction in the central government police budget over the period 2010/11–2014/15 (Her Majesty's Inspectorate of Constabulary [HMIC], 2013). After decades of generous taxpayer subsidisation compared with many other public services, the police were entering into an era of austerity.

Broadly speaking, each force had four options in making the requisite savings. The first was to reduce pay through recruitment freezes, compulsory retirement of police officers and voluntary or compulsory redundancy of police staff (HMIC, 2011: 16). The second was internal restructuring, with a focus on basic command units, workforce functions and shift patterns (HMIC, 2011: 29). The third was public sector collaboration with other police forces or local authorities so as to realise economies of scale (HMIC, 2012). The fourth was outsourcing back office and front-line services areas to the private sector for a limited duration with guaranteed savings written into the contract (HMIC, 2012: 32–3). However, these options were not operationalised evenly across the 43 forces – each charted its own pathway through austerity.

The reason for this variation was down to a mixture of economic context, organisational structure and leadership ideology. To begin with, not all forces were dependent on central government funding to the same degree because of disparities in local authority contributions, meaning some could be more selective about which options they chose to pursue than others (HMIC, 2013: 28). Furthermore, not all forces had the same amount of 'fat to trim' due to differences in scale and efficiency, meaning some forces were better placed to make savings through pay reductions and internal restructuring than others (HMIC, 2013: 36). Lastly, senior police officer attitudes towards the market diverged considerably, meaning some force leadership teams were more ideologically open to outsourcing than others (Gill, 2015). As a consequence, only 13 of the 43 territorial police forces were directly linked with outsourcing deals in the wake of the Comprehensive Spending Review – Bedfordshire, Cambridgeshire, Dorset, Gwent, Hertfordshire, Leicestershire, Lincolnshire, Northamptonshire, Nottinghamshire, Surrey, Warwickshire, West Midlands and Wiltshire Police (White, 2015). Moreover, only one of these – Lincolnshire Police – brought this process to a conclusion, signing a £229 million contract with G4S to deliver 18 services areas between 2012 and 2022, with a total saving of £36 million.

Over the past few years, policing scholars have proceeded to interrogate these developments from different angles. Crawford (2013), for instance, situates them within the broader policy initiative of mobilising the 'extended policing family' against crime and disorder. White (2015) drills down on the political dimension of this shift, focusing on the limits to market expansion. Rogers and Gravelle (2012) discuss issues of accountability, emphasising the tension between traditional chains of command embedded in the public sector and new decision making practices linked to shareholder expectations in the market. White (2014, 2018) explores the changing nature of service delivery, illustrating how outsourcing blends together public good and market logics on the front line in both intentional and unintentional ways. Through this scholarship, the dynamics and consequences of austerity-era police outsourcing are gradually being revealed. One as yet unexplored dimension, however, concerns labour force vulnerability.

That said, vulnerability has received some attention in relation to the traditional non-outsourced police labour force, especially under the conditions of austerity. At first glance, this may seem counter-intuitive. Scholarship on police occupational culture frequently depicts front-line police workers as masculinised crime-fighters endowed with considerable legal and symbolic powers which they direct towards a variety of ends, both good and bad (Loftus, 2010). Yet everyone is vulnerable and, crucially, some are more resilient than others (Fineman, 2008). As austerity-era budget cuts bite ever deeper, front-line police workers are increasingly displaying a lack of resilience. This is because they are facing resource constraints and increased scrutiny while simultaneously serving as the 'fall guys' (McBarnet, 1981: 156) of the underfunded criminal justice and health and social care systems. Foregrounding issues of vulnerability enables us to better understand their diminished resilience under such circumstances.

It is against this backdrop that Lumsden and Black (2017), for instance, explore the emotional labour of call handlers in a non-outsourced police force control room, illustrating how budget cuts in the police specifically and across the welfare state more broadly are causing time and resource pressures to mount up among front-line workers. Dehaghani and Newman (2017) likewise examine the wellbeing of custody officers facing a similar combination of pressures in two non-outsourced police custody suites. The original contribution of this chapter is to extend this line of reasoning to austerity-era outsourced front-line roles. It does so by drawing together and building upon observations from two of the aforementioned studies: Dehaghani and Newman's (2017) investigation of custody officers in two non-outsourced police custody suites; and White's (2014) analysis of front-line service delivery in the Lincolnshire Police–G4S Strategic Partnership which also covered two outsourced custody suites. This comparison serves to highlight the additional vulnerabilities faced by outsourced workers in front-line roles.

Labour force vulnerability in non-outsourced custody suites

To explore labour force vulnerability in traditional non-outsourced custody suites, this chapter reinterprets findings presented in Dehaghani and Newman's (2017) study on the wellbeing of police custody officers – findings which form part of Dehaghani's (2019) broader research on police custody. Through 23 interviews with police custody officers, combined with almost six months of field observation across two police forces, this study explores how police custody officers interpret vulnerability in relation to the appropriate adult safeguard. These data are here reframed to illustrate the vulnerabilities experienced by traditional non-outsourced police custody officers – namely, the complexity of police work, limited resources, lack of training and feeling over-scrutinised.

The first vulnerability relates to the inherent complexity of police work. Police custody officers are required not only to oversee the temporary incarceration of detainees and ensure detainees are aware of their legal rights, but also to calibrate for the variable needs of those who are below the age of 18, suffering from mental health problems, intoxicated with alcohol and/or under the influence of psychoactive substances. They are required, in other words, to bring together the specialist skill sets of a police officer, prison guard, lawyer and healthcare professional into a single role. Moreover, they are called upon to perform this feat in a highly unpredictable environment. Arrests can occur at any time, meaning they are often expected to manage large numbers of detainees simultaneously, for example in the wake of public order incidents. It is this inherent complexity which in many ways underpins all the other vulnerabilities.

The second vulnerability relates to resource limitations. Austerity-era budget cuts have left many police custody suites understaffed and officers feel little optimism that this situation will improve in the near future, for instance through redeployment from other service areas. At the same time, other public sector roles which contribute towards the running of police custody – such as drug and alcohol workers, healthcare professionals, approved mental health professionals, appropriate adults and forensic medical examiners – are also suffering from austerity-driven budget cuts. As the support functions performed by these professionals are withdrawn, officers run an increased risk of violating the Police and Criminal Evidence Act (PACE) 1984 and/ or expected provisions on detainee care. Furthermore, custody suites are more likely to become, as one officer puts it, a 'dumping ground for other agencies'. A shortage of NHS hospital beds, for example, means that crisis-stricken individuals are sometimes taken into custody as a 'place of safety' under the Mental Health Act 1984 – a resource-intensive diversion shot through with additional risks and liabilities.

The third vulnerability relates to lack of training. While police custody officers receive induction training upon first assuming the role and are given annual updates on how to assess and manage detainee care needs, some still regard their training as incommensurate with the role they are expected to perform (although to be fair others judge it to be satisfactory). Receiving adequate training on the various legal requirements emanating from PACE is a particular concern. Many officers, for example, struggle to recall the detail of PACE Code of Practice C on the requirements for the detention, treatment and questioning of suspects, admitting they find it difficult to comprehend and navigate. Such knowledge gaps not only potentially compromise the rights of detainees but also expose officers to repercussions should they fail to comply with these requirements.

The fourth vulnerability relates to the sense of feeling over-scrutinised. Police custody officers are often called upon to perform complex and demanding tasks with limited resources and training, yet 'the buck stops with them' (see also Skinns, 2011). For example, any breach of PACE or the Codes may result in exclusion of evidence at trial and, at the same time, any failure to appropriately care for a detainee, particularly when this results in death or serious injury, may result in disciplinary action. As a result, officers often experience significant discomfort with the level of responsibility placed upon them. To cite a topical issue, even though death in custody is often regarded as beyond their control, it could, as one officer remarked, be a 'career-ender' (see also Wooff and Skinns, 2018). During the fieldwork, one officer was suspended from duties pending investigation. A few weeks earlier, he had been seen opening a letter – a suicide note from a detainee previously supervised by this officer. The lack of control coupled with intense scrutiny is, for many, the most difficult part of the job.

These four vulnerabilities are in many ways intrinsic to front-line police work. The complex and unpredictable nature of this work almost inevitably means there are never enough resources and training programmes to equip any given front-line worker with the necessary tools to perform their role with complete assurance of success and without risk – hence the above average levels of scrutiny. It is also important to recognise of course that it is precisely these high stakes which attract many individuals to police work in the first place and which shape the distinctive occupational culture in the field. These vulnerabilities do not therefore represent a 'problem' to be 'fixed', so to speak. Yet nor should they simply be accepted as a kind of ever present background noise, as has too often been the case. They need to be openly addressed and brought into the dialogue surrounding police work. This is a particularly pressing concern given that these vulnerabilities are clearly being exacerbated through the politics of austerity. Moreover, taking this proposition seriously requires policing scholars to become more sensitised to new vulnerabilities rising to the surface not just in traditional non-outsourced front-line roles, but in austerity-era outsourced front-line roles too, as the next section illustrates.

Labour force vulnerability in outsourced custody suites

To explore labour force vulnerability in outsourced custody suites, this chapter reinterprets findings presented in White's (2014) study of the Lincolnshire Police–G4S Strategic Partnership, a £229 million contract covering the delivery of 18 service areas between 2012 and 2022. Through 22 interviews with individuals from both sides of the Strategic Partnership conducted during 2013–14, this study explores the relationship between public good and market logics in those front-line roles included in the contract. It includes data on the working conditions of front-line workers in two outsourced custody suites. These data are here reinterpreted through the lens of vulnerability to illustrate how these workers not only experience many of the same vulnerabilities as those outlined previously, but also face three additional vulnerabilities specific to the market for policing – namely, identity crises, unwanted media attention and a particular kind of prejudice from detainees. It is important to add, though, that these workers also receive more training in relation to certain skill sets, thereby equipping them with some of the resilience needed to mitigate these vulnerabilities.

To begin with, it is important to stress that the four vulnerabilities identified previously in non-outsourced custody suites are, unsurprisingly, also present in outsourced custody suites to a significant degree. While the 15 back office service areas taken over by G4S are more routine in nature (human resources, administrative support, facilities management and so on), the three front-line service areas (force control room, police station front counters and custody suites) display similar complexities to those found in any form of front-line police work. In outsourced custody suites, for instance, it is impossible to predict who is coming through the door, how many detainees there will be or the nature of their needs. There are comparable concerns too about resource and training limitations, especially given that G4S set out to maintain or improve delivery across the 18 service areas with a £36 million cost saving to Lincolnshire Police over ten years, while also extracting a 6.2 per cent annual profit. This said, there is also a countervailing view that training has improved to some degree in those outsourced front-lines roles, thereby going some way towards ameliorating rather than consolidating these vulnerabilities, as the following discussion illustrates. Finally, a comparable sense of feeling scrutinised is also in evidence – though it is important to add a caveat here. Those occupying front-line roles in the Lincolnshire Police–G4S Strategic Partnership are civilians rather than warranted officers, meaning the 'buck does not stop with them' in the same way. This scrutiny thus has an altogether different point of origin, as the ensuing narrative shows. In sum, those performing front-line roles in outsourced custody suites exhibit parallel vulnerabilities to those in traditional non-outsourced custody suites, yet they also show signs of additional vulnerabilities too.

The first additional vulnerability concerns the identity crises bound up in the outsourcing process. Upon going live, no fewer than 575 members of staff were immediately transferred from Lincolnshire Police to G4S through TUPE arrangements.[1] While this process did not have an immediate impact upon their working practices because there was a conscious effort to prioritise continuity in the first few months of the contract, it did nevertheless mean that all civilian custodians were required to exchange their Lincolnshire Police lanyards, epaulets and email signatures for Lincolnshire Police–G4S ones. This exchange precipitated an emotional response among certain custodians (and indeed other front-line workers) who were unwilling to relinquish these symbols of their professional identity. As the Lincolnshire Police Commercial Partnership Manager explains: 'I think people felt like that's the police, the ID card I've got is the police … some really did think you're taking Lincolnshire Police away from me and replacing it with something different.' One custodian remembers the experience as follows: 'The phrase was "I'm not G4S by choice". TUPEd over staff did not join G4S by choice. The fact that they're working for G4S is not their fault.' The extent to which this resentment results from their commitment to the public service ethos of Lincolnshire Police or their antipathy towards the profit-maximising values of G4S is difficult to say – it is likely some combination of the two. Either way, for some custodians the outsourcing process clearly precipitated an identity crisis and therefore further contributed towards their vulnerability.

The second additional vulnerability relates to unwanted media attention. By the time the Strategic Partnership went live, a polarised and emotive 'police privatisation' debate was already taking shape within the media, dominated by a campaign to 'save' what is often regarded as a core public service from the profit-maximising logic of the market. Against this backdrop, photographs of the new Lincolnshire Police–G4S lanyards and epaulets were released by G4S in an attempt to generate positive publicity. Contrary to expectations, however, these photographs were put to use by the anti-privatisation wing. 'The epaulet thing went viral', one G4S Managing Director reflects, 'it was one of our guys who took the picture to show people what they'd be wearing next week in a positive way, but it was taken

---

[1] TUPE is the common abbreviation for the Transfer of Undertakings (Protection of Employment) Regulations 2006, which protect the rights of employees when their employer changes through, for instance, the sale or outsourcing of physical assets.

in such a negative way by a lot of people. That was us taking over the police force.' Fired up by the subsequent failure of G4S to satisfy the terms of its London Olympics security contract, together with the first round of Police and Crime Commissioner elections, this debate eventually became so toxic that it contributed towards the derailment of the deals being negotiated by the 12 other forces engaged in the outsourcing process. For present purposes, though, the salient point is that the new epaulets and lanyards worn by custodians (and others) in the Strategic Partnership became the focus of critical media attention and thus added to their sense of vulnerability.

The third additional vulnerability relates to prejudice from detainees. As front-line workers responsible for depriving individuals of their basic liberties, all custodians inevitably face a certain degree of verbal abuse. After the Strategic Partnership went live, however, this abuse became increasingly laced with the anti-privatisation rhetoric articulated in the media. 'When we were Lincolnshire Police staff and the epaulet just said Lincolnshire Police they [detainees] knew we were all the same', one custodian recalls; 'when we had G4S put on our epaulets they started to say, "Well you're only a security guard I don't want to deal with you. I don't want to be booked in by G4S staff".' Again, it is impossible to tell whether this particular form of verbal abuse emanated from a principled opposition to police outsourcing or if it was simply another vehicle through which to express anger and frustration at being detained in custody. Either way, it folded into the vulnerabilities faced by these front-line workers.

At the same time, however, the Strategic Partnership fostered resilience against some of these vulnerabilities. For instance, G4S introduced new training programmes and promotion opportunities. 'If Lincolnshire Police had tried to sort out its problems without outsourcing, nothing like this would ever have changed. Nobody was driving things forward', one custodian explains; 'custodians didn't know who to go to if they wanted to suggest a change. G4S are knowledgeable and savvy in the custody environment and are making changes that wouldn't have happened.' One Custody Sergeant reinforces this impression: 'The level of training improved through G4S. Not only captures, but also food hygiene, mental health issues. In those areas they improved the professionalism of the suite and the way custodians can progress through a career structure.' Through better training and professional development pathways, then, the outsourcing process helped to enhance the resilience of custodians in the face of longstanding vulnerabilities. Despite this positive note, however, it seems clear that on balance those performing front-line roles in austerity-era outsourced custody suites experience more vulnerabilities compared with those in traditional non-outsourced custody suites.

Conclusion

This chapter has shown that in addition to traditional police labour force vulnerabilities such as the inherent complexity of police work, limited resources, lack of training and feeling over-scrutinised, those working in austerity-era outsourced front-line roles may also suffer from identity crises, unwanted media attention and a particular kind of prejudice from detainees. Before reflecting on the broader implications of these findings, however, it is necessary to consider briefly the generalisability of the case from which they arise. The Lincolnshire–G4S Strategic Partnership is by some distance the largest outsourcing deal in UK policing history and, moreover, the only one struck in the immediate aftermath of the Comprehensive Spending Review. As such, the intensity of any resulting identity crises, media attention and prejudice from detainees was perhaps always going to be especially acute. It seems quite likely therefore that such vulnerabilities will be less prominent in future outsourcing deals (should they come into effect). Yet at the same time they are unlikely to fade away entirely. If nothing else, the Lincolnshire Police–G4S Strategic Partnership suggests that there are at least some specific labour force vulnerabilities bound up with the outsourcing process.

As a consequence, it is important to take seriously the broader implications stemming from these findings. In analytical terms, they demonstrate that labour force vulnerability is not just one more austerity-specific issue to be considered alongside already examined questions of policy, politics, accountability and service delivery, but also connects with the experiences of front-line workers right across the policing landscape. In other words, we should address labour force vulnerability when debating austerity-era police outsourcing more specifically and police work more generally. In practical terms, these findings suggest that policy makers tasked with planning future police outsourcing deals should think carefully about how these deals will impact upon the experiences of front-line workers. As previously stated, such vulnerabilities should not be approached as a 'problem' to be 'fixed', for they are in many ways intrinsic to this line of work; but there should be some recognition of them and, by extension, some strategies in place to alleviate their worst affects. A front-line labour force whose vulnerabilities are well managed is undoubtedly better positioned to serve the public – and that surely is the ultimate goal here.

Finally, it is important to emphasise that these analytical and practical conclusions may also find resonance elsewhere in the criminal justice landscape. Over the past couple of decades, no fewer than 14 prison estates and/or workforces have been outsourced to the likes of G4S, Serco and Sodexo and, in more recent years, low- and medium-risk probation services have been contracted out to 21 regionally organised Community Rehabilitation Companies. While scholars have duly considered many of the challenges and difficulties experienced by front-line workers during the course of these transitions (Ludlow, 2014; Robinson et al, 2016), vulnerability has not been part of their vocabulary. As such, transferring insights from the foregoing discussion into these neighbouring fields of criminal justice scholarship may prove to be a productive process. Indeed, given the controversial renationalisation of the G4S-run prison HMP Birmingham in August 2018, and the announcement that all the contracts to run probation services awarded by the Ministry of Justice in 2015 will be terminated prematurely in 2020 due to widespread performance issues, there may never be a more opportune moment for a wider debate about vulnerability and criminal justice outsourcing.

References

Bank of England (2008) *Financial Stability Report*, October 2008, Issue no. 24, London: Bank of England.

Crawford, A. (2013) 'The police, policing and the future of the extended policing family', In J. Brown (ed) *The Future of Policing*, London: Routledge, pp 203–20.

Dehaghani, R. (2019) *Vulnerability in Police Custody: Police Decision-Making and the Appropriate Adult Safeguard*, London: Routledge.

Dehaghani, R. and Newman, D. (2017) 'We're vulnerable too': an (alternative) analysis of vulnerability within English criminal legal aid and police custody', *Onati Socio-Legal Series*, 7(6): 1199–228.

Fineman, M.A. (2008) 'The vulnerable subject: anchoring equality in the human condition', *Yale Journal of Law and Feminism*, 20(1): 1–23.

Gill, M. (2015) 'Senior police officers' perspectives on private security: sceptics, pragmatists and embracers', *Policing and Society*, 25(3): 276–93.

HMIC (2011) *Adapting to Austerity*, London: HMIC.

HMIC (2012) *Increasing Efficiency in the Police Service: The Role of Collaboration*, London: HMIC.

HMIC (2013) *Policing in Austerity: Rising to the Challenge*, London: HMIC.

Loftus, B. (2010) 'Police occupational culture: classic themes, altered times', *Policing and Society*, 20(1): 1–20.

Ludlow, A. (2014) *Privatizing Public Prisons*, Oxford: Hart.

Lumsden, K. and Black, A. (2017) 'Austerity policing, emotional labour and the boundaries of police work: an ethnography of a police force control room in England', *British Journal of Criminology*, 58(3): 606–23.

McBarnet, D. (1981) *Conviction: Law, the State and the Construction of Justice*, London: Macmillan.

Robinson, G., Burke, L. and Millings, M. (2016) 'Criminal justice identities in transition: the case of devolved probation services in England and Wales', *British Journal of Criminology*, 56(1): 161–78.

Rogers, C. and Gravelle, J. (2012) 'Policing after Winsor: outsourcing and the future of policing', *Police Journal*, 85(4): 273–84.

Skinns, L. (2011) *Police Custody: Governance, Legitimacy and Reform in the Criminal Justice Process*, Oxford: Willan.

White, A. (2014) 'Post-crisis policing and public–private partnerships: The case of Lincolnshire Police and G4S', *British Journal of Criminology*, 54(6): 1002–22.

White, A. (2015) 'The politics of police "privatization": a multiple streams approach', *Criminology & Criminal Justice*, 15(3): 283–99.

White, A. (2018) 'What is the privatisation of policing?' *Policing: A Journal of Policy and Practice*, available from: https://doi.org/10.1093/police/pay085 [accessed 30 March 2020].

Wooff, A. and Skinns, L. (2018) 'The role of emotion, space and place in police custody in England: towards a geography of police custody', *Punishment and Society*, 20(5): 562–79.

8

Marketisation or corporatisation? Making sense of private influence in public policing across Canada and the US

Kevin Walby and Randy K. Lippert

Introduction

In 2015, one of us attended a conference in the United Kingdom on policing and markets. Coming from Canada, the tone and tenor of the discussion about the expanding role of the private sector in policing was striking. For most attendees from the public police and the security industry blending in among the academics, private penetration of the public policing realm was deemed a fait accompli. Conference goers used phrases such as 'the ship has sailed' and 'the genie is out of the bottle', to refer to seemingly irreversible inroads of private security into police practices. Correspondingly, security industry representatives at the event made formal and informal pitches to woo public police, seeking to sell cost-saving packages and security management solutions, and encourage administrators to further divest. There was discussion of 'core tasks' of criminal justice and how to create 'efficiencies' via privatisation (Hancock, 1998). Notable criminologists (for example Spitzer and Scull, 1977; Shearing, 1992) have been alerting scholars and seeking to make sense of this trend for some time.

For us, the shocking part of observing these UK developments first-hand is that in Canada the public police presence is not receding. Instead, public police budgets are mostly growing; public personnel numbers are not in sharp decline. Though there is some mild civilianisation, there is no hollowing out, and there are few public–private partnerships. There are no scenarios like in the UK where entire front and back offices of police are outsourced to G4S

(Dehaghani and White, Chapter 7, this volume). Currently in Canada that is unfathomable. Police are starting to charge 'users' for some items but are not selling off the institution to the private sector.

Of course, Canada has a robust private security industry, with private security personnel easily outnumbering public police several fold. Yet the status of private security is much lower, and private security is thought to be distinct from public police even though some private security personnel occasionally seek to act as public police. Though Canadian governments have outsourced and privatised numerous other Crown and state entities, such as energy and telephone ministries, there is little appetite in Canada to apply those ideas to police. Even though Canadians spend an inordinate amount of tax dollars on public policing – approximately 25–30 per cent of most municipal budgets in cities across the country – the idea of turning to the private sector as even a partial replacement or any privatisation of public police remains distasteful to the Canadian palate. In the city in which one of us lives, for example, the public police are requesting from the municipal government a 6 per cent increase in their budget again this year.

Public policing in Canada has not, however, avoided change. New forms of private influence are emerging in Canadian public policing. This includes private sponsorship of public police and donations to emergent police foundations (Walby et al, 2017), as well as what is called 'user pay' policing. In this contribution, we suggest that how public police departments are mutating is better conceived as corporatisation than commodification, privatisation or even marketisation. Our reflections are meant to describe shifting public policing and market influences in Canada but also to bring conceptual clarity to these discussions. This contribution explores key concepts in criminology and criminal justice studies and gauges their applicability to private sponsorship and donations and user pay arrangements in public policing. We compare definitions and applications of marketisation and corporatisation. First, we describe several key concepts and the subtle but vital differences between marketisation and corporatisation. We attempt to clarify these debates occurring within police studies, as well as in criminology and criminal justice studies more broadly. Second, we elaborate some changes (police foundations, user pay policing) that reflect corporatisation of public police, in Canada but also in the US. Most literature on corporatisation has focused on public utilities, however, we argue the process is also relevant to public policing. Finally, we assess the international implications of the foregoing.

Key concepts defined

Corporatisation, commodification, privatisation and marketisation are key terms used to explain changes in policing and criminal justice. Corporatisation is similar to the term 'managerialism' (Davids and Hancock, 1998) or the 'new public management' that promises more efficient use of public police resources. Yet these terms are at times conflated or erroneously invoked. Here we attempt to untangle them. We want to develop an analytically defensible understanding of public police corporatisation and show its purchase beyond the profit-seeking private corporations that the terms commodification and privatisation invoke.

More and more criminal justice, including policing, practices are being described as marketised (Stacey, 2012). This term assumes a full-fledged shift to treating people as customers and assumes open competition. Whitfield (2006: 4) defines marketisation as the penetration of market forces into public services, including commodification of services, restructuring of state for competition and market play, and embedding of business interest in the state. The question is whether corporatisation differs from marketisation: We think it does. It can involve similar outcomes but does *not* involve the same penetration of the state by the market.

Corporatisation differs from marketisation, privatisation or commodification of public policing. The latter three concepts are interrelated because markets entail private actors producing, buying and selling commodities. Marketisation requires a market, privatisation entails private actors and commodification assumes commodity production. Commercialisation is a related though less often invoked idea that is a corollary to commodification (Ayling, 2014). Although there is affinity among them, there is no necessary or essential link between corporatisation of public police and public policing's marketisation or privatisation.

McDonald (2014, 2016) helps distinguish corporatisation, noting it is analytically distinct from marketisation and privatisation. Marketisation entails more direct private sector participation, and privatisation entails large-scale sell-offs of public services and goods. Corporatisation is thus distinct from privatisation, or even marketisation. For McDonald (2014), corporatisation creates new forms of management in the public sector that 'create arm's length enterprises with independent managers responsible solely for the operation of their own immediate organisation, and where all costs and revenues are accounted as though it were a stand-alone company' (McDonald, 2014: 1–2). It is a shift in governance structure but not a shift in ownership. This approach to corporatisation is associated with new public management, and is accompanied by new performance measures for workers (Hoque et al, 2004). McDonald argues that corporatisation is also linked to market-friendly public sector cultures and policies (McDonald, 2014: 2). This process can involve commodification and commercialisation, though not necessarily marketisation or privatisation. Again, marketisation entails more direct private sector participation and market competition, and privatisation entails large-scale sell-offs of public services and assets.

Corporatisation takes three forms. Firstly, corporatisation can refer to new managerial forms of control, revenue streams and organisations run more like for-profit businesses, which is potentially relevant to security corporatisation. Secondly, it can mean new forms of arm's length administration. This can include boards of directors and separate legal statuses for organisations and entities on whom are bestowed new capacities to govern. This could lead to privatisation or commodification, though these processes would be offshoots of a corporatisation process. Thirdly, corporatisation can refer to forms of public–private integration, including public–private partnership expansion, and private corporate interlocking with public bodies and their membership.

Corporatisation can also appear to be market oriented, which is why it is often conflated with marketisation. Neo-liberal corporatisation involves applying 'market-oriented operating principles' to stand-alone, state-owned entities (McDonald, 2016: 107). This approach leans the furthest toward market intervention and partnerships in state projects. However, the distinction is that corporatisation entails state agencies functioning with a business model, not a business appropriating goods from the state. An offshoot of neo-liberal corporatisation involves commodification of the goods and services provided by state agencies. Government practices and services can become commodified and monetised, and offered at a cost, which sometimes erodes the public accessibility of the good or service. This is not the fundamental restructuring of the state that marketisation and especially privatisation entail.

Examples from Canada and the US

Police foundations

An overlooked marker of corporatisation is the creation of private foundations to channel private donations and sponsorships into government operations. Our focus is on police foundations as one indicator of corporatisation of public police. McDonald argues that corporatised government entities 'typically have a separate legal status from other public service providers and a corporate structure similar to publicly traded private sector companies, such as a board of directors' (McDonald, 2015: 11). Police foundations are registered as private charities and are not public entities under Canadian law, and thus have a legal status separate from public police. These foundations are not privately endowed. Rather they are established as charitable organisations under Canada's federal tax laws. Foundations either register as a 'charitable organisation', as with the Calgary and Edmonton police foundations, or under the legal term 'public foundation', as with the Vancouver and Delta police foundations. The former designation's requirements are that the organisation:

- is established as a corporation, a trust, or under a constitution
- has exclusively charitable purposes
- primarily carries on its own charitable activities, but may also gift funds to other qualified donees[1] (e.g., registered charities)
- more than 50% of its governing officials must be at arm's length from each other[2]
- generally receives its funding from a variety of arm's length donors
- its income cannot be used for the personal benefit of any of its members, shareholders, or governing officials. (Canada, 2019)

The 'public foundation' differs from this only in that it cannot be established 'under a constitution' and that it 'may carry out some of its own charitable activities' rather than 'gift funds to other qualified donees' (Canada, 2019).

Police foundations have a board of directors. For McDonald (2015: 12), the goal of these new organisations is to 'create arm's length enterprises' to help 'reduce political interference'. Police foundations

---

[1] A qualified donee is an organisation that can issue official donation receipts for gifts it receives from individuals and corporations.

[2] https://www.canada.ca/en/revenue-agency/services/charities-giving/charities/charities-giving-glossary.html#arms

meet McDonald's criteria for corporatisation. Yet foundations may create the potential for furtive conflicts of interest to go on unabated.

We located more than 250 foundations in the US, 4.3 per cent (11 foundations) of which reported incomes greater than US$1 million, with the lead New York City Police (NYCP) Foundation reporting US$19.9 million. In Canada, there are fewer police foundations, but more are being established. Using the online Charities Listing database of Canada Revenue Agency, we identified eight Canadian municipal police foundations: the Abbotsford Police Foundation, Calgary Police Foundation, Delta Police Foundation, Edmonton Police Foundation, Saskatoon Police Service Foundation, Royal Canadian Mounted Police (RCMP) Foundation (formerly Mounted Police Foundation), Vancouver Police Foundation and the Fondation du service de la ville de Montreal (SPVM Foundation). In 1976 the first foundation in Canada was created: the Vancouver Police Foundation, only five years after the NYCP Foundation. The Vancouver Foundation began small but has since undergone exponential growth in private funds. The Vancouver Police Foundation reported roughly CA$8.2 million in 2015, a record year, making it the second wealthiest police foundation in North America. The richest, the NYCP Foundation, reported US$7,936,387 in revenues for 2015. The province of British Columbia has led in the creation of police foundations, with three out of the seven in Vancouver, Abbotsford and Delta. The next foundation established after Vancouver was the national RCMP Police Foundation (1994), followed by police foundations in Edmonton (2000), Delta (2004), Abbotsford (2005), Montreal (2008), Calgary (2010) and Halifax (2017). The police excitement about foundations was summed up by Jim Chu, former Chief Constable of the Vancouver Police Department, on the foundation website: 'When the public needs help, they call the police. When the VPD needs help, they call the Vancouver Police Foundation.' Other municipal and provincial police forces in Canada are considering creating police foundations.

Establishing a police foundation is not without challenges for advocates. An article in the *Saskatoon Star Phoenix* newspaper reported in January 2016 that the provincial Saskatchewan Police Commission had terminated its policy of allowing citizens and police departments to establish police foundations. Previously, it was reported that Saskatoon City Councillor Charlie Clark had discussed with the Saskatoon Board of Police Commissioners the establishment of a police foundation to boost that police department's budget. According to the Chair of the Saskatchewan Police Commission, Neil Robertson, it was decided to prohibit the creation of police foundations in Saskatchewan for fear of corruption allegations that might accompany it. As Robertson put it: 'Policing isn't a charity. It's an essential public service' (Tank, 2016). Robertson added, 'We're open to being persuaded' (Tank, 2016). It appears the Commission was persuaded, since with no press release or newspaper coverage, the Saskatoon Police had quietly registered its foundation as a charity by April 2018. More honestly than most, it included 'Service' in its title, revealing the direct link between it and the police department. The foundation's website provides no details as to how this came about, its 'history' merely reporting that it was not humanly devised, but something of an act of nature: 'The foundation began *naturally* as a fundraising event that was organised by officers of the Saskatoon Police Service and community partners who desired to give back to their community' (Saskatoon Police Service Foundation, 2019; our emphasis). But this mutation toward public–private partnerships and private influence is anything but natural.

Police foundations in the US and Canada are used to shore up police service's demands for resources. They fund many initiatives, from purchasing equipment such as bulletproof vests, to supporting technological upgrades to police facilities, to more community outreach and youth-oriented programmes. Police foundations, premised on funding programmes outside a police department's regular budget, may begin by funding more community and at-risk youth-oriented programmes. As foundations receive more donations, however, the focus can broaden, especially as large private corporations with vested interests in police department purchase of their products, equipment or technological capacities enter the fold. Do such corporatised exchanges create conflicts of interest like those observed in other domains where foundations have risen to prominence?

While it is difficult to argue that many foundation initiatives obviously commenced with a conflict of interest, the logic and mechanisms through which police foundations operate increases opportunities for abuse of due process, and erosion of public trust. Many police foundations such as the NYCP Foundation claim they are part of an *anti-corruption and pro-transparency drive* in policing. The original idea for the NYCP Foundation came from Eliot Lumbard, a private New York City attorney, in the early 1970s. Lumbard presented the idea to the Police Commissioner, who embraced the idea of creating a police foundation as 'an anti-corruption opportunity' (Delaney et al, 2014: vi). While donations made directly to police could be better managed independently by an external foundation, this is not all that police foundations do. Police foundations also solicit donations, a practice from which most police departments are prohibited (Davis, 2010). They also capitalise on the professional capital and network connections of corporate actors recruited for or otherwise sitting on their boards (Butler and Delaney, 2010). Foundations therefore raise serious questions about private influence on public police budgets and operations.

Police foundation practices can remain opaque and can adhere to Canadian tax laws because of pithy reporting requirements. In Canada an annual report is required to maintain charitable status and there is decidedly little information in it available for public consumption to ensure transparency, other than dollar amounts concerning 'assets' and 'expenditures', and somewhat vague categories used to describe activities on the Canada Revenue Agency's website (the federal department responsible for overseeing Canada's tax laws, including charitable organisation status), which maintains a searchable database of charitable organisations. If a citizen or would-be donor searched the Calgary Police Foundation, they would learn from its 2017 mandatory 'Registered Charity Information Return' that its annual revenue was almost CA$2.3 million and that almost CA$1.4 million was transferred out as 'gifts' in 2017. The largest of the three gifts was sent to the Calgary Police Service that year. However, how the Police Service used these funds is unclear, with the mandatory reporting field in the return simply stating the foundation 'funds programs that focus on education prevention and early intervention in order to reduce Youth victimisation and involvement in criminal activity. These initiatives they support are a collaboration between the Calgary Police Service and its community partners.' The vital other side of this is that it is also uncertain from the return (but not necessarily from what the foundation *chooses* to publish on their website) precisely what entities contributed to the approximately CA$1.9 million in gifts, the vast majority of which had receipts issued. The foundation website lists major oil and gas private corporations as five of the six 'founding donors' that gave CA$1 million or more such as Talisman Energy Inc., while annual donors also include private corporations of various kinds (Calgary Police Foundation, 2019). The website also reports that some donors are anonymous. We note that the amounts given to the foundation are immune from taxation, a process which could have generated public revenues then spent on public policing or other public initiatives under the oversight of elected officials responding to public demand and priorities.

Other than revenues and expenditures sorted into vague categories, almost all that we learned about these foundations had to be derived from information they happened to publish on their websites or release to media or through privately arranged interviews. Foundations are not subject to Canada's Freedom of Information laws and our efforts to access them were denied, even after appeals.

There is earlier scholarship on private influence on public policing (for example Spitzer and Scull, 1977; Shearing, 1992). Foundations comprise a new dimension in this field. However, we argue that privatisation, commodification and commercialisation as terms are misplaced if applied to foundations. Organisations governing and providing security can become corporatised and adopt key features of corporations without becoming businesses that sell or produce commodities for profit in a security marketplace or selling off parts of the institution (see also O'Malley and Hutchinson, 2007). Liaising with foundations mirrors this process. There is no divestment involved, and public police remain at the centre of these murky operations, with their coffers fuller than before.

User pays policing

Many police departments in North America and beyond now offer 'user pays' public policing. This kind of policing in Canada and the US, as well as in Australia and the UK, has been surprisingly neglected given its prevalence. The premise of 'user pays' is that those who use public police security services for private benefit should pay, and the more they use the more they should pay. This involves selling security services to individuals and organisations for street festivals, funeral escorts, concerts, parades, film production shoots and retail establishments. These arrangements entail uniformed officers providing a security presence to these 'users' via a temporary assignment, typically of between four and eight hours per officer. The generated revenue from users is transferred mostly to the officers, with only 10–15 per cent kept by the public police department.

Canadian police departments call this arrangement 'special duty' or 'paid duty', sometimes under a larger umbrella of 'charge-back', whereas state police departments in the US call it 'paid detail' or 'off-duty' security-related employment. Regardless of the moniker, all officers receive extra pay to provide these services beyond their salaries and it is often lucrative for the officers involved. The average addition to regular officer salaries in one large regional police department was CA$6,000 annually according to a police administrator (Police Representative 5). This varied across officers, with some making many times more than that in departments.

The extent of user pays policing in North America is significant. A recent US survey of non-federal police departments revealed that four out of five departments allow officers to engage in these security assignments (Stoughton, 2017: 1847). One ex-police officer who oversees these assignments in a large US state noted:

> It's very common ... the vast majority of police officers who work for cities and counties and even some state agencies work ... an off duty police service assignment and what they do is they supplement their income by working with varying degrees of permission from their agencies ... usually directly for private businesses or corporations in a highly industrialized area ... There is ... everything from churches to retail stores to office buildings to refineries it's *very, very, very common* to hire an off duty police officer. (Paid Detail Police Representative 1; emphasis added)

The number of assignments to mostly private users varies across police departments and is indexed to a department's size. According to police logs obtained through our Freedom of Information requests, the large San Francisco police department (more than 1,500 officers) in 2015 had almost 11,000 assignments; the mid-sized police department in Hamilton, Canada, with more than 650 officers, had more than 3,500 assignments; and the tiny Saanich Police in Canada, with only 45 officers, had only 22 assignments that year.

Our research shows that user pays funding arrangements involving corporate and other mostly private entities are evident across North America. Like foundations, user pay policing is not without controversy. In Toronto, the high cost of paid detail services, especially when charged to City of Toronto departments, has been problematised (Lippert and Walby, 2014). This was due to the high visibility of uniformed officers standing around road construction sites in the city. This led to curtailing assignments and replacing traffic duty officers with flag persons (Lippert and Walby, 2014). Elsewhere in Canada, an assignment procedure that randomises officers interested in a pay duty assignment was introduced following concern about cash being paid directly to officers at night's end, and officers 'owning' venues to which they would return each week. There and elsewhere this has been due to the optics of hired police potentially 'looking the other way' rather than enforcing law. Police administrators are increasingly aware of what their officers might do or might have happen to them, in users' private spaces far beyond police administrators' oversight. Thus, officers' lucrative forays into mostly private sites and events come with moral and physical risks to officers and ultimately the police department. In Jersey City and Seattle, 'user pays' policing has recently become associated with full blown corruption. This has ironically led to the public police, at taxpayer expense – in this case the Federal Bureau of Investigation – having to respond to the corruption through arrests and charges being laid, which in turn has led to some officers being fired and jailed, again at further and great public expense.

There is a history of piece work in public policing (Spitzer and Scull, 1977), which has always troubled a firm division between public and private policing. But this has typically been assumed to represent privatisation of policing. However, we would caution against viewing paid duty policing as privatisation or as commodification and commercialisation. We have also argued against seeing paid duty policing as marketisation since these operations typically started long before the onset of neo-liberalism and it is not the market that sets the terms, it is police departments. There is no open competition; police have a structural advantage and thus are not so much selling security as demanding payment. This is especially true where increasingly corporatised police department administrators decide, with no input from the public or their employees, which events held on public property will require officers and then how many before they will approve a permit so the event can be held. More importantly for our argument, there is no divestment involved, and public police remain at the centre of these operations, which line the pockets of individual police officers. There is a private demand for the public good of policing, and paid duty policing indicates a corporate outlook on the part of police to create a supply, often for other corporatised actors.

Conclusion

In many countries, public policing is changing rapidly and drastically. Though the changes seem less stark in Canada, this does not mean things are set in stone. Indeed, as we have noted, the dynamics of market influence on policing are playing out in unique ways in Canada. Paid duty policing and private sponsorship of public police may at first glance appear to resemble commodified forms of social control, but as we have argued these must be analysed empirically rather than assumed through predetermined lenses. This is generally true of social inquiry. Commodification, privatisation or marketisation might be the predominant trend in some jurisdictions but not in others. Little attention is paid to developing corporatisation as a concept or exploring how it relates to commodification, privatisation or marketisation.

The situation in the UK regarding public policing may be best described as marketisation (McLaughlin et al, 2001; Maquire, 2012). We have argued that corporatisation may be the concept most applicable to Canada, and perhaps to the US as well. Corporatisation as a concept highlights a process that neither automatically nor inevitably entails (and sometimes rebuffs) private sector participation and sell-offs of public assets. Changes in the business world might compel change in public policing (see Davids and Hancock, 1998; O'Malley and Hutchinson, 2007), but this varies. Corporatisation directs attention to corporate boards and consciousness that intertwines with foundations. This seems to be because, in Canada at least, citizens cling to the notion of publicness as a basis of critiquing such developments, as we have shown for both police foundations and user pay policing. The notion of publicness in Canada has so far been a more effective firewall against privatisation than elsewhere, although the resulting mutation this has caused is perhaps advanced corporatisation now entrenched in public policing. This trend does not exclude government or unions but compels them to act more like, or to adopt features of, corporations without engaging in restructuring, divestment or displacement of the state. Future research should explore why some criminal justice systems become more amenable to marketisation and privatisation versus corporatisation, especially in policing but also in corrections, probation and parole. Being more analytically and conceptually precise is vital for activists, academic, and policy makers who seek to confront corporatisation and its serious effects on the public interest.

References

Ayling, J. (2014) 'Trading in security: issues in the commodification of public security', in M. Gill (ed) *The Handbook of Security*, London: Palgrave Macmillan, pp 936–58.

Butler, D. and Delaney, P. (2010) 'Starting a police foundation: lessons learned', *Police Chief*, 77(2).

Calgary Police Foundation (2019) 'Our supporters', available from: http://cpf.cpsevents.ca/donate-cpf/supporters/ [accessed 31 October 2019].

Canada (2019) 'Charities and giving glossary', Canada Revenue Agency, available from: https://www.canada.ca/en/revenue-agency/services/charities-giving/charities/charities-giving-glossary.html#pub [accessed 31 October 2019].

Davids, C. and Hancock, L. (1998) 'Policing, accountability and citizenship in the market state', *Australian & New Zealand Journal of Criminology*, 31(1): 38–68.

Davis, R. (2010) 'Thoughts on starting a police foundation', *Police Chief*, March.

Delaney, P., Brody, J. and Andrews, W. (2014) *Investing in Community Safety: A Practical Guide to Forming and Sustaining Police Foundations*, Washington, DC: Office of Community Oriented Policing Services.

Hancock, L. (1998) 'Contractualism, privatisation and justice: citizenship, the state and managing risk', *Australian Journal of Public Administration*, 57(4): 118–27.

Hoque, Z., Arends, S. and Alexander, R. (2004) 'Policing the police service: a case study of the rise of "new public management" within an Australian police service', *Accounting, Auditing and Accountability Journal*, 17(1): 59–84.

Lippert, R. and Walby, K. (2014) 'Marketization, knowledge work, and "users pay" policing in Canada', *British Journal of Criminology*, 54(2): 260–80.

McDonald, D. (2014) 'Public ambiguity and the multiple meanings of corporatisation', in D. McDonald (ed) *Corporatisation and Public Services in the Global South*, New York: Zed Books, pp 1–30.

McDonald, D. (2015) 'Back to the future? The curious case of "public" services', Paper prepared for the UIC Urban Forum Chicago, 17 September, p 11.

McDonald, D. (2016) 'To corporatize or not to corporatize (and if so, how?)', *Utilities Policy*, 40: 107–14.

McLaughlin, E., Muncie, J. and Hughes, G. (2001) 'The permanent revolution: New Labour, new public management and the modernization of criminal justice', *Criminal Justice*, 1(3): 301–18.

O'Malley, P. and Hutchinson, S. (2007) 'Converging corporatisation? Police management, police unionism, and the transfer of business principles', *Police Practice and Research*, 8(2): 159–74.

Saskatoon Police Service Foundation (2019) 'History', available from: https://saskatoonpoliceservicefoundation.org/history/ [accessed 31 October 2019].

Shearing, C. (1992) 'The relation between public and private policing', *Crime and Justice*, 15, 399–434.

Spitzer, S. and Scull, A.T. (1977) 'Privatisation and capitalist development: the case of the private police', *Social Problems*, 25(1): 18–29.

Stacey, C. (2012) 'The marketization of the criminal justice system: who is the customer?' *Probation Journal*, 59(4): 406–14.

Stoughton, S. (2017) 'Moonlighting: the private employment of off-duty officers', *University of Illinois Law Review*, 5: 1847–1900.

Tank, P. (2016) '"Policing isn't a charity," Saskatoon board of police commissioners told', *Star Phoenix*, 23 January, available from: https://thestarphoenix.com/news/local-news/policing-isnt-a-charity-saskatoon-board-of-police-commissioners-told [accessed 31 October 2019].

Walby, K., Lippert, R.K. and Luscombe, A. (2017) 'The rise of the police foundation: implications of public policing's dark money', *British Journal of Criminology*, 58(4): 824–44.

Whitfield, D. (2006) 'A typology of privatisation and marketisation', European Services Strategy Unit, ESSU Research Report No. 1.

9

Marketisation and competition in criminal legal aid: implications for access to justice

Tom Smith and Ed Johnston

Introduction

Legal aid, particularly in criminal justice, is a divisive subject. For its most devoted proponents, state funding of legal representation and advice for those accused of crime is a vital public good which helps to uphold values of fairness, justice and equality. For its most virulent critics, criminal legal aid is a wasteful, bloated relic from a bygone era of state intervention, serving primarily to help criminals escape justice. These are perhaps caricatures; but most opinions on criminal legal aid lie nearer to one or other extreme. This chapter examines how, like many areas of criminal justice, criminal legal aid has been subjected to (relatively) modern notions of marketisation, managerialism and competition. We aim to provide some critique of this by both exploring its development and briefly examining two 'case studies', which arguably demonstrate the impact of neo-liberal ideology on criminal legal aid.

While criminal legal aid should not be immune to criticism, there has been consensus for decades that the right to legal representation is fundamental and that legal aid is vital to securing this. In England and Wales (E&W), all persons detained in police custody have a right of access to a legally aided lawyer. This is, in theory, universally available and not based on a person's financial circumstances. In contrast, a person *may* be entitled to a legally aided lawyer if they are charged and brought to court as a defendant. If one is available, a state-funded duty lawyer – that is, a lawyer who works 'on call' to provide representation to any accused person without it – may be able to assist a defendant. However, if the duty lawyer is not available, defendants will need to rely on their 'own' lawyer. This is subject to a test of both merits and means; if the defendant does not fall below the qualifying threshold for legal aid, they must pay for their own lawyer. If they cannot afford one, the defendant may self-represent before a court or not attend at all.

The importance of legal representation in criminal proceedings – and by extension, legal aid – can be couched in terms of both the procedural benefits (such as the check on police power and adversarial scrutiny of prosecutions) as well as the language of welfarism. Funding such representation, for people who are often indigent and marginalised, can be rationalised as a method of protecting the most vulnerable and deprived in society, and ensuring that such people are not unfairly disadvantaged by a lack of means or social status (see Newman and Smith, 2017). Such thinking drove a significant expansion in the scope of criminal legal aid in the second half of the 20th century, in terms of both the budget for legal aid and the number of defendants receiving it (see Smith and Cape, 2017). While a 'tipping point' is hard to identify, one might argue that criminal legal aid started to drift and then descend into decline somewhere in the mid- to late 1990s. The fees paid to legal aid providers have been effectively frozen for more than two decades due to a failure to implement any real terms increase (Deloitte, 2013; House of Commons Justice Committee, 2018: para. 15). Successive governments have made active attempts to reduce the cost of criminal legal aid through reforms and cuts. The narrative has markedly shifted from one emphasising the benefits of criminal legal aid, towards its costliness and unsustainability. This suggests that, ideologically, criminal legal aid is now couched in terms of neo-liberal values of managerialism, competition and efficiency, rather than that of post-war welfarism.

Competition and marketisation

The place of private and public deliverers in legal aid

The provision of criminal legal aid might be described as indirect, in that suspects and defendants are not directly provided with funding for a lawyer by the state. The Legal Aid Agency (LAA – an executive arm of the Ministry of Justice) contracts with a number of 'providers' who offer legally aided representation (either on a duty or own client basis) to accused persons (clients) (Legal Aid Agency, 2018a). In a police station, a legally aided lawyer should be provided to any suspect who requests one, regardless of means, whereas eligible defendants at court must obtain a representation order to secure this service. This system provides us with the first indication of the role of marketisation in criminal legal aid; that is, private organisations are contracted to deliver legal services as opposed to a directly funded state body. This so-called 'judicare' model has been part of the delivery of criminal legal aid in E&W since its inception (Smith and Cape, 2017: 65). Traditionally, private firms of solicitors provide representation and assistance in police stations and magistrates' courts, while self-employed barristers are instructed by solicitors to provide advocacy services in the Crown Court. An exception is the Public Defender Service (PDS), a state provider of legal aid services, employing salaried solicitors and advocates. Piloted in 2001, the PDS was touted as a means of 'benchmarking' the private legal aid market and plugging gaps in provision (Lord Chancellor's Department, 1998). For various reasons, the PDS did not expand and therefore plays a small part in the landscape of criminal legal aid (see Bridges et al, 2007). Private providers continue to dominate.

Providers can, to a certain extent, choose their clientele. They must, however, offer a certain amount of duty representation (in both police stations and courts) on a rota basis as part of their contract with the LAA. Therefore, while criminal legal aid does involve private businesses operating in a free market (albeit funded, normally, by the state), they are obliged to accept a proportion of their client base without question. This is an interesting and unusual manifestation of a free market approach to delivering state services, in part created by the mandatory requirement that a significant number of clients *must* be provided with the service. In terms of who gets to deliver such services, contracts to offer representation are allocated by the LAA based on tenders from prospective providers. They must specify the extent to which they can provide both duty and own client representation. Unsurprisingly, success is at least partly determined by capacity and economy – that is, the ability to provide more service for lower cost (although quality of service is, in theory, a significant part of the process). Again, this demonstrates the place of competition in criminal legal aid; potential providers must battle to secure a slice of the available market, the rationale being that this will drive down costs and drive up quality.

Marketisation, competition and managerialism

From the early 2000s onwards, the goal of 'marketising' legal aid was fully embraced. Among the arguments in favour of this were the belief that legal aid was subject to 'supplier-induced demand' (that providers were driving demand for their work) (Bevan, 1996: 98); that the 'cottage industry' nature of the legal aid market meant it was bloated and fragmented; and that the generous nature of legal aid funding meant that lawyers delivered services in a less than efficient manner. After initial, tentative experiments with tendering (such as the Legal Services Commission contracting pilot), the Carter Review recommend moving towards a system of best value tendering (Carter, 2006). Lord Carter recommended a 'market-based approach' to private provision of legal aid, with a necessary restructuring of the fragmented market – primarily, by larger firms swallowing smaller firms through mergers. This would grow the average size of criminal legal aid providers and shrink the size of the market – a goal of successive governments over the last two decades. In 2009, the New Labour government moved to implement best value tendering; however, this was abandoned over fears of unsustainable 'suicide' bids by some providers who would be desperate to maintain a share of the market (Criminal Bar Association, 2009).

In 2013, the Ministry of Justice consulted on a similar tendering scheme in its paper *Transforming Legal Aid: Delivering a More Credible and Efficient System* (Ministry of Justice, 2013). The paper stated that Carter's vision remained a desirable model, encouraging firms to competitively tender for work by offering the best quality at the lowest price. It rationalised this on the basis that firms would deliver greater volumes of work and therefore provide 'increased opportunities to scale-up to achieve economies of scale', leading to a more efficient service (Ministry of Justice, 2013: 14). This, it argued, would mean firms that were successful could offer a full range of criminal defence services, from police station representation to representation at trial. However, to achieve this, the size of the market would need to be constricted substantially. Under the 2010 Standard Crime Contract, there were approximately 1,600 criminal defence firms offering representation. In contrast, the 2013 proposals envisaged only 400 providers – a reduction of 75 per cent in the size of the market. This system – dubbed Price Competitive Tendering (PCT) – never came to fruition. In her criticism of the proposal, Welsh cited the Rushcliffe Committee report (whose initial recommendations preceded the Legal Advice and Assistance Act 1949) which stated that defence firms needed to be remunerated adequately because the adversarial process is dependent on the effective preparation of each side's case (Welsh, 2013: 28). PCT would not, she argued, achieve this. Kemp echoed these sentiments, suggesting that lawyers sometimes struggled to offer 'quality' when hampered by inadequate remuneration (Kemp, 2010). Cape and Smith suggested that the practical realities of delivery, in the context of a smaller pool of providers, would mean slower and less efficient processes, thereby defeating both the objectives of the reforms and (at the court stage) the overriding objective of the Criminal Procedure Rules (HM Government, 2015: rule 1.1). For example, they suggested that lawyers may be delayed in attending at police stations due to greater volumes of work – but with no more personnel to deliver this. Ultimately, this risked increased numbers of unrepresented suspects and defendants (Smith and Cape, 2017: 77). Arguably, this not only raises the prospect of injustice (in a system designed around adversarial procedures), but can increase both inefficiency and cost.

The emergence of a more competitive approach to legal aid was accompanied by the rise of managerialised criminal justice. This is best exemplified by Lord Justice Auld's review of the criminal courts, which formed part of New Labour's goal to modernise the criminal justice process of E&W and eradicate inefficiencies (Auld, 2001). In the government's view, the criminal justice system should divert offenders from a life of crime; implement fast-track, efficient procedure from arrest to sentence; deliver improved services to witnesses and victims; and ensure the component parts of the system are performing to their maximum potential (McLaughlin et al, 2001: 307; HM Government, 2003: § 69).

In 2003, the Criminal Procedure Rule Committee was established in order to help achieve these goals. It was charged with creating a single set of rules that was to be 'simple and simply expressed' and would ensure that 'the criminal justice system is an accessible, fair and efficient instrument' (Auld, 2001: para. 271). The resulting Criminal Procedure Rules (CrimPR) now govern the practice and procedure to be followed in all criminal proceedings from magistrates' courts through to the Court of Appeal. A key part of this codification process was, again, maximising the efficiency of criminal justice. However, while posited as an inherent good, the notion of 'doing justice' both quickly and cheaply raises serious questions about fairness of proceedings and, consequently, accuracy of verdicts. Indeed, a potential casualty of this agenda is traditional adversarial criminal justice, with constant piecemeal changes in the name of efficiency arguably tantamount to 'killing it by a thousand cuts' (Johnston and Smith, 2017: 212). Nonetheless, the pursuit of efficiency as a central goal has shown no loss of momentum.

The implications for criminal legal aid within this culture of minimalisation, cost saving, speed and cooperative working are stark. The scope and delivery of legally aided representation must fit within this redefined environment, which emphasises that costs must be driven down; conflict (arguably an inherent part of adversarialism) must be avoided if possible; and only those who 'need' legal aid should receive it (a term open to significant interpretation). Those who deliver such services must do so within a more restricted, challenging and competitive context, while satisfying the goals of efficiency and economy. There are potential risks arising from this combination of pressures; a primary example would be the temptation to cut corners when dealing with clients, or 'processing' them more quickly, perhaps by actively persuading them to plead guilty as early as possible (see Newman, 2013). This may or may not be appropriate – but one must wonder how easy it will be for providers to objectively consider what *should* be done when they are subject to an increasingly managerialised process and increasingly challenging financial climate.

Contradictions and 'false economies' in legal aid reform

It is also arguable that the marketised approach to criminal legal aid is marked by contradictions which undermine the ultimate objectives of competition: to increase quality and reduce the cost to the consumer. The market has been deliberately – and arguably, artificially – reduced, both through decreases in the overall budget allocated to criminal legal aid and via the introduction of tendering. The aforementioned aim (not yet achieved) of shrinking the provider base by more than 1,000 firms was a primary example, and one which appears deeply anti-competitive.

Indeed, evidence suggests (notwithstanding the failure to implement PCT) that the criminal defence profession is reducing in size. Between May 2014 and January 2018, the overall number of practising solicitors in E&W rose by 7.8 per cent; in contrast, the proportion specialising in criminal work fell by 9.4 per cent over the same period (FDA Trade Union, 2019: 8). In 2012–13, the number of providers contracted to deliver criminal legal aid work was 1,599 (Otterburn Legal Consulting, 2014: 10); in 2017, this stood at 1,299 – a 20 per cent decrease (Legal Aid Agency, 2018b: 40).[1] This is particularly problematic for the future of criminal legal aid because of the now well-recognised issue of an 'ageing' criminal defence profession. In April 2018, the Law Society

---

[1] Legal Aid Agency (2018b): statistics from June 2018 claim that the volume of provider officers fell by 8 per cent over five years; although it should be borne in mind that '[a] provider may consist of a large firm with several offices around the country or a single office location at which one or more individuals are based'. As such, the drop in provider locations would arguably not be as steep as the drop in overall providers (Legal Aid Agency, 2018c).

highlighted that the average age of a criminal duty solicitor in E&W was 47, and published a 'heat map' showing the scale of the problem (The Law Society, 2018a). In several areas of the country, more than 60 per cent of duty solicitors were over 50 (compared with 27 per cent for the entire solicitor profession in E&W) (House of Commons Justice Committee, 2018: para. 39). Some areas (particularly rural counties such as Norfolk and Cornwall) had no defence solicitors under the age of 35 (House of Commons Justice Committee, 2018: para. 39). As such, the pool of available representation is shrinking due not only to increasingly challenging financial circumstances (causing providers and individuals to leave such work), but also to the retirement of experienced practitioners coupled with a lack of 'young blood' to replenish the ranks of the profession. As the Law Society have argued, 'government cuts to criminal legal aid are deterring young lawyers entering the field of criminal defence work' (House of Commons Justice Committee, 2018: para. 40). Similarly, research by the Young Legal Aid Lawyers Association found that

> low salaries and high debt levels were a 'significant barrier' to pursuing a career in legal aided areas of law, and that stress, lack of support and juggling legal aid work is affecting retention in the profession. (The Law Society, 2018b: 3; cf Young Legal Aid Lawyers, 2018)

The gravity of the situation was summarised in evidence to the Justice Committee in 2018:

> Lawyers are retiring. Lawyers are dropping out of the schemes. Lawyers are choosing to go off and do other types of work. Young lawyers are not coming in to replace them. The schemes will continue to shrink and shrink, and there is nothing happening to turn that trend around. (House of Commons Justice Committee, 2018: para. 42)

Another issue is the reality that private providers are inevitably bound to accept certain clients and work which is, essentially, unprofitable. A traditional private market would not necessarily provide such services – but clearly they are essential, much like healthcare or education, and therefore must be provided by someone. Providers wishing to remain sustainable and viable depend not only on the funding provided by the state but on the ability to grow a client base and retain work. Currently, the market, as structured, is particularly unfair to small practices as it is dependent on economies of scale; this creates inevitable pressure on providers to either fold (reducing client choice and competition); cut corners with clients or provide inappropriate service (lowering quality) (Bindman, 2018; Hyde, 2018); overstate what they can deliver (affecting quality and cost); or merge (again, reducing choice and competition).[2] Ultimately, a reduction in the choice of providers leaves clients at a disadvantage, left only with the providers that are available – not necessarily those of good quality.

The economic squeeze on providers may lead to injustices, such as mistakes and miscarriages of justice; delays and inefficiency; unavailability of lawyers and restriction of access to justice; and providers pulling out of the market, leaving an advice vacuum. All of these problems, flowing from the desire to reduce the initial cost of criminal legal aid, ultimately create costs later on, leading to false economies. The remainder of this chapter will examine two 'case studies', which demonstrate how this approach to criminal legal aid provision has created unique problems: the rise of litigants-in-person and the outsourcing of police station legal advice to 'agents'.

The impact of criminal legal aid reform: Case studies

The rise of criminal litigants-in-person

The term 'litigant-in-person' (LiP) is used to describe an individual who represents themselves during proceedings at court. *The Equal Treatment Benchbook* suggests several reasons why those accused of crime may not have a lawyer (Judicial College, 2013: 4-1 and 4-2). They may not qualify for legal aid but may be unable to afford defence representation, or they may simply distrust lawyers, and believe they are better off alone (Judicial College, 2013: 4-2). Regardless of the reason, it is generally acknowledged that LiPs are a problem for both 'judges and the court system' (Woolf, 1995). This section will examine some of the ways in which LiPs can pose challenges for the criminal justice process, by referring primarily to a recent report by the Ministry of Justice (MoJ), entitled *Unrepresented Defendants* (Ministry of Justice,

---

[2] A recent example is the announcement of a merger between two large criminal legal aid firms (Steel and Shamash and Edward Duthie) in May 2019. In 2018, Gerald Shamash (founder of the former firm) noted that '[t]he pressure on firms now to become larger or merge is huge'; while Shaun Murphy (Senior Partner at the latter firm) felt that legal aid cuts had 'put ... more and more pressure upon us. It creates an imperative for economies of scale' (Reyes, 2018; Fouzder, 2019).

2016).[3] This report, among other sources, suggests that restrictions on and reform of criminal legal aid – particularly the shrinking of the provider market – may have given rise to a greater number of LiPs in criminal proceedings. However, it should be noted that, as yet, there is little robust research to establish a firm causal link between legal aid cuts and an emergence of LiPs in the criminal process.

A key problem for a LiP is understanding the accusation levelled against them and how to respond to it without assistance. The MoJ report found that LiPs generally had limited comprehension of the court process, with judicial and Crown Prosecution Service (CPS) interviewees believing they lacked even basic understanding of how to present evidence at trial (Ministry of Justice, 2016: 9). An adversarial trial is founded on the notion of zealous representation, in which the prosecution and defence present competing evidence and arguments to ascertain the truth. LiPs may simply be passive bystanders during a criminal trial; or, at the other extreme, they may be so hyperactively engaged that they constantly disrupt and delay proceedings. Indeed, the MoJ report suggested that LiPs were either reminiscent of a 'rabbit in the headlights ... where they have not a clue about what is going on' (Ministry of Justice, 2016: 9), or intervening 'every five seconds, even when it is not their turn to talk' (Ministry of Justice, 2016: 9). Alongside the inherent unfairness of casting an unqualified and untrained lay participant into this process, we might also highlight the apparent false economy. For example, the Justice Committee commented on the 'perception that unrepresented defendants' cases had longer hearings and case progression was slower' (House of Commons Justice Committee, 2018: para. 83); and the belief that LiPs were 'a barrier towards achieving early guilty pleas because they had a less detailed understanding of the discount scheme' (House of Commons Justice Committee, 2018: para. 83). If one accepts the argument that criminal legal aid reform has led to more LiPs (of which, according to the Justice Committee, there is 'emerging evidence'), then this is clearly self-defeating and unlikely to help fulfil the overriding objective of the CrimPR of dealing with cases justly (see also Magistrates' Association, 2015; Transform Justice, 2016).

Generally speaking there is a level of engagement between defence lawyers and the CPS in advance of pretrial hearings. In contrast, evidence suggests that this interaction does not occur when a defendant is self-represented. The MoJ report argued that LiPs are

---

[3] The report remained unreleased until, after pressure, it was published via Buzzfeed News in June 2018.

suspicious of the prosecution (which is not surprising considering they are the adversarial 'enemy'). Moreover, it was suggested that this was exacerbated by the attitude of some CPS lawyers who believed that only limited assistance could be offered to LiPs, branded as 'the other side' (Ministry of Justice, 2016: 11). LiPs also struggle to handle pretrial disclosure. The legal profession itself is mired in difficulties in this area; notwithstanding this, LiPs are expected to discharge the same disclosure obligations. The majority of participants in the MoJ study, unsurprisingly, found this conceptually difficult to accept. LiPs would not know what to ask for, with one judge giving an example of a LiP asking for '50,000 pages of documents ... and the Lord Chief Justice to give evidence' (Ministry of Justice, 2016: 11). Such problems were deepened by the natural distrust of the CPS, stopping defendants releasing relevant and required documents.

It is also arguable that LiPs cannot effectively examine or assess the weight and quality of the evidence against them; as such, they do not know if the case against them is strong (or even what the case against them is) (Ministry of Justice, 2016: 14). With a sentence discount of a up to a third for an early guilty plea, it may be tempting for an uninformed and confused LiP to simply cut their losses and accept guilt. Yet this may not be the right decision for them; a defence lawyer, possessing a fuller understanding of the implications of their case, may advise them otherwise. In this sense, there may be a difference in the outcome for unrepresented and represented defendants. In contrast, when LiPs refuse to enter a guilty plea when an otherwise represented defendant might do so (particularly when the case against them is strong), the objectives of efficiency and economy might be defeated, as recognised by the House of Commons Justice Committee (2018). Trials may take place that need not do so, wasting time and money, and potentially causing unnecessary distress to witnesses. Indeed, the Justice Committee noted 'concern about unrepresented defendants' affect upon witnesses, with particular worries about defendants undertaking cross-examination, including of their alleged victim' (House of Commons Justice Committee, 2018: para. 83).

Nearly all of the participants in the MoJ study thought that proceedings involving LiPs took longer than those where defendants were represented, for reasons including the lack of an early guilty plea; misunderstanding of the procedural and evidential provisions; or confusion about and detachment from proceedings, requiring the court to repeatedly check on their engagement (Ministry of Justice, 2016: 15). Putting unfairness to defendants aside, if the objective which underpins notions of competition, marketisation and managerialism is to increase efficiency, then the criminal justice process needs to minimise the currently unknown number of LiPs populating the criminal courts, who may (unintentionally) drive a 'coach and horses' through this agenda (Ministry of Justice, 2016: 16). More importantly, it is questionable if such cases can truly be dealt with justly, pursuant to the multifaceted overriding objective of the CrimPR. The potential outcomes in the most serious cases (involving jury trials) could be severe, with a defendant risking the loss of their liberty for many years and an impact on the rest of their lives.

The outsourcing of police station representation to 'agents'

Anyone who is detained in police custody on suspicion of committing a criminal offence is entitled to privately consult with a solicitor at any time (Police and Criminal Evidence Act 1984: § 58). This universal access reflects the importance with which police station representation is regarded, emphasised in the European Court of Human Rights case of *Salduz v Turkey* (2009) 49 EHRR 421. Case law and research suggest that access to a lawyer is of great importance in reducing the incidence of police malfeasance and, ultimately, miscarriages of justice. The police station stage of the criminal process is loaded with both significance and risk; what happens at this point in proceedings will shape much of what follows, including any potential charge; the plea entered by a defendant; or any eventual trial.

Since the codification of this right in 1985, the nature of police station representation has varied. During the 1980s and 1990s, research suggested that non-solicitors routinely provided legal advice to suspects and that the quality of the service provided by them was mixed. In an effort to address this, an accreditation scheme for non-solicitors was introduced in 1995. This category of advisers, known as Accredited Representatives (ARs), has continued to play a major role in fulfilling the promise of universal access to a lawyer in police custody. While the improvement in training since the mid-1990s has appeared to positively affect quality, a crucial influence is money – specifically, the provision of and arrangements for legal aid. As outlined earlier, firms of solicitors are contracted to provide police station advice (funded by legal aid). For many years, firms have directly employed both solicitors and ARs to fulfil their obligations. However, in recent years a new phenomenon has emerged, most recently explored by Vicky Kemp in 2018, which is arguably a direct result of the evolving landscape in legal aid funding – independent 'agencies' of ARs (Kemp, 2018).

These agencies operate outside of the normal framework applicable to traditional solicitors' firms, although they are accounted for in the current Standard Crime Contract (Legal Aid Agency, 2018a: para. 3.2). They do not have a direct contract with the LAA to provide legally aided police station advice and have no specific internal supervising solicitor (which is required for firms employing ARs – although firms are contractually responsible for 'properly' supervising agents (Legal Aid Agency, 2018a: para. 3.3)). Instead, individual agents employed by the agencies are 'hired' on a temporary basis by firms, who do have a contract to provide police station advice. The firm – by virtue of hiring the agent – provides a form of 'surrogate' supervision. In essence, agents act in a similar manner to temporary or casual employees in other sectors, brought in for support on an ad hoc basis. Since agencies do not have a provider contract, they are not paid directly by the LAA; instead, the firm (which does have a contract) will pay a fee to the agency, which will then provide an agent to deliver the service on the firm's behalf. One might question how robust this arrangement is as a check on quality, considering that such agents are unlikely to have the same working relationship with a supervising solicitor as a firm's employees, and are not subject to the LAA tendering process to acquire work (although the LAA can require that agents appointed by a firm 'possess such experience, qualifications, or membership of such panel, or hold such accreditation as we may specify' (Legal Aid Agency, 2018a: para. 3.5)).

We might question why separate agencies exist and why firms rely on them. From the perspective of the firm, provision of police station advice is both contractually required and valuable. It not only provides a reliable form of income (albeit an increasingly unprofitable one), it also enables firms to acquire new own client work by converting duty clients into long-term customers. Losing such work would affect not only a firm's short-term income stream but its long-term client base. In this context, firms with a contract will strive to retain such work. This will depend on the firm's ability to provide defence representation when requested; as such, if the firm receives a request for advice it will do everything it can to avoid losing this to a competitor. Failing to accept and deliver on a request for legal advice will not only mean lost income but suggest that the firm cannot fulfil its contract – which may affect its future prospects when such contracts are reallocated in the future. It may also make a firm more vulnerable to other forms of business rationalisation, such as redundancies, merger or closure.

However, in the increasingly challenging climate of modern legal aid funding, firms may have limited capacity to deliver – for example, where they lack employed solicitors or ARs to service demand. A firm may receive multiple requests for legal assistance while their employed solicitors and representatives are already engaged with other clients. As a result, another modern phenomenon is 'stacking' – where firms accept cases regardless of their immediate ability to deliver legal advice. In essence, the client joins a queue. While this ensures the firm retains the work, this arguably does not serve the best interests of clients in police stations, due to delays in receiving advice.[4] One method of relieving this problem is for firms to obtain external assistance – hence, the use of agencies who provide temporary cover when firms cannot adequately service the cases they have accepted.

In terms of their operation, the evidence from Kemp's study raises a number of concerns about the independent agency model. In interviews about the quality of police station legal advice, solicitors suggested that agents were primarily interested in providing a swift service rather than a good quality one, which could leave clients feeling 'rushed' (Kemp, 2018: 25). This might be at least partially attributed to the fixed fee model used for police station advice (that is, the provider is paid the same amount regardless of time spent), which can 'dis-incentivise ... attendance on a client for a minute longer than is necessary' (Kemp, 2018: 25). Clearly, this might affect legal advisers from a firm and from agencies alike. However, it was also suggested agencies were not underpinned by the same ethos of criminal defence practice as firms of solicitors, which cultivates a client-oriented culture.[5] Ultimately, the implication was that the use of agencies was primarily about maximising profit (for both the firm and the agency) rather than providing quality legal advice. This does not appear to be in the best interests of clients, which is the conceptual, ethical and contractual litmus test for provision of such representation (Legal Aid Agency, 2018d: para. 4.11). Notwithstanding this argument, it is clear that this model provides opportunities and experience for budding criminal defence practitioners who would otherwise be driven away from the sector, which might go some way to alleviating the retention problems discussed earlier. The concern, however, is that these benefits would come at the expense of a quality legal advice service at a vital stage in the criminal justice process.

---

[4] This may have serious negative consequences; research has suggested a key reason for clients either proceeding to interview without a lawyer or confessing guilt is an unwillingness to wait for advice (see Skinns, 2011).

[5] Although for a more critical view of this claim regarding the ethos of criminal defence lawyers, see Newman (2013).

It might also be questioned whether the use of agencies, and any subsequent poor service, might eventually impact on the reputation of the hiring firm and therefore provide limited long-term benefits.

At present, little information is available about this phenomenon as it is under-researched and not widely discussed in literature. What is clear from the evidence provided by Kemp is that the agency model has, for better or worse, emerged in response to a changing market, and that the challenges presented by increased competition among a smaller number of providers for decreasing financial reward have driven an unplanned and possibly negative evolution in the delivery of criminal legal aid services.

Conclusions

The last three decades have seen concerted attempts to both reduce the cost of criminal justice and eradicate inefficiency. Increased marketisation and competition in criminal legal aid practice forms a significant part of this agenda. However, unforeseen consequences of this approach (perhaps due to wilful blindness) have begun to emerge in the form of both LiPs and police station agents. Arguably, these phenomena raise the risk of diluting the quality of criminal justice. The CrimPR, and its overriding objective of dealing with cases justly, sought to use fewer resources more effectively, yet the long-term cost has not been sufficiently acknowledged.[6] In criminal justice terms, effectiveness should ideally be synonymous with a factually accurate outcome underpinned by a fair and legitimate legal process. However, both LiPs and outsourcing to agents suggest that justice is not being done effectively, but cheaply. The conclusion is perhaps that the modern criminal justice system can be either effective (within the definition given previously) or efficient – but not both. We have only been able to briefly raise such issues in this chapter. We would argue for further research on and discussion of these issues, as well as of the secondary impact of marketised legal aid more generally. We hope that these case studies present a compelling argument for focusing more on quality and effectiveness rather than speed and low cost.

References

Auld, R.E. (2001) *A Review of the Criminal Courts of England and Wales*, London: The Stationery Office.

---

[6] Although this may change after the conclusion of the Ministry of Justice's ongoing review of criminal legal aid (due in Summer 2020).

Bevan, G. (1996) 'Has there been supplier-induced demand for legal aid?', *Civil Justice Quarterly*, 15: 98–114.

Bindman, D. (2018) 'Disciplined solicitor blames failings on legal aid cuts', *Legal Futures*, 25 September, available from: https://www. legalfutures.co.uk/latest-news/disciplined-solicitor-blames-failings-on-legal-aid-cuts [accessed 1 November 2019].

Bridges, L., Cape, E., Fenn, P., Mitchell, A., Moorhead, R.L., and Sherr, A. (2007) *Evaluation of the Public Defender Service in England and Wales*, Legal Services Commission, available from: http://orca.cf.ac. uk/44472/1/1622.pdf [accessed 1 November 2019].

Carter, P.R. (2006) *Legal Aid: A Market-based Approach to Reform*, Lord Carter's Review of Criminal Legal Aid Procurement, available from: https://webarchive.nationalarchives.gov.uk/20081205143452/ http://www.legalaidprocurementreview.gov.uk/docs/carter-review-p1.pdf [accessed 31 October 2019].

Criminal Bar Association (2009) 'Response to Ministry of Justice Consultation Paper entitled "Legal Aid: Funding Reforms" dated 20th August 2009', available from: https://www.criminalbar.com/ wp-content/uploads/files/cba-responses/120215162934-Response DocumentSecondDraftforapproval22ndSeptemberPKPMformattin gamendments.pdf [accessed 31 October 2019].

Deloitte (2013) 'The government's proposed legal aid reforms: a report for the Law Society', available from: https://www.lawsociety.org. uk/policy-campaigns/consultation-responses/documents/annex-a---deloitte-report/ [accessed 31 October 2019].

FDA Trade Union (2019) 'Manifesto for justice', May, available from: https://www.fda.org.uk/home/Getinvolved/manifesto-for-justice. aspx [accessed 31 October 2019].

Fouzder, M. (2019). 'Legal aid heavyweights to merge', *Law Society Gazette*, 30 May, available from: https://www.lawgazette.co.uk/ practice/legal-aid-heavyweights-to-merge/5070432.article [accessed 21 February 2020].

HM Government (2003) *Courts Act 2003*, available from: https://www. legislation.gov.uk/ukpga/2003/39/contents [accessed 31 October 2019].

HM Government (2015) *The Criminal Procedure Rules 2015*, available from: https://www.legislation.gov.uk/uksi/2015/1490/contents/ made [accessed 31 October 2019].

House of Commons Justice Committee (2018) 'Criminal legal aid: twelfth report of Session 2017-19. Cmd HC1069', available from: https://publications.parliament.uk/pa/cm201719/cmselect/ cmjust/1069/1069.pdf [accessed 31 October 2019].

Hyde, J. (2018) 'Solicitor who sent 102 texts to prison inmate avoids strike off', *Law Society Gazette*, 20 February, available from: https://www.lawgazette.co.uk/news/solicitor-who-sent-102-texts-to-prison-inmate-avoids-strike-off/5064883.article [accessed 21 February 2020].

Johnston, E. and Smith, T. (2017) 'The early guilty plea scheme and the rising wave of managerialism', *Criminal Law and Justice Weekly*, 181(13): 210–12.

Judicial College (2013) *Equal Treatment Benchbook*, London: Judicial College, available from: https://www.sentencingcouncil.org.uk/wp-content/uploads/equal-treatment-bench-book-2013-with-2015-amendment.pdf [accessed 1 November 2019].

Kemp, V. (2010) 'Transforming legal aid: access to criminal defence services', Legal Services Research Centre, available from: http://eprints.nottingham.ac.uk/27833/1/Kemp%20Transforming%20CD%202010.pdf [accessed 31 October 2019].

Kemp, V. (2018) 'Effective police station legal advice – country report 2: England and Wales', available from: http://eprints.nottingham.ac.uk/51145/1/Country%20Report%20England%20and%20Wales%20Final%20.pdf [accessed 1 November 2019].

The Law Society (2018a) 'Criminal duty solicitors: a looming crisis', available from: https://www.lawsociety.org.uk/policy-campaigns/campaigns/criminal-lawyers/ [accessed 1 November 2019].

The Law Society (2018b) 'Parliamentary brief – criminal duty solicitors: a looming crisis', available from: https://www.lawsociety.org.uk/policy-campaigns/documents/parliamentary-briefing-criminal-duty-solicitors-a-looming-crisis/ [accessed 1 November 2019].

Legal Aid Agency (2018a) '2017 Standard Crime Contract standard terms', available from: https://assets.publishing.service.gov.uk/government/uploads/system/uploads/attachment_data/file/819173/Standard_terms_-_version_2__current_version___effective_from_25_May_2018_.pdf [accessed 1 November 2019].

Legal Aid Agency (2018b) 'Annual report and accounts 2017–18. Cmd HC118', available from: https://assets.publishing.service.gov.uk/government/uploads/system/uploads/attachment data/file/718157/laa-annual-report-2017-18.pdf [accessed 31 October 2019].

Legal Aid Agency (2018c) 'Legal aid statistics quarterly, England and Wales, January to March 2018', available from: https://assets.publishing.service.gov.uk/government/uploads/system/uploads/attachment data/file/720647/legal-aid-statistics-bulletin-jan-mar-2018.pdf [accessed 1 November 2019].

Legal Aid Agency (2018d) 'Standard Crime Contract 2017 specification', available from: https://assets.publishing.service.gov.uk/government/uploads/system/uploads/attachment_data/file/818987/Specification_-_version_5__current_version___effective_from_22_July_2019_.pdf [accessed 21 February 2020].

Lord Chancellor's Department (1998) 'Modernising justice. Cmd 4155', London: HMSO.

McLaughlin, E., Muncie, J. and Hughes, G. (2001) 'The permanent revolution: New Labour, new public management and the modernization of criminal justice', *Criminal Justice*, 1(3): 301–18.

Magistrates Association (2015) 'Survey on litigants in person and unrepresented defendants', London: Magistrates Association.

Ministry of Justice (2013) 'Transforming legal aid: Delivering a more credible and efficient system', available from: https://www.gov.uk/government/consultations/transforming-legal-aid-delivering-a-more-credible-and-efficient-system [accessed 31 October 2019].

Ministry of Justice (2016) 'Unrepresented defendants: perceived effects on the Crown Court in England and Wales and indicative volumes in magistrates' courts', published via Buzzfeed News in June 2018, available from: https://www.documentcloud.org/documents/4489882-DRAFT-29-02-16-Unrepresented-Defendants.html [accessed 1 November 2019].

Newman, D. (2013) *Legal Aid Lawyers and the Quest for Justice*, Oxford: Hart.

Newman, D. and Smith, T. (2017) 'Alienated advocates: applying Marx's labour theories to criminal legal aid', *Socialist Lawyer*, 75: 26–9.

Otterburn Legal Consulting (2014) 'Transforming legal aid: next steps, a report for the Law Society of England and Wales and the Ministry of Justice', available from: https://consult.justice.gov.uk/digital-communications/transforming-legal-aid-next-steps/results/otterburn-legal-consulting-a-report-for-the-law-society-and-moj.pdf [accessed 1 November 2019].

Reyes, E. (2018) 'Interview: Gerald Shamash', *Law Society Gazette*, 1 October, available from: https://www.lawgazette.co.uk/profiles/interview-gerald-shamash/5067730.article [accessed 21 February 2020].

Salduz v Turkey (2009) 49 EHRR 421, European Court of Human Rights.

Skinns, L. (2011) 'The right to legal advice in the police station: past, present and future', *Criminal Law Review*, 1: 19–39.

Smith, T. and Cape, E. (2017) 'The rise and decline of legal aid in England and Wales', in A. Flynn and J. Hodgson (eds) *Access to Justice and Legal Aid: Comparative Perspectives on Unmet Legal Need*, Oxford: Hart, pp 63–86.

Transform Justice (2016) 'Justice denied? The experience of unrepresented defendants in the criminal courts', London: Transform Justice, available from: http://www.transformjustice.org.uk/wp-content/uploads/2016/04/TJ-APRIL Singles.pdf [accessed 1 November 2019].

Welsh, L. (2013) 'Does tendering create travesties of justice? Lucy Welsh discusses the government's proposals on legal aid', *Criminal Justice Matters*, 93(1): 28–9.

Woolf, H. (1995) *Access to Justice: Interim report to the Lord Chancellor on the civil justice system in England and Wales*, London: Lord Chancellor's Department.

Young Legal Aid Lawyers (2018) 'Social mobility in a time of austerity', available from: http://www.younglegalaidlawyers.org/sites/default/files/Soc%20Mob%20Report%20-%20edited.pdf [accessed 1 November 2019].

10

Holding private prisons to account: what role for Controllers as 'the eyes and ears of the state'?

Joanna Hargreaves and Amy Ludlow

Introduction

> The role of the Controller is critical to the effective monitoring of [privately managed prison] contracts. They need to have ... the skills to understand and monitor the complex contractual relationship between private contractors and the Commissioner for Correctional Services. Their relationship with the senior managers in a contracted-out prison is of fundamental importance. (NAO, 2003: 55)

As has been referenced more than once in this volume, the UK operates the most marketised prison system in Europe. This chapter focuses on a specific relationship – that of the Controller and the Director – in order to examine how accountability is practised within this highly marketised system. There are currently 14 contracted-out prisons in England and Wales, with plans for more in the pipeline. In each, there is a Crown servant – a Controller – permanently based on-site. The Controller role was established in the late 1980s to mitigate concerns around diminishing state accountability for punishment in the face of prison privatisation. The 1991 Criminal Justice Act (CJA 1991) formalised the role, making Controllers responsible for reviewing the running of contracted-out prisons and investigating complaints against prison custody officers, reporting directly to the Secretary of State (SoS). Padfield (2018) describes Controllers as the 'eyes and ears of the State'. Despite Controllers' legal and political importance and their apparent centrality in holding private prison providers to account, there is little existing research about the role or its effectiveness (Padfield, 2018). Observers from the outside view the role as unclear, ideologically constrained and misunderstood (Le Vay, 2018). Further, the Controller role in England and Wales is unique. While there are similar 'monitor' roles for private prisons across other jurisdictions, for example in the US and Australia, they are not legally and/or organisationally conceived in the same way as Controllers.

Controllers in England and Wales are responsible for overseeing the operational delivery of the contract by providers. This is achieved by monitoring various prison performance metrics, such as levels of self-harm as well as provider compliance with contract delivery indicators and prison service instructions. Controllers can apply financial remedies against the contract in the event of noncompliance or poor performance, as specified in each contract. Together with their Senior Leaders, Controllers can invoke a rectification notice (performance improvement plan) that, if not achieved, may culminate in contract termination. Additionally, Controllers retain some operational responsibilities such as agreeing to Home Detention Curfews, Release on Temporary License and the award of prison custody officer powers. Controller autonomy is more ambiguous owing to the constant shifting of the overarching governance of private prisons. Controllers are now line managed by Senior Contract Managers who cover a cluster of private prisons. Controllers' decisions on financial remedies are ratified at quarterly meetings with their line managers and the provider. Major decisions on rectification are escalated at least to the Deputy Director of Contracted Prisons, if not the Chief Executive Officer of Her Majesty's Prison and Probation Service (HMPPS).

The most recent of these major contractual decisions, namely the public sector's 2018 'step-in' at privately managed HMP Birmingham, has given renewed impetus to questions about Controllers' roles and the effectiveness with which the State is able to hold private prison operators to account. In his letter of 16 August 2018 to the SoS, triggering the Urgent Notification procedure, the Chief Inspector of Prisons described 'an abject failure of contract management and delivery' at the heart of HMP Birmingham's crisis. Later, on 20 August, in an interview on the BBC Radio 4 *Today* programme, the Chief Inspector said:

> How is it that in 18 months a prison which is supposedly being run under the auspices of a tightly managed contract ... how has that been allowed to deteriorate? There are Ministry of Justice officials on site permanently and yet somehow there seems to have been some form of institutional inertia that has allowed this prison to deteriorate to this completely unacceptable state ... What on earth has been going on in terms of managing that

contract and delivering the contract and making sure that the terms of the contract are being fulfilled?

In this context, the first author of this chapter conducted a study in fulfilment of the requirements of the MSt degree in Applied Criminology, Penology and Management at the University of Cambridge, which explored the nature and significance of the Controller role. The study focused particularly on exploring the relationships between Controllers and Directors, and their implications for accountability (Hargreaves, 2018). Through individual semi-structured interviews with ten Directors and 11 Controllers, many of whom were working in the same establishments, the study shed new light on the complexity of the Controller role. It highlighted the challenges and limitations that the wider Prison Service context places on the extent to which Controllers feel able to carry out their role effectively. Critically, the research emphasised the centrality of the Controller–Director relationship for engendering meaningful accountability in private prisons, and despite the increasingly actuarial climate, a relational and dialogic approach is considered more effective. This aligns with Albertson and Fox's argument that relationships must be at the centre of criminal justice and are the thread that binds the system at an organisational, as well as personal, level.

In this chapter, we share some of the key findings of this study. In the following section we present data to illuminate the complexity of the Controller role, then we make the case for the Controller–Director relationship to be understood dialectically. Next we describe how power flows and is experienced within the Controller–Director relationship and how differences shape the quality of accountability achieved in practice. Finally, we present a model of five relational states that emerges from the data predicated on key dimensions demonstrated in effective or ineffective relationships. We suggest an 'optimal' accountability relationship, referred to as 'productive discomfort', to advance understanding of Controllers' roles as the 'eyes and ears of the state'. This includes reflections on the expertise, resilience and moral vision needed to build and sustain such relationships in a role that is complex, poorly understood and closely scrutinised.

The Controller role as multifaceted and ideologically confused

The little existing research about Controllers critiques the role as confusingly complex, requiring the role holder to pursue multiple, often conflicting, goals within a multiplicity of other accountability organisations and mechanisms. Accountability, as a concept, is associated with everything from ensuring democratic processes and legitimising the state, through to assuring value for money and testing compliance with processes (Bovens, 2007). It is often impossible to achieve all of these aims simultaneously, and the means by which some aims are achieved may not be easily reconciled. Existing empirical data on Controllers highlight substantial variation in how Controllers understand the nature of their role, its priorities and its position relative to private prison providers and headquarters (NAO, 2003). Some Controllers pursue what has been described in other accountability relationships as a collaborative 'partnership' approach, while others adopt a 'stewardship' approach, focusing on contractual compliance and performance (Morgan and Maggs, 1985).

Echoing these existing findings, Controllers in this study reflected on the diverse and sometimes diverging demands of their role. For some, the role was principally being the SoS's representative on-site, undertaking compliance, audit and assurance activity to ensure value for public money and guarantee a minimum standard of service. For others, the role was about driving improvements in delivery, ensuring the moral and ethical treatment and humanity of people held in private prisons. For a few, the role was about facilitating the Director in operational delivery. Controllers and Directors were generally confused about their position within the wider accountability landscape. Controllers conceived of themselves as 'system integrators' (Controller 7) trying to corral a haphazard and multifaceted accountability network.

Whether or not a Controller had previous operational experience played an important role in shaping responses about the purpose of the Controller role and what they considered to be effective. Controllers with operational experience focused on service delivery and prisoner treatment, guided by their experience. Controllers without previous operational experience tended to emphasise a compliance, audit and 'steward' approach, with the contract at the centre, or, as one Controller described, by putting a 'contractual stamp' on their work, not an 'operational stamp' (Controller 7).

> I'm an operational senior manager so my driver is about prisoner welfare and decency ... if the operator runs a good prison, then the contract will be delivered. (Controller 4 – operational experience)

If you weren't operational how do you know what you're seeing when you go out there? You have no idea what you're looking at whether it's right or wrong ... staff who are operational can obviously have you over. So to me you need an operational head you really do. (Controller 10 – operational experience)

We are pretty much onsite permanent auditors ... it's [the contract] best value for money. (Controller 5 – no operational experience)

I'm not walking around saying as a prison governor does ... 'you don't want to do that you want to do this' ... I'm looking at it purely from a sake of, does it comply with the contract? Does it comply with the compliance tool? (Controller 7 – no operational experience)

Despite this nuance in approaches, while Le Vay's (2018) analysis of the public sector's step-in at HMP Birmingham links the prison's decline to the 'tendency of Controllers to retreat into a bureaucratic box ticking role', all Controllers in this study were agreed about the importance of being 'out and about' in the prison in order to hold the provider to account. Here, Controllers prioritise the insight they glean from being relationally involved with the prison as opposed to a more transactional form of accountability fulfilled in the collation and interpretation of performance reports and data. As Controller 4 put it:

the real story of what's happening at the prison is not on a spreadsheet, it's not on a computer, it's out there with the prisoners and staff so we computerised the contract so we can spend as little time as reasonably practical in the office and as much time out there seeing what's going on at the point of service.

Despite a shared sense of the importance of being 'hands on', many Controllers described an 'increasing drive for tighter assurance, compliance and reporting' that 'can keep you at your desk' (Controller 6). Controllers and Directors both commented on how the Controller role had evolved, becoming more focused on commercial and compliance activity. This influenced not only how Controllers spent their time – whether on the wings or in their offices – but also, as the data given previously suggest, the approaches and questions Controllers took to their work in interaction with prisoners, staff and managers. These findings resonate with research documenting the influence of New Public Management (NPM) on prisons, arguing that its ideological orientation has reduced the complexity of accountability, imprisonment and its moral implications to the generic processes of any business (Bennett, 2014). The risks of the Controller role becoming a bureaucratic exercise in 'tick box' accountability were acknowledged in the very earliest studies of accountability in private prisons (NAO, 2003).

Although some Controllers in this study articulated a moral vision for their work that put judgement and values at the heart of their conceptualisation and practice of the role, others elaborated a narrower, actuarial and risk assessment orientation, with contractual targets as central and without a clear link to the moral outcomes such targets achieved. This is, perhaps, unsurprising given the ever-growing complexity of the contractual landscape, and growing pressures on Controllers further to high-profile cases of underperformance by providers, including most recently at HMP Birmingham (Ludlow, 2017). There are, however, risks that Controllers become mere 'conduits of the wider [new penology] managerial culture' (Liebling and Crewe, 2013: 284) at the expense of assuring moral outcomes (a similar idea is highlighted in Chapter 6 in this volume regarding the fine balance of achieving performance metrics while testing innovative approaches to rehabilitation). While our data highlight the potential risk of Controllers 'overreaching' by adopting an overt interventionist role, our data also highlight the need for Controllers to be able to balance increasingly contrived, centrally mandated and overly simplistic audits with a relational presence.

The dialectic nature of Controller–Director accountability relationships

Having explored something of the multifaceted and complex nature of the Controller role, and the varied ways in which it is put into practice, we turn now to focus on the nature of the Controller–Director relationship and its significance for accountability. Just as the NAO described the relationships between Controllers and senior managers in a contracted-out prison as 'of fundamental importance' (NAO, 2003: 55), so Controllers and Directors in this study described the exercise and experience of power between them as critical to their ability to practise their roles effectively. Effective working relationships required Controllers to go beyond a 'naked' exercise of power, which relied only on their formal status, as Controller 8 reflected:

> [S]ome Controllers ... they walk about as though they are the Secretary of State ... there was an air of arrogance 'I am the Secretary of State and you will do what I tell you to do' ... you don't get anywhere with that, because they immediately resent you.

Controllers described relying on 'the tactics of talk' (Liebling, 2011: 490) – 'you can't use rank, you can't use demands' (Controller 3):

> [O]bviously you've got the authority of the contract then but ... you're doing a lot of persuading and influencing. To get people to do what obviously is the right thing to do, rather than being able to say you must do that or you must do the other. (Controller 9)

Controllers also described under-using formal power and exerting power relationally as key to achieving positive outcomes:

> I have an assumed authority because of the role that I'm in and they know that. I don't have to rub their faces in it ... I've got a level of authority I don't need to exert it. (Controller 8)

Some Directors described strategies to build more equal, or in practice sometimes subordinating, relationships with their Controllers. These strategies included Directors 'mentoring' Controllers to develop their understanding of commercial elements of contracts (for example Director 4) and, in command situations, embedding Controllers within the Director's team (for example Director 2: 'I've just said to the Controller, "look I'm just going to use you as part of the team"'). Some Directors viewed, or used, Controllers as 'an absolutely free compliance service' (Director 9).

At its best, the Controller–Director relationship was described as an effective means through which common goals are pursued. As Director 3 put it:

> I think as long as you accept you're working for different organisations and those organisations have got different pressures. But actually ... 80 or 85 percent of your work ...

meets in the middle. Because as I said before they don't want the prison to be a failing prison. Why would they? ... So if they're going out and doing audits ... can we have a system of joint audits where you lead and my people come along so that we've got a common framework. So that's maintaining everybody's integrity and accountability but a kind of joint approach.

That Controllers and Directors highlight the nuanced and varied ways in which power flows within their relationship, and its importance to whether or not they can work effectively, is somewhat expected. Accountability has been described as a 'specific social relation' that makes power holders answerable to others for their actions by giving an account of what has taken place (Bovens, 2007: 450). Power can be held and exercised more or less effectively, and more or less legitimately, but that it is exists and is shaped reciprocally in relation to others finds wide support within the literature (see for example Bottoms and Tankebe, 2012). However, as Black argues, existing analyses of accountability all too often present a 'linear model of accountability', envisaging power 'flowing in one direction: from accountee to accountor' (Black, 2008). Our reading of the data, together with the wider literature on accountability, is that the relationship between Controllers and Directors is not unidirectional but rather, as Giddens (1984) argues in respect of all social relations, dialectic. We take this dialectic approach as our starting point in the section that follows, exploring how differences in the exercise and experience of power within the Controller–Director relationship shape the quality of accountability achieved in practice.

A model for Controller–Director relationships and their significance for accountability

The interview data from Controllers and Directors about their experiences of relationships with each other 'at their best' and 'at their worst' gives rise to a model of five relational states (Figure 10.1). In each of these states, the relationship is formed of differing degrees of key dimensions which will be explored here – proximity and opacity; formality and trust; and means and ends. This model draws the findings together with existing management literature to examine the potential implications for accountability in practice. Firstly, we will describe the dimensions and then how they manifest in the relational states identified.

Figure 10.1: A model of accountability

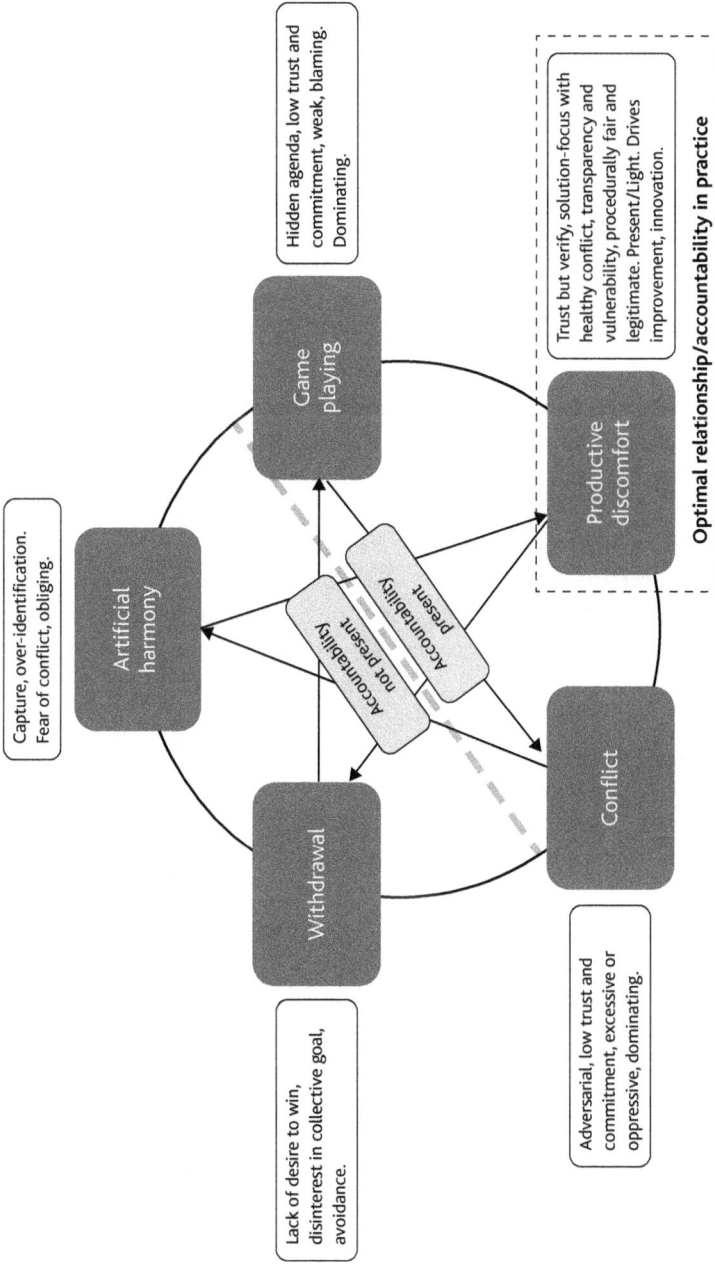

Artificial harmony — Capture, over-identification. Fear of conflict, obliging.

Game playing — Hidden agenda, low trust and commitment, weak, blaming. Dominating.

Productive discomfort — Trust but verify, solution-focus with healthy conflict, transparency and vulnerability, procedurally fair and legitimate. Present/Light. Drives improvement, innovation.

Optimal relationship/accountability in practice

Withdrawal — Lack of desire to win, disinterest in collective goal, avoidance.

Conflict — Adversarial, low trust and commitment, excessive or oppressive, dominating.

Accountability present

Accountability not present

Source: © Joanna Hargreaves, reused here with permission

Proximity and opacity

Proximity relates to closeness or distance between Controllers and Directors. Many participants described either party being 'outcast' or 'withdrawn' from the relationship, or overly close to the provider – as distinct from 'engaged' or 'present' – as dysfunctional. As Controller 10 put it, describing a relationship in which s/he was outcast by the Director:

> The relationship wasn't good, wasn't good at all. They were very closed, wouldn't share information and it's funny because, the way that the Contract Director decides to take the contact forward is obviously the driver for everybody else's behaviour in the prison. Absolutely. So if you get an edict from the Contract Director that says you will not talk to the Controller team, you will not go into those offices and sit with them, they don't do it.

Similar to 'outcast' relationships, Controllers also described relationships with Directors as dysfunctional where Directors were absent because of withdrawal from, or disinterest in, the contractual relationship. In one particular case, Controller 11 explained that a Director decided not to attend any meetings, including the monthly formal meetings between Controllers and Directors. This resulted in Controller 11 having to approach each issue formally in quarterly meetings, unable to achieve anything through informal channels. By contrast, relational closeness and mutual presence were described as supporting effective practice. There were risks in getting too close, occasionally reflected in the use of terms such as 'professional friendship' (Controller 2) to describe an optimum balance between closeness, familiarity, distance and boundaries. Getting the balance right was described as difficult but critical. As Controller 4 put it, for example:

> Professional distance is something which is very, very important. You don't get too far away that you're out of touch but you don't get so close that you change the relationship from being friendly but business-like into being friends.

While Controllers spoke of their concern about over-identifying with the providers or being 'in cahoots' (Controller 8), none gave examples of this in practice. Theoretically, this is 'capture' (Harding,

1997) whereby those responsible for monitoring the contract start to advocate for the provider. What you may expect to see in a relationship such as this is hyper proximity and overt transparency on behalf of the Controller. A Controller who is considered too close to providers compromises their objectivity by oversharing confidential information, avoiding applying penalties or developing personal relationships. Thus, the right sort of 'closeness' and 'friendliness' enabled trust building and transparency while retaining objectivity and a clear sense of the distinct responsibilities and positions of both parties.

Transparency was also referred to as 'openness' (Director 1) and 'honesty' (Controller 10). Director 5 explained how s/he practised transparency:

> The Controller is invited to the morning meeting, so they see everything. I don't have any clandestine pre-meets or anything like that ... I'm also very clear with the senior team about the fact that, never lie, never miss anything out and even if it's going to hurt, I'd much rather take it to them and go and tell them what's happened ... no one is ever ever going to come to my door and talk to me about openness of reporting, or integrity of any of those sorts of issues.

Critically, as Director 5 highlights, for many Directors and Controllers, transparency entailed a 'warts and all' (Controller 10) approach to what was shared. Controllers also spoke of how one instance of dishonesty could undermine the relationship. As Controller 10 put it, 'if you don't tell me then it comes down to me ... that to me is the honesty of this relationship gone'.

Formality and trust

The second key dimension that appeared critical for Controller–Director relationships concerned formality and trust. Trust was built and expressed through transparency and the appropriate exercise of discretion. This included informal and relational means of resolving issues, consistency and mutual professional respect. Director 8 describes high- and low-quality relationships in action through by comparing two Controllers:

> The relationship between the Controller and ... myself, or rather the previous Director was not a good relationship. It was very adversarial. Very formal, very very business-like ...

And if we couldn't provide, let's say for a recruitment reason we couldn't provide an intervention what they would do immediately is, or what this Controller would do, is take the money away. But what this Controller does, 'listen I'm not going to take the money away I'm going to wait to spend it, but let's look at a different way with another intervention ... because it's about the prisoner it's not about the contract, it's not about the MoJ, it's not about the provider'.

Here, the second Controller is exercising discretion and proactively seeking to resolve issues to support the prison. However, the first Controller is demonstrating 'low trust' through the immediate triggering of a formal process in the face of the provider's challenge to deliver a service. In effective relationships, there is a view that 'nothing should be too problematic that we can't solve it at this level' (Controller 10) and that 'if we escalate it, it's a failure' (Controller 7).

The 'we' in both of these statements refers to the Controller and Director working together to achieve a solution. This leads to the professional respect that underpins higher quality relationships. As Director 8 goes on to say:

What I'd expect from a Controller in terms of trust is to believe us. To believe, you know I come with 30 years of service operating at very senior level ... trust my operational knowledge and trust my gut instinct and trust that I can, I can run a jail.

Controller 4 reflects similar ideas around the importance of trust in effective relationships:

The trust element's right and this is where consistency of approach is absolutely vital. ... I can't resort to it being personal, it's always professional, it's always objective and it has to be reasonable.

Means and ends

Finally, and perhaps most critically, Directors and Controllers differentiated high-quality from low-quality relationships based on 'means and ends'. At their least effective, Controllers and Directors described relationships that were characterised by adversarial 'ends', bullying 'means' and game playing interactions. Controller 6, for example, described receiving 'really offensive emails' from one Director, while Controller 10 explained how a series of fallouts led to 'ridiculous' arguments between the pair: 'one morning standing at the water heater up there making a drink and they said, "oh you're using my electricity" ... I said, "I think you'll find that I pay your wages within the contract".' Controllers and Directors both explained how the relationship 'at its worst ... can actually feel like you're being bullied' (Controller 9). Director 9 described a meeting where the Controller was 'trying to bully me into a certain way', stating 'it's not a very good working relationship'. A less aggressive form of relationship, which was nevertheless experienced as dysfunctional and detrimental, was described as 'game playing':

> It's a game ... know where the skeletons are hidden. It helps. It helps if you've also been senior to the people ... So I ran one prison where they had the Controllers team, every one of them used to work for me, that helps. (Director 4)

> To be truthful, it's a game. And sometimes we win and sometimes they win. And sometimes neither side wins. And somewhere in the middle we meet and we talk about it and sometimes we have a very knowing conversation ... but we both know it's a game. (Controller 4)

Game playing was exemplified by experiences, such as those of Director 8, of the Controller taking senior managers to see 'the worst places in the prison' and never to see 'any of the good work'. Director 8 described the Controller as 'lining all this up as if they had a vendetta against the prison'. Relationships in which Controllers looked for any opportunity to identify and formalise technical breaches were experienced as 'punitive' (Director 9), and 'personal' rather than 'professional'. Such orientations to practice were described as inimical to the vulnerability required to be open and transparent. As Director 9 put it, when Controllers 'operate within a punitive way, you're less likely to engage in a sensible discussion'.

By contrast, shared values and goals for the prison, and a common focus on the benefits these could create if the Director and Controller got their relationship 'right', were seen as the basis for effective working relationships. As Director 1 described:

> I would find it very hard to work well with someone who didn't share my values in respect of how prisons should be

run and how prisoners should be treated. And I would, absolutely find it very difficult to have an honest, open collaborative relationship with someone who wasn't truthful and who didn't, who went out to try and maybe prove a point and just look for failure for the sake of it.

As such, a joint approach to tackling issues within clearly understood distinct roles was seen as effective:

> So actually I would hope that my Director would say to you that actually if [s/he] has an issue, it's ok to come and tell me that there's a problem because what we will do is we will look at how that can be fixed as opposed to me slapping them with whatever kind of contract measure I can find to begin with. It's about giving them the opportunity to remedy things as well. (Controller 5)

> At times we're going to be at different points of view and what we've got to do is put the issue in the middle of the table and sort it out so that both parties believe that it's right. And if we're not doing we're not working hard enough at it. (Director 5)

Director 5 alluded to a feature of high-quality relationships which they later expressed as 'sometimes [feeling] uncomfortable'. Despite the discomfort and challenge a relationship such as this can bring, it is also 'hugely helpful' (Director 5). Director 7 explained this in action:

> The Controller at the moment, very much takes us to task you know, if we're not dealing with something they will challenge us on it, they will give us a chance to sort it out and if we don't get things sorted out if they need to put some financial penalties our way they will do that. But they are also incredibly supportive as well and part of what they talk about, as I said is, well what can I do to help you to achieve, what can I do to make that a little bit smoother ... I think sometimes that healthy challenge helps to keep you on the ball all the time ... I know some people might think it would do, but it doesn't do you any favours having a Controller who's not on the ball and challenging you ... that's a healthy dynamic I think a healthy tension I think.

Overall, high-quality Controller–Director relationships are not ones that exist without challenge or tension but rather anticipate and manage that challenge through transparency, trust and a shared sense of values.

The model of relational states

From the data outlined thus far, we propose a tentative conceptual model of five relational states between Controllers and Directors. To garner the different dimensions explored previously, this model adapts Lencioni's work (2002) on team dysfunctions, and Rahim's (1983) theory of conflict management patterns. Lencioni's model describes five key team dysfunctions that create negative, or stagnant, outcomes for organisations through a lack of team cohesion. These dysfunctions include an absence of trust, a lack of commitment, a fear of conflict, avoidance of accountability and inattention to results. Rahim's dual-concern model develops five conflict management patterns between the self and the other. These five patterns are:

- dominating – high concern for self, low concern for other;
- avoiding – low concern for self and other;
- obliging – low concern for self, high concern for other;
- compromising – moderate concern for self and other; and
- integrating – high concern for self and other.

Each of these patterns has a different impact on how conflict is, or is not, resolved between parties. Using these management theories together with the dimensions of proximity and opacity, formality and trust, and means and ends, we can discern five different relational states between Directors and Controllers. These are 'artificial harmony' (Lencioni, 2002: 91), 'withdrawal', 'conflict', 'game playing' and 'productive discomfort' (see Figure 10.1). Each has different consequences for accountability.

The first four of these states represent lower quality Controller–Director relationships. These states feature either overly distant (withdrawal) or close (artificial harmony) accountability relationships. For example, *withdrawal* represents a state where there is no relationship to speak of and a member of the pair is absent from the contractual relationship (described earlier by Controllers 10 and 11). This aligns with Lencioni's dysfunction of 'inattention to results' characterised by a 'lack of desire to win' (Lencioni 2002: 218) or disinterest in the collective goal. In these situations, the relationship between the

Controller and Director is stagnant, reflective of Controller 11's comments (earlier) about the challenges of doing the job without a Director's buy-in. Additionally at play is Rahim's 'avoidant' conflict management pattern whereby one, or both, of the parties evade conflict and disengage from the relationship. This resonates with Controller 10's struggle having been cast aside by the provider, and Director 7's assertion that 'I've had another controller incredibly laid back … challenged us on next to nothing and that wasn't healthy, it wasn't good for any of us'. In these states the optimal proximity has not been achieved.

Artificial harmony represents a state where the Controller is 'in cahoots' (Controller 8) or too close with the provider, echoing two of Lencioni's dysfunctions, namely 'fear of conflict' and 'avoidance of accountability' (Lencioni 2002: 202–14). These dysfunctions often manifest as avoiding challenging performance and difficult issues. Rahim conceives of this as an 'obliging' pattern – the Controller has no concern for themselves or their organisational goals but a high level of concern for the Director. As a result, some Controllers acquiesce to Directors, rarely imposing sanctions. In both states, either through disinterest (in the case of 'withdrawal') or over identification (in the case of 'artificial harmony'), accountability is not facilitated. Either the Director is not giving an account, or the Controller is not seeking one. As such, there is no dialectic or specific accountability relationship (Bovens, 2007; Black, 2008). Instead, there is a relationship born from inappropriate proximity: information is either not shared, or it is 'artificial', rather than the 'warts and all' approach typified in higher quality relationships.

Low trust and hypervigilance can move the Controller–Director relationship into two further states that represent lower quality Controller–Director relationships – *conflict* and *game playing*. These relationship types share an apparent lack of professional respect and focus too greatly on the 'means' – a more formal, punitive accountability. *Game playing* is a state where both the Controller and Director are engaged in a point-scoring exercise, choosing when to conceal, when to reveal and masking their intentions with hidden agendas. Likely manifestations of this are Controllers proactively 'making hay' (Controller 11), seeking out ways to apply punitive measures and leaving Directors 'second-guessing' (Director 8) Controllers' motives. Both *conflict* and *game playing* are characterised by the dysfunctions of 'absence of trust', or the ability to be vulnerable with your colleagues, and 'lack of commitment' related to shared goals (Lencioni, 2002: 196). This, together with a pervading fear of failure, makes vulnerability in Controller–Director relationships altogether less likely. This resonates with Director 1's concern (earlier) to share a common moral ground with their Controller and corresponds to literature that an audit culture has led to systemic fault finding, criticism and mistrust (Rustin, 2004). This is further reflected in data from Directors who felt Controllers were pursuing failure for its own sake, where relationships were opaque and hyper formal. The data demonstrate the damage *conflict* and *game playing* cause to the legitimacy and flow of power between Controllers and Directors, curtailing the transparency needed for higher quality relationships. These states reflect the 'dominating' pattern – a high concern for self and low concern for other; an orientation to power that attempts to persuade, and impose, one's position (Rahim, 1983). Accountability in these states is excessive and/or weak as the relationship is bound to deteriorate.

We suggest that a high-quality accountability relationship strikes the appropriate balance in the dimensions the data present. *Productive discomfort* envisions and practices an accountability relationship that is proportionate, robust and focused on mutually agreed moral 'ends'. At 'peak rapport' (Controller 11), the data show how relationships overcome Lencioni's dysfunctions by recognising each other's legitimacy and that respectful conflict can produce 'the best possible solution in the shortest possible time' (Lencioni 2002: 202–3). For Directors, this involves vulnerability and exposing potential issues to Controllers without fear of excessive sanction. For Controllers, this involves courage, leaning into the 'interpersonal discomfort' (Lencioni, 2002: 212) challenging under- or non-performance in an objective, outcome-oriented way, 'solely based on evidence' (Controller 3).

In this state, trust and professional respect allow the relationship to function in ways that prevent the relationship deteriorating. Here, Behn's (2001) theory of 'professional friendship' – a term used by Controller 2 to describe their relationship – unpacks 'trust' further. Behn's theory asserts that trust need not be total but there must be 'an element' (Controller 10). Trust should not 'preclude a willingness to discipline defectors' so long as it is proportionate (Behn 2001: 161). Putting this into practice, Controllers are protected from becoming too close to providers by taking a 'trust but verify' (Behn, 2001) approach. As Controller 1 explained, 'If somebody [the provider] says that it's rainy outside I would need to go and check'. Beyond 'trust but verify', consistency is core to *productive discomfort* relationships. In our data, Controllers and Directors agreed that 'consistency of approach is absolutely vital' (Controller 4). Pairs must trust the relationship will 'continue to function' within 'understood professional norms of reciprocity' (Behn, 2001: 161). An 'integrating' or 'compromising' conflict management approach is used with Controllers and Directors showing high concern for both self and other and a determination to find midway solutions (Rahim, 1983). In this space Controllers also appear to be exercising limited professional discretion and taking on more regulatory approaches, proactively seeking to improve prisons above retrospective accounts of performance and compliance. Clearly this poses some challenges for consistency across prison sites, between Controllers and contracts, which may also link to the complexity of their role and the system they oversee. While potentially messier, in this relational state, accountability is balanced, drives service and contract improvement and is embedded in a shared moral vision, focused on humane outcomes for people in the prison's care (Liebling and Crewe, 2013; Bennett, 2014). Deeper understanding on *productive discomfort* may support a better framework for how to create and sustain such a relationship. In turn this could flatten inconsistencies between Controllers and Directors, by identifying the relationship's strengths and deficits and moderating accordingly.

Conclusion

The ongoing foothold of private providers in the criminal justice sphere, particularly prisons, taken together with the serious contractual failings at HMP Birmingham warrants further analysis, not speculation, of Controllers as specialists in accountability. A deeper examination of the role of Controllers and their relationships with Directors exposes the complexities and challenges of balancing the competing aims of accountability, the influence of NPM and increased scrutiny and bureaucracy. From our data, it appears that Controllers are often locked in a zero-sum game where audit is prioritised at the expense of reality, and no attempt has yet been made to describe a vision of accountability that marries the two. This lack of clarity at a system level filters into personal interpretation, allowing Controllers to determine where their skills are used best – sometimes at a desk, sometimes on a wing and, occasionally, often by luck more than design, a useful blend of both.

That said, to view Controllers as standalone would fall foul of seeing accountability as a unidirectional relationship as opposed to the dialectic, social relationship it is. As we have sought to demonstrate, understanding the nature of power flowing between Controllers and Directors is critical in any proper appraisal of the nature and effectiveness of the Controller role. We have argued that three key dimensions – proximity and opacity, formality and trust, means and ends – and their greater or lesser extent in a relationship will determine the quality of that relationship and, therefore, the quality of accountability achieved. From the data we have discerned five relational states that describe differences between Controller–Director relationships and their impacts for accountability outcomes, arguing that the 'optimal relationship' is one of 'productive discomfort', characterised by vulnerability, courage and shared moral 'ends'.

Our data pose a number of questions for further exploration, including how to articulate the Controller role so it is explicitly rooted in moral outcomes and the skills and experience needed to maximise Controllers' accountability relationship with the provider. This includes what training for Controllers and Directors ought to look like, including approaches to power, courage and vulnerability building. What is apparent is that quality Controllers, engaged in quality accountability relationships, are far from 'box tickers' and that the relationship between Controller and Director is front and centre. The longer the caricature of Controllers goes unexplored and unchallenged the more the expertise, skill and care required to be effective as the 'eyes and ears of the state' will be underestimated and misunderstood.

References

Behn, R. (2001) *Rethinking Democratic Accountability*, Washington, DC: Brookings Institution Press.

Bennett, J. (2014) 'Resisting the audit explosion: the art of prison inspection', *Howard Journal of Criminal Justice*, 53(5): 449–67.

Black, J. (2008) 'Constructing and contesting legitimacy and accountability in polycentric regulatory regimes', *Regulation & Governance*, 2(2): 137–64.

Bottoms, A.E and Tankebe, J. (2012) 'Beyond procedural justice: a dialogic approach to legitimacy in criminal justice', *Journal of Criminal Law and Criminology*, 102(1): 119–70.

Bovens, M. (2007) 'Analysing and assessing accountability: a conceptual framework', *European Journal*, 13(40): 447–68.

Giddens, A. (1984) *The Constitution of Society*, Cambridge: Cambridge University Press.

Harding, R. (1997) *Private Prisons and Public Accountability*, Buckingham: Open University Press.

Hargreaves, J. (2018) 'Understanding the role of the Controller in private prisons and how accountability operates in the Controller/ Director relationship', Unpublished MSt Thesis: Institute of Criminology, University of Cambridge.

Lencioni, P. (2002) *The Five Dysfunctions of a Team: A Leadership Fable*, San Francisco, CA: Wiley Imprint.

Le Vay, J. (2018) 'How prisons go bad', available from: http://www. julianlevay.com/articles/archives/08-2018 [accessed 1 September 2018].

Liebling, A. (2011) 'Distinctions and distinctiveness in the work of prison officers: legitimacy and authority revisited', *European Journal of Criminology*, 8(6): 484–99.

Liebling, A. and Crewe, B. (2013) 'Prisons beyond the new penology: The shifting moral foundations of prison management', in J. Simon and R. Sparks (eds) *The SAGE Handbook of Punishment and Society*, London: SAGE, pp 283–307.

Ludlow, A. (2017) 'Marketising criminal justice', in A. Liebling, S. Maruna and L. McAra (eds) *The Oxford Handbook of Criminology* (6th ed), Oxford: Oxford University Press, pp 914–38.

Morgan, R. and Maggs, C. (1985) 'Called to account? The implications of consultative groups for police', *Policing*, 1: 87–95.

NAO (National Audit Office) (2003) *The Operational Performance of PFI Prisons*, London: The Stationery Office.

Padfield, N. (2018) 'Monitoring prisons in England and Wales: who ensures the fair treatment of prisoners?' *Crime, Law and Social Change*, 70: 57–76, available from: https://link.springer.com/article/10.1007/ s10611-017-9719-x (accessed 26 April 2018).

Rahim, M. A. (1983) 'A measure of styles of handling interpersonal conflicts', *Academy of Management Journal*, 26: 368–76.

Rustin, M. (2004) 'Rethinking audit and inspection', *Soundings*, 64: 86–107.

11

A flawed revolution? Interrogating the Transforming Rehabilitation changes in England and Wales through the prism of a Community Justice Court

*Jill Annison, Tim Auburn, Daniel Gilling
and Gisella Hanley Santos*

Introduction

The advent of Transforming Rehabilitation (TR) was proclaimed a 'revolution' in the Coalition government's 2013 consultation paper, which announced:

> These reforms will make a significant change to the system, delivering the Government's commitment to real reform. Transforming rehabilitation will help to ensure that all of those sentenced to prison or community sentences are properly punished while being supported to turn their backs on crime for good – meaning lower crime, fewer victims and safer communities. (Grayling, 2013: 5–6)

The operationalisation of TR in 2014–15 impacted on policy and practice aspects of the criminal justice system as a whole and on the staff and service users of probation in particular. While TR brought about new structural and governance changes – most specifically the rupture between the National Probation Service (NPS) and the mainly privatised Community Rehabilitation Companies (CRCs)[1] – it

---

[1] The Target Operating Model for TR stated that the NPS was to be responsible for 'advice to courts, management and rehabilitation of MAPPA cases, high risk of serious harm and other public interest offenders, and delivery of their sentences', while the 'CRCs will have responsibility for the management of the majority of offenders in the community' (Ministry of Justice, 2013: 8).

is suggested in this chapter that this should have been viewed not as a new development, but rather as an enforced adaptation that was in alignment with neo-liberal penal reforms which had taken place over a longer period (Garland, 2001; Deering and Feilzer, 2019).

Of relevance in this respect were the strategies associated with the new penology which had been incorporated into probation and prison practice in England and Wales since the early 2000s. Actuarial assessment of offenders undertaken at sentencing, or at the pre-release stage from prison, informs the allocation of offenders according to risk levels, thereby sorting 'individuals into groups according to the degree of control warranted by their risk profiles' (Feeley and Simon, 1992: 459). The use of actuarial tools such as OASys (Offender Assessment System) provides assessments of risk in relation to individual offenders and thereby enables the overall management of levels of supervision, with the intention that the level of intervention should match the level of risk (Bonta and Andrews, 2017).

The rise of neo-liberal principles with which risk is associated (Hardy, 2014) became of increasing importance for probation over this period when resources were diminishing (Kemshall, 2012), with concerns being expressed by the then Chief Inspector of Probation about 'the "silting up" of probation caseloads with low risk offenders [which] is a major problem for an already over-stretched workforce' (Morgan, 2003: 7). In some probation areas different projects and collaborations were developed in relation to such low-level offenders in partnership with other services and third sector organisations,[2] with the intention of diversion to community resources, rather than ongoing engagement with statutory agencies in the criminal justice system. It is to one such project and data from the related research project that this chapter now turns in order to explore and illustrate these issues and then to apply this analysis to critique the underpinning rationale and operationalisation of TR. Analysis of the quantitative and qualitative data from this Community Justice Court (CJC) research project (2012–14) provides insights into the stress points that were to impact on the operationalisation of TR and, in particular, engages critically with the risk-based rationale which underpinned the changes.

---

[2] Partnership work had also been one of probation's targets in the late 1990s, when 5 per cent of a service's budget was intended to be allocated to such schemes (see Mair and Burke, 2012: 154).

The Community Justice Court case study

The CJC setting that is focused on here commenced its operation in line with the New Labour government's initiative in 2007 to mainstream community justice principles and practices and to introduce a new way of 'doing justice' (Gilling and Jolley, 2012). This development drew on the experiences of other community courts which had started several years earlier, primarily the Red Hook Community Justice Center in New York and also the North Liverpool Community Centre in England.[3] Both of these were situated in buildings where other agencies could be co-located. In contrast, the CJC in this location operated only one day a week within the existing local Magistrates' Court complex, with limited accommodation for staff from other agencies. It should also be noted that this CJC did not conduct reviews of progress of the defendants appearing before them, as often happens in other such settings (Berman and Fox, 2010).

This specialist court, operating in a large English city, had the remit of directing therapeutic justice to low-level offence cases,[4] encapsulated within an offender-centred approach (Wexler and Winick, 2003). As part of the proceedings staff from the associated third sector organisation could conduct problem-solving meetings and provide short-term assistance and signposting to other relevant agencies.[5] This aligned with the aim outlined previously of diverting low-risk offenders away from statutory probation supervision.

While there was commitment from local personnel to facilitate the running of the CJC, it increasingly operated in the face of wider obstacles, not least the falling away of interest on a national level when the New Labour government lost power in 2010. While the court continued to sit, it was impacted by the neo-liberal policies of austerity Britain (O'Hara, 2014), which were central to the approach of the Conservative–Liberal Democrat Coalition government (2010–15) and were continued by the subsequent Conservative government.

---

[3] While the Red Hook Court continues to operate, it was announced by the Ministry of Justice in October 2013 that the North Liverpool Community Justice Centre was to close.

[4] In this respect the CJC was intended to be in alignment with Winick's view of therapeutic jurisprudence as having a 'particular focus [on] the effect of law on the health and mental health of the individual' (Winick, 1997: 191).

[5] The proposal to hold a problem-solving meeting was usually made in the court hearing by the magistrates. As well as a staff member or volunteer from the third sector agency, these were normally conducted together with the community police officer and/or the duty probation officer, who were also assigned to these court proceedings.

Structural support networks and interventions at national and local community levels were increasingly dismantled, thus reducing the scope and availability of holistic rehabilitative packages as part of the therapeutic form of intervention propounded by the CJC.

While the rhetoric of the court proceedings demonstrated a motivation to engage with therapeutic and preventative goals (Hannah-Moffat and Maurutto, 2012), the limited availability of interventions for such defendants brought about a double bind: assessment as low-level offenders within the prevalent risk paradigm meant they did not reach the increasingly high thresholds for interventions by local agencies, but simultaneously, 'by reconceptualizing offenders as "clients" with choices, the discourse used in these courts reframes and responsibilizes the penal subject as having "opted-in"' (Quirouette et al, 2016: 373).

In the operation of the CJC there were stated intentions to carry out 'joined-up' processes across different criminal justice staff and agencies, but conflicting targets and the pressures of day-to-day schedules meant that practice was often driven by other considerations. The strictures of new managerialism, such as meeting key performance indicators within each organisation, tended to take priority, frequently resulting in tensions within and between the local statutory and voluntary agencies. This also sometimes led to a lack of continuity if there was an adjournment of a hearing, with cases being allocated away from the specialist CJC to another Magistrates' Court in the same setting in order to prioritise 'speedy justice'.[6] This came into sharp focus on occasions for defendants who experienced distinct modes of justice, sometimes in relation to the same case, within the different Magistrates' Courts sitting in this court complex.

Methodology of the research project

The data that is drawn on here comes from the research study conducted by the authors from 2012 to 2014. The scope of our research project with its four 'work packages'[7] saw qualitative and quantitative data gathered and then triangulated against records from

---

[6] The Department for Constitutional Affairs promoted this approach in 2006 in the document 'Delivering Simple, Speedy, Summary Justice' (Gilling and Jolley, 2012).

[7] The research project was funded by the ESRC Grant ES/JO10235/1. There were four work packages; this chapter focuses mostly on the data relating to work package 1, which was 'Impact of the Community Court on recidivism, re-offending and other measures associated with desistance from crime'.

police, court, probation and the third sector service. This strategy provided a uniquely in-depth data set which has been revisited here, with the qualitative responses from defendants giving insights into the problems and obstacles they faced, both at the time of their court appearances and then several months later.

Collation of data from the court and third sector agency records facilitated a detailed review of a sample of 85 defendants who appeared in the CJC over a one-year period (September 2012–August 2013). The 'modal' offender was:

- male,[8] with previous conviction(s);
- unemployed and in receipt of benefits;
- living in rented accommodation in the middle to most deprived neighbourhoods in the city;
- using drugs habitually, particularly cannabis;
- charged with an alcohol- or drug-related offence (usually possession), other public order offence, theft, assault (sometimes of a police officer); the offence 'trigger' was often having consumed excess alcohol.

No general health issues were reported in the sample but mental health issues (such as depression and anxiety) were pervasive.

While most of the defendants were charged with relatively low-level offences, the cumulative range of problems, their visibility to the police and patterns of (re)offending often resulted in sequential court appearances (not necessarily heard in the CJC), and outcomes which were progressing up the sentencing tariff. Moreover, as shown by the issues in the points listed, such defendants faced an interconnected constellation of personal, social and structural difficulties. Hannah-Moffat's research and analysis is perceptive in this area:

> I do not suggest that agency and individual responsibility are unimportant – just that there is also a need to empirically examine how socio-structural processes and factors interact with and inform agency. (Hannah-Moffat, 2016: 35)

Many defendants subject to such therapeutic justice found their personal problems being focused on in a way that brought about

---

[8] There was only a small number of female defendants. Their personal trajectories tended to have a different profile to the male offenders and raised gendered issues in relation to the TR programme (Annison et al, 2018).

personal responsibilisation but were decontextualised from the wider social and structural problems that constrained their pathways out of crime (Cowe et al, 2010).

Exploring the situations of 'low-risk' defendants in the Community Justice Court

For many of the defendants appearing in the CJC, their lack of social capital and the tentacles of social control that they faced on a daily basis were apparent. Such issues were exemplified in the qualitative interviews which were conducted as a further strand of the research project. These interviews provided 'snapshots' of some of the defendants' situations and their perceptions of their problems. While many appeared to appreciate the interest shown in them as individuals as part of the CJC procedures, the entrenched structural problems they faced, within conditions of economic marginality, rendered the prospect of (re)integration and rehabilitation largely illusory.

The lived experience of such personal and social problems was talked about by one defendant (Respondent D04, male, aged 26, and identifying as White British), in an interview six months after his court appearance:

> I've been staying out of trouble but I'm still homeless and that, nothing has changed there ... I'm all over the place. I'll stay a couple of days here, a couple of days there, and just move back ... The main difficulty really is just surviving ... Some of the places where I've got to stay it's trying not to use as well, which is even harder again. (Respondent D04 – follow-up interview)

In response to a question about his substance misuse he said:

> If they're all using and then it gives me the craving to use and I've not got any money so then it's, where can I get some money from? So that's when I would go out shoplifting. But then it's like, no, I'm not going out shoplifting. I'm just going to end up risking it and end up getting sent down again. It isn't going to do me any favours because then I'm just going to get my suspended sentence and whatever they do me for on top. I could end up in a completely different court again which they're just going to say, 'Bollocks to your

circumstances' and do me for it anyway. (Respondent D04
– follow-up interview)

These comments indicate the challenges for an offender in such a
situation to sustain a non-offending lifestyle and move towards
desistance in a holistic sense (Healy, 2012). The court records with
regards to this defendant's case revealed that he received a 12 months
conditional discharge for his current offence of shoplifting, having
previously served two prison sentences (he had never received a
community sentence). In terms of the implementation of penal policy,
the punitive elements of sentencing were apparent in the custodial
sentences, but supportive pathways out of crime via the criminal
justice system seemed much more elusive, not least because of the
limited range of interventions available locally.

The zig-zag pathway to desistance

The cases we examined and who were also known to probation were
reviewed to find out the risk of harm level that had been assigned
to these offenders via the use of risk assessment tools. It should be
emphasised that at the point they came to our attention the defendants
had been identified by the police and court officials as 'low level' cases
and thus appropriate to be dealt with by the CJC. In alignment with
this we that none had been identified as high or very high risk
of harm within probation records, and indeed most had been assessed
as low risk (this covered risk to children; risk to public; risk to a known
adult; risk to staff). Nevertheless, we did find in the 80 relevant cases:[9]

- 11 cases where the offenders were identified as medium risk to
  the public;
- 12 cases where the offenders were identified as medium risk to a
  known adult;
- three cases where offenders were identified as medium risk to staff.

Further investigation of probation records also identified:

- one case where domestic violence issues had been registered;
- one case where street crime had been registered;
- one case where (unspecified) vulnerability issues had been noted;
- one case where (unspecified) victim issues had been registered;

---

[9] Some cases had more than one of these risk aspects identified.

- one case with several issues noted, including that the offender was associated with a child on the child protection register, that there were (unspecified) victim issues and risk of suicide.

This additional information (which was unavailable to the CJC and the third sector agency at the time of the defendants' court appearances) shows that risk assessment is not, and should not be considered as, just a technocratic, depersonalised task, and moreover that it should encapsulate wider issues relating to justice, social exclusion and rehabilitation (Hannah-Moffat, 2005). It also needs to be acknowledged that risk is dynamic and that individual situations can change rapidly. For instance, Respondent D02 (male, aged 37, and identifying as White British) attributed his offending to:

> A failed relationship and a daughter to fight for; it's kind of hard also while you're trying to fight off a drug addiction and trying to turn your life around, so yeah, it's kind of overwhelming and very stressful. And that's kind of what's made it hard emotionally on me, on the mental side, you know, depression and stuff like that. (Respondent D02 – first interview)

The accounts so far have focused on the potential for risk to increase and for offenders' situations to deteriorate. However, Respondent D02 was an interesting case insofar as his life became more stable. In the follow-up interview six months later he reported that:

> Well, there have been quite a few positives, you know. My self-esteem, getting a new job, completing my order, being able to buy some new clothes, having some money for a change, you know being able to pay off some debts, being able to buy some things, you know, for my parents and people ... Being my true self, rather than, you know, a bit of a shadow of who I'm supposed to be. So yeah, you know, losing my job and that, it's kind of being like, 'oh, I don't want to slide back into', you know, 'the way I was before' ... Just take it a day at a time, you know, living a normal person's life ... It's a bit upsetting, you know, because it also reminds me of the life that I've lived, you know, that I'm not proud of, that I don't like, you know. I wish it had never gone that way, you know, but I can't

change that now ... All I can do is to hope to change the future. (Respondent D02 – follow-up interview)

The range of personal and structural issues that this respondent spoke of addressing in his move away from crime clearly link with the findings of desistance research (McNeill et al, 2012). His reflections on the difficulties in his life also emphasise that his moves towards a pro-social lifestyle took time and, moreover, encompassed an interaction between both personal and structural factors (LeBel et al, 2008).

In contrast to the positive steps forward in Respondent D02's life, an interview with Respondent D07 (male, aged 34, and identifying as White British) indicated the challenges faced by staff endeavouring to work with 'involuntary clients' (Trotter, 2015). This respondent stated that he had not been on probation since he was young and although he was experiencing health problems from excessive use of alcohol he was not registered with a GP, nor had he engaged with a community-based substance-misuse service. His account of his problems identified the death of his father as a key traumatic event which 'just messed with my head – and I started drinking and then I just didn't stop'. His responses indicated some of the problematic issues in this respect:

> I don't think I need help ... I've been in the court for drunk and disorderly before and they said 'Oh, do you want some help?' And that, 'We can help you', and I said 'No, I just want this over with'. (Respondent D07 – first interview)

In the subsequent interview six months later Respondent D07 indicated that he was still drinking heavily. In response to questions about this he said:

> Well it don't hurt no one, does it, really? It's only hurting me, I suppose ... I've told them I don't really want to know (about available services). I'm just happier when I'm drinking, so I won't stop it ... I don't like to be arrested, but yeah, it's just when I get drunk, that's usually when I end up getting arrested. (Respondent D07 – follow-up interview)

The challenges posed by such constellations of problems and the potential lack of engagement and motivation can often lead to a downward spiral of removal from the community via 'revolving door' short-term prison sentences for such individuals.

At its most positive, the operation of therapeutic justice within the CJC setting and the associated problem-solving interventions reported on here did provide an opportunity for constructive engagement and to catch 'the key therapeutic moment to effect behavioural change' (Gilling and Jolley, 2012: 56). However, the enactment of neo-liberal policies and, in particular, the constraints imposed by the extended period of austerity meant that wider structural factors increasingly put impediments in the way (Garland, 2017).

Implications for Transforming Rehabilitation

The data presented within this chapter have illustrated the range of complex problems experienced by offenders who came into the low risk of harm/low level offences categories. Implicit in the diversion to the CJC and its problem-solving element was a 'defining-down' of such deviance (used here in Garland's sense of 'a specific bureaucratic strategy' (Garland, 2001: 248)). When put in the context of developments within probation early in the new millennium and the wider influences of neo-liberal penal reforms, the fault lines can be detected in the planning for TR, as shown in a speech made by the then Secretary of State for Justice ahead of the implementation of TR:

> My vision is very simple. When someone leaves prison, I want them already to have a mentor in place to help them get their lives back together. I want them to be met at the prison gate, to have a place to live sorted out, and above all someone who knows where they are, what they are doing, and can be a wise friend to prevent them from reoffending. And also to have training or rehab lined up, because this government is determined to do more to address the root causes of offending: to get drug and alcohol users into recovery, and to address mental health needs. (Grayling, 2012)

The oversimplification of such situations and the underestimation of the resources that would be needed for such an approach were subjected to in-depth interrogation around that time by the Justice Select Committee, but to no avail. These aspects have subsequently been shown to be key elements in the problems emerging from the operationalisation of TR as evidenced by reports from HM Inspectorate of Probation and the National Audit Office.[10]

---

[10] See collated information at Webster (2019).

By looking through the prism of cases heard in the CJC it is possible to see that, where austerity cuts have hit hard, risk has been redefined in such a way so as to impose punitive conditionality (Wiggan, 2012). This is displayed most clearly in the TR contractual arrangements which have brought so little in the way of constructive interventions for those supervised by the CRCs, and especially those subject to 'Through the Gate' provision (HM Inspectorate of Probation, 2019). The cases of Respondents DO4 and DO7 show the perilous situations that face such individuals, whereby risk and needs often seemed to become elided and conflated (Donohue and Moore, 2009) and attempts to move towards desistance on a personal level are thwarted by wider structural problems inherent in the neo-liberal approach of TR (Corcoran and Carr, 2019).

Conclusion

To return to the quote at the beginning of the chapter, a 'significant change' has indeed been brought about to this part of the criminal justice system in terms of organisational structures and practices, but one which downplays and ignores the moral and human elements of rehabilitative interventions (Burke and Collett, 2016). Based on our observations of the CJC it can be suggested that far from being a 'revolution', these changes in fact continued the neo-liberal penal reforms that had been impacting this part of the criminal justice system in the recent past.

Our findings are supportive of the view that what is required to bring about any substantive rehabilitative change is a more joined-up and holistic approach: statutory and third sector agencies were already struggling to liaise in a meaningful way given the cutbacks imposed by austerity measures, and TR has made this still more difficult. In turn, within the target-driven and performance-related business model of the CRCs, offenders have been met with increased conditionality in terms of access to interventions and services.

At the time of writing TR is subject to review and revision and moving towards the implementation of TR2 but is still located within a framework of a market-driven, neo-liberal approach. The thrust of the argument within this chapter, drawing on our empirical research data, is that the complexities of problems that many so-called low-risk offenders are experiencing have been downplayed, with emphasis on personal responsibilisation and constraints imposed by narrow technologies of governance. For effective interventions to take place in terms of community sanctions, including the therapeutic justice approach explored here, the myopic, underfunded and punitive rationale of TR needs to be overturned, with social justice and rehabilitation being (re)placed as central pillars of the criminal justice system.

References

Annison, J., Auburn, T., Gilling, D. and Hanley Santos, G. (2018) 'The ambiguity of therapeutic justice and women offenders in England and Wales', in P. Ugwudike, P. Raynor and J. Annison (eds) *Evidence-Based Skills in Criminal Justice: International Research on Supporting Rehabilitation and Desistance*, Bristol: Policy Press, pp 397–419.

Berman, G. and Fox, A. (2010) 'The future of problem-solving justice: an international perspective', *University of Maryland Law Journal of Race, Religion, Gender and Class*, 10(1): 1–24.

Bonta, J. and Andrews, D. (2017) *The Psychology of Criminal Conduct* (6th ed), Abingdon: Routledge.

Burke, L. and Collett, S. (2016) 'Transforming Rehabilitation: organizational bifurcation and the end of probation as we knew it?' *Probation Journal*, 63(2): 120–35.

Corcoran, M.S. and Carr, N. (2019) 'Five years of Transforming Rehabilitation: markets, management and values', *Probation Journal*, 66(1): 3–7.

Cowe, F., Brayford, J. and Deering, J. (2010) 'Introduction', in F. Cowe, J. Brayford and J. Deering (eds) *What Else Works? Creative Work with Offenders*, Cullompton: Willan, pp 3–18.

Deering, J. and Feilzer, M. (2019) 'Hollowing out probation? The roots of Transforming Rehabilitation', *Probation Journal*, 66(1): 8–24.

Donohue, E. and Moore, D. (2009) 'When is an offender not an offender? Power, the client and shifting penal subjectivities', *Punishment and Society*, 11(3): 319–36.

Feeley, M.M. and Simon, J. (1992) 'The new penology: notes on the emerging strategy of corrections and its implications', *Criminology*, 30(4): 449–75.

Garland, D. (2001) *The Culture of Control: Crime and Social Order in Contemporary Society*, Oxford: Oxford University Press.

Garland, D. (2017) 'Punishment and welfare: social problems and social structures', in A. Liebling, S. Maruna and L. McAra (eds) *The Oxford Handbook of Criminology* (6th ed), Oxford: Oxford University Press, pp 77–97.

Gilling, D. and Jolley, M. (2012) 'A case study of an English Community Court', *British Journal of Community Justice*, 10(2): 55–69.

Grayling, C. (2012) *Rehabilitation revolution: The next steps*, speech made on 20 November, available from: https://www.gov.uk/government/speeches/rehabilitation-revolution-the-next-steps [accessed 7 September 2019].

Grayling, C. (2013) 'Ministerial foreword', in *Transforming Rehabilitation: A Revolution in the Way We Manage Offenders*, Consultation Paper CP1/2013, available from: https://consult.justice.gov.uk/digital-communications/transforming-rehabilitation/supporting_documents/transformingrehabilitation.pdf [accessed 7 September 2019].

Hannah-Moffat, K. (2005) 'Criminogenic needs and the transformative risk subject: hybridizations of risk/need in penality', *Punishment & Society*, 7(1): 29–51.

Hannah-Moffat, K. (2016) 'A conceptual kaleidoscope: Contemplating "dynamic structural risk" and an uncoupling of risk from need', *Psychology, Crime & Law*, 22(1–2): 33–46.

Hannah-Moffat, K. and Maurutto, P. (2012) 'Shifting and targeted forms of penal governance: bail, punishment and specialized courts', *Theoretical Criminology*, 16(2): 201–19.

Hardy, M. (2014) 'Practitioner perspectives on risk: using governmentality to understand contemporary probation practice', *European Journal of Criminology*, 11(3): 303–18.

Healy, D. (2012) *The Dynamics of Desistance: Charting Pathways through Change*, London: Routledge.

HM Inspectorate of Probation (2019) *Post-Release Supervision for Short-Term Prisoners: The Work Undertaken by Community Rehabilitation Companies*, Manchester: HMIP, available from: https://www.justiceinspectorates.gov.uk/hmiprobation/wp-content/uploads/sites/5/2019/05/Post-release-supervision-inspection-report.pdf [accessed 7 September 2019].

Kemshall, H. (2012) 'The role of risk, needs and strengths assessment', in F. McNeill, P. Raynor and C. Trotter (eds) *Offender Supervision: New Directions in Theory, Research and Practice*, Abingdon: Routledge, pp 155–71.

LeBel, T. P., Burnett, R., Maruna, S. and Bushway, S. (2008) 'The "chicken and egg" of subjective and social factors in desistance from crime', *European Journal of Criminology*, 5(2): 131–59.

McNeill, F., Farrall, S., Lightowler, C. and Maruna, S. (2012) *How and Why People Stop Offending: Discovering Desistance*, Institute for Research and Innovation in Social Services, available from: http://www.iriss.org.uk/sites/default/files/iriss-insight-15.pdf [accessed 7 September 2019].

Mair, G. and Burke, L. (2012) *Redemption, Rehabilitation and Risk Management*, Abingdon: Routledge.

Ministry of Justice (2013) *Target Operating Model: Rehabilitation Programme*, available from: https://www.justice.gov.uk/downloads/rehab-prog/competition/target-operating-model.pdf [accessed 15 September 2019].

Morgan, R. (2003) 'Thinking about the demand for probation services', *Probation Journal*, 50(1): 7–19.

O'Hara, M. (2014) *Austerity Bites: A Journey to the Sharp End of Cuts in the UK*, Bristol: Policy Press.

Quirouette, M., Hannah-Moffat, K. and Maurutto, P. (2016) '"A precarious place": housing and clients of specialized courts', *British Journal of Criminology*, 56(2): 370–88.

Trotter, C. (2015) *Working with Involuntary Clients: A Guide to Practice* (3rd ed), Abingdon: Routledge.

Webster, R. (2019) *Transforming Rehabilitation Resource Pack*, Available from: http://www.russellwebster.com/transforming-rehabilitation-resource-pack/ [accessed 12 September 2019].

Wexler, D.B. and Winick, B.J. (2003) 'Putting therapeutic jurisprudence to work', *ABA Journal*, May: 54–7.

Wiggan, J. (2012) 'Telling stories of 21st century welfare: the UK Coalition Government and the neo-liberal discourse of worklessness and dependency', *Critical Social Policy*, 32(3): 383–405.

Winick, B.J. (1997) 'The jurisprudence of therapeutic jurisprudence', *Psychology, Public Policy, and Law*, 3(1): 184–206.

PART III

Marketisation and the voluntary sector

12

Constructive ambiguity, market imaginaries and the penal voluntary sector in England and Wales

Mary Corcoran, Mike Maguire and Kate Williams

Introduction

In the 1990s, the idea of the marketplace as a terrain where communities of practice from business, government and the voluntary sector might tackle entrenched social problems found traction as a seemingly progressive route to reforming criminal justice. Initially associated with the so-called Third Way thinking of the New Labour government, a blend of market reforms and communitarianism found their way into subsequent Conservative–Liberal Democrat Coalition (2010–15) and Conservative (2015–) policies for encouraging civil society, local authorities and private companies to assume greater responsibility for penal welfare and 'offender management' functions. Since then, policy discourse has been replete with claims as to the transformative power of marketising approaches for saving public ('taxpayer') money, making criminal justice more efficient and responsive to public security, embedding local justice and reducing reoffending. Unconvincing, incoherent and wasteful as these claims have turned out to be in many cases (see Conclusion, this volume), the pace and scale of outsourcing was considerably accelerated under the austerity programme following the general election of 2010.

The 'mixed market' model was developed to incentivise non-governmental providers such as voluntary/third sector organisations and commercial businesses to take on the contracted delivery of prison, probation and rehabilitative activities (Hucklesby and Corcoran, 2016; Tomczak, 2016). Within the voluntary sector, the corporately organised, larger charities have consistently been most welcoming of this model, having since the 1990s actively lobbied government to allow commercial and charitable contractors to 'replac[e] the state' in many fields as providers of public services (ACEVO, 2003, 2014).

Prompted by the reconstruction of penal welfare as an entrepreneurial domain, there is also a wider tendency among voluntary sector organisations (VSOs) to brand their marketable attributes as innovative, flexible, niche or specialist, softly anti-establishment, locally embedded and whole person-oriented entities. This language is often contrasted with the supposed impersonality, inefficiency, controlling impulses and bureaucratically bound characteristics attributed to state public services.

Existing literature differs on the position of the voluntary sector under these conditions. At the end of the last century, commentators were already warning that the large-scale expansion of public funding for the voluntary sector was effectively institutionalising it as a dependent 'shadow' of government (Wolch, 1990). This confirmed to some that VSOs were further jeopardising their distinctive roles and purposes by aligning their interests with those of corporate philanthrocapitalist or state agendas (Seddon, 2007). With privatisation and the increased responsibilisation of local agencies for crime control services this century, relationships between the voluntary, public and private sectors have become even more intertwined. These trends fuel theories of a burgeoning 'non-profit-penal complex' wherein civil society actors become unconscious or unwilling facilitators of carceral expansionism (INCITE!, 2007).

Taking an approach which questions oversimplified accounts of co-optation, Corcoran et al (2018, 2019) propose that outsourcing and competitive tendering are linked to an array of mutually sustaining actuarial and regulatory rationalities which come under the rubric of 'marketised governance' (see Swirak, Chapter 6, this volume). In order to function optimally in penal service marketplaces, providers (whether public, voluntary sector or for-profit) are obliged to operate within cognate managerial, financial and performative frameworks which are intrinsic to marketised public service provision. These interconnected disciplinary fields are just as influential as direct funding for drawing the voluntary sector closer towards normative policy goals. In other words, in competing with business on corporate (or the state's) terms, VSOs themselves have come to adopt a heightened commercial disposition. This increasingly business-oriented response tends towards oligopoly and monopoly, thus diminishing the diversity of social provision. For example, the need to remain in the competitive game demands that VSOs further comply with pressures to 'professionalise' their activities (Corcoran et al, 2017, 2018), commoditise services, be willing to play a part in criminal sanctioning interventions (Maguire et al, 2019), open up new service areas and push further into new localities. These developments also interact with penal net widening tendencies towards 'govern[ing] through crime' (Simon, 2007), it is argued, as crime control agendas move 'beyond the state' to engage community partners in the 'social control efforts ... [of] official crime control agencies' (Garland, 2001: 123–7). In short, contemporary 'co-optation' is varied, indirect and fluid, occurring within horizontal (such as consortia) as well as vertical structures (such as supply chains).

Some scholars argue that critical research on marketisation takes an 'excessively macro level approach' which permits little appreciation of the 'heterogeneity' of agencies' relationships with funders (see Wong and Macmillan, Chapter 14, this volume) or 'neglects diversities in scale' and therefore potential variation in levels of dependency (Tomczak, 2016: 34–6). We agree that there is no inherent correlation between an organisation's size or wealth and its likelihood to go along with government or for-profit funders, although equally we note the research consensus that very large charitable contractors are most likely to form such highly interdependent relationships (Clinks, 2017). Fisher (2013) contends that large charities might be just as likely as small 'independents' to adopt explicitly critical positions towards 'elite interests'. Much is made too of the chameleon stance of the third sector, with its capacity to seemingly conform with, and at other times consciously oppose, state or corporate agendas (Salamon, 2015). Finally, a new strand of analysis highlights the potential for creatively engaging in profit-based penal markets as a means of achieving penal reductionist ends. Such tactics are associated with 'humonetarianism'[1] (sic), which holds that charities can yield 'virtuous profits' by persuading governments that they can save money while investing in alternatives to imprisonment (Aviram, 2015).

In response, we (Corcoran et al, 2018, 2019) have contended that as market ideas and practices are such critical components in the structural transformation of the penal welfare field, they are salient to analysing the changing conditions relating to agency and self-determination among penal voluntary sector actors. That work documents the versatility and range of adaptive responses to market governance, acknowledging that actors exercise degrees of conformity, resistance, negotiation and contestation *within* the dominant paradigm.

---

[1] 'Humonetarianism', as defined by Aviram (2010), is a political-economic ideology which focuses on a supposed scarcity of resources at a time of crisis. The founding elements of humonetarianism are an emphasis on an economic, social or fiscal emergency, which motivates short-term discourse, a lack of consideration of political alternatives and an emphasis on economic approaches such as cost and (monetisable) benefit analyses to justify (or otherwise) social investment (Aviram, 2010).

However, less well understood are questions concerning the extent to which penal voluntary sector personnel 'choose' to adopt 'pro-market' characteristics, what they think about 'the market', what their perceptions are of the prevailing rules of engagement in their sphere or how relationships between different actors – funders with providers, services with service users – are shaped by these rules.

We examine these questions as reflecting tropes of adaptability in the narratives deployed by senior voluntary sector personnel in our research interviews to explain how they were managing their projects in the face of unusually disruptive conditions. The primary data capture took place in England and Wales between April 2015 and November 2017 and was designed to investigate the voluntary sector's adaptive responses to change.[2] Our participants described significant ideational shifts in their experience of marketisation in penal services, which entailed an enhanced emphasis on competitiveness, greater willingness to take market advantage and a need to tailor methods to performance- and outcomes-based payment incentives, to degrees that they had not previously encountered. Taking Charles Taylor's (2004) concept of 'social imaginaries', we devised the term 'market imaginaries' to summarise these in terms of the tacit and fundamental understanding of the new obligatory rules of engagement in the penal marketplace. Although owing some debt to Gramsci's concept of hegemony, Taylor observed that ideas become naturalised as *commonsensical* through socialisation and shared practice: that is, through ways that people 'imagine their social existence, how they fit together with others, how things go on between them and their fellows, the expectations that are normally met and the deeper normative emotions and images that underlie these expectations' (Taylor 2004: 23). Although ruling ideas originate with elite ideological or political agendas, they find traction at lower echelons in society through interactive exchanges and experiences. Dominant ideas and values are established as standard, shared norms through routine transmission, so that '[t]he social imaginary is not [just] a set of ideas; *rather it is what enables, through making sense of, the practices of a society*' (Taylor, 2002: 91, emphasis added).

In this chapter, we establish how senior personnel came to form shared understandings of (and differences in) ideas about the importance of commercialisation and the impact of market competition to their organisations, and to the sector more broadly. Deconstructing how the language and concepts of the 'market' and

---

[2] 'Voluntary sector adaptation and resilience in a mixed economy of resettlement'. Funded by the Leverhulme Trust (RPG 2014-419).

market-oriented behaviour in criminal justice (and especially penal and probation services) were used by voluntary sector managers, we found significant areas of convergence, but also of divergence. There was a fundamental consensus about the inescapable influence of market paradigms as the primary frames of reference through which they made decisions about future strategy. In particular, there was widespread concurrence that the predominance of competitive outsourcing had pulled the voluntary sector 'firmly towards the market' (Salamon, 2015: 36). However, staff also strained to balance commercialisation and competitiveness on the one hand, while protecting their existing mission and values, types of programmes, beneficiaries or links with localities on the other hand. Likewise, while respondents adopted the linguistic codes and trappings of 'market culture', in most cases this was transposed onto their existing socially oriented structures and practices. Others positively embraced the opportunities which outsourcing and competitive contracting offered, and regarded performance incentives and outcome targets as essential to efficient and professional contract delivery. Three strategic responses from VSOs are laid out here to illustrate the trends: (i) a greater tendency towards service diversification and commoditisation; (ii) mergers, acquisitions and seeking a place in larger consortia; (iii) and varied dispositions towards market adaptive strategies, which we interpret from Hirschman's (1970) options of 'exit, voice and loyalty'.

Commoditisation and diversification

Although the voluntary sector has operated for decades within competitive contractual frameworks and grant programmes, the contraction of public spending after the 2007 global financial crisis, and later the UK government's austerity agenda, created unprecedented levels of instability for funding (Clinks 2017). This amounted to the retrenchment of practically all grant funding programmes from central government compounded by the severe curtailment of local authority funding (which is historically the most significant source of charitable funding). Against the prospect of having to discontinue programmes or even close down, most senior managers reported intensified activities to ascertain where funding might be secured. Thereafter, the main options were bidding for contracts against for-profits and public sector providers to deliver outsourced services, becoming subcontractors to larger contractors, commercialising their services, and applying to foundations and trusts or local criminal justice partners as potential funders. Several discussed how they were recalibrating their existing 'offer' towards 'new markets' (in line with emerging policy priorities in relation to specific groups, such as youth offenders, those with mental health needs and military veterans, among others). Under these conditions, new funding opportunities appeared like windfalls, notably the large-scale commissioning exercise in 2013–14 under the Transforming Rehabilitation (TR) programme (the ambitious and ill-fated partial privatisation of the probation service in England and Wales) (Marples, 2013). Responding to this seemingly promising opportunity, several voluntary organisations had spent the previous few years and considerable funds preparing to become sub-contractors to the 21 Community Rehabilitation Companies (CRCs) who were the new 'prime contractors' for probation services. Retrenchment in their existing markets was the primary spur to diversification, although one director (not untypically) argued that they had always innovated and sought new funding opportunities, even before the advent of competition from the commercial sector, and that the intensified need to do so did not mean that they would indiscriminately 'chase the money'. At the time of interview (November 2015), the board of this organisation took the view that their reputation, track record and quality of their outcomes would win out:

> We are much more engaged, I suppose, than ever in trying to find alternative forms of income. The mantra is always that you must become somehow self-sustaining. But that kind of idea of you must become a business, you need to sell anything that you can, we get that all the time. You know, politicians come in here saying the same things. (Director, drugs service)

Marketing entails an element of 'cultural performance' (Munro, 1999: 619), where organisations and managers make their products or services 'visible' and 'available' while sending out messages 'about worth and competence' to peers, funders and consumers. Yet this director attached different motivations to the performative aspects of 'selling' his organisation which appeared to transmit willing compliance with the 'performed order' of the marketplace (Munro, 1999: 634–5), while at the same time seeking to retain an element of control over the ethos and values of the organisation:

> And as it happens, we're pretty good at what we do, and what we do is recognised as being – and I hate this word – innovative. And so, people are trying to copy what we

do. In the last week, I've had to do the bloody tour of this place to the leader of the county council, then yesterday another county councillor, and then yesterday afternoon, Public Health England, we had to roll out the red carpet for somebody to come and see what we do. And earlier in the week, a big drug company, for some bizarre reason that even I don't understand, they also came for the visit. (Director, drugs service)

A 'general truism' in the charitable funding literature is that VSOs should avoid narrow 'resource dependence' and therefore 'seek as much diversity in their revenue streams as possible'. Indeed, 'the decree that more types of revenue – or more revenue streams – is always good has been around for a long time' (Hager and Hung, 2019: 1). Hager and Hung dispute the assumption that diversification offers greater stability or autonomy, although it may offer short-term certainty. 'Every revenue source has its own level of restriction from complete to none at all, *and this affects autonomy and adaptability*' (2019: 2, emphasis added). Their critique applies to our respondents who observed that diversification was no panacea to disruption in the funding and policy environments. Rather, diversification and commoditisation brought different kinds of uncertainty as well as resource costs arising from expanding into new localities or creating programmes for new client groups ('new markets'), mainly because these require investment in staff or other resources in order to deliver on such contracts. Managers observed that projecting 'risk appetites' and 'moving with the market' were inevitably constrained, reflecting Hager and Hung's insight that 'the fact [is] that every revenue source *requires some transaction costs*: money, time, and attention' (2019: 1, emphasis added). Thus, while adaptability to new markets secured some short-term advantages, in the longer term it was evident that VSOs had migrated from one form of dependency (based on reliance on government spending) to another (based on performance in competitive contract markets):

In the kind of glory days of the [New] Labour administration, there was an awful lot of EU money, different SRB [single regeneration budget] type funding, that kind of thing, which they grew very fast, very quickly, but I felt they kind of lost their roots, lost their vision, lost their sense of purpose … I think there is a cultural difference. I think things are becoming far more blurred now. It is getting more blurred. But I think the kind of cultural routes and the values of voluntary sector organisations, or should I say some voluntary sector organisations, because I think the bigger voluntary sector organisations are becoming far more commercialised and, you know, run like businesses. (Chief Executive, families project)

Accumulating market power: bigger is better

The race to optimise market share is increasingly manifested in mergers, amalgamations and demutualisations (changing from charitable to for-profit legal status) (Schwartz, 2001). These have also been conspicuous in criminal justice service areas (especially prison and probation) because national procurement systems tend to favour economies of scale, consistency and the large-scale roll-out of programmes (Audit Commission, 2007). This trend has contributed, largely unhindered by regulation, to the emergence of oligopolistic service markets and monopolies of provision. Resources are increasingly concentrated in the hands of these large players which gives them an unfair market advantage at the expense of smaller regional or local actors. The virtues that were claimed for marketisation – such as generating diversity and innovation – were in fact undermined by a countertendency towards homogeneity. The following discussion explores examples of two modes of expansion, often undertaken in response to economic pressures and commissioners' preferences for large-scale providers covering large geographical areas. The first concerns mergers between medium-sized VSOs to enable them to become large social enterprises, and the second involves voluntary sector and for-profit partnerships or joint ventures.

Mergers allow participants to acquire capabilities, assets, specialist expertise (especially in bid writing) and competitive advantage. Some had merged in order to avoid closure, while others affiliated with a larger group of like-minded organisations.

> We did three mergers in a year. We actively sought out mergers to move us into new geography and new markets ... And they took us into the southern market ... because unless you're in London, you can't break into the London market. (Chief Executive, social enterprise)

The previous quote is taken from an organisation that had rapidly expanded from a base in one region and in core housing support to become a major voluntary sector player with national reach. The organisation had 'almost gone to the wall' shortly after the economic downturn. Within a decade, the parent organisation had a large and complex overall structure based on a registered charity at its core with a profitmaking arm ('brand'). It had also expanded into several new service fields and had more than 50 separate projects under its aegis. On the other side of the equation, another VSO sought out a merger because it had sustained significant financial losses when it took on substantial contract commitments under the Work Programme (the controversial governmental programme which paid contracted providers to place the long-term unemployed in paid work): 'It was very, very clear that we were not going to be able to withstand that loss. So, the board started looking for merger partners and openly going out to do that' (Director, resettlement and employment project).

Where voluntary–for–profit joint ventures were concerned (often in the form of tiered 'supply chains' (Maguire, 2016)), a few organisations which had partnered with large for-profits reasoned that it gave them room to innovate and develop services that they had not been able to provide as long as they were trapped in multiple, short-term and smaller-scale contracting rounds. One finance director of a VSO which works jointly with a large security multinational said that the private sector offered them

> potential reach for the contracts that arguably some of the big national and global organisations might go for. They actually said, 'we're that confident we can do this, we'll put up £2 million'. As an organisation, we certainly couldn't do anything like that, but we wanted the opportunity to be able to get in and work alongside one of the bigger partners.

Some organisations which had attracted criticisms for 'empire building' responded that they were motivated by commercial altruism because their intervention revived struggling organisations which otherwise would have folded. The parent company also claimed that it did not subsequently interfere with organisations which it took over:

> We acquired a ... charity. We did that because we saw an organisation delivering work that aligned with our ethics, our values, our ethos, we liked that organisation and we could see that it was having difficulties ... And [VSO] runs alongside us as a wholly owned subsidiary of [us] but are allowed to continue the work that they're doing. (Chief Executive, multi-project social enterprise)

Commercial growth strategies were given an additional boost by the tactic of large enterprises (commercial–charitable hybrids) making several tenders simultaneously to deliver large-scale contracts in a number of regions. Commissioners often preferred large, single providers as administering these was thought to be more 'efficient' than continuing to work with several smaller providers. We were given examples of contracts for citywide or countywide drugs and alcohol services or housing being awarded to contractors with no previous history in those localities. In response to charges about predation, the contract winners reasoned that this made commercial and humanitarian sense: given the level of deprivation and lack of welfare spending by government, they were the only entities with the means to invest in large-scale programmes – in short, they were stepping in to areas which the state had abandoned. Finally, they claimed that very large social enterprises and for-profits were investing in innovation, helping struggling services survive and bringing business efficiency to the sector.

Organisational responses: exit, voice and loyalty

We asked sector leaders what they thought about offender resettlement service markets, over and above the obvious considerations of commercial continuity. Their responses have been loosely categorised according to Albert Hirschman's (1970) concepts of 'exit', 'voice' and 'loyalty'. It should be noted that this classical formulation addressed the options available to actors in the face of 'organisational decline' which can incorporate, as in this case, responses to unpredictable conditions that require urgent action and decision making. In Hirschman's view, 'voice' and 'loyalty' are available options while decline or threat is still unfolding, prompting individuals to dissent or resolve from within. 'Exit' requires actors to look for better alternatives elsewhere.

We view these as dispositions rather than fixed organisational characteristics, as respondents often worked within the different standpoints, with many combining elements of all three, albeit to varying degrees.

Exit: manifested as negative reactions to, or critiques of, those aspects of hyper-competitiveness that have sown divisions or wariness among voluntary sector personnel. Some kinds of 'exit' have more positive connotations, such as those found in the autonomous stance adopted by some organisations, especially those which concentrate on advocacy and campaigning:

I think it is more cut throat, you know, it's dog eat dog out there ... And [names a local organisation] came in here and asked to use some of our premises. And, you know, we're sitting on the fence on this. (Director, employment and training programme)

I think it's becoming more competitive. On the surface, it can look like it's more collaborative because consortiums are encouraged and things like that. But my experience of consortiums has not been good really. (Director, families project)

The approach that we've taken – and these are all interlinked – of staying small, of not taking government funding, means that we're really small and we don't have a huge amount of resources, but it allows us to still say what we think, when we think it, without worrying that that's going to cause us problems for funding. (Director, ex-prisoner legal rights)

Voice: Among the more invidious of market logics is that providers (or workers) should be willing to relocate to areas where market demand (as evidenced by potential profit) is greatest, even if this is at the expense of perceived needs and the geographical and relational bonds established with communities and beneficiaries. While some VSOs were ready and willing to transplant or expand into new 'territories', as previously discussed, most expressed some wariness about the challenges (geographic, relational and logistical) of changing their mission or client group, with the potential loss of an effective voice in a particular aspect of their area of expertise. Others observed that they had strayed from their original founding principles and constituencies as a consequence of 'chasing markets', or were changing their mission and service, or dropping their public advocacy 'voice'. The 'market' especially marginalised specialist services with 'minority' consumer bases:

Some small organisations do truly have a unique selling point and a unique inroad into a community that perhaps another organisation won't have. So, if you're looking at issues such as FGM [female genital mutilation] in a particular community, or you know, something in a particular ethnic group, you are going to be small and you're going to lose that expertise if you're not careful. (Director, families project)

Organisations within supply chains also exercised 'voice' by guarding against organisational priorities being overruled. One VSO which was sub-contracted to provide specialist employment and training support described its relationship with a CRC as sufficiently small to stay 'below the radar' of interference from the commercial contractor while maintaining continuity in their practices.

> We're part of the supply chain for both [name withheld] and [name withheld] CRCs (community rehabilitation companies), but we're kind of doing our own thing as well, you know, in line with what we see as the needs rather than what other people might see as the needs. (CEO, families project)

Most interviewees opined that organisations should be dynamic and that inertia or inability to adapt to circumstances was undesirable. Not only would inaction reflect poor commercial judgement, but 'standing still' ultimately represented losing sight of their fundamental mission and failing those who needed support. 'Voice', therefore, encompassed a mission of 'being there' to meet needs as well as to maintain an active presence in advocacy and policy networks. To quote one director of a women's project: 'We felt that if we weren't inside, we couldn't influence it. So, we could only then be outside critiquing. If you're outside critiquing, that can work to a degree but it's much slower.'

Loyalty: The most obvious case of 'loyalty' was demonstrated in the race to commercialise and expand out of the desire to improve their clients' (or prospective clients') life circumstances. Many articulated that marketisation freed them up from the prescriptiveness and bureaucracy associated with government contracts: 'It's the freedom to innovate' (Manager, youth justice charity). 'Loyalty' to their clients also manifested where individuals saw commercial opportunities, certainly, but also reflected ambitions to use difficulty as a staging point for radical change in their work. In a minority of cases, this involved changing from charitable status: 'We transformed to become a social business' (Finance Director). Yet a countermovement was evident among those who professed loyalty to a voluntary sector 'identity', which manifested itself in the stated determination to resist the imperative to continually 'chase the money' (with its risk of masking the *social* objectives of their work).

So yeah, we are forced to look around. For instance, we have a small catering business here. What we do is, we use that as a way of employing people, we don't use that in order to make some money, we do it to employ people. But that's one of the things we are trying to do here, we're trying to employ people, we're trying to *get people into work*. (Director, drugs service, emphasis in original)

Referencing Hirschman's (1970) thesis about exit, voice and loyalty, our proposition is that these are dispositions rather than fixed organisational archetypes. Competition is a social paradigm which, by its very nature, creates some 'winners' and a rather larger pool of 'losers'. There is some correlation between those VSOs which can be regarded as 'winners' and 'losers' in the current climate and the degree to which they tended to 'exit', express 'voice' or proclaim 'loyalty'. However, organisations combined elements of all three dispositions, albeit to varying degrees. Thus, some exited on the basis of being asked to undertake unacceptable types or standards of work, or compromise aspects of their values and practices (this was particularly conspicuous among providers of women's services; see Cooper and Mansfield, Chapter 13, this volume), while others 'walked away' from contracts on the basis of their lack of commercial viability. That being said, there was patterned consistency to VSOs' dispositions towards, and their fate in, the market. Market loyalty was most evident among those which actively embraced the new world of contract competition and territorial expansion, and these were generally the 'winners' in the prevailing circumstances. 'Losers' tended to be those which exited (or never entered) contract markets, or which dropped out because of failure in the market (we stress that these 'losses' are not weaknesses and are often the result of VSOs exercising agency). A minority of organisations prioritised their social voice (advocacy or campaigning), which they viewed as incompatible with delivering government contracts, while others stayed in the market but sought to influence policy makers and funders. However, the greater proportion of respondents were pragmatic adaptors who were sometimes grudgingly reliant on more powerful players, while ploughing on in the belief that the sector had no choice but to navigate through the current morass and to be around in the future to pick up the pieces. Thus, market pragmatism reflected a moral imperative of standing one's ground. As one manager put it: 'We have to survive because no one else is looking out for the most deprived.'

Discussion

The reasons given by voluntary sector managers for operating in the service contract market were varied, with some embracing the freedom to enlarge and diversify their operations, while others worked within competitive parameters with caution or scepticism. Most surveyed future cultural change as inevitable and unavoidable. For many, participation was fundamentally related to the existential question of 'adapting or perishing'. Opportunities and threats were not evenly distributed: many organisations 'chose' to make 'irrational' market decisions such as supporting loss-making enterprises, even if this was on a temporary basis or in the calculation that future funding might materialise. While theorists might celebrate state–market–charitable consortia as exemplars of 'organisational hybridity' (Evers, 1983), our findings indicate that sectoral identities currently remain durable – perhaps resilient. Even so, there are signs of change.

To summarise, the chapter explored the meanings assigned by senior voluntary sector personnel to market scoping, commercialisation and competitive activities in the past few years. It would be erroneous to conclude that greater market-oriented behaviour in penal voluntary sector organisations confirms that they have universally succumbed to radical market liberalism (although equally, there are considerable strains from working within marketised parameters). Despite closer co-production in some areas, at times forced by circumstances, the evidence does not confidently point to an easy merging or subsumption of charities' ethos and organisational identities. Rather, inferences of 'co-optation' inherent to market participation must be appreciatively nuanced and contextualised. This chapter has emphasised a number of key points that have been underappreciated in policy spheres and insufficiently addressed in the literature. Firstly, it has acted as a reminder that market-oriented behaviours and values can be fluid and contested. Secondly, it has stressed that analysis of voluntary sector reactions to dominant market discourses requires considerable nuance (although the question of dominance is not denied here). Thirdly, it has provided a rebuttal to policy common sense by demonstrating that not all charities, nor all funders, are incentivised by the profit motive. Fourthly, it has revealed how the previous consensus about the voluntary sector's 'natural' disposition (civil society orientated, human rights based and socially distributive) has been recast as an inferior and illegitimate rival philosophy to 'free market' common sense. Those who have not 'caught up' are strained between old and new positions. Finally, it has questioned the virtue of constructive ambiguity or chameleon stances in response to market ideologies and practices as a redeeming characteristic of the voluntary sector (Salamon, 2015). Successful as the voluntary sector might be in playing along with market forces, it does not deflect criticism that it may be getting too close to powerful interests. Appearing to 'go along' with the status quo (even for the greater good) may not confirm enthusiasm across the entire sector for market forces, but neither does it provide a defence against them.

References

ACEVO (Association of Chief Executives of Voluntary Organisations) (2003) *Replacing the State: The Case for Third Sector Public Service Delivery*, London: ACEVO.

ACEVO (Association of Chief Executives of Voluntary Organisations) (2014) *Remaking the State*, London: ACEVO.

Audit Commission (2007) *Hearts and Minds: Commissioning from the Voluntary Sector*, London: Audit Commission.

Aviram, H. (2010) 'Humonetarianism: the new correctional discourse of scarcity', *Hastings Race & Poverty Law Journal*, 7: 1, available from: https://repository.uchastings.edu/hastings_race_poverty_law_journal/vol7/iss1/1 [accessed 5 November 2019].

Aviram, H. (2015) *Cheap on Crime: Recession-Era Politics and the Transformation of American Punishment*, Oakland: University of California Press.

Clinks (2017) *The State of the Sector 2016/17*, London: Clinks & NCVO.

Corcoran, M.S., Maguire, M. and Williams, K. (2019) 'Alice in Wonderland: voluntary sector organisations' experiences of Transforming Rehabilitation', *Probation Journal*, 66(1): 96–112.

Corcoran, M.S., Williams, K., Prince, K. and Maguire, M. (2017) *The Voluntary Sector in Criminal Justice: A Study of Adaptation and Resilience. Summary of early findings*, Staffordshire: Keele University.

Corcoran, M.S., Williams, K., Prince, K. and Maguire, M. (2018) 'The penal voluntary sector in England & Wales: adaptation to unsettlement and austerity', *Political Quarterly*, 89(1): 187–96.

Evers, A. (1983) 'The iron cage revisited: institutional isomorphism and collective rationality in organisational fields', *American Sociological Review*, 48(2): 147–60.

Fisher, R. (2013) 'The paradox of democratic capitalism: an historical view', in R. Fisher (ed) *Managing Democracy, Managing Dissent: Capitalism, Democracy and the Organisation of Consent*, London: Corporate Watch/Freedom Press, pp 15–45.

Garland, D. (2001) *The Culture of Control: Crime and Social Order in Contemporary Society*, Chicago: University of Chicago Press.

Hager, M.A. and Hung, C. (2019) 'Is diversification of revenue food for nonprofit financial health?' *Nonprofit Quarterly* online, 10 April, available from: https://nonprofitquarterly.org/is-diversification-of-revenue-good-for-nonprofit-financial-health/ [accessed 5 November 2019].

Hirschman, A.O. (1970) *Exit, Voice, and Loyalty: Responses to Decline in Firms, Organizations, and States*, Cambridge, MA: Harvard University Press.

Hucklesby, A. and Corcoran, M.S. (eds) (2016) *The Voluntary Sector and Criminal Justice*, Basingstoke: Palgrave Macmillan.

INCITE! Women of Color Against Violence (2007) *The Revolution Will Not Be Funded: Beyond the Non-Profit Industrial Complex*, Cambridge, MA: South End Press.

Maguire, M. (2016) 'Third tier in the supply chain? Voluntary agencies and the commissioning of offender rehabilitation services', in A. Hucklesby and M. Corcoran (eds) *The Voluntary Sector and Criminal Justice*, Basingstoke: Palgrave Macmillan, pp 43–70.

Maguire, M., Williams, K. and Corcoran, M.S. (2019) 'Penal drift and the voluntary sector', *Howard Journal*, 58(3): 430–49.

Marples, R. (2013) 'Transforming Rehabilitation: the risks for the voluntary, community and social enterprise sector in engaging in commercial contracts with tier 1 providers', *British Journal of Community Justice*, 11(2/3): 21–32.

Munro, R. (1999) 'The cultural performance of control', *Organization Studies*, 20(4): 619–40.

Salamon, L. (2015) *The Resilient Sector Revisited: The New Challenges to Non-Profit America*, Washington, DC: Brookings Institute.

Schwartz, R. (2001) 'Managing government–third sector collaboration: accountability, ambiguity and politics', *International Journal of Public Administration*, 24(11): 1161–88.

Seddon, N. (2007) *Who Cares? How State Funding and Political Activism Change Charity*, London: Civitas.

Simon, J. (2007) *Governing through Crime: How the War on Crime Transformed American Democracy and Created a Culture of Fear*, Oxford: Oxford University Press.

Taylor, C. (2002) 'Modern social imaginaries', *Public Culture*, 14(1): 91–124.

Taylor, C. (2004) *Modern Social Imaginaries*, Durham NC: Duke University Press.

Tomczak, P. (2016) *The Penal Voluntary Sector*, Abingdon: Routledge.

Wolch, J. (1990) *Government and Voluntary Sector in Transition*, New York: The Foundation Center.

13

Marketisation of women's organisations in the criminal justice sector

Vickie Cooper and Maureen Mansfield

Introduction

A defining element of the women's criminal justice system for some decades has been the lack of strategic oversight and planning, particularly in relation to the role of the voluntary sector (HM Inspectorate of Probation, 2016). This lack of strategic oversight has been further compounded under the roll-out of the Transformation Rehabilitation (TR) White Paper in the criminal justice sector, published in May 2013 (see Annison et al, Chapter 11, this volume). The policy agenda set out in TR has resulted in a rapid dismantling of community-based services for economically marginalised women which, in turn, has had significant ramifications for the women's voluntary sector – the key providers of these community-based services – and for criminalised women. Blame for the dismantling of services has been predominantly apportioned to the privatisation of Probation Trusts in England and Wales and the resultant failure to commission women's services that previously provided a crucial stream of support to criminalised women. The consequences of these reforms and market-based operations include small specialist services that make up a significant portion of the women's voluntary sector being pushed out by larger, dominant players in the probation market economy. While we don't disagree with this narrative, the exposure of the women's voluntary sector to these market-based operations is not new, nor is the women's voluntary sector unfamiliar with the organisational insecurity that the private market perpetuates. In this chapter we discuss how the gendered responsive framework, which is predominantly delivered by the women's voluntary sector, previously invited small specialist voluntary organisations to participate in and commit to neo-liberal market requirements. We argue that the gender responsive penal reforms, and the tandem role of the women's voluntary sector employed to deliver and implement these reforms, has enabled the state to develop the neo-liberal market conditions that have resulted in the diminishing profile of small, specialist community services for criminalised women. The chapter begins with a brief overview of the landscape of women's service provision under conditions of austerity and the sharp decline in central and local government funding for service providers that previously catered to economically marginalised women. Second, it will outline the gender responsive framework which previously supported the expansion of the women's voluntary sector and facilitated the neo-liberal market model of funding. It will then highlight the scale of privatisation under the austerity-driven TR programme, and the resultant deleterious impact this is having upon the women's voluntary sector, which is occurring alongside the net-widening effects of this new probation regime.

The rehabilitation 'revolution', or more austerity for women?

Austerity can be understood as an economic programme that, through a distinctly patriarchal policy design, disproportionately impacts on the lives of women and therefore further marginalises already disenfranchised women and children. As we write this chapter, the precipitous effects of austerity cuts and extensive structural reform rolled out in the aftermath of the global financial crash in 2007–08 continues to adversely affect women in a range of key areas, including welfare support, housing, legal justice, child care, social care and pensions. The Women's Budget Group (2018) estimate that, by 2020, in the UK, approximately £37 billion per year will have been cut from the social security budget, and women will disproportionately shoulder the brunt of these budget cuts. Currently, the lack of housing availability, caused by an unregulated housing market and dwindling social housing investment, has directly contributed to some 120,000 children now living in temporary accommodation (House of Commons, 2019a). Not surprisingly, austerity is pushing women further onto the margins of the state and bringing them ever closer to the penal net. Sex worker activist groups, such as the English Collective of Prostitutes (2016), found a sharp rise in women moving into sex work, and/or reducing the price of sex, as a means of surviving the pernicious effects of welfare reforms and expansion of benefit sanctions.

The sharp decline in central and local government funding for support services that previously catered to economically marginalised women and children is compounding these issues further. For example, women's organisations, such as Imkaan, which represents Black and minority ethnic organisations within the violence against women and girls sector, have stated that their member organisations have had their funding drastically reduced, causing them to turn women and children away, or close altogether (Imkaan, 2016). This is occurring because austerity measures have amplified the structural inequalities between service commissioners and service providers, where women's organisations have been significantly underfunded or excluded from new funding regimes brought in as a response to austerity cuts. This is particularly the case for women's services operating within the criminal justice sector.

In 2014, the government introduced the Offender Rehabilitation Act which legislated for the privatisation of a significant portion of the probation service in England and Wales. These changes and new probation 'contracts' were rolled out in 2016, under the new umbrella of 21 Community Rehabilitation Companies (CRCs), which comprise a range of private companies and charity partnerships. This 'radical reorganisation' (Burke and Collett, 2016) of the probation sector was introduced as part of a wider fiscal consolidation programme that has resulted in austerity cuts. At the heart of fiscal consolidation programmes lies the dismantling of previously 'untouchable' public sector services where public expenditure is clawed back, business investment is crowded in and competition is ramped up (Cooper and Whyte, 2017). The Offender Rehabilitation Act 2014 (ORA) follows this long trajectory of state intervention to privatise public goods, where blame for recidivism, swelling prison populations and decaying management structures has been apportioned to the 'system', rather than a lack of resourcing or the neo-liberal ideology underpinning the system. In analysing the gendered effects and inequalities exacerbated by this privatisation and probation reform, two controversial outcomes can be evidenced: (i) the exclusion of women's voluntary services and (ii) a 131 per cent rise in recall rates for convicted women, compared with a 22 per cent rise for convicted men (House of Commons, 2019b).

How did we arrive at this critical juncture? How have women's services reached this crisis point? There can be no doubt that austerity is having damaging and pernicious effects on women and on women's voluntary services; however, we are not convinced that blame for the diminishing profile of the women's voluntary sector can be entirely located in the privatisation of probation introduced in the period of austerity. Austerity, we argue, amplified the marketisation of the women's voluntary sector, but the pattern of policy making and insecure grant funding regimes that made women's services vulnerable were already in place. In the next section we argue that the gendered responsive framework introduced in the UK around 2009 and predominantly delivered by the women's voluntary sector represents an important neo-liberal policy context that, when it was first rolled out, invited small specialist voluntary organisations to participate in and commit to neo-liberal market requirements. We argue that gender responsive penal reforms helped to carve out the strategic role of the women's voluntary sector and, in so doing, accelerated and intensified the marketisation of this sector prior to and during austerity-driven public sector reforms. Furthermore, and in this process, women's organisations were fundamentally changed and pulled more centrally into criminal justice practices, compromising their role and function.

Gender responsiveness

The principles and practices of gender responsive reform policies have been a key feature of criminal justice policy making in the UK since the 1990s. Gender responsive reforms emerged internationally, first in North America, as part of a concern that the needs of criminalised women were not acknowledged by apparently gender neutral assessment and programmes designed to address offending behaviour (Bloom et al, 2004). The central logic underpinning gender responsive frameworks is that existing penal policies and practices can be altered and reframed to meet the specific needs of women in prison, address systemic discrimination and reverse the numbers of economically marginalised and disadvantaged women coming into contact with criminal justice systems (Bloom et al, 2004). Extolled as an 'alternative' approach to the harmful treatment of women in prison, the gender responsive approach has been widely accepted and supported by politicians and policy makers. Convinced that women's prisons can be made safer by adjusting systems and practices in ways that are 'gender informed', 'woman wise' and 'women specific', UK governments have made considerable financial investment to implement and advance gender responsive penal reforms.

But prison abolitionists and anti-carceral feminists raise fundamental questions about the extent to which prisons can be made safer, given that the ideological role and purpose of prison is to function as a site of power, control and harm (Russell and Carlton, 2013). In an examination of penal reforms in Canada, Kelly Hannah-Moffat (2001) argues that gender responsive programmes are essentially a neo-liberal reform programme that reframes penal strategies in ways that facilitate self-discipline and self-governance and, as part of the organisational management of 'risk' and 'need', promote ideologies of responsibilisation and empowerment. Gender responsiveness, Hannah-Moffatt argues, is a 'flawed attempt to reconceptualise the meaning and experience of punishment to make it more "appropriate" and suitable for women' (2001: 4). Presented as an alternative and feminist response to the gendered inequalities and harms facing women in the criminal justice system, gender responsive penal reforms can be better understood as a different type of punishment. For example, a critical body of scholarship demonstrates how gendered responsive policy reforms have facilitated new strategies of 'gendered governance' that immerse women in and force them to respond to normative assumptions associated with the female norm. It has been variously highlighted that gendered modes of governance have reproduced a myriad of disciplinary techniques that seek to address women's offending behaviour through relationship surveillance (Pollack, 2007), or by regulating desires deemed to be 'anti-social' by penal institutions (Haney, 2010). Russell and Carlton (2013) further challenge the 'unitary frame of gender' produced by the gender responsive paradigm, pointing out that it ignores the historical processes of racialisation among women. For example, in the Australian context, they highlight the various ways that the gendered reform programme 'obscures the structural differences between Aboriginal women and non-Aboriginal women' (p 476).

While this body of scholarship has provided a necessary critical lens for conceptualising the ways in which gender responsive reforms align individuals with the goals and desires of the neo-liberal state, less is said about the creeping marketisation of the service providers tasked with delivering gender responsive penal reforms. With the exception of some studies, there is a dearth of critical dialogue about how the organisational identity of service providers for criminalised women has been altered and aligned to meet the requirements of the neo-liberal market. In the next section, we turn our attention to state partnerships with voluntary sector providers that emerged during the implementation of the gender responsive reforms in England and Wales.

The gender responsive policy market

In the UK, gender responsive penal reforms have played a key role in the expansion and marketisation of the women's voluntary sector. In 2007, the Corston Report (Home Office, 2007) generated a set of changes across the women's voluntary sector. Responding to the acute harms of women's imprisonment and the broader risks and vulnerabilities facing women in the criminal justice system, Corston outlined a 'radically different', 'women-centred approach', where women could be treated 'both holistically and individually' (Home Office, 2007). Underpinning this approach was a closer, more active involvement of community-based, specialist services operating from within the voluntary sector. Already equipped with the knowledge and expertise in providing creative, holistic and flexible services for women, Corston drew heavily upon the service provider Together Women Programme (TWP) – a charity organisation supporting criminalised women in the community – as an exemplary provision of women-specific services delivered at community level. Inspired by TWP, Corston asked whether a similar approach could be adopted on a broader, national scale and contemplated whether it was possible to develop a national strategy for 'sustaining and building the capacity of the women's voluntary sector' via a '*grant-making* programme' (p 82, emphasis added).

While Corston drew urgent attention to the harms facing women in prison and the deplorable conditions of their imprisonment, Corston's recommendations for penal reform can also be seen as the culmination of neo-liberal policy making, stressing the importance of market-based principles and practices delivered in the 'mixed-economy' (Corcoran, 2011; Tomczak, 2014). Arguably, the roll-out of Corston's 'women-specific' and 'radical approach' was as much about 'harnessing the local expertise of local groups' for addressing the 'practical limitations' of state-led institutions, as it was about generating reform (Corcoran, 2011). The reliance on the expertise of pre-existing women's centres and other specialist providers helped to carve out the strategic influence of the women's voluntary sector in the delivery of criminal justice interventions and, in so doing, pulled them closer to the free market ideology and political aspirations of the state.

Of course, this realignment presents several challenges for voluntary sector organisations that broadly relate ideological repositioning of values and ethics. In their account of community-based services for women in Australia, similarly commissioned under a gender responsive penal reform programme, Stubbs and Baldry (2018) conclude that 'there remains a risk that community organisations are vulnerable to being reshaped by these new arrangements reflecting government agendas' (p 140). This risk is very much echoed in England and Wales, where commissioning structures and contractual requirements have aligned the women's voluntary sector service delivery with the requirements of the neo-liberal market. The perennial issue of short-term funding and uncertainty over funding security has overshadowed the political commitments and values of women's voluntary sector work in the criminal justice system. Throughout the funding cycles, providers have had to demonstrate 'best value' to 'purchasers' at central and local government and align their work practices, organisational roles and infrastructure to develop more efficient organisational systems and enterprising techniques that meet the demands and requirements of this neo-liberal funding model.

Not long after the Corston Report was published, the Ministry of Justice secured £15.6 million in 2009 to develop a national network of women's centres. This statutory investment was partly secured by the advocacy work of the Corston Independent Funders' Coalition (CIFC), which comprised several trustees and grant making trusts, for example the Barrow Cadbury Trust, the Bromley Trust and the Nationwide Foundation (House of Commons Justice Committee, 2013). At the time, the Ministry of Justice said of the CIFC that 'we needed them' because their in-depth knowledge and experience of the area made them a strong ally and partner for the Ministry of Justice to secure government funding and roll out Corston's key recommendations. Given the nascent role and significance of the CIFC in the statutory provision and strategic development, Ministry of Justice funding was transferred to the Women's Divisionary Fund to provide start-up costs for women's community centres. In total, 24 grants were awarded, and 50 new women's centres were added to the diverse profile of community-based provision for criminalised women. Women's Breakout was established in 2011 as the umbrella organisation that oversaw the women's centres, supporting them in delivering services in ways that are 'sustainable' (National Audit Office, 2013). But it was not long after these funds were distributed that concerns began to emerge about the longevity of this annual funding programme and whether those services would receive the same funding the following year.

In 2010–11, funding powers and overarching responsibility for commissioning women's services were transferred to the National Management Offender Service (NOMS), which immediately laid out new rules and requirements for grant funding. For example, NOMS asserted that funding eligibility would be linked to *reduced reoffending* – that service providers had to evidence how their service-level activities reduced reoffending in order to secure future funding. This new funding – subject to conformity with these new eligibility criteria – was proffered after the original £15.6 million investment under the Ministry of Justice was reduced to a markedly smaller amount of £3.2 million (National Audit Office, 2013). The insistence that funding would only follow those women whose 'journey out of crime' could be statistically tracked effectively changed the focus of service providers from practices that can broadly be categorised as 'diversion away from prison' to those concerned with 'reducing reoffending'. The impact of this mission shift cannot be overemphasised: where centres had previously focused on early support with a view to preventing and diverting women from lawbreaking and the threat of custody, the new rules placed the onus on centres to reactively respond to women who had already been given a sentence or court order of some sort. This resulted in the decommissioning of some community-based services that catered to non-offending women whose needs were not explicitly aligned with a crime reduction strategy, but who nevertheless experienced the same structural neglect and marginalisation as convicted criminalised women. Service providers that previously catered to non-offending women had limited options under NOMS's new commissioning structures. Their options included (i) turning away women who did not have a conviction, (ii) subsidising this stream of work using other funding sources or (iii) severing their contractual relationship with NOMS.

Community-based services that continued to receive NOMS funding began concentrating more effort on developing administrative systems and practices to improve their evidence base on reduced reoffending, even though the production of such evidence is riddled with complications. For example, NOMS later conceded that the data collected from centres between 2009 and 2012 were not useful for understanding the effectiveness of these centres in reducing reoffending (National Audit Office, 2013). Nonetheless, service providers channelled a great deal of effort into these data gathering requirements to ensure funding security and eventually produced new systems of data administration to capture the efficiency of their organisation and evidence the positive 'outcomes' of their service-level activities (see Fox and Albertson, Chapter 2, this volume). This included but was not limited to evidencing 'value for money', 'partnership working' and providing figures for the number of women making positive progress against a list of needs such as 'skills and employment', 'drugs and alcohol', 'housing' and 'finance and benefits' (National Audit Office, 2013). Gathering this level of data is often highly technical and complex, and for some services it meant committing already stretched resources to delivering a daily service to women *and* administering complex bodies of data.

The reconfiguring of organisational practices to adhere to and survive in this neo-liberal market model raises fundamental questions about how these changes may have impacted on, or indeed weakened, pre-existing values, ethics and political commitments of those services most affected. In their report *Run Ragged*, Clinks (2014) captures the mood of community-based services that had to contend with these structural demands and concludes that services were forced to adjust in ways that drive them further from their underlying ethics and political principles. This assessment is consistent with Tomczak's (2014) study, which underlines the various ways in which structural demands and changes generated by neo-liberal penal reforms typically result in 'goal distortion', whereby voluntary sector agencies are forced to shift their attention away from campaigning and advocacy work. So, rather than mobilise on issues concerning women's imprisonment and criminalisation, the gender responsive policy framework facilitated a shift towards market-type activities that largely revolve around pursuing contracts and meeting contractual statutory requirements (Tomczak, 2014).

It is important to understand the gender responsive policy background, alongside present-day austerity machinations that have led to the privatisation of Probation Trusts and the diminishing profile of women's services. Even though the gender responsive reforms initially led to the expansion of service provision for criminalised women, as seen by a rise in community-based centres and related services available for women, those services have had to compete for and demonstrate their significance within the field, with a shrinking budget and with incongruent and inconsistent funding requirements. There is little doubt, therefore, that the gender responsive reform framework introduced women's services to a precarious policy environment, subsequently causing them to make organisational and ideological shifts that are in alignment with market-based operations and contractual funding models. This, we argue, has resulted in women's services attenuating or, at best, compromising the values and ethics that previously underpinned their 'specialist' approach to working with criminalised women.

Transforming Rehabilitation and the women's sector

If the women's voluntary sector was already beset with issues prior to 2013, the suite of austerity-driven reforms rolled out across the welfare and criminal justice sectors has further weakened their capacity and influence to reverse the growing concerns with the gender responsive policy framework. This decline can be attributed to two factors especially. Firstly, between 2010 and 2014, statutory funding for women's centres fell from £15 million to £3.8 million (National Audit Office, 2013). Secondly, the dominance of private sector CRCs facilitated the systematic dismantling of the system for delivering gender responsive services by withholding contracts and failing to fulfil commitments to commission women's specialist services that cater to criminalised women. This occurred at a time when women are disproportionately and negatively affected by austerity cuts, which has in turn increased the demand in service provision for women. But instead of responding by commissioning more women's services, CRCs were commissioning providers with no experience in supporting women, or cutting costs even further by keeping services for women 'in house' while outsourcing only the most basic provision, to the detriment of longstanding expert providers such as women's centres. In turn, the CRCs justify these strategies as reflecting the extremely tight returns, even financial losses, that they are incurring from their contract with the Ministry of Justice (Corcoran et al, 2019).

The second justification of the CRCs is that they are losing money, despite the fact that under TR, one could reasonably expect a significant increase in demand for services from the women's voluntary sector. This is because the Offender Rehabilitation Act (2014), under which aegis TR operates, made provisions for mandatory probationary supervision for all short-term *and* long-term prisoners, which brought an additional 50,000 people under probation supervision regimes. Prior to 2013, mandatory supervision was limited to people who served long-term sentences. During the consultation process on extending mandatory supervision to include short-term prisoners, penal reform organisations argued that mandatory supervision policies would disproportionately target women compared with men, because women are more likely to be given short-term sentences. Thus, the new rules would bring more women under the purview of criminal justice authorities and hold them in the criminal justice system for longer. Community supervision is a legally binding contract, where people must comply with the terms and conditions outlined in the probation licence agreement, and failure to comply can result in recall, that is, being sent back to custody without any court hearing or trial. Framed in this way, mandatory supervision can, at best, be described as a net-widening policy, obfuscated as a reformative and innovative programme.

Although the architects of TR proposed that mandatory supervision would help *more* people gain access to rehabilitation and reintegration services, there was always a substantial risk that the punitive and controlling aspects of the policy would predominate. This has come to pass in the form of an alarming 131 per cent rise in recall rates for women, compared with 22 per cent for men (House of Commons, 2019b). Preliminary evidence suggests that women are recalled for failing to 'attend probation appointments', for failing to 'keep in touch' and for 'failure to reside [at address agreed with probation]' (House of Commons, 2019b). Recall rates in England and Wales began to peak after the introduction of the Criminal Justice Act 2003 and now, since the introduction of the TR, they are rising further.

Alongside this sharp rise in women being recalled to custody, we are also seeing the fracturing of relationships previously formed with the specialist voluntary sector. As Burke and Collett (2016: 121) point out, organisational relations have become a 'battleground of antagonistic actions' in the new probation market economy because privatisation was always contested by the key agencies and actors involved, but was implemented by the pro-austerity Coalition government regardless. From the outset, the women's voluntary sector has been consumed with 'antagonistic actions', and emerging data from Clinks (2014), the Howard League for Penal Reform (2016) and the National Audit Office (2013) elucidate some of these issues (see Wong and Macmillan, Chapter 14, this volume). They reveal that some women's organisations have been both included and excluded, strategically, to suit prime contracts in bidding processes. For example, CRCs encouraged women's organisations to join consortiums in order to increase their funding opportunities, but then allocated funding to single organisations. At the level of service delivery, women's organisations commissioned by CRCs have been told to reduce their one-to-one work with their clients and instead increase more 'cost efficient' group work activities. Relatedly, in some cases organisations that did receive contracts for the CRCs have been obliged to exclude a cohort of women they previously provided a service to, because their new contractual requirements limited the client group they can work with. These contractual relations deteriorated further and reached their nadir when CRC lawyers inserted 'gagging' clauses to prevent some women's organisations from publicly disclosing how CRCs jeopardised their established advocacy work with criminalised women (Howard League for Penal Reform, 2016). When HM Inspectorate of Probation (2016) asked CRCs to provide them with the relevant data on the provision of funds to women's organisations, it noted that CRC managers could not offer any concrete information about these contracts, timescales or funding, or even provide data on the numbers of women being sent to women's centres.

These testimonies and the litany of complaints reveal how the privatisation of Probation Trusts has damaged the profile of women's specialist services and diminished the provision of support available for women. But the privatisation of probation did not occur overnight and was preceded by a creeping marketisation of the penal voluntary sector. As such, we see the gendered impacts of privatisation as a *continuation* of the struggles precipitated under the gender responsive policy framework, which marked a critical moment in the marketisation of women's voluntary organisations, encouraging them to compete with other voluntary services and prove 'better value' for money. Given the inherent struggles that marketisation brings – practical and ideological – we have also seen an organisational shift that seriously limits the capacity of those organisations to undertake advocacy and campaign work (see Corcoran et al, Chapter 12, this volume).

Not only is there a desperate lack of strategy concerning women in the criminal justice system, which would also attend to the diminishing profile of women's services, but any notion of a strategy appears to be left in the hands of private consortiums that have, manifestly, failed to cater to women's gender-specific needs in ways that prevent women from entering custody. In its recent Female Offender Strategy, the Ministry of Justice (2018: 24) announced the allocation of £1.5 million for the development of 'residential women's centres', to provide 'intensive residential support' for women who have served short-term custodial sentences. The strategy was welcomed by women's charities and advocacy groups, but only for the reason that it was a partial withdrawal on the controversial Prison Reform programme which involved the development of five 'community prisons' for women (Ministry of Justice, 2016). The watered down proposal to set up 'residential centres' is supposed to provide settled accommodation for economically marginalised women leaving custody, reduce the risk of homelessness and, directly linked to these experiences of abject poverty, prevent women from being recalled to custody (Ministry of Justice, 2018). But the strategy fails to identify mandatory supervision as a draconian and punitive policy that has brought significantly more women serving short-term sentences under the purview of criminal justice authorities; nor does it identify the litany of complaints exposing CRCs lack of provision of gender-specific services for women through the exclusion of women's organisations that provide those services. Disappointingly, the Female Offender strategy merely sits on top of existing net-widening policies and appears to support the dominance of CRCs in the probation market economy by giving them a central role in the development of residential centres. Apart from the identification of an obligatory 'women strategic lead' on each CRC, there was no clear indication of how CRCs would develop these 'residential centres' in ways that will 'benefit women who offend' (Ministry of Justice, 2018: 24). Adding to these concerns, the Ministry of Justice states that such a strategy could be 'linked to existing women's community service provision such as women's centres' (Ministry of Justice, 2018: 21), but again there was no statutory requirement, or at the very least any clear instruction, about the extent to which CRCs should involve women's community services.

There is deep concern brewing that the Female Offender Strategy lacks the clear vision 'that was so desperately needed by women affected by the CJS' (Booth et al, 2018: 432; Women in Prison, 2018). The depicting of economically marginalised women as 'productive citizens' suggests that the strategy continues to ignore the systemic oppression that contributes to people coming into contact with the criminal justice system in the first place and fails to acknowledge that the least harmful approach might be to not send vulnerable people to prison, or expect them to complete supervision orders. We concur with Booth et al (2018) that this strategy is 'history repeating itself': it espouses the same gender responsive – and 'neo-liberal-citizen' – ideologies that ignore the structural context affecting criminalised women and fails to indicate any attempt to reverse the harms facing women in the criminal justice system. As the independent charity INQUEST (2018: 4) emphatically reminds us, the situation facing women in the criminal justice system 'has never felt so desperate'.

Conclusion: towards a radical (re)organisation

It is striking that the continuing crisis in conditions for women in the criminal justice system – such as the 131 per cent rise in recall rates and unprecedented spike in deaths in custody (INQUEST, 2018) – occurred in the era of gender responsive penal reforms. While we acknowledge the meaningful support and immeasurable impact women's services have upon the lives of those experiencing systemic neglect, we argue that the 'gender responsive reform programme' proved amenable to the language of innovation in ways which facilitated the alignment of the women's voluntary services with free market ideology. In turn, this adversely exposed women's voluntary services to further structural inequalities in the service provider landscape. Seen against this backdrop, the privatisation of Probation Trusts in England and Wales amplified the marginality facing women's organisations. CRCs repeatedly failed to offer contracts to these established services, undermined the quality of their service provision and effectively curbed their capacity to reach criminalised women.

On the one hand, the advancement of the neo-liberal gender responsive reform programme raised the strategic profile of the women's voluntary sector by relying heavily upon and increasing the number of community-based services. On the other hand, the precarious funding environment and inconsistent contractual requirements that arrived with this reform programme generated operational difficulties and some services were ideologically opposed to the competitive shift that this programme initiated. In essence, the gender responsive reform programme threatened the political ethics and values that informed their unique approach to working with women and underpinned their *raison d'être*. This weakening of values may reflect what other scholars have referred to as 'co-option, or absorption' (Baldry et al, 2015: 169), which can be understood as 'a way of diverting or quietening oppositional struggle and activism' (Baldry et al, 2015: 173).

But the voluntary sector's relationship with the state is never fixed and constantly evolves. We believe that the women's voluntary sector is at a critical juncture to turn around their fate. Already coined as 'TR2', the former Justice Minister, David Gauke, revealed plans to re-nationalise the portion of the probation sector that was previously privatised under the ORA. Probation services will be brought back under the purview of the National Probation Service (a public authority) and commissioning structures will return to national and regional government. This renationalisation may at first appear as good news, but for the women's voluntary sector and for criminalised women too, this will not necessarily reverse the damage already done. The renationalisation of Probation Trusts in England and Wales will involve more bureaucratic upheaval, new contractual requirements and more organisational adjustments, necessary to capture grant funding under the forthcoming regime. And CRCs will continue to play a role in this restructuring. Given the problems we have outlined, perhaps this is a critical juncture for the women's voluntary sector to reflect on the losses and gains of their entanglement with the neo-liberal state and creeping marketisation of service provision, and to contemplate a radical (re)organisation of their relationship with the state and how centrally they are aligned with criminal justice practices.

References

Baldry, E., Carlton, B. and Cunneen, C. (2015) 'Abolitionism and the paradox of penal reform in Australia: indigenous women, colonial patriarchy, and co-option', *Social Justice*, 41(3): 168–89.

Bloom, B., Owen, B. and Covington, S. (2004) 'Women offenders and the gendered effects of public policy (1)', *Review of Policy Research*, 21(1): 31–48.

Booth, N., Masson, I. and Baldwin, L. (2018) 'Promises, promises: can the female offender strategy deliver?', *Probation Journal*, 65(4): 429–38.

Burke, L. and Collett, S. (2016) 'Transforming Rehabilitation: organizational bifurcation and the end of probation as we knew it?', *Probation Journal*, 63(2): 120–35.

Clinks (2014) *Run Ragged: The Current Experience of Projects Providing Community Based Female Offender Support Services*, London: Clinks, available from: https://www.clinks.org/sites/default/files/2018-11/Run%20Ragged%20Interim%20Report%20February%202014_0.pdf [accessed 5 November 2019].

Cooper. V. and Whyte. D. (2017) 'Introduction', in V. Cooper and D. Whyte (eds) *The Violence of Austerity*, London: Pluto Press, pp 1–34.

Corcoran, M.S. (2011) 'After Corston, the rehabilitation revolution?' *Criminal Justice Matters*, 85(1): 26–7.

Corcoran, M.S., Maguire, M. and Williams, K. (2019) 'Alice in Wonderland: voluntary sector organisations' experiences of Transforming Rehabilitation', *Probation Journal*, 66 (1): 96–112.

English Collective of Prostitutes (2016) *Decriminalisation of Prostitution: The Evidence*, London: ECP, available from: http://prostitutescollective.net/wp-content/uploads/2017/01/Online-Symposium-Report.pdf [accessed 5 November 2019].

Haney, L. (2010) *Offending Women: Power, Punishment, and the Regulation of Desire*, Berkeley: University of California Press.

Hannah-Moffat, K. (2001) *Punishment in Disguise: Penal Governance and Federal Imprisonment of Women in Canada*, Toronto: University of Toronto Press.

HM Inspectorate of Probation (2016) *A Thematic Inspection of the Provision and Quality of Services in the Community for Women Who Offend*, London: HMIP, available from: https://www.justiceinspectorates.gov.uk/hmiprobation/wp-content/uploads/sites/5/2016/09/A-thematic-inspection-of-the-provision-and-quality-of-services-in-the-community-for-women-who-offend.pdf [accessed 5 November 2019].

Home Office (2007) *The Corston Report: The Need for a Distinct, Radically Different, Visibly-Led, Strategic, Proportionate, Holistic, Woman-Centred, Integrated Approach*, London: Home Office, available from: https://webarchive.nationalarchives.gov.uk/20130206102659/http:/www.justice.gov.uk/publications/docs/corston-report-march-2007.pdf [accessed 5 November 2019].

House of Commons (2019a) *Households in Temporary Accommodation (England), Briefing Paper, No. 02110,* London: House of Commons.

House of Commons (2019b) *Recall of Women to Prisons, Debate Pack, No. CDP-2019-0038,* London: House of Commons.

House of Commons Justice Committee (2013) *Women Offenders: After the Corston Report. Second Report of Session 2013–14,* London: The Stationery Office.

Howard League for Penal Reform (2016) *Is This the End of Women's Centres?* London: HLPR, available from: https://howardleague.org/wp-content/uploads/2016/11/Is-it-the-end-of-womens-centres.pdf [accessed 5 November 2019].

Imkaan (2016) *Capital Losses: The State of Specialist BME Ending Violence against Women and Girls Sector in London,* London: Imkaan, available from: https://www.trustforlondon.org.uk/publications/capital-losses-state-specialist-bme-ending-violence-against-women-and-girls-sector-london/ [accessed 5 November 2019].

INQUEST (2018) *Still Dying on the Inside: Examining Deaths in Women's Prisons,* London: INQUEST, available from: https://tbinternet.ohchr.org/Treaties/CEDAW/Shared%20Documents/GBR/INT_CEDAW_ICO_GBR_31671_E.pdf [accessed 5 November 2019].

Ministry of Justice (2016) *Prison Safety and Reform,* London: Ministry of Justice, available from: https://assets.publishing.service.gov.uk/government/uploads/system/uploads/attachment_data/file/565014/cm-9350-prison-safety-and-reform-_web_.pdf [accessed 5 November 2019].

Ministry of Justice (2018). *Female Offender Strategy,* London: Ministry of Justice, available from: https://assets.publishing.service.gov.uk/government/uploads/system/uploads/attachment_data/file/719819/female-offender-strategy.pdf [accessed 5 November 2019].

National Audit Office (2013) *Funding of Women's Centres in the Community,* London: National Audit Office, available from: https://www.nao.org.uk/wp-content/uploads/2013/05/Funding-of-Womens-Centres-in-the-Community.pdf [accessed 5 November 2019].

Pollack, S. (2007) '"I'm just not good in relationships": Victimization discourses and the gendered regulation of criminalized women', *Feminist Criminology,* 2(2): 158–74.

Russell, E. and Carlton, B. (2013) 'Pathways, race and gender responsive reform: Through an abolitionist lens', *Theoretical Criminology,* 17(4): 474–92.

Stubbs, J. and Baldry, E. (2018) 'In pursuit of fundamental change within the Australian penal landscape: taking inspiration from the Corston Report', in L. Moore, P. Scraton and A. Wahidin (eds) *Women's Imprisonment and the Case for Abolition: Critical Reflections on Corston Ten Years On*, Oxford: Routledge, pp 129–49.

Tomczak, P.J. (2014) 'The penal voluntary sector in England and Wales: beyond neoliberalism?' *Criminology & Criminal Justice*, 14(4): 470–86.

Women in Prison (2018) 'Mass Lobby of Parliament', 19 December, available from: https://www.womeninprison.org.uk/news-and-campaigns.php?s=2018-12-19-mass-lobby-of-parliament [accessed 5 November 2019].

Women's Budget Group (2018) *The Impact of Austerity on Women in the UK*, London: Women's Budget Group, available from: https://www.ohchr.org/Documents/Issues/Development/IEDebt/WomenAusterity/WBG.pdf [accessed 5 November 2019].

14

Surviving the revolution? The voluntary sector under Transforming Rehabilitation in England and Wales

Kevin Wong and Rob Macmillan

Introduction

This chapter examines the role and fortunes of the voluntary sector (VS) in the field of offender resettlement and rehabilitation between 2014 and 2019 in England and Wales. During this period, the central government's Transforming Rehabilitation (TR) reforms saw the partial privatisation of probation services and the promise of an enlarged role for the VS (Ministry of Justice, 2013a). While TR dominated the discourse around VS commissioning it was not the only 'game in town'. The vast majority of VS agencies providing rehabilitation services *were not* commissioned through the new Community Rehabilitation Companies (CRCs) or National Probation Service (NPS) which formed the institutional structure of TR (Clinks, 2018a). Instead, their funders were primarily charitable trusts and local public bodies such as local authorities and police and crime commissioners. These arrangements have been largely overlooked, drowned out by the preoccupation with TR, its condemnation and the post-TR partial 'renationalisation' of probation services (Ministry of Justice, 2019a).

By examining how the VS and other agencies shaped the field of offender rehabilitation and resettlement, this chapter aims to redress this oversight. We revisit the sector's generally negative experience of, and seemingly marginal role within, the top-down government-driven TR commissioning processes between 2014 and 2019. We then contrast this with two case studies which tell a more encouraging story, shining a light on alternative commissioning processes by a charitable trust and by local public bodies. We demonstrate how VS organisations themselves *acted* to shape the field. We illustrate how local public bodies, through regional English devolution, wrested control from central government and shaped their own regional rehabilitation market. In doing this we highlight valuable lessons for what makes for effective commissioning. We conclude by advocating the adoption of a market stewardship approach, which better serves the interests of all stakeholders, but in particular the intended market beneficiaries – offenders and the wider society itself.

The 'voluntary sector' and 'market making' in criminal justice

Our analysis is informed by insights from field theory (Fligstein and McAdam, 2012). The starting assumption is that more or less organised groups of actors convene around common but contested areas of interests – fields – in which they variously compete and combine to pursue particular causes and secure and advance their positions. The rehabilitation of offenders might usefully be seen as one such field. Here, individuals and organisations across different sectors (such as government departments, local authorities, other public institutions, private companies, charitable and other funders, voluntary organisations and campaigning groups) engage in contrasting strategies to define its core intentions and priorities, describe how it works and should work (for example, as a 'market'), and identify who is involved, as well as what powers and resources they put to use. Field theory emphasises twin struggles over resources and meaning, combining material concerns (that is 'who gets what and how, compared with others') with contested work to frame field understandings and developments.

Understanding the role of the VS in the field of criminal justice has been the subject of growing commentary in recent years (Hucklesby and Corcoran, 2016). The sector involves considerable heterogeneity, comprising very large professionalised VS organisations with much smaller, less formally structured organisations often operating at community level, as well as newer organisations describing themselves as social enterprises (Macmillan, 2016). Many VS organisations work simultaneously in criminal justice and other fields, such as housing or substance misuse, rather than solely with offenders or victims of crime. Research on the 'state of the sector' distinguishes a core of 'specialist' VS organisations whose main purpose is working within criminal justice, and a periphery of non-specialist VS organisations who work in criminal justice and sometimes with offenders, but this is not their main purpose (Clinks, 2018b).

In the last 30 years, developments in criminal justice have increasingly been framed in the language of 'markets' and 'marketisation'. Governments and others have sought to introduce formalised competitive market processes and to enhance the role of private firms and VS organisations in what had otherwise become a field dominated by the public sector. In the terms of field theory, this has involved an effort to recast the field as a criminal justice market, or more accurately a set of markets, such as the market for rehabilitation services. Such efforts rarely go uncontested, both in practice and in academic analysis. Here 'marketisation' is linked to the 'privatisation' of public services facilitated through a wider hegemonic neo-liberal approach to public management (Corcoran, 2011), which may have reached its ultimate apotheosis under TR. Yet commentary in such terms runs a considerable risk of oversimplification, reducing a complex, differentiated and dynamic set of arrangements to a single broad-sweeping trend (Tomczak, 2017). To avoid these pitfalls, we seek to examine the voluntary sector's experience in recent years through an alternative field-oriented frame of 'market making', which highlights the efforts by different actors, including state institutions, to shape an emerging 'market' (in rehabilitation services) to secure or advance their interests (Fligstein, 2001). We suggest that this better reflects a more nuanced and varied set of commissioning arrangements which operated between 2014 and 2019, of which the 'marketisation' via TR was just one part.

In the early 2010s, the VS in criminal justice was preoccupied by uncertainty around the impact of the 2008 financial crash and its translation into a deficit reduction austerity programme by the Conservative-led Coalition government formed in 2010. The Ministry of Justice's budget was earmarked for severe cuts, alongside other central government departments and local authorities. VS surveys at the time reflect the anxieties of the situation. They refer to criminal justice VS organisations continuing to 'soldier on in difficult circumstances' (Clinks, 2013: 5), mostly maintaining or even expanding services, but also subsidising services by using reserves, making redundancies, putting more effort into generating income and recruiting more volunteers as a way of mitigating funding reductions for paid staff. Organisations reported their struggle to meet increasing and more complex needs facing service users, as welfare reform policies began to take effect and other services became more targeted or were withdrawn (Clinks, 2013, 2015). Concern also focused on how to understand and take part in the Coalition government's criminal justice policy priorities. Interest in outcome-based commissioning, including social investment, payment by results (PbR) and Social Impact Bonds, was intensifying. VS surveys highlighted the concern that commissioning processes, including the fashion for PbR, were working to the advantage of larger VS organisations (and private firms) who were in a stronger position to bear the financial risks. Smaller and medium sized VS organisations feared being squeezed out. At the same time, Conservative politicians were discussing the content of a proposed 'rehabilitation revolution' to shake up probation services in order to reduce reoffending rates. In 2014–15, at the advent of what can be regarded as a seismic change in the criminal justice field, the sector's attention and resources were already being absorbed by attempts to engage with the 'changing goalposts' of the new system – as one survey respondent noted:

> It's taken a lot of energy and resources to keep on top of a frequently changing and complicated agenda. (Clinks, 2015: 28)

The voluntary sector's experience of TR

Transforming Rehabilitation was a flagship public services reform programme for the 2010–15 Conservative-led Coalition government in the UK. It involved the partial privatisation of the public probation service. The existing institutional configuration of 35 local public sector Probation Trusts was dismantled (in June 2014), replaced by a smaller single public National Probation Service and contracts let to 21 new private sector-led Community Rehabilitation Companies. The former would be responsible for ex-offenders categorised as 'high risk' of harm, while the latter would cover those deemed low to medium risk of harm.

The idea of a 'rehabilitation revolution' to reduce offending had been discussed in Conservative Party policy circles well before the 2010 General Election (Conservative Party, 2008). Underpinned by the Coalition government's commitment to 'open public services' involving competition and a diverse market of public service providers (HM Government, 2011), policy development intensified from September 2012 when Chris Grayling became Justice Secretary. Up to this point it was envisaged that Probation Trusts would act as local commissioning bodies. But a January 2013 consultation paper proposed instead a centralised market model of commissioned services, which

> supports a wide range of lead providers, and partnerships which bring in the particular skills of local and specialist

organisations ... We are keen to see partnerships between VCS organisations, or private and VCS providers, coming forward to compete for contracts. (Ministry of Justice, 2013a: 16)

A final strategy published in May 2013 confirmed that Probation Trusts would be abolished, and a competition would be held for new contracts to begin in 2015 (Ministry of Justice 2013b).

Ministerial speeches and government documents throughout this time spoke highly of the role VS organisations could play in the new system. In July 2013, for example, the Secretary of State argued that

[t]here is no question of us paying only lip-service to the voluntary and community sector as we transform rehabilitation. I am determined to ensure these organisations are right at the heart of our approach, delivering it on the ground. (Centre for Social Justice, 2013)

The announcement of preferred bidders for the 21 CRC contracts noted that

around 75% of the 300 subcontractors named in the successful bids are voluntary sector or mutual organisations, putting them at the frontline of offender rehabilitation. (Ministry of Justice, 2014)

Five years on from this intense institutional shake-up, the relentlessly optimistic talk of promise and potential for the voluntary sector and for the new system looks rather hollow. TR has been severely criticised, reoffending rates have not changed significantly and the CRC contracts were foreshortened after an earlier bailout. In March 2019 the Chief Inspector of Probation reported that TR's probation model was 'irredeemably flawed' for its attempt to render professional probation work into a set of contract-specified transactions (HMI Probation, 2019: 3). Following an earlier consultation, the Ministry of Justice finally announced the end of TR in May 2019 (Ministry of Justice, 2018, 2019a, 2019b).

An earlier report from the Probation Inspectorate indicated that despite high expectations, the voluntary sector is 'less involved than ever in probation services, despite its best efforts' (HMI Probation, 2018: 5). Echoing this, parliamentary committees claimed that 'the extent of involvement of the third sector in delivering probations services has been woeful' (HC Public Accounts Committee, 2018: 6), and that

> the Government have failed to open up the probation market, a key aim of the then Government when they introduced the TR reforms. (HC Justice Committee, 2018: 4)

The National Audit Office referred to an 'immature' market, with still unrealised ambitions for greater VS involvement in probation, noting that only 159 VS organisations were providing services directly to CRCs as at October 2018, representing around 11 per cent of voluntary organisations working in the criminal justice sector (National Audit Office, 2019: 18).

Research led by Clinks during the first four years of TR underpinned these arguments (Clinks, 2018a).[1] Three cross-sectional surveys of criminal justice voluntary organisations between 2015 and 2017 suggested an increasingly pessimistic picture of VS engagement with TR. The final survey, involving 132 respondents, indicated four main findings. Firstly, the level of involvement in TR was low: only 35 per cent of 132 respondents were contracted to provide services by CRCs, and most of these were larger organisations. Smaller organisations were far less likely to have been able to engage in TR, even where they wanted to and despite official encouragement. The sense of frustration was palpable across the survey:

> We invested huge amounts of time engaging with TR over two years but, in spite of being told we would be contracted, eventually we're not. (Clinks, 2018a: 22)

Secondly, there were severe doubts about the sustainability of voluntary sector involvement in TR. Half of all respondents thought the changes brought by TR had a negative or very negative impact on their organisation, compared with less than one quarter seeing a positive impact. Only half of voluntary organisations funded to deliver services through CRCs considered the terms agreed to be sustainable. And

---

[1] The research – 'TrackTR' – was undertaken by a partnership of Clinks, the National Council for Voluntary Organisations (NCVO), the Third Sector Research Centre (TSRC) at the University of Birmingham, the Centre for Regional Economic and Social Research (CRESR) at Sheffield Hallam University and the Centre for Voluntary Sector Leadership (CVSL) at Open University.

to support TR services, 35 per cent of respondents had to subsidise services with their own charitable reserves, and 37 per cent had to use funding from other sources. Moreover, the probation system under TR seemed to rely on the work of the VS, but without paying for it: for example, two thirds of the VS organisations operating outside the TR system received referrals from CRCs without payment. Given the hype of VS involvement in TR prior to its implementation, this survey finding underlines the gap between government rhetoric and reality on the ground.

Thirdly, respondents reported that TR had had a negative effect on their services, service users and relationships with other organisations. Over time they had moved from a reserved judgement – 'too early to tell' – in earlier stages of the research, to reaching a more damning indictment about the impact of TR. Three fifths (59 per cent) saw a negative or very negative impact on their service users of the changes brought about by TR. The main concern focused on the lack of resources to undertake quality rehabilitation work given expected volume targets. One respondent noted that their focus had 'shifted from client facing one-to-one support to delivering [one to many] workshops and surgeries so that we can generate the volumes required', while another reported having 'to move away from a preferred model of high quality, longer term mentoring, to short interventions which are of limited value'. Only 17 per cent of respondents thought that partnerships with statutory bodies had improved since TR, compared with 43 per cent who thought they had worsened. Similarly, 18 per cent thought that partnerships with other voluntary organisations had improved, compared with 37 per cent who thought they had worsened.

Fourthly, the research highlights the possibility of a wider impact of TR on the voluntary sector criminal justice field, over and above its direct effects on the relatively few organisations involved in CRC supply chains or those on the receiving end of unpaid referrals. The survey revealed signs of some troubling unintended consequences of the introduction of TR. For example, numerous instances were cited of confusion among other funders of voluntary organisations in criminal justice about their role in the wake of TR. There were reports of funders looking to withdraw their support on the grounds that TR would now be available to fund the work instead, and a third of respondents indicated that TR had decreased their ability to access other sources of funding.

In offering suggestions for how the system could be reformed and improved, many respondents were dismissive of the changes introduced by TR. For one respondent, TR had privileged box ticking over the work of people committed to rehabilitation:

> If I could, I would go back to what we had before, but that is probably not practicable. There is, however, an urgent need for a rehabilitation regime which is designed by people who understand the process of reforming offenders rather than budget management. (Clinks, 2018a: 22)

'Same as it ever was'

Inevitably much of the debate around market making within the field of VS rehabilitation services and during the implementation of TR has focused on the commissioning of VS organisations by CRCs and the NPS.[2] This has concentrated on long held concerns about responsibility for core public services, and the effect of such funding on the independence and distinctiveness of the sector (Macmillan, 2016; Clinks, 2018a). What appears to have been overlooked is an alternative story – that of the market making role of charitable trusts and local public bodies in the field, that is 'traditional' VS funding bodies which supported VS rehabilitation provision prior to and during TR, and which will almost certainly continue to do so after TR. As well as providing additional resources in the field, these bodies also play a strategic role in shaping commissioning relationships and organising local markets in different ways. As a result, local voluntary organisations find alternative positions and pathways for delivering services, compared with the rigid supply chains associated with TR. Market making thus involves steering resources to create specific local configurations of actors involved in criminal justice, but also the use of wider connections and legitimacy to influence the context of discussion about the nature, purpose and dynamics of the field, for example what 'success' looks like, and the value of plural commissioning arrangements. To illustrate the significance of these bodies as market making actors within criminal justice, the Clinks 2018 State of the Sector survey found that in 2015–16 specialist criminal justice VS organisations received the same level of funding from local government as from central government. In the same year specialist criminal justice VS organisations with an income of between £100,000 and £500,000 received a third of their income

---

[2] Eno, B., Frantz, C., Byrne, D., Harrison, J., Weymouth, T. (1982) *Once in a lifetime*, Warner/Chappell Music, Inc, Universal Music Publishing Group.

from 'voluntary sources', which includes grants from charitable trusts (Clinks, 2018b). The same survey found that during 2015–16 non-specialist criminal justice VS organisations received more funding from local government than from central government (Clinks, 2018b). Additionally, while acknowledging the limitations of sample size and representativeness, the 'TrackTR' research found that 69 per cent of VS organisations outside of the CRC and NPS supply chains were funded by charitable trusts and foundations (including the Big Lottery Fund) to undertake their resettlement and rehabilitation work (Clinks, 2018a). In this section we detail two case studies which illustrate how, firstly, charitable grant making bodies, and then secondly, local public bodies, interacted with a segment of the market in VS rehabilitation provision during the TR period. We suggest that they provide good examples of the market shaping possibilities of arrangements with these types of funders.

Case study 1: Charitable trusts

The Transition to Adulthood (T2A) Pathway Programme was commissioned by the Barrow Cadbury Trust (BCT) in 2013 during the consultation period for the then TR reforms (Wong et al, 2017). BCT had a long history of supporting VS organisations to bring about 'socially just change' and prior to 2013 had already funded initiatives to generate evidence and influence policy around developing a distinctive approach to young adults (aged 16–24) in the criminal justice system (BCT, 2019). This included supporting the T2A Alliance – a coalition of VS and other partners committed to lobbying for policy and legislative changes with potential market impacts. The T2A Pathway Programme was commissioned through open competition – a market-based exercise aimed at garnering a range of project ideas for interventions from the VS at each point within the criminal justice system which made up the T2A Pathway (T2A Alliance, 2013). Six projects led by VS organisations were selected and received grant funding between 2014 and 2016 to develop and deliver services in six sites in England to young adults who had committed offences or were at risk of committing offences (Wong et al, 2017). The services they provided and how they delivered them arguably typified the distinctive nature of VS provision confidently defined by the sector's advocates as 'person centred interventions deeply embedded in the appropriate social and local context with significant points of synthesis with desistance theory' (Martin et al, 2016: 32). The evaluation of the T2A programme found that the relationship between BCT and the VS organisations was an important factor in the development and delivery of the T2A services (Wong et al, 2017). The funding conditions enabled the VS organisations to exhibit the distinctive features of VS rehabilitation provision: they were services which users voluntarily opted into; they were open ended, that is service user access was not time limited; and they were providing holistic support to address criminogenic and non-criminogenic needs (Wong, 2018). The programme evaluation found that BCT enabled the VSOs to develop their services in

> a safe environment which was not bound by meeting specific delivery targets ... [BCT] were understanding about the differences between the projected and actual numbers of service users which the projects worked with and the reasons for this. (Wong et al, 2017: 20)

The evaluation concluded that throughout the programme the commissioners maintained that the quality of the service provided was more important than meeting the projected number of service users (Wong et al, 2017). Such accommodation by a commissioner is perhaps rare and marked out the relationship between funder and VS provider as being more collaborative than other commissioning arrangements. This also extended to the field shaping role of BCT, supporting the VS providers by attending meetings with local agencies, giving the organisations credibility with their partners with a view to enabling them to secure succession funding for the T2A services.

The benefit of this relationship, however, was not one-sided, since the VS organisations also furthered the social change aims of BCT. At a national level, this occurred by directly providing evidence to the Justice Committee inquiry into young adults and the criminal justice system (HC Justice Committee, 2016) and the T2A Alliance (Wong et al, 2017). At a local level, the market shaping role of the VS organisations themselves arose operationally, making a case locally for treating young adults as a cohort with particular needs, through the age specificity of their target service users and their engagement with partner agencies.

Case study 2: Local public commissioning and devolution

In parallel with TR, from 2014 English local government devolution unfolded with the promise of limited justice devolution in some areas (Sandford, 2016). Of all the devolution deals negotiated between 2014 and 2016, the Greater Manchester (GM) arrangements were arguably the most comprehensive. The GM arrangements provide a second case study which explores the role of local public bodies as actors within the field of local rehabilitation services and local government devolution settlements as a contextual factor within this. Again, we suggest that this illustrates the role that local public bodies played and can play. We also examine what difference, if any, devolution made in this case, while noting that this may not be representative of other settlements. We focus on the commissioning of one particular service, the GM whole system approach (WSA) for women offenders. This was one of the more high-profile justice initiatives commenced in 2014, established as part of the preparatory arrangements in the run-up to the formal devolution arrangements across GM. Funded by the Cheshire and Greater Manchester Community Rehabilitation Company (CGM CRC), NHS England and the Financial Incentive Model (FIM), a PbR reward for a reduction in demand on the criminal justice system (see Wong et al, 2015), the WSA aimed to embed gender responsive support for women. This was one instance in which the TR-framed commissioning model (embodied by the CRC for GM) was sidestepped and harnessed to a local commissioning framework led by the GM combined authority. In this case the CRC was merely a co-funder rather than the commissioner. It is worth nothing also the GM combined authority's commissioning approach: The intention was to commission a standard level of provision across GM, but through nine individual service lots (one each for eight individual GM local authorities, and the ninth covering two authorities), rather than from a single provider with responsibility for delivering services across all ten GM local authorities. Within this arrangement the market shaping intentions of the public authority were clear. Firstly, they aimed to redress the previously patchy provision of VS rehabilitation services for women offenders across GM – some local authorities had such a service, others did not. Secondly, they aimed to retain the existing providers while attracting new market entrants to areas with no prior provision. Thirdly, they were keen to learn from a Justice Reinvestment pilot (Wong et al, 2015),[3] and implement a standard service model which would 'create efficiencies by transforming services at the point of arrest, sentence and release' (Kinsella et al, 2018).

---

[3] Justice Reinvestment seeks to reduce the cost of crime in the most efficient way possible. It involves local agencies working together to reduce the drivers of criminal justice costs through the analysis of criminal justice data, mapping of interventions, use of evidence and identification of cost-effective interventions (Fox et al, 2013).

The nine successful VS organisations were a combination of existing incumbent providers of women's services in some local authorities and new market entrants in others (Kinsella et al, 2018). As actors within this managed market, the existing women's services could have chosen to expand and tender for services outside their existing operational areas to areas with no existing provision – but decided not to. This appeared to reflect an informal pact between the existing providers to bid for provision solely within their existing areas, putting a limit on each organisation's expansion. It is unclear if this was due to their perception that they had limited capacity/capability to expand and/or because of a principled decision that they did not wish to compete with other VS agencies.

Subsequently, the public authority has maintained an overview of the services with a view to maintaining the integrity of the model but also stability of provision and through the Justice and Rehabilitation Executive, a strategic body accountable to the GM Combined Authority (Kinsella et al, 2018). This in part has aided the development of an internal alliance between the VS organisations to secure the long-term sustainability of the rehabilitation provision for women in GM. They have since developed this into a public facing body in its own right – the Greater Manchester Women's Services Alliance. This has enabled market shaping and market protective benefits, including the sharing of best practice, support, standardised reporting requirements and enhanced referral pathways between centres (Kinsella et al, 2018). Additionally, it has ensured a minimum standard of service delivery for women across GM, notwithstanding differences in the VS organisations' delivery models, and access to further funding as an alliance (Kinsella et al, 2018).

An uncertain future?

In 2019, the partial renationalisation of probation services in England and Wales was announced by the then Justice Minister David Gauke (Ministry of Justice, 2019a). This inevitably prompted questions as to how the proposed 11 new English NPS regions would work, and which voluntary and private sector providers would bid to become their 'innovation partners' (Webster, 2019).[4] Irrespective of which (and/or if any) VS organisations become partners once the dust has settled on these new arrangements, the VS will continue to be commissioned by other parts of government, charitable trusts and local public bodies

---

[4] Later in 2019 the Ministry of Justice amended this label to 'delivery partners'.

to provide rehabilitation services. In this final section we reflect on the learning from the 'TR era', and how this can be applied by the various actors involved in the future commissioning of these services. We have highlighted how the field of rehabilitation services has been organised and understood in different ways through the market shaping effort of different actors. Here we set these within the context of a 'market stewardship' approach to public service markets (Gash et al, 2013). We highlight two themes which stand out from the VS experience of commissioning during TR: the role that commissioners can play in enabling VS engagement in markets, and VS agency in influencing the market(s) in which they operate.

In this chapter we have discussed three examples of public service markets which operated during the TR era. The first is the top-down approach of TR itself, where central government set the market rules for VS engagement in bidding to run CRCs, which effectively excluded the VS from being the lead bidders. Once the CRCs were contracted, the government adopted a hands-off approach, leaving CRCs and the NPS to commission (or not) specialist VS services to support their offender supervision work. The second example is the T2A Pathway Programme, an initially open competition process (solely) for the VS where the market rules again were set by the commissioner – the Barrow Cadbury Trust. But in contrast to TR, BCT adopted a collaborative approach following the selection of providers, helping them to shape and influence the local markets within which their projects were located while also drawing on their testimony to advocate for and influence the rehabilitative services market(s) for young adults at a national level. The third example is the role of local public bodies in GM in shaping the market for VS rehabilitative services for women with convictions. They set the framework for the market by prescribing the whole system approach delivery model and then managed the market to support existing VS providers operating within their existing geographic areas while encouraging new VS entrants. Once all the individual services were commissioned (operating the WSA), the public bodies set up structures which provided a route for the providers to engage with the strategic and policy making structures within GM. This not only enabled them to shape their local market(s), but also allowed the public bodies to have oversight of the services delivered by the providers.

It is possible to discern within these three arrangements variations of a 'market stewardship' approach to public service markets, defined by Gash and colleagues (2013: 19) as the role of government, but which in our view can be applied more broadly to any funder or commissioner where market mechanisms play a central role. In Table 14.1 we have set out our summary assessment of the extent to which the three TR-era examples demonstrate each of the four elements of market stewardship proposed by Gash et al (2013), as applied to VS rehabilitation services.

Assessed against the elements of market stewardship in relation to the VS in TR, the government as commissioner adopted a laissez-faire approach to market stewardship. It was a key actor in the field in setting the basic parameters of TR, but then abdicated responsibility for monitoring the market, leaving this to the VS themselves (Clinks, 2018a) and public service inspection bodies (HMI Probation, 2019; National Audit Office, 2019). It failed to engage with VS organisations and their users during TR and likewise failed to adjust the rules of the market to meet the promise of enlarged VS involvement in TR rehabilitation provision.

In contrast, the Barrow Cadbury Trust adopted two parallel market stewardship roles. One was in relation to the commissioning and management of the T2A Pathway Programme itself, where BCT

Table 14.1: Elements of effective market stewardship

Elements of effective market stewardship	TR	T2A Pathway Programme	WSA for women offenders
Engaging closely with users, provider organisations and other interested parties across the system to understand needs, objectives and enablers of successful delivery	Limited	Occurred prior to, during and after the programme	Occurred prior to the programme and continues to date
Setting the 'rules of the game' allowing providers and users to respond to the incentives this creates	Occurred at the commencement of TR	Occurred prior to and during the programme	Occurred prior to the programme and continues to date
Monitoring market development and how providers are responding to the rules, and the actions of other providers	Limited to CRC and NPS first tier providers	Occurred during the programme	Occurred prior to the programme and continues to date
Adjusting the rules to steer the system (much of which is beyond their immediate control) to achieve their high-level aims	None in relation to the VS	Occurred within the programme	Occurred prior to the programme and continues to date

adopted a responsive approach to the VS providers, engaging with them and their service users, flexing the 'rules of the market' to enable and support service delivery (Wong et al, 2017). The other, wider market stewardship role of BCT can be seen through influencing the local rehabilitation services markets within which the T2A projects were located and nationally via their input to the Justice Committee Inquiry on young adult offenders (Justice Committee, 2016), as well as through BCT's support for the T2A Alliance – lobbying for a distinct criminal justice approach to supporting and managing young adult offenders (Wong et al, 2017).

Illustrating what could be considered to be a more traditional interventionist role for public bodies, the commissioning and oversight of the WSA for women with convictions demonstrated the potential for local public bodies to co-opt TR (via the Cheshire and Greater Manchester CRC) into a regional agenda for the provision of women's rehabilitation services. In particular, this involved setting the market rules to preserve the role of existing VS providers while also encouraging new entrants where there were gaps in services. The role then involved continuing to monitor and manage this through regional strategic, policy making and commissioning structures established through the regional combined authority.

The idea that the VS in TR was largely squeezed, exploited or ignored (Clinks, 2018a) certainly has some resonance. But it may overlook instances of VS efficacy in acting where possible to shape public service markets to their advantage. It has not been possible to assess the full extent of that influence here but it is an important topic for future research. At a national level during the TR era, the 'TrackTR' work of Clinks (2018a) highlighted the problems of VS engagement with TR while also bearing witness to the other public service rehabilitation markets that the VS were involved in and through which they were being funded. Through the T2A Pathway Programme and the WSA for women with convictions, we have highlighted examples of VSOs taking proactive steps in shaping markets with other actors. The T2A VSOs advocated for a distinct young adult approach with their local public, private and VS partners and, facilitated by their commissioner the Barrow Cadbury Trust, showcased their services to national policy makers including the Justice Committee (Wong et al, 2017). The voluntary sector providers of women's services in Greater Manchester collaborated as the Women's Services Alliance and secured funding as a coalition for cross-service interventions, while also having a 'seat at the table' engaging with regional strategic and policy making structures.

Discussion

As the post-TR era takes shape, it seems clear that we should not be thinking of a single monolithic public service rehabilitation market to which VSOs will or will not have access, or of a single trend of 'marketisation'. Instead the sector is likely to have access to a range of parallel but at the same time intersecting markets operating to their own set of rules established by commissioners and others with different and sometimes competing interests. A field-informed analysis has encouraged us to look at the importance of the market rules themselves, how they are set and the role of the commissioners and others in managing and responding to the markets that they create. Where public service markets exist, we would advocate for the adoption of market stewardship principles as a framework for commissioners, embedding a clear role for providers, in this case the VS and their users, as an integral part of the market shaping process (Gash et al, 2013). Ultimately the purpose of public service markets is to do just that – serve the public. To that end it seems clear that joining the efforts of funders and commissioners, providers and users in a fair and equitable manner is the right thing to do.

References

BCT (Barrow Cadbury Trust) (2019) 'Criminal justice', available at: https://www.barrowcadbury.org.uk/what-we-do/programmes/criminal-justice/ [accessed 30 May 2019].

Centre for Social Justice (2013) *The New Probation Landscape: Why the Voluntary Sector Matters if We Are Going to Reduce Reoffending*, London: Centre for Social Justice.

Clinks (2013) *Economic Downturn: State of the Sector February 2013: The Impact of the Economic Downturn on the Voluntary and Community Sector Working with Offenders*, London: Clinks.

Clinks (2015) *The State of the Sector 2015: Key Trends for Voluntary Sector Organisations Working with Offenders and Their Families*, London: Clinks.

Clinks (2018a) *Under Represented, Under Pressure, Under Resourced: The Voluntary Sector in Transforming Rehabilitation*, London: Clinks.

Clinks (2018b) *The State of the Sector 2018: Key Trends for Voluntary Sector Organisations Working in the Criminal Justice System*, London: Clinks.

Conservative Party (2008) *Prisons with a Purpose: Our Sentencing and Rehabilitation Revolution to Break the Cycle of Crime*, Security Agenda Policy Green Paper No. 4, London: Conservative Party.

Corcoran, M.S. (2011) 'Dilemmas of institutionalization in the penal voluntary sector', *Critical Social Policy*, 31(1): 30–52.

Fligstein, N. (2001) *The Architecture of Markets: An Economic Sociology of Twenty-First-Century Capitalist Societies*, Princeton, NJ: Princeton University Press.

Fligstein, N. and McAdam, D. (2012) *A Theory of Fields*, Oxford: Oxford University Press.

Fox, C., Albertson, K. and Wong, K. (2013) *Justice Reinvestment: Can the Criminal Justice System Deliver More for Less?* London: Routledge.

Gash, T., Panchamia, N., Sims, S. and Hotson, L. (2013) *Making Public Service Markets Work: Professionalising Government's Approach to Commissioning and Market Stewardship*, London: Institute for Government.

HC Justice Committee (2016) 'The treatment of young adults in the criminal justice system: Seventh Report of Session 2016–17', London: House of Commons.

HC Justice Committee (2018) *Transforming Rehabilitation*, HC 482, June, London: HMSO.

HC Public Accounts Committee (2018) *Government Contracts for Community Rehabilitation Companies*, HC 897, March, London: HMSO.

HM Government (2011) *Open Public Services White Paper*, London: HMSO.

HMI Probation (2018) *Probation Supply Chains: A Thematic Inspection by HM Inspectorate of Probation, April 2018*, Manchester: HMI Probation.

HMI Probation (2019) *Report of the Chief Inspector of Probation, March 2019*, Manchester: HMI Probation.

Hucklesby, A. and Corcoran, M.S. (eds) (2016) *The Voluntary Sector and Criminal Justice*, Basingstoke: Palgrave.

Kinsella, R., O'Keeffe, C., Lowthian, J., Clarke, B., Ellison, M., Kiss, Z. and Wong, K. (2018) 'Whole system approach for women offenders: final report', Manchester: Policy Evaluation and Research Unit, Manchester Metropolitan University.

Macmillan, R. (2016) 'Talking up the voluntary sector in criminal justice: market making in rehabilitation', in J. Rees and D. Mullin (eds) *The Third Sector Delivering Public Services: Developments, Innovations and Challenges*, Bristol: Policy Press, pp 237–60.

Martin, C., Frazer, L., Cumbo, E., Hayes, C. and O'Donahue, K. (2016) 'Paved with good intentions: the way ahead for voluntary, community and social enterprise sector organisations', in A. Hucklesby and M.S. Corcoran (eds) (2016) *The Voluntary Sector and Criminal Justice*, Basingstoke: Palgrave, pp 15–42.

Ministry of Justice (2013a) *Transforming Rehabilitation: A Revolution in the Way We Manage Offenders*, Cm 8517, London: Ministry of Justice.

Ministry of Justice (2013b) *Transforming Rehabilitation: A Strategy for Reform*, Cm 8619, London: Ministry of Justice.

Ministry of Justice (2014) 'Voluntary sector at forefront of new fight against reoffending', Press release, 29 October, available from: https://www.gov.uk/government/news/voluntary-sector-at-forefront-of-new-fight-against-reoffending [accessed 25 March 2019].

Ministry of Justice (2018) *Strengthening Probation, Building Confidence*, Cm 9613, July, London: Ministry of Justice.

Ministry of Justice (2019a) 'Justice Secretary announces new model for probation', Press release, 16 May, available from: https://www.gov.uk/government/news/justice-secretary-announces-new-model-for-probation [accessed 24 May 2019].

Ministry of Justice (2019b) *Strengthening Probation, Building Confidence: Response to Consultation*, CP93, May, London: Ministry of Justice.

National Audit Office (2019) *Transforming Rehabilitation: Progress Review*, HC 1986, London: National Audit Office.

Sandford, M. (2016) 'Devolution to local government in England', Briefing Paper No. 07029, London: House of Commons Library.

T2A Alliance (Transition to Adulthood Alliance) (2013) *Pathways from Crime*, London: Transition to Adulthood Alliance.

Tomczak, P. (2017) *The Penal Voluntary Sector*, Oxford: Routledge.

Webster, R. (2019) 'Probation re-nationalised (more or less)', available from: http://www.russellwebster.com/reversetr/ [accessed 16 May 2019].

Wong, K. (2018) 'Engaging offenders: alternative approaches to commissioning voluntary sector justice services', Presentation to the Academy of Social Justice Commissioning Seminar, 13 September, Manchester.

Wong, K., Ellingworth, D. and Meadows, L. (2015) 'Local Justice Reinvestment Pilot: final process evaluation report', London: Ministry of Justice Analytical Services.

Wong, K., Kinsella, R., Bamonte, J. and Meadows, L. (2017) 'T2A final process evaluation report', Manchester: Manchester Metropolitan University.

PART IV

Beyond institutions: marketisation beyond the criminal justice institution

15

Neo-liberal imaginaries and GPS tracking in England and Wales

Mike Nellis

Introduction

Electronic monitoring (EM) – locational pinpointing and the remote regulation of spatial and temporal schedules – emerged in England and Wales in a small, short pilot in 1989 under a Conservative government and was rolled out nationally (after a second, larger pilot in 1996) in 1999 by the New Labour government. The pilot evaluations proved satisfactory in narrow cost-effectiveness terms, but determination to 'modernise' criminal justice processes, to enlist the private sector in a mixed economy of penal provision and to impose a more punitive ethos on the probation service were arguably the more significant drivers of EM use (Mair, 2005). Within a nascent neo-liberal imaginary, state-based welfare in general and probation in particular were cast by both governments as anachronistic, expensive and inefficient: delivering EM commercially, under extendable five-yearly contracts with central government, was presented as a necessary public service (and penal) reform. Legislating for EM curfews as a largely standalone measure at the pretrial, sentencing and post-release stages – rather than integrating them in probation and youth justice – justified the establishment of a separate private sector infrastructure and created a new occupational group, 'EM officers', in criminal justice in England and Wales.

Probation interests and liberal penal reform groups feared EM, both as a 'privatised' service and as a penal surveillant technology incompatible with social work, hoping it would be a passing fad because some conservative commentators themselves dismissed EM as an insufficiently punitive sanction. Probation unwisely imagined EM as an isolated penal gimmick, simply to be said yes or no to, oblivious to the momentum it gained from broader techno-cultural shifts in society. After the millennium, when digitally mediated relationships, connectivity and datification were being normalised within commerce, governance and everyday life, it became more difficult to deny EM's potential utility in 'offender management', but bad rather than good uses were still expected if it. The consolidation of outsourcing companies as penal stakeholders (part of a global 'EM industry') further increased liberal pessimism.

Mainland European probation services were gradually accommodating EM within existing supervisory frameworks, but continuing institutional unfamiliarity with it in England and Wales reinforced its 'otherness' to the probation service there. Government discouraged both integrated practice across the public–private divide and probation interest in EM, although some was being shown. A rising, digitally aware younger generation of probation staff were less fazed by location monitoring but could never prioritise reshaping EM in a probation-centric way, given the relentless threats to the service. Penal reform bodies, preoccupied with traditional concerns, saw nothing but harm and danger in EM, but in refusing any engagement with EM they ceded authority on it to government, right-wing think tanks and the industry itself.

When EM's political 'moment' seemingly arrived, under the Conservative-led Coalition government which replaced New Labour in 2010, EM's opponents were too ill-informed to sense what was coming. In the aftermath of the global banking crash of 2008, and the damage it inflicted on the legitimacy of the prevailing political-economic imaginary, the Coalition seized the opportunity to reconfigure welfare and penal services. Taking cues from global business leaders, notably accounting firm Deloitte, aided and abetted by right-wing think tanks, it promised to deliver 'more for less' and to disrupt established public sector practices with new technologies of productivity and governance (Deloitte, 2012; Toynbee and Walker, 2015). Deloitte specifically pushed EM as a desirable disruptive innovation, and the events which played out in the Anglo-Welsh Ministry of Justice (MoJ) – an *attempted upgrading* of EM (to mass GPS tracking) alongside an *actual downgrading* of probation (its fragmentation into 21 under-resourced, privately run Community Rehabilitation Companies (CRCs) and a new National Probation Service (NPS) – uncannily mirrored its thinking. The EM upgrade, in fact, foundered badly, but the probation downgrade proceeded with predictably dire consequences for professional practice. Nothing was more emblematic of the MoJ's flawed imaginary than the discovery, later on, that while ministers were portentously anticipating a techno-utopian future based on the meticulous, real-time regulation of offender's lives using geolocation satellites, some cash-strapped CRCs were reducing offender supervision *to desultory telephone check-ups* made *at six weekly intervals* (Probation Inspectorate, 2017).

The rise of 'New World'

Prior to 2010 there had only been two national contracts for radio frequency (RF) EM in England and Wales, the first using Reliance, Premier and Group 4 to manage three regions, the second using G4S (Group 4 merged with Securicor) and Serco (a former partner in Premier, now solo) to manage two. A third contract was in development under New Labour and was carried over into the Conservative-led Coalition, ostensibly embedded in its broader Transforming Rehabilitation strategy. GPS tracking was always to have figured in the new contract, building on its sporadic, small scale use on (i) suspects subject to Control Orders (later called Terrorist Prevention and Investigation Measures (TPIMs)), (ii) some higher risk offenders supervised by MAPPA and (iii) such lessons as had been learned from New Labour's original GPS pilot in 2005–06. A Coalition White Paper vaguely mooted the simultaneous privatising of probation and an expansion of EM, without indicating anything about the unprecedently ambitious GPS strategy, tellingly dubbed 'New World', on which Chris Grayling, the neo-liberal ideologue who became Justice Minister in 2012, was embarking. GPS was intended to supersede obsolete and limited RF technology. Seventy-five thousand offenders per day were to be tracked by 2020, phased in from 2014, creating the largest EM scheme in the world. A new, notionally world-beating 'supertag' (combining GPS and RF) was also commissioned, rather than bought on the open market. Apart from using it at home, Grayling hoped to sell it internationally via Just Solutions International, the commercial arm of the National Offender Management Service (NOMS) he had established in 2014. Neither stakeholder consultations nor cautious GPS pilots were deemed necessary despite the manifestly *transformational* aspirations of 'New World'.

The commercial delivery structure for EM was also to be redesigned. Rather than, as in the past, appointing contractors who provided a 'full service', the MoJ devised a consortium model in which four specialised companies were to collaborate, each one's contribution cost-controlled by the Ministry itself, akin to other large-scale government IT projects. A procurement exercise yielded Capita (a large British outsourcing company, for staffing and running monitoring centres), Buddi (a small British specialist in GPS tracking technology), Airbus (an Anglo-French aerospace corporation for mapping software) and Spanish-owned Telefonica (for telephony). The Ministry of Justice's (2013) announcement at the time, 'New generation tagging contract *boosts British economy*' (emphasis added), portrayed 'New World' more as a business achievement than a penal innovation. Its anticipated scale was not publicly divulged, but the MoJ claimed that £9 million would immediately be saved on the previous contract, and £30 million in the longer term.

The emerging third contract was spared vital scrutiny by the diversion afforded by a financial scandal involving the incumbent EM providers, G4S and Serco. After a whistleblower came forward in the former, and following a subsequent MoJ investigation of both using accountants PwC, they were accused of systematically overcharging for EM since 2005, taking advantage of lax oversight by MoJ contract managers. Grayling made great public play of shaming these companies, and reviews of all their government projects created alarm among their shareholders, but they remained integral to the government's outsourcing programme and could not be dispensed with (although Serco, of its own volition, ceased providing EM). They repaid substantial sums (G4S £108.9 million, Serco £70.5 million), were barred from tendering in the upcoming probation privatisation contract and relinquished control of their two monitoring centres to Capita earlier than planned. General outrage about the overcharging, and the unprecedented referral of both companies for investigation by the Serious Fraud Office, deflected media attention from the already secretive third contract, fostering a default impression that it was safe in Grayling's hands.

The MoJ's bold all-GPS strategy and 75,000 per day target had not been plucked from thin air. They came from the think tank Policy Exchange's comprehensive 'future of corrections' report on EM, whose full potential as a crime-reducing technology, it had argued, would remain untapped if RF technology was not superseded (Geohegan, 2012). In part, the report was a fair, evidence-based critique of existing EM practice, especially the failure to integrate it with other penal interventions. It claimed, also, that the costly, centralised, top-down approach to procurement and contracting used by the MoJ impeded integration and stifled innovation in EM, favouring instead devolved contracting via 'local state' agencies – specifically Probation Trusts and Police and Crime Commissioners – which, it believed, would allow smaller, more innovative tech companies to enter the market (see also Chambers et al, 2013).

Policy Exchange's thinking was influenced by (i) localised EM contracting models in the US, (ii) the partnerships Buddi had created with Anglo-Welsh police forces since 2010 to track prolific offenders and (iii) the capabilities of the Police and Crime Commissioners (PCCs). Buddi may well have inspired Policy Exchange's technocentric aspiration to supplant RF 'presence monitoring' with GPS 'mobility monitoring', despite RF-enabled house arrest having some proven penal worth. Policy Exchange realistically acknowledged offenders' need for support services, but pitched GPS tracking as the new, crucial upgrade, the gamechanger for reducing recidivism, hence the case for using it at scale. It projected three scenarios for GPS's future, resulting, respectively, in 35,000, 76,000 or 140,000 people per day being monitored by 2020, depending on the strategy adopted. Without publicity or consultation, despite the novelty and scale of the intended disruption, the MoJ adopted the middle figure (slightly adjusted), deeming it both feasible and – an important consideration – financially attractive to a range of players in the EM industry.

The fall of 'New World'

Quite ironically, given its innovative track record with the police and its influence on Policy Exchange, Buddi, the company supplying hardware to the MoJ's consortium (crucially, the desired supertag), proved to be the first stumbling block to realising 'New World'. The Ministry's technical specifications for the supertag became increasingly unrealistic (probably impossible to fulfil) without further development work, which the MoJ was unwilling to fund. In addition, they pressured Buddi to share intellectual property with partner companies, notably Airbus (and probably, later, with Just Solutions International) despite the likelihood of their becoming Buddi's competitors elsewhere in the global EM market at some point in the future. As a result, Buddi withdrew from 'New World'.

It was rapidly replaced by Steatite (a British military hardware company), more by default than by proper procurement, because other players in the EM industry were apparently reluctant to invest time and money in Grayling's problematic vision and delivery structure. Steatite had no track record making wearable GPS and tracking devices, and they too failed to build the supertag to MoJ specifications. This, and other factors (only revealed later), delayed the onset of 'New World': not a single person had been placed on GPS by the official start date of late 2014, despite £60 million having been spent on 'development' since 2012.

In 2015 a Conservative government succeeded the Coalition, and Chris Grayling was replaced as Justice Minister by Michael Gove. Faced with potential embarrassment if Grayling's failings became public, Gove (a co-founder of Policy Exchange) pragmatically cut the MoJ's losses, paying off Steatite (with £5.2 million), turned to the open market for a tracking device and closed down Just Solutions International. Pointedly, Gove refused the advice of Reform, another neo-liberal think tank favouring both GPS over RF and localised contracting, tempered with a compromise proposal for centralised practice standards and an MoJ 'approved list' of tech suppliers (Lockhart-Mirams et al, 2015). Gove stuck with the consortium model, but created a new EM Directorate in NOMS, within the MoJ, if possible to salvage something useful from 'New World'. He briefly considered, then abandoned, a strategy for reducing the prison population, and quickly moved on from the MoJ to another ministry, and a frontman role in the emerging Brexit campaign.

In July 2017, a National Audit Office (NAO) report took the unusual, out of remit, step of querying *the very conception* of 'New World', before itemising its costly implementation failures: 'New World' had had no apparent connection, it said, with wider penal policy, nor had an evidence base been gathered to underpin it; prison, probation and court services were not treated as relevant stakeholders; pursuing a bespoke supertag was never necessary; losing Buddi was an absurd step; and Steatite was not procured properly. There had been major difficulties getting the four companies to collaborate – there had been, for example, unclear expectations and foreseeable problems left unaddressed which inexorably escalated into serious conflicts. Capita itself had disputed some costs with the MoJ and, using government specifications, began building a data centre that proved incompatible with Airbus's software requirements. Despite being the 'system integrator' Capita never had substantive authority to coordinate the consortium's work.

Three MoJ civil servants who subsequently appeared before the Parliamentary Accounts Committee (PAC) (2018) to explain this fiasco were hard pressed to disagree that 'New World' had suffered from its designer's 'optimism bias', and been 'shambolic', 'a catastrophe', 'a total disaster from start to finish', while fending off continuing PAC scepticism about the viability of the consortium model. The House of Commons Justice Select Committee (2018) further condemned 'New World' as a 'situation [that] should not have been allowed to happen in the first place', but Grayling, its primary driver, and by then both Minister of Transport and loyal Brexiteer in the 2017 minority Conservative government, received no censure.

EM outside the MoJ

While 'New World' failed to fly, innovative and interesting EM schemes were in fact developing elsewhere, outside MoJ auspices. In its original NHS medium-secure psychiatric unit project in South London, Buddi technology was initially applied as a security measure to prevent absconding. Over time it was integrated into the unit's therapeutic regime, enabling more patients to have short periods of leave than would otherwise have been granted (Hearn, 2015). Although the project was well planned and satisfactorily evaluated, its key lessons have never informed wider EM debate: it was the pioneering example of local practitioners (psychiatrists and nurses) collaborating with commercial technologists to devise monitoring hardware and software to meet particular professional needs (including a harder to remove ankle tag, requested by staff), something the MoJ contracts never allowed.

Buddi also catalysed the police-run and probation-supported Integrated Offender Management (IOM) schemes for persistent and prolific offenders, which were also created collaboratively. Driven by cuts to police budgets, they began in 2010, in Hertfordshire, and grew rapidly as word spread about the service Buddi was offering – there were 34 in 2019. Persistent and prolific offenders (released from prison) had traditionally been subject to intrusive police oversight, including daily check-ups, and mass arrests and interrogations as members of the 'usual suspects' whenever a crime occurred. This was labour intensive and costly. Real-time, 24/7 GPS monitoring, linked to crime mapping software which pinpointed offenders' proximity to – or absence from – known crime scenes, promised significant cost reductions. In the absence of a statutory framework, monitoring could not be compulsory; only offenders wanting to prove their desistance (or improve the likelihood of desistance) from crime were likely to volunteer, confident that their GPS trails would exonerate rather than incriminate them. Some tension now exists between the schemes using the person-centred emphasis on desistance of the original Hertfordshire model and those with a system-centred emphasis on the intelligence gathering capabilities of GPS technology. This latter uses various data analytics to reveal more about the behaviour, networks and lifestyles of the people monitored. The Police and Crime Commissioners have consistently championed such schemes, but neither the Home Office, the College of Policing nor the National Police Chiefs' Council have paid them much heed. They have not been systematically evaluated and lessons – likely to be varied, a mix of good and bad, given the schemes' unregulated character – are not being learned.

The London Mayor's Office for Policing and Crime (MOPAC) commissioned the American company Alcohol Monitoring Services (AMS) to run a 'sobriety tagging' pilot on 1,208 offenders between

June 2014 and June 2018, using its transdermal technology (but fitted by Capita). The pilot responded to well recognised connections between reckless alcohol consumption and crime, particularly violent crime, and drew on pioneering US practice (Bainbridge, 2019). A new Alcohol Abstinence Monitoring Requirement (AAMR), lobbied for by the then London mayor, was inserted into community and suspended sentence orders, prohibiting alcohol consumption for up to 120 days for those given alcohol-related convictions, where alcohol dependency did not apply. NPS and CRC probation officers provided some advice and support to those monitored. MOPAC's own first year evaluation showed considerable take-up by sentencers – for a wider range of drink-related offences than originally anticipated (including domestic violence), high compliance rates (92 per cent) and comparable (but not better) effects on reoffending than other sentencing options. However, in the absence of MoJ funding after the pilot, the intervention was discontinued.

Serendipitously, a creative, judge-led innovation in the civil jurisdiction indicated that establishment suspicions about 'technological solutions' were receding. A senior judge in the High Court (Family Division), for example, requested GPS tracking as a contribution to preventing two sets of Muslim parents from taking their children to the Syrian war zone in 2015; unless the parents submitted to tracking and other travel restrictions, their children were not allowed to live with them. The MoJ had previously supported using RF EM curfews in occasional child abduction cases, and despite the absence of a contractual agreement with Capita to operate GPS in the family jurisdiction, they again acquiesced.

After 'New World'

After the 'New World' fiasco, the EM Directorate was tasked with restoring credibility to GPS tracking, taking account of the NAO, Public Accounts Committee and Justice Select Committee strictures. Ministers came and went – after Gove came Liz Truss, David Liddington and David Gauke. These were all variously preoccupied with the crises that Grayling's austerity policies had set in train, for example legal aid restrictions, the overstrained courts, the violent, understaffed prisons and dysfunctional CRCs – including companies frustrated by unrealised profits. The Probation Inspectorate maintained a regular commentary on the all too foreseeable consequences of privatising probation, although the MoJ's initial response, under Gauke, to the early termination of TR contracts was a revised privatisation model rather than reversion to public ownership. Community orders, including RF EM, have dramatically declined, by 24 per cent since 2010, as magistrates have lost confidence in CRCs' capabilities and in the NPS's discretionary approach to breaching EM curfews (Whitehead and Ely, 2018). One consequence of declining EM numbers, coupled with Capita's wider financial difficulties, was the closure in November 2016 of the Norwich monitoring centre it had taken over from Serco, and a switch to nationwide monitoring from its Salford centre.

The EM Directorate's new team of civil servants injected modesty and rationality into the revised GPS programme, taking over control of 'system integration' in the consortium from Capita, accepting that it would be unwise to replace RF with GPS and allowing 'presence monitoring' to remain dominant, leaving 'mobility monitoring' to find its own level with sentencers. The name 'New World' was dropped. Operationally, a 'tried-and-tested' model for introducing EM schemes was applied: establishing and evaluating pilot schemes, and learning lessons prior to an anticipated national roll-out. An Electronic Monitoring Advisory Group (EMAG) was also established, encompassing stakeholder representatives (and including two academics), ostensibly to broaden the range of expertise on which the MoJ was drawing.

Eight pilot GPS schemes, governed by a comprehensive Code of Practice, ran between October 2016 and March 2018 and were qualitatively evaluated by NatCen Social Research (Kerr et al, 2019). A long established Israeli EM company, Attenti (formerly 3MEM, formerly ElmoTech), was procured to supply the technology. Eight police force areas were selected as pilot sites. GPS was aimed at supporting offender management, assisting rehabilitation and adding a level of restrictiveness to bail, suspended sentence orders and community orders sufficient to persuade sentencers to avoid custody in more threshold cases. It was also to be available as an option in Home Detention Curfew (HDC), as a release condition for life sentences and Imprisonment for Public Protection sentences, and as a fallback measure when offenders on probation were not complying with existing licence conditions, or where prisoners were being re-released after recall to prison. Although the monitoring was retrospective rather than real time, exclusion zones, attendance monitoring at designated locations (for example unpaid work placements), curfews (helpful for battery charging) and standalone monitoring were all to be made available.

More than 600 people were tagged in the eight pilots, fewer than anticipated (and too few to draw firm conclusions about the cost effectiveness of the intervention), but sufficient to learn some lessons. Court bail and post-custody measures were the most common uses of tagging. As in all previous EM pilots in Britain, sentencers, at least in this preliminary stage, were unenthusiastic about its use as a sentence. This may have been less to do with distaste for tracking and more with everyday imagination-stifling pressures on courts under government-induced austerity. Both CRCs and the NPS administered the orders and learned how to deploy exclusion zones (inclusion zones were not used), use tracking data for behavioural insights and risk management, and manage the expectations of victims protected by exclusion zones. The requirement of GPS as part of a bail requirement meant fewer doorstep curfew checks by the police, saving money and causing less disruption of families.

MOPAC established its own GPS pilot in March 2017, with MoJ money, but using Buddi technology, in eight London boroughs, and had more success encouraging take-up, with 73 GPS requirements in its first year, evenly split between community orders and suspended sentence orders. More than 70 per cent of the cases were actively managed by the London CRC, the rest by NPS, with monitoring integrated into casework (MOPAC Evidence and Insight, 2018). The second year saw GPS added to the existing panoply of measures for dealing with London's knife crime crisis – which has a territorial element – with higher risk offenders tracked after release from prison.

Alongside its GPS pilots, the EM Directorate initiated two alcohol monitoring pilots with AMS, one in June 2017 (for two years), with the Yorkshire, Humberside and Lincoln CRC, the other in October 2018 (for six months) in HMP Preston, where alcohol monitoring was made a compulsory licence condition. The CRC project was doubly important because it piloted a long overdue integration of monitoring into probation practice: AAMRs were formally accompanied by supportive interventions, and probation officers – trained by AMS – fitted the tags, rather than Capita. The Directorate also ran a small, short GPS pilot in HMP Kirklevington to ascertain its utility in the context of short periods of Release on Temporary Licence (ROTL), something which Policy Exchange had once favoured.

Returning to 'New World'?

The MoJ's national strategy for GPS began a phased roll-out across National Probation Service regions, and the Youth Justice Service, in November 2018, for completion by early 2020, but was officially launched by then Justice Minister David Gauke in February 2019, in the context of a major policy speech at the Reform think tank. He may have hoped to use this speech to deflect attention from the imminent NAO indictment of Grayling's probation reforms, and of his own dubious plans for fixing them. The financial collapse of Working Links, one of the leading CRC providers, in the same month underlined the deteriorating situation. Gauke made only limited reference to probation, aligning himself instead with 'smart justice', showcasing the infusion of GPS into a range of legislative contexts (including, now, Extended Determinate Sentences) and praising the 'sobriety tagging' schemes (without indicating if they had a future). Smart offender management was to be further supported later in 2019 by the 'EM Portal', an online automated decision support system with zone mapping capabilities and data analytics software. All this was to enable a very limited prison reduction agenda, premised on curtailing the use of under six month custodial sentences:

> I want a [community] regime that can impose greater restrictions on people's movements and lifestyle and stricter requirements in terms of accessing treatment and support. ... I believe we are nearing a time when *a combination of technology and radical thinking* will make it possible for much more intensive and restrictive conditions to be applied in more creative and fundamental ways outside of prison. (Gauke, 2019, emphasis added)

BBC News Online (2019) reported that 'officials estimate that around 4,000 people will be GPS-tagged in a year. There will be a maximum of 1,000 tags in use at any one time'. This was quite modest compared with the original projections for 'New World', but Gauke's vague invocation of 'technology and radical thinking' hinted that transformational aspirations still remained in play. Given that the NAO had reported that £470 million had once been available for implementing 'New World' between 2017 and 2025, the revisionist approach of the EM Directorate could yet morph in ministerial hands into something more grandiose. But the main tropes of Gauke's argument were deeply clichéd: reduce unacceptably high levels of imprisonment with tougher community penalties, *this time using more technology*. 'Find-more-credible-alternatives' has long been a prison numbers reduction strategy; this tech-heavy iteration of it signalled to established and emerging companies in the global EM industry that England and Wales intended to remain a significant customer despite the setback of 'New World'.

The EM industry had reason to be optimistic. Outside the MoJ, the Home Office was developing a long mooted, predominantly GPS (and possibly smartphone) tracking programme to become operational in 2020, ostensibly to reduce the use of detention for asylum seekers and foreign national offenders. That nine companies (including Serco, attempting a return to EM) showed initial interest in tendering for the Home Office contract suggested that the EM industry remained dynamic and confident of future profits. Panopticon Technologies, a new British company, emerged only in 2018, backed by the venture capital firm Public: in its 'technology-solves-problems' pitch it is similar to Buddi, but more 'security-oriented', and is not just selling EM. Apart from a strong and prestigious police presence on its board, it also includes the American Chief Executive of AMS and, connecting to the era in which 'New World' began, a former criminal justice lead at Policy Exchange, who had long been exasperated by the MoJ's botched implementation of the think tank's original vision for GPS in criminal justice.

Conclusion

Grayling's entwined strategy of partially privatising the probation service and establishing the 'New World' GPS programme should be understood as an attempt to adopt the (so-called) tech industries' approach to innovation: to 'move fast and break things' – that is, to disrupt existing services in the hope of facilitating longer-term, marketised penal developments. Deloitte signalled the principle; Policy Exchange envisioned the practice; austerity offered the pretext. Grayling fashioned a reckless personal project out of this neo-liberal imaginary, seeking to weaken and dismantle the old and, with mass GPS tracking, to sow the seeds of the new unscrutinised – before his intentions could be discerned and resistance mobilised. His talent was not equal to the task, but despite the officially recognised failure of both his probation reforms and of 'New World', all within five years, momentum may only have temporarily been lost. Translating the precepts of a neo-liberal imaginary invariably proceeds in opportunist stages, and is not immune to political contingencies, or, indeed, ministerial hubris. Grayling may or may not have expected actual reoffending or cost-saving outcomes from his strategy, but those may never have been his criteria of success. He wanted – and achieved – disruption of existing offender management arrangements in 2012, making probation supervision harder work, fostering staff burnout and setting a new techno-commercial dynamic in motion. This logic, he hoped, would be irreversible, whatever the timescale and despite any setbacks. It is significant that when Grayling bragged of creating something eye-catchingly world class in British criminal justice, it was GPS tracking he extolled, and the role of business in making it happen, not courts, prisons or probation.

Unfortunately, 'breaking things' (whether moving fast or not) is not a sufficient (nor even necessary) condition of progress. 'New World' failed as a specific penal strategy in 2012–15 simply because of unforeseen (if foreseeable) difficulties, and internal inconsistencies and contradictions. It did not fail because of external opposition; there was none, largely because it was secretive. The reconfigured EM/GPS strategy, without a fate-tempting name, but underpinned by 'radical thinking', retains the potential incrementally to effect dramatic changes in offender supervision, if sentencers can be persuaded of its merits. Gauke's own plans to curtail short custodial sentences, to which the use of RF and GPS were key, were abandoned by the Conservative government in August 2019 (from which Gauke resigned), shortly after Boris Johnson took over as Prime Minister. It is unlikely this has meant loss of faith in EM, and the prospect of a national roll-out of alcohol monitoring was signalled at the Conservative Party conference in October.

Future prospects for the probation service itself depend on the tenor on the government which inherits the legacy of Brexit, but the precise contingencies cannot be anticipated. Broadly, the 'populist punitive' sentiments Brexit has unleashed would be consolidated by a Conservative government which, even if it pursues increased use of imprisonment, will likely make a battleground of community supervision, and revive commercial models of it. Prison-loving populists have typically treated EM regimes with derision, but could welcome punitive versions of them as a quid pro quo for further diminishing probation's influence.

A Labour government may well restore probation to public ownership, and *should* bring EM under its auspices. It will not reject EM outright, because a great deal of recent left-wing thought, appealingly grounded in humanism, has been focussed on the socialist potential of digitisation (see for example Mason, 2019).

It will be up to penal reformers to support government in identifying the progressive potential of EM while increasing the evidence base regarding its use and hopefully opposing the all too conceivable worst uses of it.

References

Bainbridge, L. (2019) 'Transferring 24/7 Sobriety from South Dakota to South London: the case of MOPAC's Alcohol Abstinence Monitoring Requirement Pilot', *Addiction*, 114 (9): 1–9.

BBC News Online (2019) 'Electronic GPS tags to track thousands of criminals in England and Wales', 16 February, available from: https://www.bbc.co.uk/news/uk-47256515 [accessed 18 November 2019].

Chambers, M., Davis, R. and McLeod, C. (2013) *Power Down: A Plan for a Cheaper, More Effective Justice System*, London: Policy Exchange.

Deloitte (2012) *Public Sector, Disrupted: How Disruptive Innovation Can Help Government Achieve More for Less*, London: Deloitte.

Gauke, D. (2019) 'Beyond prison, redefining punishment', Speech by Minister of Justice David Gauke to Reform, London, 18 February, available from: https://www.gov.uk/government/speeches/beyond-prison-redefining-punishment-david-gauke-speech [accessed 18 November 2019].

Geohegan, R. (2012) *Future of Corrections*, London: Policy Exchange.

Hearn, D. (2015) 'Other GPS uses: Forensic mental health', *Probation Quarterly*, 5 (unpaginated).

House of Commons Justice Select Committee (2018) *Offender Monitoring Tags: Fifteenth Report of Session 2017–19*, London: House of Commons, available from: https://publications.parliament.uk/pa/cm201719/cmselect/cmpubacc/458/458.pdf [accessed 18 November 2019].

Kerr, J., Roberts, E., Davies, M. and Pullerits, M. (2019) *Process Evaluation of the Global Positioning System (GPS) Electronic Monitoring Pilot: Qualitative Findings*, London: Ministry of Justice Analytical Series 2019, NatCen Social Research, available from: https://assets.publishing.service.gov.uk/government/uploads/system/uploads/attachment_data/file/779199/gps-location-monitoring-pilot-process-evaluation.pdf [accessed 18 November 2019].

Lockhart-Mirams, G., Pickles, C. and Crowhurst, E. (2015) *Cutting Crime: The Role of Tagging in Offender Management*, London: Reform.

Mair, G. (2005) 'Electronic monitoring in England and Wales: evidence-based or not?' *Criminal Justice* 5(3): 257–77.

Mason, P. (2019) *Clear Bright Future: A Radical Defence of the Human Being*, London: Penguin.

MoJ (Ministry of Justice) (2013) 'New generation tagging contract boosts British economy', Press release 080/13, 20 August, London.

MOPAC Evidence and Insight (2018) *GPS Tagging: First Year Interim Report*, London: MOPAC.

NAO (National Audit Office) (2017) *The New Generation Electronic Monitoring Programme*, London: National Audit Office.

Parliamentary Accounts Committee (2018) *Offender Monitoring Tags Enquiry*, London: House of Commons.

Probation Inspectorate (2017) *Annual Report*, London: Ministry of Justice.

Toynbee, P. and Walker, D. (2015) *Cameron's Coup: How the Tories took Britain to the Brink*, London: Guardian Books.

Whitehead, S. and Ely, C. (2018) *Renewing Trust: How We Can Improve the Relationship between Probation and the Courts*, London: Centre for Justice Innovation.

16

Misery as business: how immigration detention became a cash cow in Britain's borders

Monish Bhatia and Victoria Canning

Introduction

In the UK's electoral cycles since 2010, there has been growing support for political parties projecting nationalism, nativism and exclusionism, which implicitly constructs foreigners (or at least, economically vulnerable foreigners) as a threat and promises a sharp cut in immigration numbers. This was arguably the backbone to the Conservative Party's electoral success and also to the 2016 Brexit vote. Although already long in existence, the then Conservative government leader Theresa May coined the term 'hostile environment' with respect to foreign migrants in 2012, leading to a radical overhaul of legislative and administrative provisions, introducing even harsher, punitive and restrictive immigration policies, rapidly drawing and expanding crime control structures into the immigration arena, creating aggressive technologies of control and outsourcing of provisions for migrants generally, and people seeking asylum specifically. Consequently, this resulted in further mistreatment of migrant groups and dramatic rights violations. Through the Windrush exposé in 2018, the wrongful and unlawful nature of the immigration control regime was made visible (again), and on this occasion led to significant public outcry. The environment experienced by wealthy or foreign nationals living in the UK, it hardly needs to be said, is rather more sympathetic.

A short history of the outsourcing of detention

In 1971, having relied on immigration to meet skill shortfalls in the aftermath of the Second World War, the British government decided to halt the 'flow' of non-white migration from the former colonies into the UK. Having contributed significantly to Britain's economic rebuilding, the increase in family resettlement and now unneeded additional labour led to invested interests closing borders which had previously been open. Alongside this was the implementation of a series of restrictive measures which has since included virginity testing, x-ray screening of minors and the increased imprisonment of illegalised,[1] mostly non-white migrants.

It was during the 1970s that the Conservative government of the day contracted Securicor – which later merged with Group 4 Falck, now G4S – to manage detention facilities, one in Harmondsworth near Heathrow airport, and a second one near Manchester airport. In 1971, Securicor Group Limited and Security Services Limited were also listed on the London Stock Exchange. Ten years later, in 1981, Securicor Chair Peter Smith was awarded the OBE for services to the security industry. This was just the beginning of a new relationship between the state and private security companies that policed people for profits. The confinement business became an inspiration, one that was drawn from the US (Jones and Newburn, 2012).

Between the late 1980s and mid-1990s, amid the ideological move toward neo-liberalism in the UK, at least two prisons were contracted out to private security companies, along with Campsfield House detention centre. Nevertheless, leading figures in the Labour Party, then in opposition, remained critical of the privatisation move. Tony Blair, for example, was concerned at the time that the private sector might begin to dominate state-led criminal justice agendas, stating:

> there is a danger that if you build up an industrial vested interest into the penal system, and as part of that interest they are designed obviously to keep the prison population such that it satisfies those commercial interests ... there is a risk that that distorts the penal policy that otherwise you would introduce ... Secondly, I believe that privatisation is a diversion of our energies from where those energies should be properly set. (Tony Blair MP, 1993; quoted in Scottish Consortium on Crime and Criminal Justice briefing paper, 2006)

---

[1] We choose to use the term 'illegalised' rather than 'illegal' to shift the terminology away from the connotations that this is a naturalised state. It is multiple processes of immigration that facilitate illegalisation based on punitive laws and social policy. For more information, see Canning (2016).

Similarly, during the election campaigns Labour MP Jack Straw made promises to withdraw the private sector involvement in prisons and bring it back under public control. However, after winning power in the 1997 elections, the by then rebranded 'New Labour' party took an apparent U-turn and entered into new privately financed prison deals. This was the point after which the industrial vested interest in prisons grew.

While the privatisation of prisons and probation services has captured criminological attention, the same has not been the case with immigration detention centres, an inconsistency which continues to this date. Perhaps this is because prisons are viewed as punitive and detention as simply administrative. There was a dramatic increase in Immigration Removal Centres (IRCs) under New Labour under the Blair (and later Brown) leaderships, and nearly all the IRC sites were managed by private companies. Further, some companies that managed prisons also managed the detention of migrants. Often, economic reasoning is used to justify the trust in the private sector and that services offered by them are more 'efficient' and 'dynamic' than publicly run services. However, it is rather difficult to trace any substantive literature or research that can confidently demonstrate that privatisation and marketisation give better value for money (or superior services for less fiscal and social cost). Further, there is nothing to assure us that privatisation will not drive profitability at a cost to non-monetised social aspirations (for example, decent terms and conditions of employment for staff or decent standards of facilities). On the contrary, prison overcrowding, diminished security, scandals and failures to meet contractual obligations have indicated the opposite (Mason, 2013).

Throughout the New Labour government (followed by the 2010 Conservative–Liberal Democrat Coalition and, from 2015, Conservative governments), several reports on excessive use of force and physical violence against detainees/deportees by Detention Custody Officers (DCO) and immigration escorts emerged. According to a 2008 report by Medical Justice, a leading non-governmental organisation (NGO) working in migrant rights in the UK, a number of detainees alleging assault were able to bring civil action cases, some of which were settled out of court. However, none of the security guards or the private companies which are their employers were ever prosecuted for any assault-related offences under the criminal law. This raises questions about whether the Home Office is outsourcing the accountability of the abuse of migrants to security companies, in part to shift responsibility from itself to those doing the state's bidding. It is to this question we now turn.

Mapping the corporate realities of privatised confinement

> It's like a hotel with a guaranteed occupancy. (Ron Garzini, promoting privatised custodial facilities; quoted in Parenti, 1999: 211)

> [W]e can be very confident that the world will still need prisons, will still need to manage immigration ... a prison custody officer can sleep soundly in the knowledge that his or her skills will be required for years to come. (Serco, 2017)

The United States was the first country to privatise confinement facilities and to embark on an incarceration binge, locking up more people per capita than any other English speaking developed country (Austin and Irwin, 2012). In 2011, the US held around 8.41 per cent of their total prison population in private facilities,[2] whereas England and Wales held 18.46 per cent and Scotland 15.3 per cent (Mason, 2013). The figures differ dramatically for immigration detention – for instance, the US holds 73 per cent of migrants in privatised detention facilities (Haberman, 2018), and the UK has a similar number, with seven out of eight long-term facilities run by private contractors. Both the US and UK have a significantly higher private sector involvement in immigration detention than comparable states. Moreover, the UK is further advanced in privatisation when compared with other European countries and has one of the largest detention estates in the EU. Furthermore, the UK is the only country in Europe that has no statutory upper limit on length of detention; it can detain migrants indefinitely.

The use of detention in the UK has rapidly expanded from 250 places in 1993 to 2,928 at the end of 2018. Around 25,000 people passed through the UK's detention estate in 2018, around 50 per cent of whom have sought asylum at some point (Silverman and Griffiths, 2019). Since the late 1990s, successive immigration and asylum legislations have turned increasingly restrictive, which in part explains the increased use of detention. Nevertheless, we cannot ignore the link between restrictive policies and privatisation as they often run in tandem with and complement each other. By shifting the focus to privatisation, we can begin to understand how the corporate lobby will be motivated to shape – and act as a driving force behind – restrictive immigration policies, designed to trap and

---

[2] The figures for the US and Scotland are from 2011, whereas for England and Wales they are from 2012.

drag people into its privatised confinement net. Of course, private contractors need constant flow(s) of migrants, and this is made possible by keeping detention under the administrative domain rather than as a formal process of criminal justice, since less stringent regulation is required to confine migrants. Although some people in detention have previously *completed* their sentences in prisons (which in itself is a double punishment; see Turnbull and Hasselberg, 2016), people who are detained in IRCs do not go through a trial: They are not convicted or serving sentences; there is no judge, jury, cross examination or testing of evidence; and the principles of fairness, equality and proportionality are not applicable. Worryingly, the Home Office is exempted from the Race Relations (amendment) Act 2000 to carry out immigration control functions and can forcefully lock up individuals simply based on their supposed precarious immigration status. Taking this into account, it could be said that people in prison have more legal and procedural safeguards than people trapped in IRC detention (although this should not be interpreted as an endorsement of prisons, institutions we are also highly critical of).

Detention in the UK is almost exclusively administered by four private companies, namely, Mitie, G4S, Serco and GEO Group. It is reasonable to suppose it is one of the most profitable privatised businesses, since a relatively steady flow of migrants, according to the previous quote, suggests 'guaranteed occupancy'. According to one analysis, the US prison company GEO Group was operating on a 30 per cent profit margin from running Dungavel IRC in Scotland, whereas G4S was making approximately 20 per cent and 40 per cent on Brook House IRC and Tinsley House IRC respectively (Corporate Watch, 2018). However, the full scale of profits is unknown, as companies protect this information on the grounds of 'commercial confidentiality'. Thus taxpayers have no way of assessing whether they are over- or underpaying for such services. Since the time of their inception, private security companies, like other capitalist ventures, have been driven by the quest for higher profits. These companies by definition are heavily labour intensive, so any such increases in profit are likely to impact upon wages and conditions of staff and the people detained – surplus value can be extracted through greater exploitation of labour and deterioration of the physical estate. It is of least surprise that staffing levels, health and safety, training and consequently care provided to those who are confined have remained a cause for concern over many years and have been raised in all the independent reviews.

There are several examples of irresponsible profit making. For instance, in June 2017 it was reported that the Home Office-backed detention labour wage rate of £1 per hour – for cleaning, kitchen and other menial tasks – accounted for paying hundreds of detained people just £887,565 in wages for 887,073 hours of work (Taylor, 2018). These 'wages' were exempted from minimum wage legislation (as with labourers in prisons), and very recently a High Court judge ruled this as *lawful* and *not* exploitative. It is speculated that private security companies have saved over £3 million by paying detained migrants well below the national minimum wage (Corporate Watch, 2018), thereby boosting profits. As noted earlier, the immigration detention 'market' is largely oligopolistic, with a few companies bidding for large government contracts. The domination of this market by corporate giants ensures that market is oligarchic, and small and medium-size companies cannot succeed in competing for business; thus prices and profit margins are kept high for existing providers. Furthermore, understaffing, high staff turnover, overcrowded and unsanitary cell conditions, cost cutting on cleanliness and insufficient recreational activities (as we will discuss later) – all translate to greater savings. This has a dire impact on migrants, as highlighted by a recent Home Affairs Select Committee Report (2019: 80):

> Low staffing levels mean that people are locked up for longer periods of time, face to face communication is limited and IRC facilities are more likely to be closed (e.g. libraries, cafés, IT facilities) all of which compound levels of frustration and mental health issues among detainees and staff. This can lead to increased levels of self-harm as well as violence among detainees and towards IRC staff. In the event of a serious incident, a lack of staff could have detrimental consequences for everyone's safety within an IRC.

As noted elsewhere (Canning, 2017), detention staff working in immigration detention are often on fairly low wages, precarious contracts and generally without the requirement of specialist experience in working with people who are living in stressful conditions. The likelihood of staff in these conditions investing scarce resources in the rights or wellbeing of the people who are detained diminishes over time, as various exposés have demonstrated.

Evidencing abuses and re-centring accountability

Apart from the obvious serious assault on liberty inherent in such practice, immigration detention centres have been plagued with reports of racial violence, sexual abuse, medical negligence, deaths in custody and other rights violations. Of seven IRCs in the UK, only one is governed by Her Majesty's Prison Service – IRC Morton Hall (Silverman and Griffiths, 2019). This facility has faced its share of public scrutiny, specifically after the deaths of four men in 2017. To this we emphasise that while Morton Hall is not a for-profit venture, the violence of immigration detention is part of a violent continuum, the difference here being the lack of emphasis on profit. In 2015, an undercover Channel 4 News recording secretly recorded IRC staff referring to detained people as 'animals', 'beasties' and 'bitches' (Channel 4, 2015), while one pregnant woman who 'refused' to 'wait her turn' in the G4S medical queue went on to have a miscarriage. A former Yarl's Wood detainee described staff openly mocking her, and putting their fingers in her eyes after she collapsed:

> What they are doing, they turn off the camera and say they do not do stuff like that. I collapsed coming out from the bathroom. They were poking my eyes, forcing me, telling me, 'You need to eat. You want to kill yourself? You are a stupid girl.' They mimic me sometimes when I say something. They repeat it in a very funny way and they laugh about it. To me, that is just not right. (Home Affairs Select Committee, 2019: 81)

In the same year, undercover filming at IRC Harmondsworth captured Home Office staff admitting that the conditions under corporate giant Mitie are 'shit',[3] and that the Home Office wouldn't allow cameras so as to avoid the bad press. In 2017, a Panorama exposé evidenced high levels of abuse. In one scene an obviously ill man was screamed at, called a 'fucking piece of shit' and choked by the DCO. Racist language and mocking of detainees by staff seemed casual and routine, and violent behaviour appeared acceptable to staff and some managers. 'We don't cringe at breaking bones ... If I killed a man, I wouldn't be bothered. I'd carry on,' one officer said (see Bhatia and Canning, 2017).

This is not to say that the exposés have had no positive effect. Not long after Channel 4's footage at Yarl's Wood was released, Nick Hardwick, then the Chief Inspector of Prisons, called the centre a place of national concern. Following the string of reports on abuse, sexual assaults and racism at the centre, Serco commissioned its own

---

[3] https://corporatewatch.org/home-office-told-to-publish-confidential-reports-on-migrant-detention-sites/

review of the centre which was published in January 2016. Serco said it was committed to 'respond to all of these recommendations'.

The same month, the 'Shaw Review', which had been commissioned by the Home Office on the detention of vulnerable people, was published by Stephen Shaw. Although its remit did not cover the overall IRC detention regime, it advocated banning the detention of pregnant women and suggested there should be a 'presumption against detention' for victims of sexual violence, female genital mutilation, people with learning difficulties, those with post-traumatic stress disorder and transgender people. Reforms were subsequently introduced which included reducing the detention of pregnant women to a maximum time of 72 hours, and only in extreme circumstance. People were to be screened to check whether they were survivors of torture or sexual violence, particularly after an external review by Women for Refugee Women (2017) which found that women who had been raped and/or tortured continued to be detained, even after the Home Office received the 64 recommendations made by Shaw.

In a critique of these reviews at the time, we argued that the crux of the issue is the overall injustice of immigration detention: It is unhealthy to remove people's liberty arbitrarily (Bhatia and Canning, 2016). Even outside such centres, the spectre of detention hangs over those awaiting the outcome of an asylum application. Moreover, we raised concerns about the likelihood of wholesale change or the improvement of the lives of people seeking asylum. The moral and ethical issue of detention does not lie simply in the complexity of individuals' histories or indeed their contemporary carceral realities, but in the removal of liberty based on neo-colonial, racialised approaches to the Othering of migrant bodies. Making surface level reforms does not address this issue, but rather detracts from the violence inherent to confining people and removing their autonomy and, indeed, stealing their time – time which cannot be retrieved or restored. As such, taking temporal sections out of migrant people's lives is – for us at least – unethical at best and an act of state-corporate violence at worst.

As time has moved on in the aftermath of the reviews, our concerns have continued to be justified. In a follow-up progress report, Shaw critiqued the 'Adults at Risk' policy which has been developed to avoid the detention of people deemed vulnerable (including survivors of sexual violence and torture) as well as continued failures in healthcare in detention – another aspect of the detention machinery which is often privatised. We highlighted the potential for facilitating a 'bad apple' approach, whereby systemic problems would be represented to arise from individual centres or staff members who violated safeguards, policies or even the law. While individual accountability is welcome for those who inflict violence through racism or sexual violence, the overall landscape does not facilitate a move away from the harms of incarceration inherent to the experience of people who are detained. It is to this point that we now move: addressing the systemic harms of immigration detention.

The broader harms of immigration detention

As other chapters in this book show, places of confinement carry problems that arise from loss of liberty. Lack of autonomy over food, ones' own time, educational or work-related opportunities and the fracturing of relationships are all integral to the prison regime. However, as Bosworth (2014) points out, IRCs are not prisons but are spaces of indefinite waiting and reduced educational or support investment. For people held in immigration detention centres, the further impacts include a fear of deportation or the potential for forced return, possibly to conflict or persecution. As in the exposés highlighted earlier, research repeatedly provides evidence of abuses of power and instances of violence and intimidation. The issues span the individual to the institutional and structural levels.

On a human level, people in detention have drastically reduced autonomy over their time, both in the everyday and in the longer term. As immigration detention is indefinite, unlike a prison sentence, people tend to count the days *up* rather than counting *down*. The most recent statistics under Freedom of Information requests to the Home Office (2014) showed that the 20 longest recorded lengths of incarceration in IRCs ranged from 722 days to 1,701 days.[4] Over one fifth of immigrants are held in IRCs for longer than two months (Silverman and Griffiths, 2019). This is not insignificant: The longer a person is incarcerated, the greater their chances of developing mental health problems. As such, although there are moves to help in the identification of vulnerable people, people are in fact *made more vulnerable* through the enforced removal of their liberty and as such reductions in their rights.

This leads us then to highlight the increase in self-harm and self-inflicted deaths in immigration detention in the UK. As Harmit Athwal noted with the Institute of Race Relations, there were 34 deaths in immigration detention between 1989 and 2014 (Athwal, 2015). This

---

[4] https://assets.publishing.service.gov.uk/government/uploads/system/uploads/attachment_data/file/387139/33568.pdf

number – of *human lives* – has since continued to increase, with six suicides in 2017, and a 22 per cent increase in suicide attempts between 2017 and 2018, when 159 attempts were recorded. Considering the points raised earlier, it seems reasonable to suppose that reduced funds and – for those run by private companies – drives for increased profit have facilitated proportional reductions in staffing, medical care and psychological support. How seriously these are taken is unclear; as Canning found in her study of border harms in Britain, Denmark and Sweden, self-harm and suicide are often conflated with attention seeking, trying to avoid deportation or facilitating a move to hospital from which to 'escape' more easily (Canning, 2019). In a system that weighs heavily proving one's history or current reality, the action of inflicting harm on one's self, or even attempting or committing suicide, is represented as misdirection or falsehood. This is in stark contrast to the very corporations entrusted to run such facilities who, despite the regular and repeated failings and rights abuses outlined earlier, continue to receive trust – or at least the benefit of the doubt – from the state that sanctions their contracts.

In a nutshell: what is the problem with privatisation?

Having outlined histories of privatisation and the harms of detention, it is worth now summarising the issues specific to the privatisation of immigration detention. What is it that makes the expansion of private investments in the confinement of migrant people so problematic?

Point 1: *Detainees have arguably become cash cows for companies.* Increases in the number of individuals and/or holding individuals for longer periods is, as we have shown, likely to result in higher financial gains. The mantra is simple: More detainees equals more profit. Despite growing evidence of poor mental health in detention, although ongoing debate ensues, there appears to be no rush to change the policy of indefinite detention. It is not just the management of migration, but management of misery and suffering which has now become one of the most profitable activities. For instance, and to name just a few, this includes housing, electronic monitoring, reporting centres, vans that transport people to detention, deportation escorts and private and commercial charter flights. Migrant misery is big business in bordered Britain.

Point 2: *The 'security market' is highly oligopolistic.* As outlined earlier, a handful of contractors systematically bid for lucrative public services contracts. Billions in taxpayers' money is handed over to these companies, despite national and global reports of abuses and harms inflicted in private facilities on migrants who are deemed vulnerable. Questions are again raised around performance, financial sustainability and superiority of service.

Point 3: *Outsourcing can reduce accountability*. The state might not offer preferable alternatives to their business counterparts in terms of conditions, but there is one key difference with state run facilities: public accountability for the individual or institutional infliction of harm or systematic violence, at least in theory if not practice. This takes various forms. The first is a question of access, which is extremely difficult where immigration detention in the UK is concerned. Although access has been granted to a number of academics studying immigration detention in the UK (see Border Criminologies website),[5] gaining entry to immigration detention is generally limited to official inspections. Even then, controversy ensued in 2015 when access to Yarl's Wood, the UK's only women and family facility, was denied to the United Nations special rapporteur on violence against women, Rashida Manjoo, who subsequently censured the UK over the denial. Secondly, access to knowledge is more restrictive: Unlike public services, companies and corporations are more likely to opt out or redact information relating to Freedom of Information requests, if they are found to be required to respond at all (that is, that their role falls under the scope of public service). Thirdly, documenting the inside workings of IRCs is notoriously difficult. When people are detained, they are denied access to most internet and social media outlets, and any personal media which has recording capacities (such as android phones) are confiscated for the duration of their stay.

Point 4: *Immigration detention also costs money*. As the Joint Committee on Human Rights highlights, the annual detention costs for the year ending March 2018 were £108 million. At the time of writing, it cost approximately £87.71 per day to confine a person in detention (Silverman and Griffiths, 2019). In addition, compensation is payable to people who have been wrongly detained – over £3 million in compensation was paid in the financial year 2016–17 (Joint Committee on Human Rights, 2019). Despite the numerous scandals, punishment of the corporations involved is limited to fines and cancellation/

---

[5] https://www.law.ox.ac.uk/research-subject-groups/centre-criminology/centreborder-criminologies

cessation of contracts. Immigration detention is so expensive, it is not clear why it remains policy.

It is important to note here that, although these are specific to private companies and corporations, the UK government and in particular the Home Office are not exempt from accountability. As noted earlier, privatisation shifts accountability, so that 'when things go wrong' there is someone to blame. However, we emphasise that *things have already gone wrong*. The privatisation and profiteering of immigration detention is the manifestation of long-running hostilities toward migrants, many of which are enforced not only by institutional actors, but by law. It was the UK government that created and maintains laws which allow for the administrative detention of migrants. Through increasingly punitive laws, most recently the Immigration Acts of 2014 and 2016, the lives of people who have migrated to the UK are made much more difficult. While privatisation allows the state to wash its hands of individualised or even institutional problems, it is the state itself that is responsible for their very existence. Corporations are paid to enforce restrictions that successive governments have created and allowed to persist.

Conclusion: the case for the abolition of immigration detention

The fact that detention has meant big business for big companies should not come as a surprise, and yet as this chapter demonstrates, the privatisation of the IRC complex has been in flow for decades. What we can see, however, is the significant expansion of private enterprise well beyond the realms of confinement, and its deep entrenchment in the everyday lives of migrants and people seeking asylum.

There is no doubt that confinement is a harmful practice. For the people we work with in academic and activist senses, we see that detention has impacts which can span years; they range from invasive memories to ongoing anxiety or fears of a repeat detention. The sound of keys is a memory that many refer back to, even many years after their experience of detention without trial. Even for those who have never experienced detention, the threat of being detained taints subsequent Home Office appointments, where people fear being subjected to arbitrary arrest, detention or enforced removal – concerns which are very rational and very real.

Since the 2016 Brexit vote, there has been a sharp rise in the numbers of EU citizens locked up in detention centres. In 2009, the number of EU nationals in detention was 768; however, in 2016 this rose to 4,701 – a sixfold increase.[6] There are indications the system will continue to find new bodies for the private sector to commodify, through new draconian legislation and renewed xenophobic and racist rhetoric. Of course, detention must be understood as a punitive act, one that deprives people of liberty and makes them suffer. However, it is also a space created and maintained by corporations for profit – a profit gained from migrant misery, and by stealing their time. Immigration detention needs to be abolished.

References

Athwal, H. (2015) '"I don't have a life to live": deaths and UK detention', *Race & class*, 56(3): 50–68.

Austin, J. and Irwin, J. (2012) *It's About Time: America's Imprisonment Binge*, Belmont, CA: Cengage Learning.

Bhatia, M. and Canning, V. (2016) *Immigration Detention: A Tale of Two Reviews*, London: Institute of Race Relations, available from: http://www.irr.org.uk/news/immigration-detention-a-tale-of-two-reviews/ [accessed 14 February 2019].

Bhatia, M and Canning, V. (2017) 'Brutality of British Immigration Centre Laid Bare', *The Conversation*, 5 September, available from: https://theconversation.com/brutality-of-british-immigration-detention-system-laid-bare-83396 [accessed 14 February 2019].

Bosworth, M. (2014) *Inside Immigration Detention*, Oxford: Oxford University Press.

Canning, V. (2016) *Timeline: The Criminalisation of Asylum*, Milton Keynes: The Open University, available from: https://www.open.edu/openlearn/people-politics-law/politics-policy-people/timeline-the-criminalisation-asylum [accessed 8 October 2019].

Canning, V. (2017) *Gendered Harm and Structural Violence in the British Asylum System*, Abingdon: Routledge.

Canning, V. (2019) 'Keeping up with the kladdkaka: Kindness and coercion in Swedish immigration detention centres', *European Journal of Criminology*, available from: https://doi.org/10.1177/1477370818820627 [accessed 30 March 2020].

Channel 4 (2015) 'Yarl's Wood: undercover in the secretive immigration centre', available from: https://www.channel4.com/news/yarls-wood-immigration-removal-detention-centre-investigation [accessed 14 February 2019].

---

[6] https://inews.co.uk/news/uk/eu-nationals-held-immigration-detention-soars-tories/

Corporate Watch (2018) 'Detention centre profits: 20% and up for the migration prison bosses', available from: https://corporatewatch. org/detention-centre-profits-20-and-up-for-the-migration-prison-bosses/ [accessed 14 February 2019].

Haberman, C. (2018) 'For private prisons, detaining immigrants is big business', *New York Times*, 1 October, available from: https://www. nytimes.com/2018/10/01/us/prisons-immigration-detention.html [accessed 25 June 2019].

Home Affairs Select Committee (2019) 'Immigration detention: fourteenth report of Session 2017–2019, available from: https://publications.parliament.uk/pa/cm201719/cmselect/ cmhaff/913/913.pdf [accessed 25 June 2019].

Joint Committee on Human Rights (2019) 'Immigration detention', available from: https://publications.parliament.uk/pa/jt201719/ jtselect/jtrights/1484/1484.pdf [accessed 2 August 2019].

Jones, T. and Newburn, T. (2012) 'The convergence of US and UK crime control policy: Exploring substance and process', in T. Newburn and R. Sparks (eds) *Criminal Justice and Political Cultures*, Cullompton: Willan, pp 135–63.

Mason, C. (2013) 'International growth and trends in prison privatisation', The Sentencing Project', available from: http://www. sentencingproject.org/publications/international-growth-trends-in-prison-privatization/ [accessed 25 June 2019].

Parenti, C. (1999) *Lockdown America: Police and Prisons in the Age of Crisis*, London and New York: Verso.

Scottish Consortium on Crime and Criminal Justice (2006) 'Prison privatisation in Scotland – briefing paper', available from: http://www. scccj.org.uk/wp-content/uploads/2011/08/Prison-Privatisation-in-Scotland.pdf [accessed 25 June 2019].

Serco (2017) *Annual Report and Accounts 2017*, available from: https://www.serco.com/media/2384/serco-annual-report-and-accounts-2017.pdf [accessed 8 October 2019].

Silverman, S. and Griffiths, M. (2019) 'Immigration detention in the UK', The Migration Observatory, updated 29 May, available from: https://migrationobservatory.ox.ac.uk/resources/briefings/ immigration-detention-in-the-uk/ [accessed 25 June 2019].

Taylor, D. (2018) 'Home Office backed "slave labour" pay for immigration detainees', *The Guardian*, 4 September, available from: https://www.theguardian.com/uk-news/2018/sep/04/home-office-pay-immigration-detainees-menial-jobs-legal-action [accessed 25 June 2019].

Turnbull, S. and Hasselberg, I. (2016) 'From prison to detention: the carceral trajectories of foreign-national prisoners in the United Kingdom', *Punishment & Society*, 19(2): 135–54.

Women for Refugee Women (2017) 'We are still here: the continued detention of women seeking asylum in Yarl's Wood', available from: https://www.refugeewomen.co.uk/wp-content/uploads/2019/01/women-for-refugee-women-reports-we-are-still-here.pdf [accessed 14 February 2019].

17

Prison education: a Northern European wicked policy problem?

Gerry Czerniawski

Introduction

Time in prison is justified as a punishment for committing an offence. But little evidence exists that incarceration of offenders affects the level of crime. On the contrary, the prison population has grown by 24 per cent since the year 2000, with an estimated official figure of 10.74 million people incarcerated worldwide (Munoz, 2009; Walmsley, 2018); unofficial figures are significantly higher. Many scholars argue that rates of imprisonment vary depending upon the level of societal trust, the extent of social welfare and the type of economic structure (Hughes, 2012; Coyle, 2016; Czerniawski, 2016).

In addition to the roles of punishment and assumed deterrence, a growing body of evidence also suggests that prison education can play a role in reducing recidivism (MoJ, 2018; Prison Reform Trust, 2018). Findings from one of the largest ever meta-analyses of prison education studies carried out in the US (Davis et al, 2013) have shown that inmates who participated in prison education programmes had a 43 per cent lower chance of returning to prison than those who did not. However, for policy makers caught between conflicting discourses around a need to combat recidivism and a need, in the eyes of the public, for punitive incarceration, prison education is what has been termed a 'wicked policy problem' (Allen, 2004). Such problems are complex, not fully understood by policy makers, highly resistant to change and seemingly immune to any evidence that is likely to bring about institutional reconstruction. While evidence indicates that education in prison can reduce recidivism, many politicians struggle to find an acceptable policy solution to the rise in prison populations.

In this chapter I explore this policy problem by looking more closely at the provision of prison education in three northern European countries: Norway, Germany and England. After examining what makes wicked policies 'wicked', I look at why making a distinction between 'education' and 'training' is important in understanding the efficacy of prison education programmes. After introducing the three national contexts, the chapter discusses their contextual specificities and their implications for policy makers when considering the impact prison education can have on genuine prisoner rehabilitation.

A wicked policy problem

Policy makers consider many factors when reviewing the extent to which prison education can or should play a major part in the rehabilitation of prisoners. Not least is the extent to which the prison system at national level is conceived as a tool for rehabilitation, retribution, punishment, incapacitation and/or deterrence. Other factors include available expenditure; the quality of prison leadership, staff development and resources; trends within adult education; and the attitudes, values and beliefs held by key stakeholders in education, including the wider teaching and teacher/educator professions. All of these will be shaped by wider social, political and economic factors that stretch beyond the criminal justice system.

Policy makers also have to be aware of, and confront, barriers to prison education that many prisoners experience. Two broad categories of barriers have been identified in a pan-European survey (Hawley et al, 2012) of coordinators of prison education in 35 countries. Firstly, there are *dispositional barriers* experienced by prisoners that include the effects of a disadvantaged childhood; previous educational failure and low self-esteem; drug and alcohol abuse; and communication, learning and mental health conditions (Munoz, 2009: 11). Secondly, there are *institutional* barriers, including the interruption of learning caused by movement of prisoners from one prison to another due to overcrowding; lack of information on what educational opportunities may be available and how these might be accessed; limited availability of places for learners (for example in classroom space or ratio of learners to teachers); a limited curriculum offer of education and training in terms of both the level and content; and a shortage of human and material teaching and learning resources (for example appropriately qualified staff and computer facilities).

Finally, with the resurgence of national populism and the far right, policy makers also have to confront the fact that fear of crime and the 'penal populism' it generates can push major political parties to wish to be seen to be 'tough on crime' by following potentially repressive policy solutions that threaten the rehabilitative potential of the prison system. This can leave prison education in danger of being depicted as permissive and counterproductive 'do-gooding'. Indeed, the United Nations General Assembly has noted:

> The all too ready willingness of politicians to reflect these fears in penal policy has led to a reluctance to embed prisoners' rights to education and to develop models of education and delivery consistent with the full development of the human personality. (Munoz, 2009: 11)

Tabloid media demonising lawbreakers as violent, parasitic and even 'sub-human' can exacerbate these competing expectations and the dilemmas associated with them. While the British media's longstanding capacity to foment fears about criminals, crime and disorder has, historically, been particularly vitriolic (Philo, 1990), the Berlin Christmas market attack in 2016 by Anis Amri and the Norwegian terrorist attacks in 2017 by Anders Breivik have added momentum internationally to a tabloid frenzy on the public perception of prisoners. Within such climates of fear it is easy for policy makers, academics and practitioners to forget the transformatory effect education can have on those behind bars.

'Training' and 'education' are not the same thing

As an educationalist I am mindful of a distinction often made within my own academic field between the words 'training' and 'education'. The former is generally (and often crudely) associated with learning how to do something and how to develop skills associated with that particular learning context (for example cutting hair, repairing boilers, amputating limbs). The latter often embraces wider, more nuanced processes of systematic learning associated with judgement, reasoning, critical reflection and personal transformation. The terms are often conflated, despite the fact that many forms of professional learning (for example those of teachers, doctors, social workers) include both elements. However, prison education is at its most effective in combating recidivism when conceived and championed as 'education' in its broadest transformatory sense and least effective when narrowly and instrumentally constructed as 'training' for employability (Coates, 2016). This is not to undermine the importance of employability training for prisoners but to recognise there is more to employability than functional 'skills' – and more to prison education than the goal of fostering employability.

This distinction is important when acknowledging that prisoners are a particularly vulnerable group of potential learners. Taking England as an example, compared with the general population, prisoners are '13 times as likely to have been in care as a child, 13 times as likely to be unemployed, 10 times as likely to have been a regular truant, [and] 2.5 times as likely to have had a family member convicted of a criminal offence' (Bracken, 2011: 7). While not ignoring the damage criminal acts inflict on their victims, these figures give some indication of the often tragic situations that prisoners themselves have experienced prior to their initial incarceration. Sadly, however, Hughes (2012) reminds us that the history of education in prisons is one of fluctuation rather than a linear tale of gradual expansion:

> The nature, level and goals of the education provided at any given time or locale are subject to the influences of prevailing views on the causes of crime as well as attitudes regarding the desirability and viability of rehabilitation of offenders as a goal of the penal system. (Hughes, 2012: 4)

While many politicians face a balancing act – bringing about positive societal change against success at the ballot box – attempts at reforming education in prisons are likely to be viewed by many voters as controversial. Nevertheless, educational reform in prisons is an imperative, both categorical and moral.

Prisoners have a right to education

While many international organisations promote the right to education as a universal entitlement, within the context of prison education this right is contested, far from absolute and subject to limitation. With less than 25 per cent of prisoners (Hawley et al, 2013: 13) receiving some sort of formalised education or training in many European countries, it is hard to realise in practice prisoners' rights to formalised education. The Council of Europe in its *European Prison Rules* states that

> every prison shall seek to provide all prisoners with access to educational programmes which are as comprehensive as possible and which meet their individual needs while taking into account their aspirations. (Council of Europe, 2006: 18)

This right is enshrined in the UN General Assembly policy documentation that 'all prisoners should have the right to take part in cultural activities and education aimed at the full development of the human personality' (UN, 2009: 9). Significant legislation from the European Union exists to ensure that this right includes the marginalised, dispossessed and incarcerated, the latter representing approximately 640,000 of the Union's population (Hawley et al, 2013: 12). Article 2 of the First Protocol to the European Convention on Human Rights decrees that 'no person shall be denied the right to education' (Council of Europe, 1950). Similarly, Article 14 of the Charter of Fundamental Rights of the European Union states that '[e]veryone has the right to education and to have access to vocational and continuing training' (European Council, 2000: C364/11).

However, despite all this policy rhetoric on the rights to an education, the Equality and Human Rights Commission has been critical of the way in which this right has been expressed:

> [T]his [right] is expressed in negative rather than positive terms, reflecting the comparatively weak protection it provides. It requires every signatory to guarantee that individuals can take advantage of existing educational institutions, but it does not guarantee an education of a particular kind or quality, or that the education will be provided by a particular institution. (Human Rights Review, 2012: 425)

In considering the 'kind or quality' of education referred to previously, three broad typologies of educational provision in prisons have been identified (European Council, 2011; Costelloe and Warner, 2014):

- Education drawn from a broad mainstream school curriculum and developed to meet the needs of adult learners in a prison context;
- Vocational training targeting basic skills for employability;
- Offence-focused programmes providing courses influenced directly by the prison context (for example anger management courses).

While acknowledging the fuzziness between these distinctions, these typologies serve as useful heuristic devices in attempting to understand differences in educational provision in prisons in the three countries that this chapter explores.

Three national contexts

The extent to which prison education (in its broadest sense) is enacted within any national criminal justice system is dependent on its positioning as one of many vehicles of social welfare. The three countries discussed in this chapter exemplify many aspects of Esping-Andersen and Myles's (2009) three welfare state types: namely, Norway's social democratic approach to welfare policy; Germany's relatively conservative and corporatist approaches; and those adopted in the more free market, liberal regimes characterised as typical of the English welfare state. Different forms of societal trust are associated with each of these different welfare regimes, said to range from relatively high degrees in Nordic social democracies such as Finland, Norway and Sweden (Stephens et al, 2004), to extremely low in the more free market, liberal democracies such as England and the US (Elliot, 2004; Patulny, 2004). I draw a further distinction in this chapter between the Nordic and anglophone clusters of countries (Pratt and Eriksson, 2012). The former adheres to what has become known as *Nordic exceptionalism*, with prisons in this region widely celebrated for more humane, welfare-orientated approaches to prison welfare, including educational provision. The anglophone cluster is associated with prison cultures deemed to be more punitive, more retributional – more austere. Starting with Norway, this section looks more closely at the positioning of prison education within these three criminal justice systems.

Norway

At just 20 per cent, Norway has one of the lowest recidivism rates in the world (World Prison Brief, 2018c). In a country with a population of 5.32 million there are approximately 3,373 prisoners in the country's 38 correctional facilities. Norway's prison population rate (per 100,000 of the national population) is 63, one of the lowest worldwide. Just under a third (30.9 per cent) of inmates are foreign nationals (foreign nationals represent 16.8 per cent of the national population). The percentage of women incarcerated has remained relatively stable in recent years, constituting 6 per cent of the total inmate population in 2018. Moreover, 0.2 per cent of Norwegian prisoners are under the age of 18. Most Norwegian prisons are relatively small institutions with 50 to 100 occupants. The combination of a small population living within a large, geographically challenging environment, plus ministerial policy that ensures that most prisoners serve their sentence close to where they live, accounts in part for the relatively large number of prisons with small prison populations. The maximum time a prisoner can spend in a Norwegian prison is 21 years, although prisoners can be released having served two thirds of their sentence.

In addition to its 38 prisons, Norway also boasts 17 probation offices, responsible for overseeing conditions of release, community sanctions and electronic monitoring.

The Ministry of Justice and Public Security is responsible for overseeing policy related to correctional institutions, including educational programmes, with its administration coming under the Norwegian Correctional Service (NCS). The task of the NCS is to ensure

> [p]roper execution of remand and prison sentences, with due regard to the security of all citizens and attempts to prevent recidivism by enabling the offenders, through their own initiatives, to change their criminal behaviour. (Kriminalomsorgen, 2018)

Prison education in Norway is viewed as a significant tool of behaviour change. All activities within the NCS attempt to align with the values of openness, respect, professionalism and commitment (Kriminalomsorgen, 2018). In many cases, these attempts are successful, with scholars arguing that with Norway's relatively small population, practitioners and politicians can relatively easily be inculcated with similar public service values (Stephens et al, 2004; Czerniawski, 2011). These values, they claim, reflect in part Norway's social democratic political system and its particular form of Lutheranism (a form of Protestant Christianity). However, while official expectations regarding appropriate values can often equate to state mandated ideals of employees, this may not affect what prison practitioners and inmates actually do *in situ*. Nevertheless, in the eyes of Norwegian courts, the sentenced offender 'has all the same rights as all others who live in Norway' (Kriminalomsorgen, 2018). The punishment element within a prison sentence is primarily focused on restriction of prisoners' liberty while they retain full citizenship rights. This emphasis on the rights of prisoners is significant when considering the status that education has in the rehabilitation process.

Broadly speaking, prisons in Norway import public services, including education, from outside the prison. Under Section 4 of the Execution of Sentences Act (MoJ, 2017) this administrative cooperation model accounts for why educational authorities in civilian society take responsibility for education and training in Norwegian prisons. As and where possible, education in Norwegian prisons teaches mainstream school curriculum subjects while also ensuring that there is a sufficient range of vocational education and training available to enhance employability when prisoners are released. Qualified teachers are contracted from local schools and colleges to teach in prisons, although they may not necessarily have received specific training to prepare them for the prison environment. This means that qualified teachers act as bridges between the communities of practice in schools and prisons. Prison officers receive three years' training, including curriculum elements from sociology, psychology, law and social work. As acknowledged citizens, and accepting the constraints of prison architecture and security, Norwegian prisoners have access to mainstream curricula. In what Manger et al (2018) refer to as 'being offered a second chance' (p 5), prison learners have the opportunity to revisit and complete their primary, lower secondary and upper secondary school education. They can also opt for general or vocational studies. All Norwegian prisons offer education up to upper secondary level and in some cases higher education, although there are not necessarily qualified teachers to teach at this higher level.

Germany

At the time of writing, Germany's population of 83.07 million includes a prison population of 62,902 (World Prison Brief, 2018a). The country's prison population rate (per 100,000 of the national population) is 76, one of the lowest in Western Europe. Foreign nationals (who make up 22.5 per cent of the national population) comprise 31.3 per cent of prisoners, and female prisoners make up 5.8 per cent of the prison population. The German criminal justice system has evolved to ensure that those under the age of 20 who have committed an offence have the right to support and education under the protection of youth welfare agencies. This means it is unusual for anyone under this age to enter the prison system, and less likely than it is in other countries. Once a prison sentence has begun, education and/or vocational training are considered a high priority for all prisoners. Just over two thirds of those in German prisons are involved in some sort of education or training programme, a figure considerably higher than the European average of 25 per cent (Prison Reform Trust, 2018).

Germany's federal structure means that individual state Ministries of Justice take localised responsibility for overseeing policy and administration in the country's 183 prisons. According to the German Prison Act of 1976, the objectives of its execution state that:

> By serving his [sic] prison sentence the prisoner shall be enabled in future to lead a life in social responsibility without

committing criminal offences (objective of treatment). The execution of the prison sentence shall also serve to protect the general public from further criminal offenses. (Bundesministerium der Justiz und für Verbraucherschutz, 2013)

According to the Prison Act, three overarching principals underpin the German prison regime:

1. Life in penal institutions should be approximated as far as possible to general living conditions.
2. Any detrimental effects of imprisonment shall be counteracted.
3. Imprisonment shall be so designed as to help the prisoner to reintegrate into life at liberty (Federal Law Gazette, 1976: 11).

While German prisons have no private or federal prison model as such, Harding (2001) has described many German prisons as 'semi-privee'. Many of its custodial functions remain with the state while support services, including education, are in many cases provided through tendered contracts. While many aspects of academic education in prisons are provided by local schools and colleges, vocational education in German prisons is subject to competitive tendering. In contrast to Norway, where education in its broadest sense is sewn into the fabric of the custodial sentence, in German prisons that thread is one wrapped around vocational training. According to the Prison Act, the aim of further training shall be to furnish the prisoner with skill and knowledge to make him capable of earning a livelihood after his release, or to preserve or promote such skill and knowledge (Harding, 2001). While the word 'training' appears 34 times in the Prison Act, the word 'education' appears just four times. The subjects taught vary from prison to prison and from state to state, but they tend to broadly come under the vocational training banner and include construction, metalwork, painting and decorating, woodwork, carpentry, hairdressing and electronics. Depending on the nature of the sentence, modern apprenticeships are offered as well as some higher-level distance learning courses.

England

England is unique in Europe for two reasons: firstly, its prison system is widely recognised as being the most privatised in Europe (Howard League for Penal Affairs, 2013; Prison Reform Trust, 2018); and secondly, along with Scotland and Wales, it boasts the highest rates of imprisonment in Western Europe, with 139 prisoners per 100,000 of the national population (Aebi et al, 2018; World Prison Brief, 2018a). With a population of 59.29 million, English and Welsh prisons currently host 82,384 prisoners. This prison population is made up of 4.6 per cent female prisoners and 11 per cent foreign nationals (foreign nationals make up 19.5 per cent of the population in England and Wales), with 0.8 per cent of this population under the age of 18.

Overseen by the Ministry of Justice, prison administration in 118 prisons in England and Wales is facilitated by Her Majesty's Prison and Probation Service (HMPPS). In a speech to the Royal Society of Arts in 2018, Justice Secretary David Gauke said he supposed the purpose of prison to be threefold:

> First, protection of the public – prison protects the public from the most dangerous and violent individuals. Second, punishment – prison deprives offenders of their liberty and certain freedoms enjoyed by the rest of society and acts as a deterrent. It is not the only sanction available, but it is an important one. And third, rehabilitation – prison provides offenders with the opportunity to reflect on, and take responsibility for, their crimes and prepare them for a law-abiding life when they are released. (Ministry of Justice, 2018)

In the same speech, education and training in prisons is constructed and positioned primarily as a tool for future employment:

> We will shortly be launching our Education and Employment Strategy that will set out our approach to helping offenders get the skills they need to find a job and avoid the activities that landed them in prison in the first place. (Ministry of Justice, 2018)

Education policy in England and Wales is characterised by both endogenous and exogenous forms of privatisation (Ball, 2004), the former associated with the importation of ideas and practices from the private sector (for example performance-related pay and short-term contracts), the latter involving opening up public services to the competitive participation of the private sector. Education contracts are awarded to Further Education (FE) colleges and private organisations through three-yearly competitive tendering. Educational providers competitively bid to manage educational departments in prisons, with, in many cases, changes in the management and employment conditions for teachers and with what has been acknowledged as a lack of continuity, consistency and quality in educational provision for prisoners (Champion, 2017). Drawing on their survey data, Rogers et al (2014) found that nearly two thirds (62 per cent) of prison educators in their study were critical of competitive tendering for prison contracts and the fact that funding is dependent on prisoners' results. They argued that a payment by results model 'rewards providers who maximise revenue by providing short, low level courses that typically secure high success and completion rates' (Rogers et al, 2014: 39). According to the government's website, education courses in prison

> are normally available to help prisoners get new skills, e.g. learning to read and write use computers and do basic maths ... most courses lead to qualifications that are recognized by employers outside prison. (HMRC Gov.uk, 2020)

The positioning and portrayal of prison education and training is one of skills-based and employment-based functionality. While provision varies, most prisons have the potential to offer courses that cover social and life skills (for example cooking, woodwork, citizenship), academic courses (GCSEs in English and Maths), creative classes (art, music); business and IT training; and vocational skills training (plastering, hairdressing). However, this potential is contingent on a number of factors including the availability of sufficient human and material resources (for example enough staff to teach; sufficient numbers of prison guards to accompany prisoners to education wings; sufficient classroom space and equipment). The government's 2016 review of education in prison carried out by Dame Sally Coates (Coates, 2016) promised much in a vision embracing engagement, progression, technology and a holistic whole prison approach to education. A number of improvements have been made in respect to prison education as a result of this review. These include an increase in prison–university partnerships in educational provision, and new funding opportunities that broaden the definition of what education is worthwhile while also reducing the emphasis on what some have described as a 'results driven mentality' (Champion, 2017). However, while the review promised much in terms of the transformation of prisoner learning, events associated with Brexit and increasing levels of mortality and violence in English prisons have dominated policy makers' concerns to the detriment of the review's potential outcomes. In a report published recently by the Council of Europe, serious concerns were raised over the lack of safety for inmates and staff in prisons in England. Causes include increasing levels of prison violence, poor governance and chronic overcrowding (Council of Europe, 2017).

Discussion

It has been argued elsewhere (Czerniawski, 2011) that cultural specificities exist that can account for the variety of ways policies are interpreted and implemented at national, regional and local levels. Nevertheless, there is much to learn from countries where prison education, in its broadest sense, is strongly supported. In increasingly globalised times, debates on and about the efficacy of prison education in the rehabilitative process need international perspectives. Obtaining accurate comparative figures for reoffending rates in different countries is difficult, not least because of the different ways recidivism is defined in different countries. With this in mind, the reoffending rates of 48 per cent in England and Wales (Prison Reform Trust, 2018), 38 per cent in Germany and 20 per cent in Norway are figures that must be treated with caution (Albrect and Jehle, 2014). But they are figures that may give some indication of knowledge, best practice and wisdom that exists elsewhere. Earlier in this chapter I stated that prison education is at its most effective in combating recidivism when conceived and championed as 'education' in its broadest transformatory sense and least effective when narrowly and instrumentally constructed as 'training' for employability. In the short term the former invariably costs more financially than the latter, but in the medium and long term the costs of recidivism extend beyond simply the economic.

Nearly three decades ago Telhaug (1992) identified a common tendency prevailing during the 1980s in Norway, Germany and the UK (despite their differences in history, culture and political systems) in which a policy shift in public service provision moved from an emphasis on the individual and society to that of the economy. By this he meant that values about social justice and personal development had been displaced by the values of competition, quality and productivity. The economic mantra of 'efficiency and effectiveness' and its accompanying emphasis on the significance of the individual are, for some, at odds with those values traditionally associated with the defining and underpinning values of social welfare provision: namely trust, equity and care. Despite various attempts, the neo-liberal project has, as yet, failed to take control of the Norwegian prison system. To what extent this is down to the values associated with social democracy, religion and so on is hard to determine. But the welfare state, in a Keynesian sense, is standing steadfast against a prevailing European neo-liberal wind. Norwegian prisons, while hardly immediate family, nevertheless remain valued cousins within the family of Norwegian welfare state institutions. As Ugelvik succinctly puts it:

> The ideals of rehabilitation and re-socialisation in prison fit hand in glove with the ambitious and generous welfare state system of care/control that developed in the years following the Second World War. (Ugelvik, 2016: 398)

In the Norwegian case a duality exists in which values at local and national level coalesce around ideas of citizenship and human rights. Earlier I stated that qualified teachers act locally as bridges between the communities of practice in schools and prisons. Costelloe and Warner (2014) argue that in Norway the person in prison is constructed primarily as a *citizen*, one who has a right to education. This enacted right to education is reinforced by values focused at local and national levels around the rehabilitative role that prisons can and must play before prisoners are released back into the community. Because of this structurally embedded system of linkages within and beyond the prison in relation to medical, educational and social services, those held in Norwegian prisons are not socially isolated during and after their sentences to the same extent as prisoners in most other countries. Education in Norwegian prisons is associated with the cognitive, social and emotional development of the prisoner, and this may be due in part to the fact that this reflects very much the values of professional teachers who come from an overwhelmingly comprehensive system. But it also reflects on overwhelming and structurally embedded belief in the transformative power of education as a rehabilitative tool.

Earlier in this chapter we saw that the German prison system, like its Norwegian counterpart, is organised around the central tenets of resocialisation and rehabilitation. On my many trips to German prisons I have been impressed at the access that German prisoners have to teachers, psychologists, social workers and social therapists. In part this is because, as I stated earlier, the country's prison population rate is one of the lowest in Western Europe – at just under half that in England. Prisons within the German criminal justice system are just one of a variety of mechanisms for punishing offenders. Eighty per cent of those convicted of crimes in Germany receive sentences as fines based on the offence and the offender's ability to pay (Turner and Travis, 2015). This is particularly significant considering that staffing ratios in German prisons mean there are more opportunities for education and training activities and sufficient prison staff available to escort prisoners from one part of the building to another to access those services. In line with the general status afforded to vocational training in the country as a whole, all prison officers undergo two years of training as part of their role. While vocational training in German prisons is very much focused on its potential to generate employability, the quality of its facilitation is enhanced significantly by the quality of both the human and material resources that are prioritised in its provision.

Not driven by what works and not evidence based, prison education policy in England and Wales is at its most 'wicked'. Political expediency and the signalling of politicians' 'toughness on crime' in different ways, at different times, determines the form it takes. That form resonates with elements in the media that construct prison as a site of punishment rather than a place for reform. Discourses associated with rehabilitation do exist; however, incapacitation and retribution are the de facto discursive constructions that policy makers enact. While the right to education for prisoners cannot be disputed in the English and Welsh context, this right exists within a discursive construction of the prisoner in which they are positioned as an *offender*. Such a positioning means that prison education is narrowly conceived in terms of its employability potential, with a particularly narrow understanding of what employability might comprise – a point enforced by Downes, who states that 'the goal of employment subordinates other legitimate goals of lifelong learning, such as active citizenship, social cohesion and personal fulfillment' (Downes, 2014: 202).

This situation is exacerbated further by the perceived cost of prison education provision to the taxpayer. A neo-liberal policy approach of competitive tendering has aimed to reduce these costs to the state while indirectly reneging on the responsibility to deal with this provision more fully in the ways suggested by European legislation. The reconstruction of prison 'education' into low-cost, job skills training has contributed to the domination of policies that speak more to public moral panic and the need to cut economic costs than to the rehabilitation of prisoners. But this reconstruction has not been successful. The Prison Reform Trust (2018) has signalled a deterioration in prisoner performance. With competing government departmental interests in the provision of education in prisons, it is difficult to see how this policy environment can effectively provide long-term, high-quality education that prisoners not only need but are entitled to. In his third annual report as HM Chief Inspector of Prisons for England and Wales, Peter Clarke stated:

> Violence, drugs, suicide and self-harm, squalor and poor access to education are again prominent themes. Another recurrent theme is the disappointing failure of many prisons to act on our previous recommendations – which are intended to help save lives, keep prisoners safe, ensure they are treated respectfully and to give a chance of returning to the community less likely to reoffend. (Clarke, 2018: 7)

In concluding this discussion, I wish to return to Costelloe and Warner's (2014) typologies of educational provision mentioned earlier. In both the Norwegian and German contexts, human and material resources are provided and developed to facilitate education, training and offence-focused programmes, albeit to varying degrees. These resources are made available because in both locations there is recognition of the right that all prisoners have to a broad curriculum and of the role that prisons can play in the rehabilitation process. In both cases the criminal justice system uses prison as a last resort in dealing with those convicted of crimes. This has an inevitable knock-on effect on the availability of resources for those employed and incarcerated in prisons. While in both countries the systems are far from perfect, they nevertheless outperform England on all the indicators I have highlighted, including prison population and recidivism rates. In contrast to the broad vocational training opportunities that exist for prisoners in German prisons, vocational training, in its narrowest sense, typifies prison education in England despite recent attempts to broaden the curriculum. In the main, prison education in England targets basic employability skills and is facilitated by a de-motivated workforce in fear of the consequences of performance-related pay and short-term contracts. This may not be the best way to deal with this particular 'wicked policy problem' – a problem exacerbated in the English context by the more punitive, retributional and austere nature of its provision.

Concluding thoughts

There is, I am sure, something quite seductive for many politicians and their policy makers about the notion of a free market economy, competition and meritocracy and its potential application to criminal justice, prisons and prison education. This notion enables, in part, the belief that the harder one works, the more one is paid, and the more successful one becomes. It can lead many to believe that privatisation and competition have the ability to save money and transform public perceptions of public sector workers (including those employed in prisons) who are sometimes perceived to be unproductive and unwilling to change. But for many sociologists of education, this logic is immediately open to challenge when looking at prison learners and how they are affected by the marketisation of education, the instrumental repositioning of education as training for employment and competitive policies on public sector work. The churning out of low-level qualifications, hastily facilitated by external providers, can certainly provide sufficient evidence to win future educational contracts with prisons; however, they can do little to repair the damage done by the many dispositional and institutional barriers prisoners will have encountered and which I have described. Low levels of qualifications have also been identified by the European Commission as having negative effects on prisoners' employment prospects upon release, one of the key factors influencing whether or not ex-prisoners reoffend (Hawley et al, 2013).

Those working in increasingly beleaguered prison institutions need to be able to draw, when needed, not just on the knowledge and best practice generated in different communities of practice, but on the enthusiasm, hope, creativity and wisdom that exists elsewhere. In this chapter, I have drawn attention to a disjuncture that exists between the discourses and legislation surrounding the rights of all prisoners to education in Europe, the mediation of those rights by policy makers and what is happening on the ground in many prisons. While a rhetoric of inclusion, entitlements and a rights-based approach towards the provision of education and training in the prison services of Europe exists, in practice, often other more dominant policies can undercut and marginalise these more humane approaches.

Paradoxically, or perhaps not, the criminal justice model least based on marketised goals of effectiveness, namely Norway's, is the most effective and efficient of the three I consider in this chapter. I do not suggest that the prison systems and educational provision in Norway and Germany are without problems. There are many documented systemic failings in both countries that this chapter has been unable to explore. However, I do highlight for those looking at improving prison education in England that it really does not have to be this way: There are lessons to be learned.

References

Aebi, M.F., Tiago, M.M., Berger-Kolopp, L. and Burkhardt, C. (2018). *SPACE I – Council of Europe Annual Penal Statistics: Prison Populations. Survey 2016*, Strasbourg: Council of Europe.

Allen, J. (2004). *Sociology of Education* (3rd ed), Southbank, Victoria: Social Science Press, Thomson Learning Australia.

Ball, S. (ed) (2004) *The Routledge Falmer Reader in Sociology of Education*, New York: Routledge Falmer.

Bundesministerium der Justiz und für Verbraucherschutz (2013) 'Act Concerning the Execution of Prison Sentences and Measures of Rehabilitation and Prevention involving Deprivation of Liberty (Prison Act)', 16 March 1976 (act updated by Article 7 of the Act of 25 April 2013), available from: https://assets.publishing.service.gov.uk/government/uploads/system/uploads/attachment_data/file/779199/gps-location-monitoring-pilot-process-evaluation.pdf [accessed 17 March 2019].

Champion, N. (2017) *Coates: One Year On*, London: Prison Education Trust.

Clarke, P. (2018) *HM Chief Inspector of Prisons for England and Wales Annual Report 2017–18*, London: Her Majesty's Inspectorate of Prisons, available from: https://www.justiceinspectorates.gov.uk/hmiprisons/wp-content/uploads/sites/4/2018/07/6.4472_HMI-Prisons_AR-2017-18_Content_A4_Final_WEB.pdf [accessed 22 January 2019].

Coates, S. (2016) *Unlocking Potential: A Review of Education in Prison*, London: Crown Copyright, available from: https://assets.publishing.service.gov.uk/government/uploads/system/uploads/attachment_data/file/524013/education-review-report.pdf [accessed 27 June 2018].

Costelloe, A. and Warner, K. (2014) 'Prison education across Europe: policy, practice, politics', *London Review of Education*, 12(2): 175–83.

Council of Europe (2006) *The European Prison Rules*, Strasbourg: Council of Europe Publishing/Editions du Conseil de l'Europe.

Council of Europe (2017) 'Report to the Government of the United Kingdom on the visit to the United Kingdom carried out by the European Committee for the prevention of torture and inhuman or degrading treatment or punishment', Strasbourg: Council of Europe CPT/Inf, available from: https://rm.coe.int/168070a773 [accessed 17 March 2019].

Coyle, A. (2016) 'Prisons in context', in Y. Jewkes, J. Bennett and B. Crewe (eds) *The Handbook on Prisons*, London: Routledge, pp 7–23.

Czerniawski, G. (2011) *Emerging Teachers and Globalisation*, London: Routledge.

Czerniawski, G. (2016) 'A race to the bottom: Prison education and the English and Welsh policy context', *Journal of Education Policy*, 31(2): 198–212.

Davis, L.M., Bozick, R., Steele, J.L., Saunders, J. and Miles, J.N.V. (2013) *Evaluating the Effectiveness of Correctional Education: A Meta-Analysis of Programs That Provide Education to Incarcerated*, Washington, DC: Bureau of Justice Assistance, US Department of Justice.

Downes, P. (2014) *Access to Education in Europe: A Framework and Agenda for System Change*, Dordrecht: Springer.

Esping-Andersen, G. and Myles, J. (2009) 'Economic inequality and the welfare state', in W. Salverda, B. Nolan and M. Timothy (eds) *The Oxford Handbook of Economic Inequality*, Oxford: Oxford University Press, pp 639–64.

Federal Law Gazette (1976) (translation) 'Act Concerning the Execution of Prison Sentences and Measures of Rehabilitation and Prevention involving Deprivation of Liberty', Prison Act, 16 March, available from: http://www.prawa.org/wp-content/uploads/2012/09/Prison-Act_Stand-17_06_2008-Germany.pdf [accessed 7 February 2019].

Harding, R.W. (2001) 'Private prisons', in M. Tonry (ed) *Crime and Justice: A Review of Research*, Vol 28, Chicago, IL: Chicago University Press, pp 265–346.

Hawley, J., Murphy, I. and Souto-Otero, M. (2012) *Survey on Prison Education and Training in Europe – Final Report*, Order 23 of the DG Education and Culture Framework Contract 02/10-Lot 1, July.

Hawley, J., Murphy, I. and Souto-Otero, M. (2013). *Prison Education and Training in Europe: Current State-of-Play and Challenges – A Summary Report Authored for the European Commission*, Brussels: GHK Publishing.

HMRC Gov.uk (2020) 'Prison life', available from: https://www.gov.uk/life-in-prison/education-and-work-in-prison [accessed 31 March 2020].

Hughes, E. (2012) *Education in Prison: Studying through Distance Learning*, London: Routledge.

Kriminalomsorgen (2018) *About the Norwegian Correction Service*, available from: http://www.kriminalomsorgen.no/information-in-english.265199.no.html [accessed 17 March 2019].

Manger, T., Eikeland, O.J. and Asbjornsen, A. (2018) 'Why do not more prisoners participate in adult education? An analysis of barriers to education in Norwegian prisons', *International Review of Education*, 7 June, available from: https://doi.org/10.1007/s11159-018-9724-z [accessed 2 April 2019].

Ministry of Justice (2018) 'Prison reform speech', Delivered 6 March, available from: https://www.gov.uk/government/speeches/prisons-reform-speech [accessed 17 March 2019].

Munoz, V. (2009) 'Promotion and protection of human rights, civil, political, economic, social and cultural rights, including the right to development: the right to education of persons in detention', UN General Assembly, 2 April, available from: http://www2.ohchr.org/english/bodies/hrcouncil/docs/11session/A.HRC.11.8_en.pdf [accessed 7 February 2019].

Philo, G. (ed) (1990) *Seeing and Believing: The Influence of Television*, Routledge: London.

Pratt, J. and Eriksson, A. (2012) *Contrasts in Punishment: An Explanation of Anglophone Excess and Nordic Exceptionalism*, London: Routledge.

Prison Reform Trust (2018) 'Prison: the facts – Bromley Briefings June 2018', London: Prison Reform Trust.

Rogers, L., Simonot, M. and Nartey, A. (2014) *Prison Educators: Professionalism Against All the Odds*, London: UCU and IoE.

Stephens, P., Egil tønnessen, F. and Kyriacou, C. (2004) 'Teacher training and teacher education in England and Norway: a comparative study of policy goals', *Comparative Education*, 40(1): 109–30.

Telhaug, A.O. (1992) *Norsk og internasjonal skoleutvikling* [Norwegian and International School Development], Oslo: Ad Notam Gyldendal.

Turner, N. and Travis, J. (2015) 'What we learned from German Prisons', *New York Times*, 6 August, available from: https://www.nytimes.com/2015/08/07/opinion/what-we-learned-from-german-prisons.html [accessed 16 March 2017].

Walmsley, R. (2018) 'World prison population list' (12th ed), London: Institute for Criminal Policy Research.

World Prison Brief (2018a) 'Country page England and Wales', available from: http://www.prisonstudies.org/country/united-kingdom-england-wales [access 21 March 2019].

World Prison Brief (2018b) 'Country page Germany', available from: http://www.prisonstudies.org/country/germany [accessed 21 March 2019].

World Prison Brief (2018c) 'Country page Norway', available from: http://www.prisonstudies.org/country/norway [accessed 21 March 2019].

18

Making local regulation better? Marketisation, privatisation and the erosion of social protection

Steve Tombs

Introduction

Since 2010, what had previously been New Labour's approach to business regulation – 'better regulation' (who could possibly object?) – has become turbocharged under conditions of 'austerity'. Within this onslaught on the social wage, even those local services which attract popular support have been vulnerable, not least some of those which fall under the rubric of regulatory services. For example, one of the areas compromised by 'the cuts' since 2010 has been fire protection: In December 2018, HM Inspectorate of Constabulary, Fire and Rescue Services reported that fire safety inspections across England had fallen by 42 per cent since 2010–11, according to the new watchdog for fire and rescue services – a somewhat chilling fact in the light of the fire at Grenfell Tower in June 2017 which killed 72 people and devastated the lives, for the rest of their lives, of many more (Tombs, 2019). Perhaps most alarmingly in light of Grenfell, the same National Audit Office (NAO) report noted that the government had 'reduced funding most to fire and rescue authorities with the highest levels of need … as defined by the social and demographic factors'. In other words, the cuts to fire and rescue services have fallen hardest on the poorest – just like all austerity cuts (Cooper and Whyte, 2017).

More generally, since the cuts began to bite, capacity to enforce regulation of businesses at local authority level – designed to enhance social protection in areas such as food safety, pollution control, trading standards and workers' health and safety – has fallen into virtual disrepair. This is because most councils – albeit not the Royal Borough of Kensington and Chelsea Council, the wealthiest local authority in England, within which Grenfell Tower, and its relatively poor residents, stood – have reached rock bottom in terms of their ability to maintain services (Ryan, 2017). As an Environmental Health Officer in Merseyside put it to me, 'we are at that point now, public health and protection is being eroded'.

But this is not simply a sorry tale of anti-regulatory zeal, of austerity and cuts, of the non-enforcement of regulation, nor simply of the broader undermining of social protection. Rather, *this is about a process of the long march of profit-seeking institutions through what was public service and public provision – a process characterised by privatisation, marketisation, de-democratisation and deregulation for the business world.*

Reframing regulation: neo-liberalism and state-corporate crime

The broad frame for this discussion is what we might term 'crimes of the powerful', a phrase introduced in 1976 in the eponymous title of Frank Pearce's book (Pearce, 1976). With no little irony, that book appeared at the same time as the neo-liberal project was being rolled out in Chile, the UK, the US and then across much of the world.

Among its many effects, neo-liberalism ushered in a period of official state antipathy to government regulation of business (deemed 'interference') – so that deregulation became a favoured policy objective of governments of all political stripes. Deregulation either entailed explicit removal of regulations, or the undermining of the capacity or will to enforce existing regulations of business. In so doing, it reversed the effects of business regulation which had emerged as a form of social protection – effects which forced the costs of that protection, whether for workers, consumers or the environment, onto the producers of risks, that is, businesses, through their commercial activity. Deregulation, then, is not about actually or effectively removing rules which limit business activities, it is about shifting the non-market costs of production – what economists call 'externalities' – away from producers, so that the benefits of private production are privatised (in the form of profits), while the harmful effects of that activity are socialised (in the form of harm to lives, the environment, costs of healthcare, welfare, clean-up and so on).

Over the subsequent decades these tendencies have produced significant increases in inequalities within and between states, and not coincidentally in corporate power. And in one contribution to analysing the overall structure that produced corporate crime in the neo-liberal period, Laureen Snider (2000) notes that strategies of accumulation realigned the balance of social forces in capitalist economies in a contradictory form. On the one hand, neo-liberalism created fertile conditions for producing corporate crimes; on the other hand, it diminished public capacity to describe and respond to them. Corporate crime, for Snider, was effectively being defined out of existence by neo-liberal ideals and the policies that followed those ideals.

In a very obvious sense, then, the new realignments of neo-liberalism shifted the nature of the crimes of the powerful. Prior to that period, a principal concern for critical scholars and pro-social activists and campaigners might have been corporate crimes per se – illegal acts or omissions that are the result of deliberate decision making or culpable negligence within a legitimate formal organisation, committed by or on behalf of the corporation in pursuit of its formal goals (cutting costs, increasing market share, profitability, innovation and so on).

But it is no coincidence that the consolidations of neo-liberalism brought with them the emergence of a new object of focus. First developed by scholars in the US in 1990, state-corporate crime is defined by Kramer and Michalowski (2006: 20) as 'illegal or socially injurious actions that occur when one or more institutions of political governance pursue a goal in direct co-operation with one or more institutions of economic production and distribution'. State-corporate crime captures crimes committed in the context of increasingly complex relationships between states and the private sector, where private providers increasingly deliver 'public' functions instead of, or work alongside, public authorities.

For Kramer and Michalowski, state-corporate crime is either initiated or facilitated by states. When such crime is initiated by states, corporations engage in illegality at the prompt of or with the approval of state institutions; when facilitated, this refers to situations where state actors fail to prevent, respond to or collude with such illegality. More recently, Kristian Lasslett has expanded upon these subcategories, identifying corporate-initiated state crime, which occurs 'when corporations directly employ their economic power to coerce states into taking deviant actions'; and corporate-facilitated state crime, which occurs 'when corporations either provide the means for states' criminality, ... or when they fail to alert the domestic/international community to the state's criminality, because these deviant practices directly/indirectly benefit the corporation concerned' (Lasslett, 2010).

Finally, it should be emphasised that integral to neo-liberalism, the realignment of state–corporate relations and indeed any of the processes detailed in the rest of this paper is the phenomenon of marketisation. Whitfield (2006) characterises marketisation as 'the process by which market forces are imposed in public services', identifying a series of elements within this general process (Whitfield, 2006: 4). Crucially, for us, are processes whereby markets replace, and market forces undertake the role of, regulation –which will be discussed later. As indicated earlier, regulation is ultimately about forcing the externalities associated with economic activity back onto corporations, so that the costs of these are borne by those who create the costs, even if at the expense of profitability; marketisation as a replacement for public regulation displaces these costs onto external constituencies beyond the profit making organisation. In this sense, two further points need emphasis. Firstly, these processes are redistributive: in protecting profits and socialising costs, they effectively shift costs from the wealthy (those who own and control businesses) to the poorer (consumers, communities, workers). At the same time, secondly, they are de-democratising – regulation, where it proceeds through the state, holds the potential for democratic accountability, while marketisation, as a privatising phenomenon, breaks any such links with publicly elected officials and thus ruptures any potential for such accountability.

From better regulation to austerity at local authority level

In 2004, New Labour's Chancellor of the Exchequer Gordon Brown established the Hampton Review, with a remit to reduce regulatory 'burdens on business' across all (63) major, national regulators, as well as 468 local authorities (Hampton, 2005: 13, 3).

Hampton's subsequent 2005 report, *Reducing Administrative Burdens: Effective Inspection and Enforcement*, proved to be the consolidation of what had already been termed 'Better Regulation', a formal policy shift from enforcement to advice and education, a concentration of formal enforcement resources away from the majority of businesses onto so-called high risk areas, and consistent efforts to do more with less. 'Better Regulation' proved to be remarkably effective in reducing regulation. Combining ideological attacks on regulation per se, undermining the role and capacity of regulators, and engaging in pro-business legal reform (Tombs, 2016), it had produced, by 2010, significant downturns in all forms of enforcement activity across a swathe of national and local forms of regulation.

Five years later, at the General Election of 2010, changes to law coupled with downward pressures on inspection and formal enforcement meant that, both nationally and locally, much in the regulatory landscape across the UK had been transformed. Of course, in the intervening years the financial crisis had erupted, resulting in massive state bailouts and a tide (albeit short-lived) of criticism of the poor regulation of 'the banks'. Yet, quite remarkably, the political consensus, at least in the UK, remained that business was overregulated – and all three mainstream political parties campaigned on manifestos to reduce regulation further. The five years of Coalition government which followed went on to act on that commitment with a feverish intensity. Nor did the post-2015 Conservative government relent in its attack on regulation and enforcement – even if its regulation-hating rhetoric had to be toned down, temporarily at least, in the wake of Grenfell.

In what follows, I focus down to local authority level as a means of examining what these trends mean in the context of unfolding austerity – and how they have ushered in opportunities for a reframed, that is, specifically, privatised and marketised, form of regulation.

From 2009 to 2010, local government funding from the UK government in Westminster (London) came under pressure. Indeed, of all the cuts to government departments between 2010 and 2016, the Department for Communities and Local Government (DCLG) was impacted most of all. Further, analyses of the distribution and impacts of these cuts indicate overwhelmingly that they impact most heavily upon poorer local authorities:

> Councils covering the 10 most deprived areas of England – measured according to the index of multiple deprivation – are losing £782 on average per household, while authorities covering the richest areas are losing just £48 on average. Hart district council in Hampshire, the least deprived local authority, is losing £28 per household, while in Liverpool District B, the most deprived area, the figure is £807. (Sparrow, 2014)

One of the most deprived regions in the UK is Merseyside – and the following sections of this chapter draw upon a case study of regulation and enforcement in the local authorities which make up this region. Merseyside is a populous conurbation: The combined population of the five local authorities under examination here is 1.4 million.[1] There are some 40,000 businesses registered across these authorities. Merseyside is also one of the poorest regions in England, if not the poorest. On the English Index of Multiple Deprivation (Department for Communities and Local Government, 2015), Knowlsey is the second poorest local authority area in England, Liverpool the fourth

---

[1] Knowsley, Liverpool, St Helens, Sefton and Wirral.

poorest. Residents across all five areas are particularly reliant upon their local authority for a range of welfare, social and public services, as well as employment opportunities, so that changes in any of these impact disproportionately upon local people, as residents, consumers and workers (Centre for Local Economic Strategies, 2014).

In a series of interviews with 35 Environmental Health Officers (EHOs) across Merseyside during 2014–15,[2] the strongest, most consistent theme to emerge focused around 'the cuts'. For example, and most starkly, staffing levels across each of the functions across all of the local authorities had, virtually across the board, been radically reduced. It is worth noting that the absolutely low numbers of staff resource at issue here, in any authority in any year, but notably by the final year for which data are provided, that is, 2017. At its most extreme, by April 2017, Knowsley had no dedicated pollution control EHOs, and neither Liverpool nor Sefton had any dedicated health and safety EHOs – rather, food EHOs would 'keep an eye out' for health and safety issues.[3] It is little wonder, then, that during interviews I heard remarkably similar phrases from EHOs, to the effect that local authority enforcement capacities had been so undermined that public health and safety were endangered.

There are various dimensions to these staffing reductions – as well as other pressures on local authority enforcement – which are worth greater exploration in the context of this edited collection.

The reach of the private sector into public service

Alongside the resource constraints within which local authorities are struggling to meet their statutory duties as regulators is a related development, the creeping influence of the private sector in those regulatory efforts. Here we find clear instances of politics meeting economics and, in their combination, changing the role of local regulation and enforcement, perhaps irrevocably. This not only undermines the idea that regulation is something which is aimed at guiding business towards socially efficient operations, but it creates an increasing democratic deficit, as public services designed for social protection come under ever increasing private influence.

---

[2] In four of the five authorities; one refused access.

[3] In May 2013, a change to HSE's National Enforcement Code had effectively banned preventative health and safety inspections at a local level (DWP, 2013).

Educating EHOs

We can see the creeping influence of the private sector in changes to the education of EHOs. EHOs attain professional status through a university degree course accredited by the Chartered Institute of Environmental Health (CIEH). In 2011, the curriculum was overhauled, partly, in the words of one interviewee, a programme leader of one such course at a north-west university, to reflect 'the shift in the profession from not being seen as inspection focused'. In the words of another respondent, a student EHO, 'CIEH is increasingly making the content of degrees more private-sector friendly'. This process had already begun as a result of local authorities' inability to offer paid placements for students, while students require placements in order to complete the main assessment on their degree course. Several respondents told me that local authority-funded students simply no longer exist – the one student EHO I interviewed was working in the authority part time, and unpaid. More commonly, since students still have to undertake a placement, they now take these where they can be paid, or at least receive expenses, that is, in the private sector – Asda, Sainsbury's and Tesco were all mentioned as significant sites for such placements in the food sector. Obviously, and as was said to me, this also means that the values and perspectives of the private sector (the potentially regulated) are prioritised for the student EHO over those of the regulator (and hence the public). In such subtle ways are the mindsets and thus practices of a profession shifted.

The Primary Authority scheme

The transformation of social protection is not simply about non-enforcement – it also involves a concerted effort to change the relationship between the state, the private sector and regulation. Indeed, this changing relationship is increasingly one in which the private business, ostensibly the object of regulation, becomes a key shaper of that regulation. A paradigmatic instance of this is being achieved through the Primary Authority (PA) scheme, itself illustrative of how the economics and politics of Better Regulation have combined to produce a fundamental shift in the practice and principles of regulation and enforcement. The PA scheme was introduced by the New Labour government in 2009, but given considerable impetus by the Coalition government from 2010, notably following the establishment of the Better Regulation Delivery Office (BRDO) in 2012, for which oversight of the scheme was a key priority.

According to the BRDO, the scheme

> allows businesses to be involved in their own regulation. It enables them to form a statutory partnership with one local authority, which then provides robust and reliable advice for other councils to take into account when carrying out inspections or addressing non-compliance. The general aim is to ensure that local regulation is consistent at a national level, but sufficiently flexible to address local circumstances. The business can decide what level of support it requires, and the resourcing of partnerships is a matter for the parties concerned. A primary authority can recover its costs. (Better Regulation Delivery Office, 2014: 2)

When this statement was issued, in April 2014, 1,500 businesses had established PA relationships across 120 local authorities. The PA 'industry' has mushroomed in recent years. As of 27 March 2017, there were 17,358 such relationships across 182 authorities. In a prelude to the Enterprise Act 2017, the government stated that '[t]he number of businesses in Primary Authority is expected to increase from 17,000 to an estimated 250,000 by 2020 and simplification of the administrative arrangements for the scheme is required to support this expansion' (Regulatory Delivery, 2017: 4).

The PA scheme applies across a vast swathe of areas of regulation, but its main areas are pollution control, occupational health and safety and other local environmental health enforcement areas, such as food safety, trading standards, fire safety, licensing, petrol storage certification and explosives licensing. It allows a company – and, since April 2014, franchises and businesses in trade associations – operating across more than one local authority area to enter an agreement with one specific local authority to regulate all of its sites, nationally. Thus, a supermarket such as Tesco may have stores in every one of the local authorities in England and Wales and, under the PA scheme, it can reach an agreement with one local authority to regulate its systems across all of its stores in every local authority for complying with a relevant body of law – occupational health and safety or food hygiene, for example.

To regulate its systems, the company makes a payment to the local authority, agreed through contract. It should be immediately clear that this structure through which contracts are agreed enormously favours the businesses – these are few – in contrast to the many local authorities who want the contract (and, given central government cuts, need the money) from the business. Such highly unequal terms of trade should be thought of as a distorted market of few sellers and many buyers, leaving local authorities potentially pitted against each other in a 'bidding war' of ever more lax regulation in order to access the funding which follows PA contracts.

Aside from the power to impose more rather than less favourable contractual conditions, the key benefit of the PA agreement per se for the company is the absence of effective oversight in the vast majority of its sites. These can be visited in other areas, but any enforcement action needs to be undertaken through the local authority which is the PA. Should a local authority wish to prosecute a company in a PA agreement, for example, it can only do so with the permission of the local authority which is party to that agreement. Then, under the scheme, any consideration of a potential prosecution must entail prior notice being given to the company; the company can then request that the matter be referred to the BRDO for determination (Williams, 2013).

Government advice on this to businesses is explicit:

> Primary authorities generally report low levels of enforcement action against the businesses they partner with. In the event that an enforcement officer decides to take action against a business that is in a direct partnership with you, or covered by a co-ordinated partnership with you, he or she is required to notify you via the Primary Authority Register. As a primary authority you can direct against (block) an enforcement action being taken against the business when you have issued relevant Primary Authority Advice and the business was following it. (Office for Product Safety and Standards, 2018)

While civil servants at the BRDO stated that the PA scheme was 'a big success',[4] it was proving highly problematic for local regulators, even as they sought to enter into PA agreements in order to generate income – 'this is why we are really pushing the PA scheme', one local authority interviewee told me. But as another respondent put it, while 'in theory it could work well, in practice it protects large companies from local authority enforcement'. Others noted similar problems with the scheme, for example: 'under PA they [companies] only have to demonstrate the existence of systems'; local authorities have a 'disincentive to take enforcement action because PA schemes are

---

[4] Two interviews were conducted at the BRDO, May 2014.

a source of income'; PA schemes 'protect companies from inspection and enforcement'; they operate 'in my experience at the level of a tick-box rather than real co-operation or taking responsibility'; PA schemes 'work on paper only, there are hundreds of businesses in the scheme and I can't see how these can all be genuine'.

In general, then, as one enforcement officer noted, 'Primary Authority has had a real impact on what we can and cannot do'; the claim was made at length that businesses 'pick and choose' with which local authorities to enter into PA agreements, with the insistence that 'they wouldn't pick an authority like Liverpool', they will pick the 'no-one knows anything authority', that is, local authorities with no experience of the particular industry or business. Moreover, in the processes of negotiation to draw up the contract which represents the PA agreement, local authorities are at a distinct disadvantage – there is an 'asymmetry of expertise' (Social Enterprise UK, 2012) between local authority negotiators and private companies in such contractual negotiations, as well, of course, as a structural power accruing to private companies operating across numerous authorities to drive down the terms of contract with any one local authority by threatening to move to another.

Outsourcing and privatisation

The PA scheme represents a fundamental shift in the nature of local regulation and enforcement. It is a classic vehicle of Better Regulation, since it reduces inspection, builds in checks against regulation and enforcement, exacerbates the power imbalance between regulators and regulated, and operates on a marketised, contract-based system. Discussion of the PA scheme was, then, inevitably used as a way of discussing the future trajectories of local regulatory services. When respondents were asked where they thought their service might be in five to ten years, responses were variations on a theme, encapsulated pithily by the response, 'I don't know if I'll be here in one year let alone five years'. Those who expanded upon this rather dispirited response indicated that the function would become marketised or privatised or likely some hybrid of the two – reflecting more general prognoses of how local authorities would respond to the pressures of funding cuts (Hastings et al, 2013).

Such indications are hardly pure speculation. The wholesale outsourcing of regulatory functions has been realised in two local authorities. In October 2012, North Tyneside Council announced the transfer of 800 employees to Balfour Beatty and Capita Symonds.

Then, in a much bigger contract, in August 2013, the London Borough of Barnet saw off a legal challenge to a contract to hand over its services to two wings of Capita, under what has become known as the 'One Barnet' model. In this model, business services – estates, finance, payroll, human resources, IT, procurement, revenues and benefits administration, and customer and support services – have been outsourced to Capita in a ten-year contract worth £350 million. A range of other services – including regulatory services – were contracted to its subsidiary Capita Symonds, in a £130 million contract, also for ten years. From January 2016, Burnley Council's environmental health services were outsourced to Liberata.

These wholesale shifts from public to private provision are the mere visible tip of a significant iceberg. Councils in Bromley, Chester West, Cheshire and Wandsworth have all publicly considered wholesale privatisation of regulatory services. Moreover, recent research by the New Economics Foundation for the Trades Union Congress (TUC) calculated that '[e]nvironmental and regulatory services is the sector with the second biggest proportion of expenditure paid to external contractors, at 44 per cent' (TUC and the New Economics Foundation, 2015: 59). The arrangements under which this outsourcing proceeds are complex and opaque, confounding accountability and often even transparency (under the usual clauses of 'commercial confidentiality'), and include diverse arrangements such as the use of strategic service partnerships (SSPs), joint venture companies (JVCs), shared services and collaborative outsourcing (TUC and the New Economics Foundation, 2015: 59).

Discussion: from social protection to social murder

> We're dying in there because we don't count. (Cited in Wynne Jones, 2017)

So spoke one teenage resident on the morning of 14 June 2017 as he stood outside Grenfell Tower, which continued to burn. Both the fire and 'not counting' are partly the outcomes of the economic and political initiatives outlined in this chapter.

Once regulation is successfully cast as a problem to be reduced, a drain on state resources, private entrepreneurship and economic growth, and once that view is furthered through regulatory, legal and institutional reform, then the momentum against regulation becomes virtually unstoppable. If less state regulation and enforcement are always to be preferred, how little is little enough?

As has also been indicated in this chapter, the rationale for regulation has shifted during this period – from one ostensibly claiming to deliver some level of social protection to regulation as a vehicle for private growth and profitability. At local levels, this shift has been stark, with local authorities increasingly servicing private business rather than providing public service, and even with public provision being replaced wholesale by private regulation of private capital. In other words, what is at issue here is not just reducing, but changing the shape and nature of, local government, even if any focus on local responsibilities for social protection are often absent from even critical analyses of this process (McMahon, 2015).

The trends at issue in this chapter, therefore, also amount to a process of de-democratisation. It is in this context – de-democratisation – that Tenants' Management Organisations (TMOs), such as the Kensington and Chelsea TMO, might be understood; for a TMO is effectively an arm's length organisational arrangement within local neo-liberalism which breaks lines of accountability and undermines democracy. And this is also the context within which we better understand both the conditions in which residents of Grenfell Tower and the Lancaster West Estate within which it sits lived and, most crucially, their relationships with the Royal Borough of Kensington and Chelsea (RBKC) Council and the Kensington and Chelsea Tenants' Management Organisation (KCTMO), to which the Council had transferred the management of the borough's entire council housing stock, 9,700 homes, in 1996 (Boughton, 2017).

Stanning has argued that KCTMO was universally hated by those it housed across the borough, a hatred which 'goes beyond the usual suspicion of residents towards those who have power over them. KCTMO has for years been an unaccountable and deeply resented part of life for many Kensington and Chelsea residents' (Stanning, 2017). I think this relationship is best characterised as one of contempt by the KCTMO for Grenfell residents (Tombs, 2019), nowhere better captured than in the refurbishment of the tower, which was ultimately to prove fatal for at least 72 of its residents – and the disastrous decision to clad the tower 'because it was an eyesore for the rich people who live opposite' (Akala, musician and local resident, C4 News, 15 June 2017). Such relationships typify wider processes of gentrification and social cleansing in many of the UK's inner cities, but most notably in London.

Formed in 2010, the Grenfell Action Group (GAG) joined with Unite Community Membership in 2015 principally as a result of concerns about the refurbishment of the tower block (Grenfell Action

Group, 2015a). In this context, the Group documented 'threatening and intimidatory tactics' being used by the TMO and Rydon, the lead contractor in the tower's refurbishment, to get access to flats – access which had been denied in response to what GAG saw as substandard and dangerous work. The Group set out a long list of residents' 'primary concerns with regards TMO/Rydon', at the top of which was the '(l)ack of meaningful consultation with residents and feeling of total disregard for tenant and leaseholders' well-being' (Grenfell Action Group, 2015b). Safety concerns relating to the lack of fire safety instructions, power surges, the single staircase egress in the event of a fire and the exposure of gas pipes within the flats as a result of the refurbishment were commonly expressed. As GAG posted at 5 am on the morning of the fire as the tower was still in flames,

> [r]egular readers of this blog will know that we have posted numerous warnings in recent years about the very poor fire safety standards at Grenfell Tower and elsewhere in RBKC. **ALL OUR WARNINGS FELL ON DEAF EARS** and we predicted that a catastrophe like this was inevitable and just a matter of time. (Grenfell Action Group, 2017, emphasis in original)

The starkest of these warnings had been published in November 2016, under the apocryphal but prescient headline 'KCTMO – Playing with fire!', which included the following, chilling passage:

> It is a truly terrifying thought but the Grenfell Action Group firmly believe that only a catastrophic event will expose the ineptitude and incompetence of our landlord, the KCTMO, and bring an end to the dangerous living conditions and neglect of health and safety legislation that they inflict upon their tenants and leaseholders. … [O]nly an incident that results in serious loss of life of KCTMO residents will allow the external scrutiny to occur that will shine a light on the practices that characterise the malign governance of this non-functioning organisation … (Grenfell Action Group, 2016)

Such chillingly prescient words were ignored, as virtually all of the claims, warnings and concerns of local residents were ignored by a Council who not only did not represent them but would have preferred to have them out of the borough, allowing luxury developments for the world's super-rich to expand north-westwards. While it was the fire which caused loss and devastation of lives, it was in many respects a class contempt which was the cause of this outrage – a contempt that continued in the wake of the fire through the initial absence of the national and local state, and then through the lies, broken promises and half-truths which characterised the response of state actors and bodies when they did eventually arrive on the scene (Tombs, 2019).

Grenfell illustrates better than anything that the processes outlined in this chapter do not amount to a story about rules, regulations and red tape. Rather, this is a story about social harm and social inequality – lives lost and shortened, the health of communities, workers, consumers made poorer. It is a story about the concentration of wealth and power in the hands of the few and the insatiable desire of these few for yet more. It is a story about contempt for those who, in the eyes of the powerful and the rich, simply 'don't count'. It is a story about the intentional removal of social protection – and thus a story about avoidable business generated, state facilitated violence: social murder.

References

Better Regulation Delivery Office (2014) *Regulators' Code*, Birmingham: Better Regulation Delivery Office.

Boughton, J. (2017) 'A perfect storm of disadvantage: the history of Grenfell Tower', *inews*, 26 July, available from: https://inews.co.uk/essentials/news/perfect-storm-disadvantage-history-grenfell-tower/amp/ [accessed 18 November 2019].

Centre for Local Economic Strategies (2014) *Austerity Uncovered*, London: TUC.

Cooper, V. and Whyte, D. (2017) 'Government austerity demands that we die within our means', *Open Democracy UK*, 23 May, available from: https://www.opendemocracy.net/uk/vickie-cooper/government-austerity-demands-that-we-die-within-our-means [accessed 2 September 2019].

Department for Communities and Local Government (2015) *The English Indices of Deprivation: Statistical Release*, London: Department for Communities and Local Government.

Grenfell Action Group (2015a) 'A collective voice for residents as "Grenfell Community Unite" is formed!', 31 March, available from: https://grenfellactiongroup.wordpress.com/2015/03/31/a-collective-voice-for-residents-as-grenfell-community-unite-is-formed/ [accessed 31 March 2020].

Grenfell Action Group (2015b) Minutes from the Grenfell Tower Emergency Residents Meeting (17/03/15), 27 March, available from: https://grenfellactiongroup.wordpress.com/2015/03/27/minutes-from-the-grenfell-tower-emergency-residents-meeting-170315/ [accessed 31 March 2020].

Grenfell Action Group (2016) 'KCTMO – playing with fire!' 20 November, available from: https://grenfellactiongroup.wordpress.com/2016/11/20/kctmo-playing-with-fire/ [accessed 2 September 2019].

Grenfell Action Group (2017) 'Grenfell Tower fire', 14 June, available from: https://grenfellactiongroup.wordpress.com/2017/06/14/grenfell-tower-fire/ [accessed 2 September 2019].

Hampton, P. (2005) *Reducing Administrative Burdens: Effective Inspection and Enforcement*, London: HM Treasury/HMSO.

Hastings, A., Bailey, N., Besemer, K., Bramley, G., Gannon, M. and Watkins, D. (2013) *Coping with the Cuts? Local Government and Poorer Communities*, York: The Joseph Rowntree Foundation.

Kramer, R.C. and Michalowski, R. (2006) 'The original formulation', in R.J. Michalowski and R.C. Kramer (eds) *State-Corporate Crime*, Brunswick, NJ: Rutgers University Press, pp 18–26.

Lasslett, K. (2010) 'Crime or social harm? A dialectical perspective', *Crime, Law and Social Change*, 54(1): 1–19.

McMahon, W. (2015) 'Thinking the unthinkable: the coming revolution in local government', *The Project: A Socialist Journal*, 13 January, available from: http://www.socialistproject.org/issues/thinking-the-unthinkable-the-coming-revolution-in-local-government/ [accessed 2 September 2019].

Office for Product Safety and Standards (2018) 'Primary authority: a guide for local authorities', available from: https://www.gov.uk/guidance/primary-authority-a-guide-for-local-authorities#areas-covered-by-primary-authority [accessed 2 September 2019].

Pearce, F. (1976) *Crimes of the Powerful: Marxism, Crime and Deviance*, London: Pluto.

Regulatory Delivery (2017) *Unlocking the Potential of Primary Authority: Implementing The Enterprise Act 2016. Government response to consultation*, available from: https://assets.publishing.service.gov.uk/government/uploads/system/uploads/attachment_data/file/631401/pa-consultation-implementing-the-enterprise-act-2016-response.pdf [accessed 2 September 2019].

Ryan, F. (2017) 'In Liverpool, Tory cuts have brought a city and its people to breaking point', *The Guardian*, 23 March, available from: https://www.theguardian.com/commentisfree/2017/mar/23/liverpool-tory-cuts-city-benefits-poorest [accessed 2 September 2019].

Snider, L. (2000) The sociology of corporate crime: an obituary (Or: Whose knowledge claims have legs?), *Theoretical Criminology*, 4(2): 169–206.

Social Enterprise UK (2012) *The Shadow State: A Report about Outsourcing of Public Services*, London: Social Enterprise UK.

Sparrow, A. (2014) 'Councils in poorest areas suffering biggest budget cuts, Labour says', *The Guardian*, 25 August, available from: https://www.theguardian.com/society/2014/aug/25/councils-poorest-areas-biggest-cuts-labour-says [accessed 2 September 2019].

Stanning, J. (2017) 'At Grenfell, a lack accountability was deliberate – and residents were treated with contempt', *Open Democracy UK*, 19 June, available from: https://www.opendemocracy.net/uk/jake-stanning/grenfell-tower-lack-accountability-deliberate-residents-contempt [accessed 2 September 2019].

Tombs, S. (2016) *Social Protection after the Crisis: Regulation without Enforcement*, Bristol: Policy Press.

Tombs, S. (2019) 'Grenfell: the unfolding dimensions of social harm', *Justice, Power and Resistance*, 3(1): 61–88.

TUC and the New Economics Foundation (2015) *Outsourcing Public Services*, London: Trades Union Congress.

Whitfield, D. (2006) *A Typology of Privatisation and Marketisation*, Co. Kerry: European Services Strategy Unit.

Williams, C. (2013) 'Tesco gave green light to prosecution', *Environmental Health News Online*, 10 April, available from: http://www.ehn-online.com/news/article.aspx?id=8790 [accessed 2 September 2019].

Wynne Jones, R. (2017) '"We died in there because we don't count" – fury of the Grenfell Tower survivors', *The Mirror*, 15 June, available from: http://www.mirror.co.uk/news/uk-news/were-dying-because-dont-count-10631261 [accessed 2 September 2019].

19

The 'fearsome frowning face of the state' and ex-prisoners: promoting employment or alienation, anger and perpetual punishment?

Del Roy Fletcher

Introduction

Wacquant (2009) has argued that a transnational political process is under way to exert social control over the poor. Harsh penal policies ('prisonfare') and social policies ('workfare') seek to control marginal populations created by economic liberalism and welfare state retrenchment. Prisonfare is characterised by burgeoning prison populations and the movement of the penal system away from notions of rehabilitating inmates to merely warehousing them. This theorisation has been highly influential but was developed with close reference to the US case. The UK prison population currently stands at record levels but we have not witnessed the development of hyper-incarceration emblematic of the US approach. Similarly, UK welfare reforms have increasingly made the receipt of welfare benefits conditional on the behaviour of recipients enforced by harsh benefit sanctions. In Wacquant's (2009: 91) terms claimants are 'saddled with abridged rights and expanded obligations'. This chapter explores the relevance of Wacquant's ideas to the UK by drawing upon new primary research that has explored offender experiences of both prisonfare and workfare.

The prison is an institution that poses unique challenges to the reintegration of ex-prisoners. The 'free market society' can also be viewed as a form of prison for those of limited means. However, there has been no consideration of the impact of prison on the ability of benefit claimants to meet the intensified behavioural requirements of the welfare system. This chapter begins by showing how prison intensifies the social atomisation associated with economic liberalism before articulating key welfare reforms which have intensified behavioural conditionality. The author then explores the impact of imprisonment on their ability to engage with the benefits system. A key finding is that long-term imprisonment leaves a legacy which frequently results in sanctioning and may propel many out of the welfare system and into further criminal activity.

Prison: institutionalising atomisation

Economic liberalism champions the free market liberated from the shackles of the state. Yet this erodes the social bonds and civic ties upon which market economies depend. Individuals are encouraged to maximise their own subjective choices in conditions of growing market anarchy policed by an authoritarian state, as Polanyi (2001) diagnoses in *The Great Transformation*. This is also associated with the progressive loss of a 'moral economy' of mutual obligations and the growing atomisation of society. The triumph of economic liberalism may ultimately bring about Hobbes's (1651) vision of 'war of each against all' (cited in Sparks et al, 1996: 35).

Prisons are dominative institutions in which people are confined against their will, in intimate daily contact with others whose company they have not chosen, under conditions they would not choose and can do little to change, attended by staff who are empowered to regulate their lives at a minute level of detail (Spark et al, 1996). Prisons not only are called upon to manage the social disorders created by economic liberalism but also intensify and institutionalise growing social atomisation. There are three key processes at work.

Firstly, the process of incarceration isolates individuals from their social ties. Prison limits horizons, and the ways in which some prisoners deal with this restriction compounds the problem. A Scottish study found, for example, that prisoners often collaborated in this limitation, which meant they struggled upon release to reconnect with loved ones and to find their place in society (Schinkel, 2015). Weaver and McNeill (2007) argue that prison is destructive because it undermines strong and positive social ties, reinforces the offender label and places individuals in close contact with other offenders. Similarly, Farrall et al (2011) conclude that prison often hinders identity transformation and desistance from crime.

Secondly, atomisation is facilitated by the way prisoners cope with their loss of security. This is a source of 'acute anxiety' because the threat of victimisation continually calls into question the individual's ability to cope with it (Sykes, 1958). 'Prison is a barely controlled jungle where the aggressive and the strong will exploit the weak, and the weak are dreadfully aware of it' (Keve, 1974: 54). McCorkle (1992: 161) finds that many prisoners 'believe that unless an inmate can convincingly project an image that conveys the potential for violence, he is likely to be dominated and exploited'.

Finally, prison officer power is an important driver of isolation because they control access to food, possessions, contact with family and so on. Mathiesen (1965) argues that this means that prison inmates are essentially 'lonely individuals' lacking solidarity and peer support. From this perspective inmates are in a position of psychological and material weakness and their dependency leaves them in a childlike situation unable to contest parental power. Sykes (1958) also argues that prisoners are infantilised by being deprived of the right to make even small decisions about their activities. Similarly, more recent participant observation research has concluded: 'A consequence of putting men in cells and controlling their movements is that they can do almost nothing for themselves' (Conover, 2001: 234).

Prison life is widely understood as a reflection of both external cultural influences and efforts to cope with the pains of imprisonment (Gover et al, 2000). Similarly, Wacquant (2009: 205) finds that studies have consistently found that the 'incarcerated develop their own argot roles, exchange systems and normative standards, whether as an adaptive response or through selective importation of criminal and lower-class values from outside'. More recently Wacquant (2014) suggests that the US prison has been 'ghettoised' as rigid racial partition has led to the 'predatory culture of the street' supplanting the 'convict code' that had traditionally organised 'inmate society'.

The impact of imprisonment on psychological well-being is most negative in the earliest stages, and harsher prison environments are more likely to have more negative effects (Van Ginneken, 2015). Consequently, the psychological harms may have grown due to the increasingly harsh conditions of confinement and the reduced emphasis on rehabilitation (Haney, 2001; Huey and McNulty, 2005). Moreover, the indications are that this may represent a significant impediment to post-prison adjustment (Van Ginneken, 2015).

Welfare reform: intensifying behavioural obligations

There were 82,773 prisoners in England and Wales as of 30 June 2018 and 262,758 offenders on probation as of 31 March 2018. This gives a total of around 345,000 people serving a custodial sentence or undertaking a period of supervision (Ministry of Justice, 2018). More than 71,000 individuals were released from prison in England and Wales in 2017 and only 17 per cent of those leaving prison were in P45 employment (that is paying income tax and/or social insurance) a year later (Prison Reform Trust, 2018). Many were claiming out-of-work benefits.

Access to unemployment benefits has traditionally been made conditional on unemployment being involuntary. Since the mid-1980s a series of reforms have tightened eligibility and increased the severity of sanctions. The original maximum sanction of six weeks' loss of benefit, which existed from 1911 to 1986, was increased to 28 weeks in 1988 and three years in 2010, which equates to the 'most punitive welfare sanctions ever proposed by a British government' (Slater, 2014: 949). A quarter (24 per cent) of all Jobseeker Allowance (JSA) claimants between 2010 and 2015 received at least one sanction (National Audit Office, 2016). This has been likened to a 'huge penal system, rivalling in its severity the mainstream judicial system but without the latter's safeguards' (Webster, 2014: 8).

A single JSA claimant aged 25 years or over loses £300 for a four week sanction (National Audit Office, 2016). Sanctions differ from other financial penalties such as court fines in that they take immediate effect and individuals lose their only source of income, causing disproportionate hardship (Adler, 2016). Although sanctioned claimants are eligible to apply for Hardship Payments (at a reduced rate, available after a two week waiting period of no income), the Department for Work and Pension (DWP)'s (2013) survey found that tiny proportions applied. Deep poverty and a growing reliance on food banks are often the result. Those using food banks are more likely to be unemployed and have experienced a benefit sanction (Perry et al, 2014). The rise in food bank use is concentrated in communities where more people are experiencing benefit sanctions (Loopstra et al, 2015).

The present research

The data presented in this chapter were generated by an Economic and Social Research Council (ESRC) funded study (2014–18) of the efficacy and ethicality of welfare conditionality in England and Scotland.[1] The study comprised an international literature review, interviews with 52 national stakeholders and 27 focus groups with front-line welfare practitioners. The interviews with national

---

[1] See www.welfareconditionality.ac.uk

stakeholders included senior policy makers, representatives of political parties, campaigning and practitioner groups and charities. The core was qualitative longitudinal research undertaken with three waves of annual repeat interviews with 481 welfare recipients in the first wave. All interviews were recorded and transcribed.

This chapter discusses the 57 offender interviews drawn from the first wave of interviews conducted between August 2014 and September 2015 in Bristol, Edinburgh, Glasgow, London, Manchester, Peterborough and Sheffield. More than three quarters (79 per cent) of interviewees were male and three quarters (74 per cent) were aged between 25 and 49 years. Virtually all had been imprisoned and many of those had spent much of their adult lives in prison. Ex-prisoners are an acutely disadvantaged group (see Table 19.1). Most interviewees suffered multiple barriers to work with poor mental health, drug and alcohol misuse, literacy and numeracy difficulties, and homelessness being pronounced. Over half (56 per cent) of the sample had received a benefit sanction, compared with just over a third (38 per cent) of the total sample. Furthermore, a fifth had received between two and five sanctions, and 5 per cent had received more than five.

Table 19.1: A profile of the prison population in England and Wales

	Prisoners (%)	General population (%)
Excluded from school (2)	49	1
Reading below the level expected of an 11 year old (2)	37	16
No qualifications (2)	52	15
Suffer from two or more mental health disorders (3)	72 of men 70 of women	5 of men 2 of women
Drug use in the previous year (3)	66 of men 55 of women	13 of men 8 of women
Treatment for a drug problem (1)	44	N/A
Hazardous drinking (3)	63 of men 39 of women	38 of men 15 of women
Treatment for a drink problem (1)	16	N/A
Attempted to take own life (1)	24	N/A

Sources: (1) Ministry of Justice (2012); (2) HM Government (2005); (3) Social Exclusion Unit (2002)

Findings

Interviews explored family, employment, housing, health and criminal justice histories and experiences of support and sanctions. Institutionalisation was frequently mentioned especially by those that had been in social care prior to their imprisonment. A Sheffield man, aged 39 years, acknowledged: 'I'd been in the system, kids' home, Borstal, prison the lot since I was twelve years old. I'm now coming up forty.' Institutionalisation had often left a legacy of:

- dependency;
- alienation from the reformed welfare system;
- suspicion, aggression and violence.

Dependency

Many of those incarcerated become dependent on the prison to make most of their personal decisions. This dependence on the institutional structure was often apparent, with individuals frequently articulating the need for more support from Jobcentre Plus and complaining that they had received more help during their incarceration. This occasionally included vocational training but was often more mundane: 'Just like arranging appointments and things like that or putting in for community care grants and that to get back into the community' (Glasgow man, aged 38 years).

Prison was also valued by some as a means of providing a daily routine. A Bristol man, aged 50 years, had served 29 years in prison and described his usual reaction to imprisonment: 'I have kind of sighed with relief though when I was arrested and sent to prison … I do appreciate the luxury of sleep and the comfort of a bed and three meals a day and the facilities of the gym.' Moreover, prison was often a refuge from poverty, drug addiction and violence. A Glaswegian, aged 38 years, indicated that prison was valued by many offenders as a place of sanctuary. 'Some people would prefer to go back in jail, you know you'll get fed and you're safe, you're back away from drugs again.' Consequently, imprisonment often follows and perpetuates a history of deeply ingrained social structural disadvantage (Van Ginneken, 2015).

Alienation

Alienation has been viewed as either an objective condition of society or a subjective 'state of mind'. Seeman (1975) has identified several dimensions of perceived alienation, some of which were manifest in the lived experiences of respondents, including:

- powerlessness
- meaninglessness
- normlessness
- self-estrangement

Powerlessness: Powerlessness is the sense of low control or mastery over events. A Bristol man, aged 38 years, expressed his frustration at being unable to explain his inability to meet the terms of his benefit claim due to an undisclosed drug addiction: 'I never had the mental faculties to tell them, to explain it to them.'

Another individual pointed out that:

> A lot of people in prison do not have that ability. They can't read, they can't write, they don't know how to put a sentence together. So they're slightly left by the wayside. (Edinburgh man, aged 41 years)

Powerlessness often lay behind the reluctance to appeal the imposition of benefit sanctions. A London man, aged 42 years, explained: 'You can't really win and there's no way of fighting against them because they're above you ... we don't have our say in the Jobcentre, they just make their rules and keep them.' Similarly, an illiterate Sheffield man, aged 26 years, explained his decision not to appeal a sanction levied for his inability to complete a written record of job search activity: 'I still feel it's wrong for the way that they did it [imposition of a sanction], but you can't stop them, you can't.' He was sanctioned within a couple of weeks of his release and was imprisoned again just over a year later.

Meaninglessness: Many were caught in a setting whose complexity they were unable to fully comprehend. Mental illness and drug and/or alcohol addictions meant that many simply did not understand what was expected of them. A London man, aged 38 years, described his experience of claiming benefits: 'Look, I'm confused as hell. Help me out. No-one did; all they seemed to want to do is get someone out of the door.' This incomprehensibility was often exacerbated by episodic imprisonment.

> I never used to bother with benefits. Because I used to come out of prison, be out three months, banged up for

> like two, three years, and then do the same. I've never had
> to use benefits ... so I don't really understand a lot of it.
> (Peterborough man, aged 34 years)

The specific behaviours required to make a claim for benefits were sometimes incomprehensible. The mainstay of back-to-work support for jobseekers is the self-directed use of the Universal Jobmatch website which works by matching job openings with certain skill sets. Most jobseekers are required to use the site but many respondents simply did not have the requisite digital skills. Some had incurred sanctions because of their inability to comply with online obligations. An Edinburgh man, aged 34 years, had received a four week sanction because he was unable to cut and paste job search information: 'Well they've got all the computers and they want you to use computers and that, but yet if you ask for assistance there's nobody to help you.' Others thought that this was a meaningless box ticking exercise.

> You're applying for all these jobs that you know for a fact
> that you're not going to get, all these jobs on Universal
> Jobmatch, I've never got a reply from one of them ... I
> just think it is pointless. (Peterborough man, aged 39 years)

Normlessness: Some were able to prevail upon family and friends to cope with the loss of benefits. However, the impoverishment of personal social networks frequently placed limits on this source of support. A London man, aged 24 years, reported: 'I didn't really like asking my nan or any of my friends because they're all in the same predicament as me.' Drug or alcohol problems also meant that many were estranged from family members. An Edinburgh man, aged 27 years, noted: 'I've got no-one I can ask for help ... because I'm the black sheep of the family.'

Consequently, many reported that they had engaged in 'survival crime'. 'I'd go into shops and steal whatever just to make do basically. And I used to rig my meter when I had my house' (Glasgow woman, aged 34 years). However, it was sometimes difficult to disentangle 'survival crime' from wider patterns of criminal behaviour. 'I was shoplifting because we had no money. Otherwise we wouldn't have had any food or anything. And because we [she and her partner] had a drug habit as well' (Peterborough woman, aged 26 years). Nevertheless, most indicated that criminal behaviour was a legitimate response to benefit sanctioning. A London man, aged 38 years, explained: 'That's [benefits pay for] what they eat and if they get sanctioned, they have nothing to eat. So in essence, you're going to make people starve or you're going to force them to do something illegal.'

Self-estrangement: The depersonalisation of employment support was emblematic. A Sheffield woman, aged 34 years, complained: 'I know they [Jobcentre Plus staff] see thousands of people, but like I say we're not all numbers, we are people.' Moreover, some also believed that staff behaviour, including the imposition of sanctions, was determined by the need to meet organisational targets. An Edinburgh man, aged 41 years, observed: 'There's a lot of resentment that comes from it. The fact that staff are pulling flankers left, right and centre. You know to hit the figures.'

Wacquant (2009) argues that the purpose of welfare reform is to push individuals into poor work. This was reflected in the work histories of most interviewees. A Sheffield man, aged 57 years, pointed out: 'There's no work out there, and if there is work you're working for a pittance.' Most had worked in low-skilled, male dominated manual jobs and had undertaken informal labour to make ends meet. The sense of minimal work control, the denial of self-respect on the job, and the chronic insecurity of employment and its inability to function as a route out of poverty were emblematic. Some individuals had been recycling through the lower reaches of the labour market for decades and had had a series of menial jobs interspersed with unemployment and imprisonment. 'Just labouring, stuff like that. Trying to jump from job to job, really. I would take anything that's going. But you could be working for one day or four days' (Glasgow man, aged 41 years). Consequently, work alienation was another aspect of powerlessness.

Suspicion, aggression and violence

Welfare reform has resulted in greater levels of surveillance of the behaviour of those claiming work-related benefits. Consequently, many were highly suspicious of the motivations of Jobcentre Plus front-line staff. Despite not receiving a benefit sanction, a Glasgow man, aged 41 years, reported: 'I don't get orally threatened, but I sense it. I sense it ... Call it paranoia.' A few thought that social control was the primary purpose of welfare reform: 'They're keeping you in a controlled state ... like cattle' (London man, aged 43 years).

Some are affected by 'compounded conditionality' in that they have to comply with many different rules and meet a myriad of requirements set by a range of agencies such as the National Probation Service, Community Rehabilitation Companies, Jobcentre Plus, drug treatment providers and hostels. A strong antipathy towards government support perceived as unwanted surveillance was frequently evident. 'I've got to meet probation once a week, I've got to meet a hostel man once a week where I am. I don't want to see all these fucking people. Well maybe I want support, but not them, fuck, not their support, not government support' (Bristol man, aged 47 years). Furthermore, some experience these different systems as similar intrusions into their personal lives and interconnected sources of alienation.

The ability to project a tough veneer was frequently a liability following release. An Edinburgh man, aged 45 years, complained that his social worker accused him of minimising his previous offences which included murder and rape. 'I've sat with my social worker and I've had major barnies with them and they always say that I come across as quite aggressive but most of the time I'm just letting off steam.' Many respondents articulated histories of confrontation and aggression in their relationships with front-line staff: 'Jobcentres, places like that ... we don't get on. Now last year I managed to get myself barred for 12 months from every Jobcentre in Sheffield' (Sheffield man, aged 37 years). This individual received another custodial sentence shortly after our interview.

Nevertheless, some were intimidated by front-line staff. A Sheffield woman, aged 34 years, with a history of self-harming reported: 'I don't engage with them [Jobcentre staff]. I don't like them, they scare me. They give me panic attacks.' The process of receiving a benefit sanction was a profoundly hurtful experience for some individuals:

> I was utterly humiliated. In fact I was in tears when I left the building. Well I'm going to be homeless. How am I going to feed myself? It had a serious impact on my health. I'm on heavy medication [anti-depressants] now. (Edinburgh man, aged 29 years)

Conclusions

Previous research has highlighted the problems that some vulnerable groups have meeting their expanded welfare obligations (see Homeless Link, 2013; Crisis et al, 2014). The Social Security Advisory Committee (2010) has also shown that problem drug users experience high rates of benefit sanctions and highlighted the lack of evidence that sanctions influence their behaviour. However, there has been little consideration of the role played by the state in constraining the ability of some to meet the behavioural conditions of their benefit claim.

Yet prison is increasingly being used to manage marginal populations. The US population behind bars has risen from 380,000 in 1975 to 2.4 million today and hyper-incarceration has been finely targeted, first by class, second by race and third by place (Wacquant, 2014). The prison population of England and Wales also rose by over 90 per cent between 1990 and 2015 (Allen and Dempsey, 2016). Inmates are first and foremost poor men. Furthermore, there is a large body of research conducted over the past 60 years which has documented the social and psychological adaptations made by prisoners and which shows that prison intensifies social isolation and is antithetical to reintegration. Imprisonment further disadvantages a vulnerable population and reinforces structural problems and social inequalities. The present research has shown that this leaves many unable to meet their expanded responsibilities with institutional dependency, alienation and ill-discipline frequently resulting in suspicion, conflict and repeated benefit sanctions.

Moreover, the destructive potential of imprisonment has intensified. Firstly, prison overcrowding combined with staff reductions have meant that prisoners are being denied the necessary pre-release support. When asked about the preparations made for her release, a Sheffield woman, aged 34 years, reported: 'Nothing, just about £60 cash, that's it out you go.' Secondly, the ongoing crisis in the UK prison system means that many have been exposed to an increasingly brutal regime. The 12 months to 2016 witnessed the highest number of deaths, prison homicides and rates of self-harm on record – with the latter rising by nearly 40 per cent in just two years (Prison Reform Trust, 2016). Thirdly, the swing towards the penal treatment of poverty has led to the resurgence of private incarceration. 'Inconceivable just twenty years ago, the private prison is an inescapable component of the US penal landscape of today' (Wacquant, 2009: 169). The spiralling financial costs of hyper-incarceration coupled with the ideology of commodification have been key drivers. The US experience is that commodification has supported the dominant penal philosophy of making incarceration an ordeal. The ideal of 'rehabilitation' has been jettisoned in favour of 'neutralisation' and the correlative toughening of the conditions of confinement (Wacquant, 2009).

Australia, South Africa and the UK have also introduced private prisons. Some of the problems of allowing prisoners to be treated as a commodity to be exploited for profit are becoming evident. UK private sector providers have recruited less well trained staff, paid them less and introduced staffing levels and patterns of working which are dangerous (Howard League for Penal Reform, 2017). US studies have traced the lack of effective correctional services directly to efforts to control costs and thus maximise profits (see Greene, 2003). Furthermore, privatisation has 'produced a much worse record of deprivation, violence and abuse than is found in the public prison system' (Greene, 2003: 65). However, the momentum has stalled on privatisation, and prison contracts in England and Wales have required higher levels of service delivery enforced by financial penalties. Nevertheless, acute concerns about a lack of control over prisoners at HMP Birmingham has led to the state taking back control of the prison from a private provider (Guardian, 2018).

Wacquant (2009) argues that the state increasingly presents a 'fearsome and frowning' face towards the poor via the development of harsh penal and social policies which seek to impose insecure labour as the normal horizon of work. Despite the development of harsher carceral sanctions many interviewees preferred prison life to the growing sense of alienation they experience in the 'free market society'. Furthermore, the present research suggests that prisonfare leaves a 'heavy imprint' of alienation and ill-discipline, which means individuals are likely to be punished by benefit sanctions and further contact with the criminal justice system. Many interviewees had engaged in 'survival crime' to cope with the loss of benefits. 'I had to go out and steal and it didn't feel wrong because I just thought if I get caught it would be doing me a favour. I would have gone to the court and said "Look don't let me back out because I've no option and I'm going to do it again"' (Peterborough man, aged 28 years). Some indicated their experiences had made them discontinue benefit claims. A Bristol man, aged 27 years, reported: 'I just gave it up [the benefit claim] and didn't bother with it again. Carried on just going out every day thieving.'

References

Adler, M. (2016) 'A new leviathan: benefit sanctions in the twenty first century', *Journal of Law and Society*, 43(2): 195–227.

Allen, G. and Dempsey, N. (2016) 'Prison population statistics', House of Commons Library Briefing Paper Number SN/SG/04334, 4 July.

Conover, T. (2001) *Newjack: Guarding Sing Sing*, New York: Vintage.

Crisis, Homeless Link and St Mungo's (2014) 'The programme's not working: Experiences of homeless people on the Work Programme', available from: https://www.homeless.org.uk/sites/default/files/site-attachments/The%20Programme%27s%20Not%20Working%202012.pdf [accessed 31 March 2020].

DWP (Department for Work and Pension) (2013) *The Jobcentre Plus Offer: Final Evaluation Report*, London: DWP.

Farrall, S., Hough, M., Maruna, S. and Sparks, R. (2011) *Escape Routes: Contemporary Perspectives on Life after Punishment*, London: Routledge.

Gover, A., MacKenzie, D. and Armstrong, G. (2000) 'Importation and deprivation explanations of juveniles' adjustment to correctional facilities', *International Journal of Offender Therapy and Comparative Criminology*, 44: 450–67.

Greene, J. (2003) 'Lack of correctional services', in A. Coyle, A. Campbell and R. Neufeld, *Capitalist Punishment: Prison Privatization and Human Rights*, London: Zed Books, pp 56–66.

Guardian (2018) 'MoJ seizes control of Birmingham prison from G4S', 19 August, available from: https://www.theguardian.com/business/2018/aug/20/moj-seizes-control-of-birmingham-prison-from-g4s [accessed 18 November 2019].

Haney, C. (2001) *The Psychological Impact of Incarceration*, Washington, DC: US Department of Health & Human Services, Office of the Assistant Secretary for Planning and Evaluation.

HM Government (2005) *Reducing Re-offending through Skills and Employment*, Cm6702, London: Secretary of State for Education and Skills.

Homeless Link (2013) 'A high cost to pay: The impact of benefit sanctions on homeless people'. London: Homeless Link.

Howard League for Penal Reform (2017) 'The role of the prison officer: research briefing', available from: https://howardleague.org/wp-content/uploads/2017/11/The-role-of-the-prison-officer.pdf [accessed 31 March 2020].

Huey, M. and McNulty, T. (2005) 'Institutional conditions and prison suicide: conditional effects of deprivation and overcrowding', *Prison Journal*, 85(4): 490–514.

Keve, P. (1974) *Prison Life and Human Worth*, Minneapolis: University of Minnesota Press.

Loopstra, R., Reeves, A., Taylor-Robinson, D., Barr, B., McKee, M. and Stuckler, D. (2015) 'Austerity, sanctions, and the rise of food banks in the UK', *British Medical Journal*, 350: 1–6.

McCorkle, R. (1992) 'Personal precautions to violence in prison', *Criminal Justice and Behavior*, 19(2): 160–73.

Mathiesen, T. (1965) *The Defences of the Weak*, London: Tavistock.

Ministry of Justice (2012) *Surveying Prisoner Crime Reduction Wave 1 (Reception): Samples 1 and 2 Technical Report*, London: Ministry of Justice.

Ministry of Justice (2018) *Offender Management Statistics Bulletin, England and Wales*, 26 July, London: Ministry of Justice.

National Audit Office (2016) *Benefit Sanctions: A Report to the Comptroller and Auditor General*, London: National Audit Office.

Perry, J., Williams, M., Sefton, T. and Haddad, M. (2014) 'Emergency use only: understanding and reducing the use of food banks in the UK', available from: http://policy-practice.oxfam.org.uk/publications/emergency-use-onlyunderstanding-and-reducing-the-use-of food-banks-in-the-uk-335731 [accessed 18 November 2019].

Polanyi, K. (2001) *The Great Transformation: The Political and Economic Origins of our Time*, Boston, MA: Beacon Press.

Prison Reform Trust (2016) 'Prison: The facts', Bromley Briefings, Summer, available from: https://futuresunlocked.org/images/summer2016briefing.pdf [accessed 31 March 2020].

Prison Reform Trust (2018) 'Bromley Briefings Prison factfile', Autumn, available from: http://www.prisonreformtrust.org.uk/Portals/0/Documents/Bromley%20Briefings/Autumn%202018%20Factfile.pdf [accessed 31 March 2020].

Schinkel, M. (2015) 'Adaptation, the meaning of imprisonment and outcomes after release: the impact of the prison regime', *Prison Service Journal*, 219: 24–9.

Seeman, M. (1975) 'Alienation studies', *Annual Review of Sociology*, 1: 91–123.

Slater, T. (2014) 'The myth of "broken Britain": Welfare reform and the production of ignorance', *Antipode*, 46(4): 948–69.

Social Exclusion Unit (2002) *Reducing Re-offending by Ex-Prisoners*, London: Social Exclusion Unit.

Social Security Advisory Committee (2010) Report of the Social Security Advisory Committee Made under Section 174(2) of the Social Security Administration Act 1992 on the Social Security (Welfare Reform Drugs Recovery Pilot Scheme), Regulations 2010, London.

Sparks, R., Bottoms, A. and Hay, W. (1996) *Prisons and the Problem of Order*, Oxford: Clarendon Press.

Sykes, G. (1958) *The Society of Captives: A Study of a Maximum Security Prison*, Princeton, NJ: Princeton University Press.

Van Ginneken, E. (2015) 'Doing well or just doing time? A qualitative study of patterns of psychological adjustment in prison', *Howard Journal of Criminal Justice*, 54(4): 352–70.

Wacquant, L. (2009) *Punishing the Poor: The Neoliberal Government of Social Insecurity*, Durham, NC: Duke University Press.

Wacquant, L. (2014) 'Class, race and hyper-incarceration in revanchist America', *Socialism and Democracy*, 28(3): 35–56.

Weaver, B. and McNeill, F. (2007) *Giving Up Crime: Directions for Policy*, Edinburgh: Scottish Consortium on Crime and Criminal Justice.

Webster, D. (2014) 'Inquiry into benefit sanctions policy beyond the Oakley Review', Evidence submitted by Dr David Webster, 12 December.

Conclusion
What has been learned

Kevin Albertson, Mary Corcoran and Jake Phillips

In the Introduction we noted the distinction between privatisation and marketisation, and we argued that this book is necessary because criminal justice has been the site of marketisation to a greater extent than it has privatisation. Yet this concept of marketisation has been underexplored. The chapters in the book demonstrate the sheer scale of marketisation that has occurred in criminal justice in the UK. There is evidence that similar marketisation has occurred in other states around the world (Walby and Lippert, Chapter 8; Swirak, Chapter 6).

As this book demonstrates, there is a whole array of other means by which the market has been used to shape the delivery of experiences of criminal justice. The chapters in this book expose a range of modes of governance and accountability that are at play and demonstrate the ways in which marketisation has impacted on criminal justice at macro-, meso- and micro-levels. Importantly, they have shown what the impact of this has been on the broader field, the individuals working within those fields and the service users that are subjected to systems of power delivered in newly formed markets. In this concluding chapter we attempt to draw together some of the themes that run across the chapters and consider what the future might hold for criminal justice and marketisation.

The language of the market

Ironically, or perhaps not, the concepts of free markets, marketisation and privatisation have so well captured the public discourse, we must employ them in highlighting their problems (Corcoran, Chapter 1; Swirak, Chapter 6; Corcoran et al, Chapter 12). We may talk, for example, about costs and benefits, about innovation, responsibility and accountability. Thus, we critique marketisation on its own terms here: in costs and benefits (Corcoran, Chapter 1). Yet despite allowing the market to choose its own grounds on which it might be justified, there are significant problems with the model as currently realised, even on its own terms.

Competition and its discontents

One of the key themes to come out of these chapters is the importance and role of competition. While one would expect competition to be a key feature of marketised services, it is the implications that are of concern. In general, under competition, the logic of the market dictates participants must necessarily be partitioned into 'winners' and 'losers', the former being those whose business models will succeed, and the latter those who will eventually be driven out by competitive pressure.

In the context of criminal justice, it is not clear how productive this competitive process is. As those providers unable to compete on the terms that have been set are driven out, markets generally become more concentrated (Corcoran et al, Chapter 12) and standardised. Standardisation may lead to efficiency, and hence competitive advantage, but it also may lead to impersonalisation. For example, in the context of probation in England and Wales the competitive structure introduced by Transforming Rehabilitation (TR) has led to the deterioration of gender specific services for women in the community. Thus, service users are not getting the services they need or deserve (see Annison et al, Chapter 11; Cooper and Mansfield, Chapter 13).

More generally, the impact of competitive market forces may bring with it impacts which are not necessarily socially constructive. In the competitive struggle, there is the potential for the corruption of targets, dilution of service quality and deprofessionalisation of the labour force (Phillips, Chapter 4). Linked to the competitive nature of markets is distrust. In general, no competitive firm is likely to see much return from adding to the business model of competitors, through adding to the knowledge base of 'what works' for example.

Competition is said to facilitate a process of creative destruction – an evolutionary never-ending process of fomenting change. However, change must be distinguished from progress, and the benefits of stability and the cost of competitive change are often not recognised and seldom evaluated. Whether the 'creation' of innovation generates sufficient benefits to offset the costs of the 'destruction' of pre-existing modes of delivery ought not to be taken for granted (Albertson and Fox, Chapter 5; Nellis, Chapter 15).

Accountability

Where democratic government is, in theory at least, held to account by the electorate, markets are held to account by the profit (or at least break-even) imperative. In the UK, because of commercial confidentiality, the citizenry may not even be able to find out the actions taken in their names as firms pursue marketised contracts. Yet it cannot be taken for granted that market transactions taken in the pursuit of monetised profit are always in the best interests of the wider citizenry (Gacek and Sparks, Chapter 3). Walby and Lippert (Chapter 8) sound a useful caution in this regard with respect to public policing.

In practice, we see significant issues in relation to democracy and accountability arising from the increased marketisation of criminal justice. Indeed, as Bhatia and Canning (Chapter 16) note, to the extent that public services are delivered by large corporations responsible to foreign stakeholders, the market in criminal justice might not even represent the best interests of the nation as a whole. They argue that application of market forces has the potential to result in state-corporate violence. Another example of this is highlighted by Tombs (Chapter 18). There we see evidence that the increased involvement of the private sector meant that local authority health and safety regulation became much more focused on the retail and food/catering sector to the neglect of social goals such as building regulations. This relative neglect of social costs contributed to the deaths of 72 people in Grenfell Tower.

Responsibilisation

A strong theme to emerge from the analyses presented here is that of responsibilisation (Annison et al, Chapter 11). Responsibilisation is closely linked to neo-liberalism, the atomisation of society and the need to achieve better outcomes with diminished financial resources. In practice it means that criminal justice systems are increasingly placing responsibility for change – be that at the service level or the service user level – on to the shoulders of agencies other than the state. Nowhere do we see this more than in Swirak (Chapter 6), where it is argued the burden of desistance is placed on those who are already marginalised. Responsibilisation serves to highlight the distancing of the state from issues of criminal justice. To assign responsibility for change to the marginalised, those with the least power, may reduce political risk, but it is unlikely to lead to social progress (see for example Fletcher, Chapter 19).

Innovation, modernisation

As Nellis (Chapter 15) argues, the modern, innovative solution may be so alluring as to be assumed to be more efficient. This will be particularly true in a time of ongoing austerity (itself caused in part by the government's necessary response to the unsustainability of financial innovation). Marketisation superficially would appear to promote such innovation and even perhaps harness financial innovation for social impact (Fox and Albertson, Chapter 2). However, in this regard, marketisation, perhaps because of competitive pressures, has rather led more to replication of existing, tried and tested models (Albertson and Fox, Chapter 5) than innovation.

The transactional and the relational

Although many chapters point to the problems of competition and the reliance on the transactional (for example Fletcher, Chapter 19), some of our chapters also highlight the antidote to these developments. Ultimately, markets will put a price on social goods, whereas it is in the relational sphere that values may be attributed to such goods (cf Swirak, Chapter 6). For example, in Hargreaves and Ludlow (Chapter 10) we see the importance of the relational as a more effective means of creating accountability, while in Smith and Johnston (Chapter 9) the importance of expertise is seen as a more effective way of obtaining justice than the move towards limiting access to legal aid. Indeed, the irony of the reforms to legal aid is that cases now cost more than previously. This is due to litigants, unable to access professional legal advice, not knowing how to represent themselves in court and concomitant delays to proceedings.

The importance of relationships also ought to be highlighted throughout criminal justice – relationships, that is, both between different service providers and between service users and services providers. However, such relationships require time and resources – which may be in short supply in marketised services operating under an austerity agenda. Because market forces create homogeneity, there is a tendency to work towards the modal or median which will not work for everybody, perhaps for none. The process of marketisation in probation meant that probation workers had very little say over their role. Marketisation can be seen as a form of violence, diminishing the influence of the employee organisations (Phillips, Chapter 4), meaning much valuable implicit knowledge of what works may have been lost. There is evidence marketisation has resulted in lower morale among staff and poorer services (Phillips, Chapter 4). See Dehaghani and White (Chapter 7) also in this regard with respect to the role of policing, and Czerniawski (Chapter 17) with regard to the impact of marketisation on prison education.

Ultimately

Together, the chapters contribute to a volume which demonstrates that marketisation and privatisation in criminal justice is not restricted to the sale of prisons or calling for tenders for probation contracts. Rather, it has, over the years, made its way into almost all aspects of criminal justice, and the practice of marketisation furthers, and is furthered by, its language and objectives (Corcoran et al, Chapter 12) in a chain reaction. This has gone largely uncontested. Walby and Lippert (Chapter 8), for example, note how easily the UK relinquishes public ownership and custodianship compared with Canada.

This collection of chapters shows how marketisation and privatisation, alongside austerity, have often resulted in less justice for victims and people engaged in the criminal justice system, less effective systems of punishment and rehabilitation, and lower levels of accountability for the state and service providers. What is particularly interesting is that while some of the developments in this book have resulted in improved outcomes – improved efficiency for the state, increased profits for financiers and contractors (in some cases) and better (or at least not worse) services offered to the marginalised – this is by no means universal: rather the opposite. It is thus by no means clear which stakeholders have benefited from this experiment in governance through markets.

The contribution of this volume, therefore, is not just in its analysis of particular aspects of privatisation and marketisation in criminal justice, but that these case studies taken as a whole may serve to illustrate the costs and benefits of privatisation and marketisation more widely (Phillips, Chapter 4). Markets (like wine, so it is said), make a good servant but a poor master. Ultimately, as Wong and Macmillan (Chapter 14) conclude, and it bears repeating, 'the purpose of public service markets is to do just that – serve the public'. To do so, they must be managed on terms that the public themselves determine, not adopted haphazardly for reasons of political expediency or the pursuit of profit. The change of the language of debate – away from political expediency and towards democratic legitimacy; away from the financial and towards the social; and away from the transactional and towards the relational – is long overdue.

Index

Note: Page numbers for tables appear in italics.